OF

FICTION

the MAGIC of fiction

CRAFTING WORDS INTO STORY

The Writer's Guide to Writing & Editing

BETH HILL

TITLE PAGE BOOKS
ATLANTA

For DLB and CAS,
to fulfill a promise made too many years ago

Contents

Part Three: Major Story Sections

Part Four: Getting Specific: A Few Detailed Details_

Part Five: Style Issues: Little Details, Big Effects

The double dagger symbol (‡) identifies chapters that contain articles, whole or in part, first published at The Editor's Blog.

A Definition

Magic—

The supposed art of influencing the course of events
and of producing extraordinary physical phenomena
by the occult control of nature or of spirits.

("Magic," def. 1)

fig. An inexplicable and remarkable influence producing surprising results.

("Magic," def. 2)

This definition of magic comes very close to a definition of the craft
of fiction, of writing and editing stories. Not a match, but it's close,
close, close. And the figurative definition is nearly perfect.

Writing and editing *are* arts. They *do* produce extraordinary phenomena through hidden control and manipulation, but manipulation
of the writing and fiction elements, not nature and spirits. And editing
certainly has a remarkable influence on stories, one that produces
surprising and marvelous results.

We read of the fictitious practitioner of magic who has to train,
who must wed hours of practice to his natural abilities in order to
produce his results, and we wonder *just how long was the sorcerer's
apprentice an apprentice?*

If his training was anything like what a typical apprentice in the
Middle Ages went through, the sorcerer's apprentice trained for years
before he was qualified to practice magic on his own.

In the very same way that the magician's apprentice must train, the
writer and editor of fiction must master his craft, joining learned and
practiced skills to his natural gifts. High-quality fiction doesn't
manifest instantaneously, conjured from nothing; writing, rewriting,
and editing require work and the honing of skills. They require time.
They require perseverance.

They require attention to detail and, most certainly, imagination.

Contrary to our desires, there's no incantation that can create a literary masterpiece at the utterance of a few mystical words, no wizardry that weaves stories at the slight wave of a wand.

The creation of high-quality fiction requires a different kind of magic, one that produces no less startling results but that requires expertise and patience as well as the mind of a technician, the eyes and ears of an artist, and the heart of a dreamer.

Fiction demands a blend of skill and creativity, craft and artistry, and each writing project requires its own particular balance of these elements, a mix necessary to produce powerful stories.

Writing and editing fiction *is* magic of a kind. With a nod to the Shorter Oxford English Dictionary, crafting a work of fiction is

> the art of influencing the course of story events and of producing extraordinary fictional phenomena by the hidden control of words, punctuation, and the elements of fiction.

In *The Magic of Fiction*, we'll explore the related crafts of writing and editing fiction as a means of honing your skills, skills that you can then wed to your natural abilities in order to create captivating fiction.

INTRODUCTION
WHY THIS BOOK

SO WHY A FICTION-WRITING HANDBOOK with a decided emphasis on editing? The simple answer: I see a need.

You can find many fabulous books on writing, at least on certain aspects of the craft. And there are numerous resources that cover some facets of rewriting. But there aren't many books easily accessible to all writers that address each of the fiction elements and major sections of a story, at least not with an orientation toward reworking and perfecting those elements, not with the objective of helping writers learn how to edit those elements.

Writers deserve more than an introduction to the fiction elements. Knowledge of how to rewrite and edit, how to work through problems, and why rewriting and editing are crucial is information every fiction writer should have.

Learning how to work the craft shouldn't be restricted to writers who attend writing programs or workshops. All writers should have access to writing tips and strategies useful to not only complete a first draft, but to change a first draft into a polished piece of fiction.

This knowledge is especially important for writers intending to self-publish. If writers are going to bypass traditional gatekeepers such as agents and editors, they need a few extra resources to help them put together the best stories possible.

With e-publishing making the opportunity to self-publish relatively simple for writers, more writers than ever are taking their stories directly to the public. And those stories often don't get the editing attention that traditionally published books get.

Self-published books (e-books and print books) shouldn't be shorted the opportunity of a good edit. But if you eliminate the traditional publisher, you also eliminate many of the tasks performed by the publishing company, including editing and proofing. All novels should be edited; they deserve the attention. Even more so when you consider what they face in the marketplace.

Writers with drawers of manuscripts are pulling those manuscripts out and, for a relatively few dollars, they're making them available without a publisher's help, guidance, or backing.

And some of those manuscripts are no doubt written by popular authors, which means not only a glut of self-published books, but self-published books from authors that readers are likely to gravitate to first because of reputation.

That's a lot of competition for books from untried writers. And a big inducement to get it right.

For the known author, the ability to produce books that compare favorably with those released by a publishing house is just as crucial.

The opportunities for self-publishing make knowing how to re-write and edit manuscripts, how to form them into entertaining books, essential skills for all writers.

EXPECTATIONS

While I'm not going to delve into the sales statistics of self-published books (often e-books, but print books as well) of an unknown author, I will remind you that for most writers, the number of sales is low. Very low. Extremely low.

Yes, a few unknown authors hit it big. And we're all encouraged when one does. There's no doubt that some self-published books are fantastic and even more entertaining than books vetted and published in the traditional manner. But those big, big sales are still rare. Maybe that will change as self-publishing continues to evolve, but don't count on it. Not for your first effort. Especially if you don't have an established name or reputation.

You're still one writer among thousands, among many thousands. And those thousands all have the same idea—to be a best-selling author. So with self-publishing increasingly popular, how many more novels will enter the marketplace every year?

Hundreds? Thousands?

Will the number of readers go up to match the numbers of new books? Maybe. Will readers buy more books if the cost is lower than that for traditionally published books or if they can download directly to personal devices wherever they are? Again, maybe.

So more readers may be looking for more books. But *you* still have to do something to make your books stand out.

To get noticed, you can set up an eye-popping web presence with a website and a blog and blog tours and membership in different online groups. And you'll probably want to explore all these options, maybe try a marketing or publicity approach that no one else has explored. You'll want to try whatever is working for other writers even as you devise your own methods for introducing yourself and your books to an audience.

I'm not a publicist or marketing expert, but I am an editor of fiction, and I can suggest another way to make your stories rise to the attention of readers:

> Write an entertaining story in a recognizable genre that takes readers on an engaging journey into a captivating world in the company of fascinating characters, and tap into reader emotions while you're doing it.

Give readers a good story well told.

Sound familiar? Yes, that part is no different from what good writers have always done. It was true for Mark Twain and it was true for writers before his day and it'll be true for writers for the foreseeable future: you've got to have an entertaining story and you've got to tell it well.

Readers want good fiction. *Believable* fiction. And they don't want to be reminded that they're merely reading—they want to imagine they're living the adventure your characters are living. Or at least imagine that the adventure could be possible.

They want to see and touch your worlds, feel your characters' emotions. They want more than static words on a page or screen. They want color and motion and *e*motion and action and conflict. They want ups and downs, highs and lows. They want characters who act on their beliefs no matter what it might cost them.

And they want satisfaction when they reach the end. They want something that they can't get in their jobs or hobbies or sports. They want what only fiction provides.

Can you deliver for them? Can you write an entertaining story that locks readers inside a fictional world and can you make that world real? Can you touch the emotions of your readers? Can you *manipulate* the emotions of your readers? Can you write such a compelling story that *from page 1 to the end,* readers are not once distracted by the mechanics or the foundations of the story but only caught up in the trials, ordeals, and victories of your characters?

Can you make your readers yearn for your fictional world as if it were a tangible place where they can taste the foods and walk the streets and defeat the bad guy or fall in love?

I intend to give you help to do just that.

Easy access to self-publishing is going to be around a while, at least until the next evolution in publishing, so why not try self-publishing? At the same time, why not give yourself every advantage?

Even if you intend to pursue the traditional route to publishing, make your stories as strong as possible, as flawless as possible. No, agents and publishers won't reject your story simply because it's got a few errors. But they could easily reject a story that isn't as tight as it could be, one that shows weaknesses in major fiction elements. One that's all telling, no showing, or that opens with pages of back story before the current story begins. Show off your stories by increasing your skills.

Tips for rewriting and self-editing should give you a leg up. If not that, how about a toehold? At the least, editing advice will put you ahead of where you were before, with manuscripts hidden away, too frightened to show themselves in public.

My intent is to light a fire under you, one to match the fire inside you, a fervent flame that'll have you not only rewriting and editing, but impatient to write and publish even more stories.

FICTION BASICS AND BENCHMARKS

I can't distill every bit of writing and editing wisdom and fold it into this book any more than a tech writer could put all there is to know about computing inside a single book. There are too many issues and permutations and possible digressions.

Still, I do want to give you the basics and more. I also want to share suggestions for areas you may not have considered. And I want to get you thinking about options, about writing elements or areas of fiction that you may know nothing about.

It's difficult to know what's wrong with a section of text without a means of comparison, without a benchmark. That is, to see how and where a story or any one element is off track, you have to know where the story should be at any given time and where it's ultimately headed. You need to know the elements of fiction, their purposes and how they fit with other elements, and know how to manipulate the elements to create intended effects and strong stories.

In *The Magic of Fiction* you'll find plenty of information concerning the fiction elements—what each should accomplish and ways to achieve those ends—enough to enable you to compare the particulars of your manuscript with basic standards.

And while this book is primarily a resource for fiction writers, any writer or editor can benefit from the suggestions, tips, and examples you'll find here.

Use the recommendations to make your manuscripts irresistible to readers, whether those readers are fans and critics, beta readers and critique partners, or agents and publishers.

Don't be surprised to come across the most basic topics and suggestions or, conversely, topics you've never heard of. By necessity, this is a book for any fiction writer at any level. And that means that some of the suggestions here will be familiar to you, something you learned in middle school or in college or in your writing group. But a lot of this material is going to be new to a great many writers, writers who've never formally studied writing or literature or fiction. New to the man who's dreamed all his life of writing but who's been working

70 hours a week for 25 years building and growing his own business. New to the woman who devours mysteries and finds she has an engaging character in mind for a mystery series, one she knows she could write. New to the recent college graduate determined to get his or her writing career underway.

For those who've been traditionally published, who've had editors point out these issues and rules before, the suggestions in this book should serve as reminders of editing suggestions you're familiar with. But if you've never been through a professional edit, the majority of this information may be unfamiliar.

If this advice is new to you, published author or not, you're in the right place.

I encourage you to take the initiative and seek out additional resources for more information on any topic. The Internet has made research easy, so take advantage of it and of writers forums and your writing group. Ask questions and keep asking until you're satisfied. And let your research be both deep and broad. Learn all you can about an issue and then see how that issue relates to other issues. Keep learning. Keep refining your craft.

VALUE OF A FIRST NOVEL

The value of your first novel in incalculable. It's an effort worth celebrating and celebrating well. Putting a story together, following plot threads, characters, and events from the beginning to an ending 350 pages later is a major achievement.

But no matter how dear and precious that first novel manuscript is, it may not be worthy of being published.

Some manuscripts will never be publishable. And many writers' first efforts fall into that category.

I mention this point now because I want to raise the caution flag for the eager writer intent on rushing to publish, especially one rushing to self-publish a first novel.

You may be the exception, a writer who writes a blockbuster novel with your first effort. And you may be able to edit that first effort, that first novel, to perfection. But that's not a likely scenario. Not for most writers.

The first novel of most writers isn't suitable for the public.

An artist doesn't try to sell his first painting. A composer doesn't expect his first try at creating a symphony to be performed by an elite orchestra. An architect doesn't expect a major corporation to use the first rendering of his first building as the design for their new corporate headquarters.

No craftsman or artist assumes his first effort is a masterpiece.

No one wants to show off their worst works. No one, it seems, except overeager writers who don't consider what such exposure could mean for their reputations or future sales.

If your reputation says you can't write, that your plotting or technique is laughable, how many readers will try your next novel and the one after that? Yes, your technique will improve with each effort, but there's no reason to showcase the worst of your weaknesses with a bad first novel that's either released before its time or published when instead it should be used as a training exercise.

A first effort at writing a novel is probably not worth publishing. Yes, yours may be the exception. But it probably isn't.

You should act as if it isn't.

Don't self-publish your first novel, especially if it hasn't been edited by someone other than you. If it hasn't been *read* by someone other than you.

Have someone help you decide whether that first manuscript is worth publishing. If you've written only one full-length fiction manuscript, I'd bet that it shouldn't be published, not even self-published. I might be betting against a sure thing in one out of millions of instances, but most of the time that first novel isn't worth releasing.

Sure, a few noted authors wrote a famed first novel, a superspectacular one in terms of sales or reputation. But many more writers have written first novels read only by the writer's family and no one else, and then only under threat or because of bribes or deep love.

And who's to say that the first novel published by those noted authors was actually the first each had ever written? Those novels may have been only the first submitted to a publishing house.

Your first novel, like a painter's first effort, is not likely a masterpiece. How could it be? It's simply your first novel. Don't assume that merely completing a novel means that it's a great one or even one worth sharing.

Writing a first novel is a learning experience that deserves to be covered in its own book. For now, let's leave it with the recommendation that you not self-publish your first novel, especially if it hasn't been professionally edited and you've never formally studied the craft. And maybe consider not publishing a second or third effort either.

Don't rush to publish any story that's not been revised and edited, whether this means that you do the editing yourself, you hire someone, or you go the traditional publication route and work with an editor at a publishing house.

And while we're considering firsts, never publish a first draft. We'll talk about first drafts later, but for now, recognize that a first draft is incomplete and not ready for publication.

Do have a critique partner or beta readers help you out.

Yes, I highly recommend that you have someone who knows something about fiction read the story and give you feedback, feedback that you will then follow through with.

If you've requested comments and a reader takes the time to point out events that don't make sense or wording that she doesn't understand, check out whatever is causing confusion. If she tells you she doesn't believe a character would do what you had one do, listen to her. If she says she doesn't like a character or that she found herself rooting for the bad guy, knowing she should have been rooting for the main character, *listen to what she's telling you.*

If she said she got bored or couldn't finish the story, find out where she lost interest.

Turn off your defense mechanisms, tell the ego to hush, and see if what your reader said has merit. You might save yourself embarrassment and improve your story in one shot.

Do you have to listen to every suggestion? Listen, yes. Check it out? Yes. Follow a recommendation? No. You still make the decisions about what goes on the page. You decide what makes the final cut for your stories. But do take a moment or three to investigate your reader's comments. Maybe she didn't know how to pinpoint the true problem but only tells you what bothers her in general terms. Maybe she actually found a story thread that was out of balance or a character who wasn't used enough or who acted out of character. But even if she can't diagnose the story's weaknesses, that doesn't mean she can't point out that there *is* a problem. Thank your reader and consider what she took the time to mention.

Yet even if you have someone else read your manuscript, you have an obligation to make your stories the best they can be. One way to do that is through self-editing. Learn a few skills and apply them to your manuscripts to bring them to a condition worth reading. *Learn how to do it yourself.*

LIMITATIONS

So, even though I can't share the entirety of an editor's knowledge and experience in this book, I can give you the basics and more on crafting entertaining fiction. I can address common mistakes and their fixes. I can offer suggestions derived from experience. And I can give you lists of must-dos and a few never-dos. I can encourage you to write, rewrite, and polish the best book you're capable of putting together at this moment in your writer's journey.

I started a blog several years ago (www.theeditorsblog.net) solely for the purpose of helping writers craft strong stories and compelling fiction. But now, with so, so many writers going the self-publishing route, this book is my effort to reach even more writers with in-depth suggestions before they publish. Whether they plan to self-publish or pursue traditional publishing options, there's no reason for writers not to be equipped to edit their own manuscripts.

And by the way, you'll find some of the same information from this book on the blog. It was appropriate when I wrote it for the blog and, updated and expanded, it's appropriate for this collection of advice. Chapters that contain articles from the blog (all or in part), are marked with a double dagger symbol (‡).

Publishing is different now from what it was three to five, maybe seven to ten years ago. And in *those* days, publishing was different from the way it had been before the 1960s and 1970s, before independent book publishers were bought up by corporations and the big publishers became bigger publishers.

E-publishing is a major change in the field, one that has blasted open the publishing doors. Publishing may swirl around this innovation for a long while or something new and as equally revolutionary might be unveiled next year. But there's no reason to wait for the next breakthrough. Why not take advantage of this opportunity that thousands of writers before you didn't have?

But be prepared. Do what you can to ready your stories for the public or for agents and publishers.

Write the best story you can. Rewrite and edit to make it shine.

PARTICULARS OF THIS GUIDE

To help you write, revise, and edit, this guide provides lists and questions and explanations and options.

Some chapters are short, with suggestions in easy-to-follow bullet lists. Other chapters offer explanations for how to use a particular writing or fiction element and tips on ways to check your manuscript for the use or absence of that element.

You'll find examples in many chapters. Since I don't want any confusion about incorrect options, examples that point out the wrong way to do something are marked with a lovely **X**.

Numerous sections include questions. Lots of questions. The questions are there to encourage you to consider options and possibilities, maybe get you thinking of choices you've never imagined before. Get you thinking of choices as they relate to your manuscript.

Get you thinking the same way an editor's prompts and questions would get you thinking and reevaluating sections of your text.

THE MAGIC OF FICTION

Because I didn't want any one list to be incomplete, you'll find similar topics or advice in several sections because the information is integral to the subject matter in multiple chapters. This arrangement of the material allows you to read chapters out of order so you can zero in on the topics you need to cover without missing out because you skipped a section.

So while you can read from front to back, you don't have to. If you're looking for suggestions for a specific topic, feel free to jump ahead or skip around.

The final sections of many chapters contain questions and a list of issues you'll want to consider as you edit. If you want to skip explanations and details about a topic, go directly to the ends of chapters for recommendations and reminders.

The book is separated into seven parts to help you explore different aspects of the writing and editing of fiction.

Part 1 Getting Started

Part 1 focuses on what you should know before you rewrite and edit.

Part 2 Major Elements of Fiction

Part 2 offers a review of the major fiction elements and includes questions to ask yourself in relation to your use of those elements in your story. These chapters will give you great ideas for what to look for as you rewrite and edit. The information about the fiction elements can also help as you create your first draft.

Part 3 Major Story Sections

Part 3 looks at story issues by studying recognizable sections of text. Topics include hooks, introductions, notable story moments, scenes, and beginnings, middles, and ends. You'll be able to use the questions, suggestions, and examples in these chapters to rework sections of text without limiting yourself to individual fiction elements, to help you smooth out your story's big picture, and to remember to include important story moments in your novels.

Part 4 Getting Specific: A Few Detailed Details

Part 4 covers specifics for punctuating dialogue, rules for handling numbers in fiction, and tips for grammar and punctuation. It also includes a list of common mistakes and their fixes.

Part 5 Style Issues: Little Details, Big Effects

The focus in part 5 is on details that may seem insignificant but that nonetheless make a big impact on story. Topics include word choice, symbolism, and author preaching and intrusion.

Part 6 Focus on Editing

Part 6 contains a handful of editing checklists and a chapter on editing a manuscript the way an editor does. Use the checklists as you rewrite and edit, but also allow the topics you find in them to guide your first draft and even your original outline as well.

Part 7 Putting It All Together

The chapters in part 7 will help you focus on the needs of your readers as well as on your strengths as a writer. You'll also find encouragement for finishing your writing projects.

> Please don't let the number of pages in this book dishearten you. It's likely that you already know and practice more than a few suggestions included here. Take what you need and be encouraged to be the best writer, the best self-editing writer, you can be.

MORE THAN EDITING TIPS

Although this guide has a decided focus on rewriting and editing, the writer who begins a novel with the knowledge highlighted here will be ahead when it comes time to rework the manuscript. In order to make changes to your text, you need to know how to create—and manipulate—the necessary components. In other words, it helps to know what you're aiming for and how to hit the target.

If you've never formally studied writing, this may be the only place you find such information. You may think it's too late to incorporate what you learn here into the project that you intend to publish soon, but I hope you'll find solid advice that will help, no matter what stage of the writing process you're in. You'll definitely be able to use this information for a work in progress and for your next novel.

Many writers—most writers—will turn to an editor or a critique partner or a really good friend or a blackmailed family member for help at some point; there's simply too great a benefit in having others vet our stories to not make that choice. But other writers won't ask for help. Not when they think they must do it all on their own.

But every writer—every single one—can benefit from a second pair of eyes attached to a person unafraid to be honest.

We all need someone to see what we, with our personal blinders, can't see. Someone to read our stories with an impartial eye and point out missed connections, tangents, wacky plotting, or wrong words.

If you don't have someone to act as that trusted outside eye, I hope this book will serve as a substitute. And if you do have friends or others who help you improve your stories, I hope this book will be one more resource to help you write better fiction.

Because there's so, so much to writing a novel, having resources to prompt you to use all the elements of fiction in the right manner, in the right measure, and at the right times—a resource that teaches as well as encourages—is a must.

There's more to telling a story than relaying events, weaving in description, and plopping in dialogue. And there's more to editing than correcting punctuation and cutting out words. Learn what *more* means for writing, for rewriting, and for editing. Learn the ingredients that go into entertaining fiction, including into the revision stages.

Make your stories stand out for reasons that make you proud and satisfied, not embarrassed.

Write that heavenly story.

And then edit the hell out of it.

THE MAGIC
OF
FICTION

Part One

GETTING STARTED

1

THE MAGIC OF FICTION

CREATING A WORLD, populating it with people, designing parameters for it, and then dreaming up dramatic dilemmas to bedevil the people of that world, that's magic. Or sorcery. Or it's the unique gift of the fiction writer who, armed with only his imagination, a mind full of words, and a few tools, builds stories out of nothing.

Writing fiction—entertaining fiction that keeps readers enthralled—isn't magic of the unexplained kind. It's the magic of our trained magician.

Crafting story out of the void is a marvel, yet no sleight of hand is involved. Fiction that can stand up to readers isn't the product of false magic. No, this is the real thing. It's the creation of a reality where previously nothing else existed.

And it's powerful, this fiction magic.

It not only creates people and worlds, but when it's manipulated just right, it has real people living the adventures of the created people. It has real-world humans *seeing* imaginary events, empathizing with imagined people, and feeling *real* emotions.

If that's not potent magic—touching and moving people through the power of words—then I don't know what it should be called.

A formidable force exists within words. Words create. They direct. They influence.

And this is no less true of words in fiction than for words written for any other purpose.

You can work fiction magic by writing, rewriting, and editing. You can create worlds from nothing. You can influence readers.

You can produce extraordinary fictional phenomena.

The Magic of Fiction is one more tool to help you create believable fictional worlds, fascinating characters, and entertaining stories.

- It's a handbook for the writer just starting out, the writer unfamiliar with all the fiction elements and their purposes, unfamiliar with revision and the need for self-editing.

- It's a guide for the writer who wants to perfect her stories before submitting them to agents and publishers.

- It's a manual for the writer who intends to self-publish, whose stories may never be touched by a professional editor.

- It's a textbook for the writing student eager to learn how to piece together a work of long fiction.

- It's a resource for the educator who needs a comprehensive guide for the classroom.

- It's a primer for the beginning editor learning new skills.

- It's a review for editors who want a refresher.

This book focuses not solely on the creation of a story but on the development of that story through revisions and editing, from draft to edited masterpiece.

Multiple writers have been credited with saying some variation of *all writing is rewriting*. Many have said something similar because rewriting is what produces the end product, a satisfying novel that can transport readers to new worlds and introduce them to new people without causing them to trip over confusing sentences and grammar or oddities that don't belong in the fictional world.

> It's in the manipulation of words and the fiction elements—it's in change and revision—that powerful story is created.

My intention is to provide you with ways to work and rework your story—to write, rewrite, and polish words and phrases, the fiction elements (including characters, plot, and dialogue), and major sections of text (including first pages, scenes, and the climax)—until you've created a story world and characters that can support the scrutiny and skepticism of real-world readers.

Because so much of the craft of writing fiction deals with rewriting and editing, we're not going to leave off after the creation of the first draft. Actually, that will be our start point and not the end point.

We're going to cover the major fiction elements, major novel sections, and writing practices all the way through the completion of a novel (or any piece of long fiction). We're going to make sure you have strategies and tips and a mindset for completing every necessary component of your stories.

Work and rework your fiction. Craft words into stories and stories into powerful moments that resonate with readers.

Touch real-world people with the power of your words.

Create fiction magic.

2

WHAT YOU SHOULD KNOW BEFORE YOU START

WRITING A NOVEL involves a whole lot more than dropping a character into unfamiliar circumstances, much more than following characters around a world that suddenly makes no sense to them. If you've finished at least one draft of one manuscript, you know that's true. If you've been through a couple of rewrites or a couple of novels, you're laughing at my understatement. But a reminder, even a reminder of the fundamentals, can be timely.

Writing the basic story is only the first step. Rewrites follow the first draft and editing follows rewriting.

And if you're self-publishing and self-editing, you've added other time-consuming but vital tasks to your duties.

When you estimate the time needed to finish a novel-length manuscript, remember to factor in not only writing time but time to rewrite and edit. Rewriting and editing may well take weeks or months. Be realistic concerning how long revising will take and don't skimp on the hours you allow yourself to get your manuscript into shape.

You give yourself time to write; allow yourself time to rewrite and edit as well.

Let's consider a few details useful to know before you begin your novel and points to review before you rewrite and edit.

MISTAKES

Your novels won't be free of mistakes. I'm saying this one up front so you'll know it's unlikely that you'll publish an error-free book. And if you self-edit and/or self-publish, you're going to be the one making most of those mistakes. Unless you know every detail about punctuation, grammar, and the elements of fiction, your books will have errors. Unless you're the perfect typist, your books will have errors.

Even after a professional edit and a pass by a proofreader or two, a novel will likely *still* contain errors.

I'm not saying you should accept dozens of errors, but you could make yourself crazy or delay publication forever if you try to ferret out every last one.

Decide on your threshold—how many errors will you allow? What type? What mistakes will you never permit? Devise a plan for finding and correcting errors of any kind—in technical/mechanics issues, in plotting and story issues, in style choices, and in facts.

But to save your sanity, acknowledge that errors will still creep in.

CONNECTIONS

Novels, to be cohesive, need to have connections. Story threads are elements that weave through a novel from beginning to end. They can be related characters or plot twists or setting props or themes or colors or touch points or . . .

They can be *anything*, these threads that bind parts of a story together. They can be character motivation or goals that move characters and readers from chapter 1 to chapter 35. They're the story elements that let us know we're reading one cohesive story and not a half dozen unrelated tales.

As family members have ties that even outsiders recognize, so should our stories.

A daughter may favor her mother in the eyes, either in the physical traits, through shape or color, or in the way they study others. So when we see the daughter squint and stare, we're reminded of the mother, and with that reminder we're led to think about other details we know about the mother.

In a similar manner, there are story moments that make us think of other moments in the story. For example, an action scene that concludes in chapter 15 is a direct result of what was set up in chapter 2, mentioned in chapter 7, and then unleashed in chapter 14. And the repercussions of that action scene may well extend past chapter 15 and through the end of the story.

Story events and reactions build on what came before. Marvin can't attack his boss out of the blue in chapter 20—there must be a setup or a cause or a motivation. And the characters he attacks (and/or those with a relationship to them) must have reactions so that the story wheel keeps turning. Action or event leads to response leads to action leads to response and so on.

It's up to you to make sure you've made connections at every level and story point, using a variety of fiction and writing elements.

If you're self-publishing, you don't have an editor or reader at the publishing house asking about dropped story threads or unnecessary characters. You don't have anyone to point out weak story ties or plot events that don't make sense or aren't deep enough that the reader feels them or aren't tight enough that they can't be easily unraveled. You definitely don't want a story that's too loose, that can be shaken and pulled apart by a casual read.

Even if you're not self-publishing, you still want your manuscript as tight as it can be before you submit to agent or publisher.

If the plot can unravel too easily, you haven't tied it with enough threads or haven't pulled the threads tight.

The tighter the story threads, the more cohesive the story elements. Tightly woven story elements lead to stories with depth and provide a more involving read for readers.

The inclusion of lots of tight threads makes a story's events seem inevitable. Not predictable, as if the reader would invariably guess what would happen, but inevitable, in that events—given the characters' personalities and all that's happened—couldn't play out any other way. That inevitability without predictability appeals to readers.

Be sure you've created enough connections. And not only between characters but between characters and events and between setting and character. Between setting and character motivation. Between major plot and subplots.

Weave story threads in as you write, even setting them up beforehand in your outline if you use one.

You can add story threads in an edit, but when you've created places and reasons for threads as you write, that element of the story is already strong before you get to the edit stage. Add linking elements and threads during an edit if you overlooked them in the writing stages, but if you can plan ahead, do so. Know that you'll need story connections to give readers the sense that they're reading one full story and not a series of unrelated episodes.

BEFORE YOU START WRITING, KNOW THE GENRE

Do you write to genre specifics and expectations? Readers who read by genre have expectations—do you know how to satisfy them? Does your romance (in the modern sense of the word) have a happily ever after or at least a happy for now? Is your mystery solved by your sleuth? Does your dystopian novel have a sufficiently somber mood?

Maybe you think you can write a romance because they're all straight formula. Stick in a few character names, a locale, a popular career for the hero and heroine, and boom, you've got a romance.

Or maybe the success of erotic romances has you thinking it would be a breeze to string together a few sex scenes and call it a book. After all, everyone knows about sex, so how hard could it be to write a novel filled with it? Hint: Good sex scenes are notoriously difficult to write well.

Good fictional sex is more than part A goes into slot B. There's more to sex scenes than grunting, sweating, four-letter words, and grinding body parts. And there's more to both romance and erotica than sex scenes.

Or maybe you think that coming up with a new way to murder someone means that your mystery can almost write itself.

There's certainly more to writing mysteries than devising a new way to murder the victim.

There's more to every genre than familiar tropes and formula.

Romance readers, and that includes readers of erotica, want more than a few repeated phrases—*Harder. Yeah, that's it. Harder and deeper.* Romance readers want to see the triumph of characters overcoming the very real challenges that work to keep them separated. They want to see characters fall in love despite differences or conditions that should keep them apart. Readers want to see love victorious in seemingly impossible circumstances.

Mystery lovers want challenge and surprises. They want a puzzle to solve. They want to beat the protagonist to the answer of how it was done or who done it.

Readers of literary fiction want beautiful words and creative phrasing, but they also want to gain insight into the main character. They want to explore a character's depths.

Readers of *every* genre have expectations. And you've got to know those expectations before you can write a satisfying novel for them.

BEFORE YOU START WRITING, LEARN ABOUT THE ELEMENTS OF FICTION

You may be a marvelous writer as a technician, knowing all the rules of writing, grammar, and punctuation, but do you also know what goes into a piece of long fiction? Do you know how to carry a story through multiple events and across time and into a number of story locations, with events relayed and played out by a cast of unique and memorable characters?

Do you know how to manipulate the elements of fiction? Do you know how they can play off one another to create memorable stories?

There's more to fiction and writing a novel than having a plot idea; an idea alone would be pretty thin stretched over 400 pages. You have to include events and dialogue and engaging characters. You need to include highs and lows and foreshadowing and surprises and setting details and conflict and character reactions.

You have to include characters who make readers laugh or cry and chapter-ending hooks that compel readers to turn pages. You have to touch readers through their emotions as well as their minds.

You need the full spectrum of fiction elements and you need to link them in ways that are arresting and satisfying for the reader.

If you've never studied the elements of fiction, start your studies. Learn what those elements are and how to use them. Learn their strengths and weaknesses.

We'll cover the major elements in this book, but there's always more to explore and learn. Expand your knowledge and skill set by studying the fiction elements.

BEFORE YOU PUBLISH OR SUBMIT, REWRITE *AND* EDIT

I'll say this several times, so I hope you don't get tired of hearing it— a first draft is not ready for, not suitable for, publication. Rewrite that first draft, maybe the third and fourth and seventh drafts as well.

Don't assume that you're an anomaly, the miracle novelist, the only writer who doesn't have to rework his stories. Every manuscript deserves rewriting. Every story deserves your best, and a first draft isn't your best.

Yes, you might have some truly awesome writing in your first draft. But you've also got plot holes and inconsistencies and incongruities and characters acting contrary to their personalities. You've got annoying word repetition and weak word choices and a dragging, sagging middle.

You've overplayed the theme or allowed dialogue to turn into monologue. You've spent too much time in a character's thoughts at the expense of action or you've ignored character thoughts altogether or you've ignored emotion, emotions of both character and reader.

You've given the reader more back story than he could ever want or a protagonist without a believable motivation for his behavior.

You've dropped a story thread that seemed promising in order to follow the new thread you introduced in chapter 5, never resolving or cutting out the first thread.

You rushed the climax and/or resolution or you drew them out for so long that readers will get bored.

Unless you planned and plotted and anticipated every story moment before you began writing—you plotters who love outlines know exactly what I'm talking about—then it's likely your first draft is incomplete. And even if you plotted out the wazoo before you put one line on the page, it's still likely you didn't get every word or line of dialogue or story event just right as it flowed from your fingers.

No matter what you hear from other writers who say they pretty much published their first drafts, don't believe that a first draft is the best you have in you or that it's the best for your story. Rewrite and edit. Your stories deserve the attention. They deserve to be complete.

A first draft is a blueprint; it isn't the novel itself.

Maybe your words and sentences are each a work of art. That doesn't mean you've successfully tied the story elements together in ways that make sense. That doesn't mean that you've chosen the best secondary character to reveal vital information to your lead character. That doesn't mean you haven't rushed too quickly through some scenes, taken way too long with others.

Just because you've written pretty sentences, that doesn't mean your story structure doesn't need work or that your dialogue couldn't use sprucing up or that you chose the right viewpoint character for pivotal scenes. Unfortunately, being an expert in the mechanics of writing in general doesn't equate to being a thrilling storyteller.

Conversely, you may have written an awesome adventure, with twists and turns designed to pull the reader deep, but have limited grammar skills and no knowledge of how to vary the rhythm of your sentences and no aptitude for choosing the best words for a scene.

You no doubt possess strengths either in storytelling or in the basics of writing, maybe in both. But at the same time, you've also got weaknesses. And if you've never explored them, never tried to improve those weaknesses, your novels will suffer from weaknesses as well.

Granted, certain writing weaknesses may not be evident until you've written thousands and thousands of words and tried to make sense of the mess in your hands. If you've not tried writing a novel-length manuscript, concepts such as pacing, rising and falling tension, and character growth may be foreign to you. Don't beat yourself up for lack of experience; do be alert to a lack of knowledge. No, you can't know what you don't know that you didn't know, but you *can* acknowledge there are writing truths you haven't yet come across.

Bottom line? Remain aware that there's always more. Don't imagine that you should stop exploring the elements of fiction and the rules of writing. Be on the lookout for what you don't know. Read a book on craft or grammar. Take a class. Join a writers group.

Never stop learning.

And rewrite as many times as necessary to tell the story you want to tell in the way that best suits it.

BEFORE YOU EDIT, UNDERSTAND WHAT EDITING CAN DO FOR STORIES

Editing deals with far more than proofing for punctuation and spelling. While you need to make sure grammar, spelling, and punctuation are correct, you've also got to consider story issues, the fiction elements, genre requirements, *and* the way every piece of story fits with every other piece.

Editing can cut lifeless phrases and elements that add nothing to a story, elements that actually reduce the impact of other elements.

Editing can add life and connections and passion.

Think of editing as cutting away the dross that weighs down story. Use it to remove the scum that prevents the reader from seeing clearly, from experiencing your characters and their adventure in a way that entertains and touches the reader's emotions.

Think of editing as a way to add and enhance as well. Use your editing passes to stir emotions and crank the story engine hotter.

> Editing uses both addition and subtraction, so be sure to use both to hone every fiction element and strengthen your story. You don't want to be so fixated on one area, on one editing concern or fix, that you ignore the others.

And you don't want to focus on only what you do well. As a matter of fact, editing is a time to focus on your weak skills. But don't let that scare you away from editing. Instead, run toward those areas that you know need work. (Or use this guide to help you discover areas you didn't even know you had to check.) Each time you edit a manuscript, you strengthen your skills so that the next manuscript will have fewer errors and weaknesses. Use an edit to not only improve the quality of that one story, but the quality of every story your write thereafter.

Don't think that a focus on a story's weaknesses or your own means that we won't also look at strengths. You've got to be aware of strengths, otherwise you might end up cutting out the heart of your stories. Play up your strengths and those of a particular manuscript, but also work at strengthening those areas that need extra help.

PREPARE TO GET CREATIVE

Just as you're creative with words and sentence construction when you write your story, be creative when you rewrite and edit. You don't want every change to sound the same.

So, for example, if you have many sentences with participial phrases that show simultaneous action for what should be sequential actions, be careful not to correct each the same way.

> Original: Dashing down the street, Elliot rushed into the hospital. *X*

> Corrected: After dashing down the street, Elliot rushed into the hospital.

Although the corrected sentence is a legitimate way to order sequential or consecutive actions, you wouldn't want to use this construction every time. The word *after* would get noticed and the result would be boring text.

Other options—

> Elliot dashed down the street and then rushed into the hospital.

> Elliot dashed down the street before rushing into the hospital.
>
> Elliot's dash down the street was inelegant and graceless. But his galumphing was nothing compared to the frenzied way he cartwheeled into Mercy General's emergency room.

Use as much creativity with your edits as you do with the creation of your first drafts.

DON'T RUSH

Don't cave in to pressure or excitement and submit that first draft or any early draft that has only been proofed for spelling and missing words. A first draft is not a finished novel; it's not a *complete* novel. If you're self-publishing, don't upload a first draft. Finish the story first.

Offering a book *before it's ready* is shooting yourself in the foot. Put your best work out there; a first draft is not your best work. You don't want readers, agents, or publishers seeing an incomplete work.

And you don't want to merely polish that first draft, as if making it pretty will make it a solid story.

Rewrite. That may mean taking out characters, entire plot threads, and events. That may mean changing the point of view or the major viewpoint character. Rewriting may mean a new antagonist or even a new protagonist.

Rewriting typically means major changes in the foundation or structure of your story. So before you publish or submit . . . before you proofread . . . before you edit . . . rewrite scenes and chapters and large sections as many times as you need to. Make every version the best you can make it. Give each step of the writing process time and focused consideration. From research to writing to rewriting to editing to taking that final proofing pass to eventually submitting or self-publishing, give your novel the stamp of excellence.

Write a good story. Rewrite until it's a story that makes sense and engages readers. And then edit with that same attention to detail and care. Only then should you think about introducing the world to your characters and their adventure. Don't rush to publish. The rush isn't worth the complications.

EDIT WITH A PLAN IN MIND

When you reach the edit stage, approach your edit with a plan. Know where you want to start and what you want to cover. There are a couple of standard approaches to editing—the chapter "Rewriting, Editing, or Proofreading" provides details on the two major approaches. When you're working the first approach, you can begin anywhere and with any issue. Use the editing checklists in this book to help you decide where to start or go to chapters that feature issues that you know need reworking.

In the second approach, you'll be reading your novel as a reader (and as an editor) would, from story beginning to final page.

Because editors, like writers, may use any number of methods to strengthen a story, I won't recommend one edit path for you as you're working through that first edit approach. Decide what you want to look at first and what should follow.

Do consider, however, looking at big-picture and story-wide issues first. And complete major rewriting before you begin editing. If you make changes to plot threads or characters or setting in ways that affect large sections of the story, you don't want to have wasted your time making changes in the details before that point. A major change might require the deletion of a whole scene—there's no reason to work through the fine details in that scene only to eventually cut it.

Yes, this might happen anyway, and that's simply part of the creation process. But you reduce the chances it will happen if you give thought to the big picture before editing.

Be realistic in terms of time—edits can take longer to do well than it takes to write a first draft. Budget your time.

And remember that you need to edit for both the technical issues—grammar, punctuation, and word choice—and the fiction elements. Since it's likely you have an affinity for one over the other (or for one fiction element over another), make a point of covering every issue and not just your favorites.

Write out your plan and then follow it. You can make deviations along the way, but don't be sidetracked from covering all the issues simply because an unexpected one shows up.

And don't think you need some elaborate and micro-detailed plan. Simply create a list of issues and tasks, based on the edit checklists, that you need to cover. And then start working your list.

I've included a chapter on the second edit approach—"Working Through the Text"—that provides tips on how to read the manuscript from beginning to end and how to make edit notes on the hard copy. But working the first approach will be different. And it will be different for every writer and for every manuscript.

Begin that first approach, looking at different issues and at different sections of text, once you've finished your major rewriting. Use the checklists in this book to guide you, but develop your own edit hierarchies and rhythms.

When you're done with the individual elements and sections of text, then tackle the second edit approach.

BEFORE YOU CHANGE ONE WORD

Make a plan for backing up your drafts and then follow it. Whether you create new files every so many days or after a certain number of changes, make sure you save different versions—with understandable file names—so you can go back to earlier versions if you have to.

You don't have to go overboard, but use a backup system that works for you.

If you cut scenes or interesting tidbits, save them for your website. Your fans will love the extra scenes and goodies featuring your story world and characters.

Yet before you can make changes, you've actually got to get the first draft written.

Let's take a few moments and use the next chapter to look at the first draft.

3

THE FIRST DRAFT

STORY IDEAS CAN come from anywhere, and it makes no difference where they come from. The importance of the initial story idea is its ability to keep the writer on track to create 90,000 words of clear and entertaining fiction.

And just as story ideas can come from anywhere, the writing of stories can begin anywhere.

You can start with the kernel of an idea and simply run with that, sitting down to write with no more than the excitement of that kernel to guide you. Or you can plot out every move your characters make, outline every event that transpires in your as-yet-unwritten story.

Or you can begin somewhere in between, with more than a kernel but less than 100 pages of outline.

Or your idea spark can lead to research that leads to more ideas before you discover *the* idea that has you sitting down and writing.

Plotters are known for writing out story events before they write one word of their novel. And pantsers are known to write by the seat of their pants, writing with some sense of where they're going or what's going to happen to their characters along the way, but also with an attitude of freedom—they'll include anything that strikes them as fitting or relevant.

Both pantsers and plotters can reach the story's end and connect all the points between beginning and end, so either system does work. The key for writers is to learn which method produces the strongest stories in the most efficient manner *for them*.

Plotters typically spend more time planning up front while pantsers typically spend more time rewriting. Both methods still require editing once the rewriting is done.

Plot or pants through your stories—or use a blend of the two methods—but get your story down.

Write events and dialogue and scenes. Write description. Get the basics on the page. Get more than the basics down. Move your characters from A to B to M and then to T, U, and V before you end up at Z. But write. Whatever the story is for you, get it written.

If you know you need a scene between two other scenes but don't know exactly what it should contain, leave a note in the text—*add a scene with protag, add a scene in Leila's POV, add fight between Bob and John.*

There's nothing wrong with skipping ahead. You may discover the perfect scene a hundred pages later as you're writing a different scene.

> I promise that it's okay to skip scenes as you're writing.
> And doing so will become easier the more you write.

You can use the same method to skip a section of dialogue or a bit of action. If you don't know all the details, type something like MORE or XXX (and maybe highlight the word) and then keep writing. You can always, always come back and fill in the gaps.

And then when you're done with the first draft, you'll have something to refashion. You'll be able to work your skills and use your imagination to turn that initial draft into a complete story. You'll be able to bring your strengths and abilities to bear on every scene and passage. You'll have something on which to work your craft.

Now, some writers rewrite as they create. And other writers rework sections along the way, cleaning up their manuscripts at the start of a new writing day. But many writers reserve the majority of their rewriting for a time when they've got a complete story ready to be worked on.

You'll discover what works best for you, but I advise that you don't get caught up in rewriting while you're writing the first draft. Definitely don't feel that you must edit as you're creating.

WRITING APPROACHES

Approaches to writing are as varied, maybe as quirky, as writers.

▪ You may write scene by scene, chronologically, starting at the beginning and writing until you reach the end. And you may know the end before you start writing, but maybe you don't.

While I typically suggest using whatever method works to write a first draft, I also suggest that knowing where a story's headed is a good idea; it's much easier to direct a story if you know where it's supposed to end up. And knowing an end point will let you know when you've arrived. If you don't know where you're going, you won't know you've gotten there.

Rewriting and editing are infinitely tougher if you only stumble into your ending place; there's so much to do when you must go back to shade and direct *every* story component with the ending in mind. Every scene, every smidgen of character background and thought, every bit of dialogue, the pace, the mood and tone, the rising and falling tension, the conflict, and even the order of events will all need enhancing to fit an ending devised after those elements were written.

I won't say that a writer absolutely couldn't produce a solid and entertaining story without first knowing the ending, but the creation of such a story is vastly more difficult. And most writers would find their writing experience much more rewarding if they spent time deciding where the story was headed before they wrote fifty or sixty thousand words. Even better might be to know where the climax will take place, who will be involved in that scene, and how that scene will play out.

▪ Maybe once you know the ending, you start writing that scene before anything else. Yet maybe you don't. Maybe you begin with major events earlier in the story, first creating the moments of highest tension and emotion and later linking those events.

▪ If your characters have been yakking at you, you might begin with major dialogue scenes.

▪ You might create what you imagine will be your favorite scenes first or you may choose to reward yourself by holding out on writing those until you're almost finished, waiting until the end of the creation stage to let loose with those scenes that you know will be knockout wonderful.

Whatever your approach to getting the first draft done, recognize that others may follow a different path to the completion of their first drafts and that it's okay to have different paths to the same out-come—a finished first draft. Recognize also that the first draft isn't the end. The first draft is simply the bare bones of the story.

Some first drafts are more complete than others, this is true. Some are closer to outlines while others are closer to books. Many more fall between the extremes.

Most are missing scenes. Most have too many words and too many inexact words.

Some are missing character motivation or character goals while others are missing necessary characters.

Some are light on dialogue, heavy on description. Some have the opposite problem.

Many feature dialogue that's too exact or direct.

Many first drafts have little conflict and few emotionally charged scenes. Many are too cool or distant.

Many first drafts have way too much back story doled out with a generous hand.

Some first drafts inadvertently feature ghost towns—locales popu-lated by only major characters and no background characters—or story worlds that are as clear as fog, with no discernible characteristics or details peculiar to that world.

Many have the same steady pace throughout, no speeding up and no slowing down. No sense of events approaching a high or low point. No sense of rising excitement or easing back on excitement.

Many have an unintentional mix of points of view, the wrong viewpoint character performing narrator duties, and uneven narrative distance from scene to scene.

Many are missing the buildup to the climax. Some are missing the climax itself.

Most have characters who hedge or who don't follow through. Many have no memorable characters who stand out.

Some have way too much explanation. Some feature summary and a whole bunch of telling with only a few scenes depicted in real time.

Some first drafts lack setting details and references to sounds, tex-tures, or scents. Some have few visuals. Many lack color.

Still others have no subtext, no depth of any kind, only surface actions and the most superficial insight into the characters.

Many first drafts suffer from all of these shortcomings.

For all first drafts, many words are simply wrong. They're the wrong words for meaning or they're used in the wrong way. They're wrong for the sound of the sentence. They're repetitious. They don't fit the character. Don't fit a scene's mood. Don't fit the genre or era. Don't fit the words around them.

> First drafts have all sorts of problems, and yet weaknesses in a first draft are okay. *Okay for that first draft.*

Writing a first draft is all about getting the events on the page, putting the characters into place, and establishing some sense of genre, mood, and setting. It's not about perfection, although you may discover the perfect event or character motivation as you write. You may even discover a perfect section of dialogue that lasts intact throughout the revision process. Still, writing the first draft isn't about composing perfect sentences, devising lyrical metaphors, or creating fiction gold *although you might do any of these things to some degree in a first draft.*

> The first draft is allowed to be messy and bloated and full of holes. It's allowed to be a little of this and a lot of that. It's allowed to be too much and too little at the same time.

The first draft is allowed to be the *first* draft. Which means there will be more drafts. Which means that you get to take that first draft and change it, mangle it, rip it apart, and reform it.

The first draft is only the beginning. You don't ever need to be ashamed of a first draft. At the same time, you don't need to show it to others either.

It's not ready for an audience.

Except for the truly beautiful streaks that run through it here and there, the first draft is ugly and raw, and it doesn't need critics poking at it. *You* don't need critics poking at it. It does, however, need your diligent care and all your varied skills to help it grow into a story of beauty and strength.

The first draft is allowed to be lacking. It's just not allowed to remain that way. (Exceptions if you decide to toss the story because you discovered it won't work with the setup or characters you've given it.)

START WRITING

Sometimes what you'll want to do is to simply write fast and feverishly, getting that churning out of you and onto the page. This means the word choices won't be perfect, the grammar will be wild, and some of what you write won't make sense.

But when you write this way, the intensity bleeds through. The sentence rhythms are probably close to what you want for a particular scene, especially an emotion-filled scene. Truth is likely to come pouring out of you when you take off writing, your internal editor not only muted but turned off.

As a matter of fact, force your inner editor into silence—or banish her from your mind completely—when you write your first draft. A picky editor has no place in the writing of the first draft. If you're too worried about saying it right, it's likely you'll never produce soaring phrases. Sometimes the rules have to take a back seat to creativity, and the period of writing the first draft is one of those times.

There will be opportunity enough to fix excesses later.

> During the creation phase, create. Use your imagination. Don't limit yourself to rules and to doing the *right* thing—be open to everything.

Write your first draft with abandon. Don't worry about getting everything right; you won't and that's okay. You won't get every word, every fiction element, or every emotional component perfect as you create, and if you insist upon trying to perfect them, you'll miss opportunities to create truly inventive phrasing and wildly creative—and memorable—story moments.

And even if you do "perfect" words and noteworthy moments as you're writing the first draft, it's likely you'll be changing a whole lot of words anyway, even the perfect ones, as you rewrite and edit.

Writing a perfect first draft is virtually impossible since along the way you're likely to discover that you need additional events, scenes, and details that you hadn't planned for, even if you typically plot to the nth degree. And that means that after you decide you need those additional scenes and details, you'll need to change the scenes where the new details need to be added. *And* you'll need to make adjustments to other scenes, both before and after the changes, to make those additions work in relation to other scenes and plot threads.

This also means taking out sections which refer to the original story elements that you cut to make room for the new text.

Maybe you discover a tidbit of a character's back story that links several story moments, a tidbit you hadn't imagined.

Maybe you find a character has changed or needs to change to better complement other characters.

Maybe you find your setting isn't vibrant enough.

Maybe you find you don't have enough story events. Maybe your plot is flat, nothing that readers could get lost in. Maybe the plot's topic is simply uninvolving. Even if the words are perfectly crafted, if the story itself is boring, that story is incomplete.

Maybe your characters think too much but don't actually do anything noteworthy.

Maybe you discover all your characters sound alike, like hip teens or professors or corporate attorneys.

Maybe you neglected to meet genre expectations.

> The major point I'm trying to make is that it's okay to write a first draft that stinks (even though *stink* is relative). The second point is that it's not okay to leave the first draft in that stinking state and call it a finished book.

My intent is to help you change your first draft into a book, one that readers can enjoy. The suggestions and information in this guide are here to help you fashion that incomplete first draft into a piece of fiction worth getting lost in, worth reading, maybe worth crying over and remembering.

While you can use anything you find in this book to guide your first drafts—as you no doubt already use everything you learn about writing to make each subsequent story a more complete one, even in a story's early stages—I'm going to assume that you'll get the most use out of this guide as you revise and self-edit. After all, if all writing is rewriting, that's where you'll be spending most of your time and effort, with reworking that first draft into a second draft and beyond that into a polished book.

So by all means read about the fiction elements and peruse the edit checklists before you begin a story, before you write that first draft. But dig into the meat of this guide when you're ready to move from first draft into subsequent drafts and the finished product.

> Don't write your first draft with this or any other writing guide open, continually checking rules and recommendations. Just write. Don't stifle the free flow of creativity by repeatedly shifting from writer to editor or from writer to student. Do, however, prop open your reference works when you rewrite and edit.

And don't imagine that you need to address every issue or problem with every new draft.

For example, it's likely that the second draft will feature new scenes or new characters, maybe a new arrangement of scenes, maybe a new beginning or a new ending. But it's not likely that the second draft will contain *all* of these changes. It's also unlikely that draft two will contain word-perfect and rhythm-perfect dialogue, fully fleshed-out characters, and just the right amount of conflict per scene.

Rewriting and editing are done in stages, not all at once. You'll rewrite more and work though more editing passes for stories that require more changes, tackle fewer rewrites for stories that are more fully developed in their first drafts. And you'll certainly spend more time rewriting and editing with longer or more complex stories.

Realistically, assume that you'll create *at least* three drafts; a complex or long story might require eight or ten. Don't limit yourself based on what you've heard that other writers do. You have your own approach, and each of your stories has its own needs. Write, rewrite, and edit according to your writing style and the needs of each story.

And after you have what you assume is the final draft, recognize that the draft still needs work, still needs improving and tweaking. It still needs polishing.

Don't forget that proofreading follows rewrites and edits.

THE TAKEAWAY

Using whatever method and mix of approaches works for you, write your first draft. Get the basic story down, knowing that you'll be making changes—some drastic—to strengthen every story element and every scene when you rewrite and edit.

Write with abandon rather than with an eye toward the rules. Allow yourself to explore and experiment. Writing the first draft is a time for creativity to come to the fore. There will be plenty of time to follow the rules when you edit.

It really is easier to rein in excesses during an edit than it is to push beyond the common when you're rewriting. Not that you can't beef up your story in a rewrite or while editing, because you certainly can and you will have to. But in my experience, more writers need to push harder and go deeper with their early drafts rather than constrain their writing. Rather than go overboard in early drafts, most writers don't go far enough. Allow me to encourage you to go farther and push deeper with that first draft.

I'm talking about pushing deeper into the emotions and into meaning, into action. I'm talking about not stopping a tour-de-force dialogue scene before it's run its course. I'm talking about pushing at an emotional scene to wrest all the emotion from it that you can.

I'm not talking about padding a first draft with unnecessary words. I am talking about adding depth and breadth.

So push when you create your first draft. Go for some excesses. You can always trim and cut back if you're too liberal with any element. In contrast, adding later can be much harder.

Still, the key is to get the basics and more put together for that first draft. And after that you get to dive into the meat of the craft with your rewriting and editing, with crafting scenes, sentences, and words into adventures, love stories, mysteries, literary gems, and every other manner of appealing fiction.

Give yourself something to work with in a first draft, and then go to work. Tackle the deep and wide tasks of rewriting and editing.

4

REWRITING, EDITING, OR PROOFREADING?

REWRITING, EDITING, AND PROOFREADING are related but different tasks. Still, there is overlap. Especially when a writer will be editing and proofing his own work.

Let's look at an overview of the three tasks so you'll have a sense of what each entails.

REWRITING

Rewriting is typically what happens to a manuscript between the first draft and subsequent drafts. It involves adding or removing scenes or changing major sections of the text such as events, characters, or secondary plots. Rewriting may include changing the setting, perhaps the locale or era. Rewriting might entail a change in point of view (POV) or narrative tense.

Rewriting often focuses on changing chunks of text. The emphasis is not on details but it's not necessarily on the big picture either—the focus is typically on one issue at a time, although that issue can be big in terms of importance to the story or the amount of page time devoted to it. Rewrite to add what you left out and to cut sections or story threads that prove superfluous once the full story takes shape.

Rewriting also involves moving the pieces around, perhaps shifting one scene to a spot earlier in the story and another to a later section. Or perhaps you decide to feature a different secondary character in a scene and so must rewrite that scene.

These big changes don't mean that you won't be rewriting individual sentences here and there as you rewrite. But in general, rewrites deal with comparatively large sections of text or large-scale changes.

Rewriting is often intuitive—you read your manuscript and realize you omitted a key scene; you discover your protagonist's motivation isn't strong enough, that it wouldn't be rousing enough to get him to mow the lawn much less leave home to slay dragons; you have the feeling that a change in POV from third-person to first would solve half a dozen major problems. So you rewrite to correct these issues.

But you could approach rewriting in a more systematic way.

Use the questions in the edit checklist—specifically those dealing with large-picture elements such as character, plot, and setting—to guide you as you rewrite. Use the chapters featuring those same elements—"Shaping Characters," "Inspecting Plot," and "Showcasing the Setting"—to prompt changes in major story elements.

Consider rewriting to be a large-scale restructuring. For example, you don't necessarily push deep into details or even at links between elements when you rewrite. You don't typically look at word choice and sentence construction, at the effects of one element on another element, at the way elements such as mood, tone, pace, and rhythm are affected by changing story components. But you do eventually need to deal with these issues.

These are tasks best undertaken when editing.

EDITING

When you're satisfied with POV, narrative tense, major characters, scene arrangement, and plot events—with what happens, the order of events, and the characters involved—you're ready to begin editing.

As a matter of course, you'll no doubt have already covered some issues traditionally considered part of editing as you were rewriting. We look at the two activities as separate, but they do intersect at times. Still, *rewriting* is often concentrated on one scene, paragraph, or chapter—on one section of text—or on one character or plot thread.

Although rewriting may ultimately change large sections of text as well as many different sections of text throughout a novel, the focus—on one scene or paragraph at a time—is narrower.

Editing takes into account what changes to that one scene, paragraph, chapter, character, or plot thread mean to the surrounding scenes and to linked scenes in other chapters. Rewriting may also focus on a single fiction element, such as dialogue or setting, that crosses many scenes. But that focus is on the one element, the dialogue or setting. Editing covers every story element, every connection, every word. Even every punctuation mark.

Editing starts with an evaluation of story components, the fiction elements as well as technical elements. You'll read sections of the story (and then the whole manuscript) looking for the absence and presence of elements and decide whether the use and blend of elements work to create the effects you intended to create, the *story* you intended to create. Yet at some point you'll no longer be evaluating what you intended to create but rather what was actually created.

Editing will involve rewriting, even major rewriting. But it also involves attention to detail. It involves evaluating the big picture and the smallest particulars.

Editing looks at every issue, from plot, setting, character, dialogue, description, and conflict to grammar, punctuation, and word choice. When you edit, you'll be making choices about any element found in—or missing from—your stories.

Editing brings all the elements together to create the best possible story given the limitations of those elements.

Editing is like juggling dozens of objects of different size, shape, and weight. The editor recognizes that a change in any one element can upset the balance, necessitating changes in other elements which then lead to even further changes. When you *rewrite* a scene, you may simply be concerned with making that one scene perfect. When you *edit*, you must be concerned with how every element and every change influences dozens of other scenes and story components.

Editing is finished when the manuscript's components produce a complete story with a pleasing balance of elements that holds together for the length of the story *and* when the blend of elements fulfills genre requirements and the specific requirements of the story.

You're finished editing when the elements are no longer individual pieces but have blended into that good story told well, when there's nothing left to be moved or cut out, polished, or tweaked.

DUAL APPROACHES TO EDITING

It's likely that you'll approach editing in two ways as you work through your manuscripts. Yet you won't be choosing between the approaches but making use of both.

Using the first approach, you'll work through issues one at a time or maybe you'll tackle related issues together. Use the checklists in this guide and the questions and quick lists at the ends of chapters to remind you what kinds of issues you need to take on and to help you as you work through those issues. Use suggestions and examples from the chapters to guide changes for your own text.

This approach focuses on the fiction elements (plot, setting, character, dialogue, etc.) *and* sections of text (scenes, beginnings, middles, and ends). This first approach is similar to the approach for rewrites, except with editing you'll want to be more structured and less intuitive in deciding which elements to look at. (Although you should always listen to your intuition while you edit.) In editing, you'll want to check *everything*. And often multiple times.

The second edit approach, which you'll work through only after you finish the first approach, involves reading the full story text from beginning to end and marking it for errors, noting sections you want to rewrite, and making notations about missing elements (whether that means a word; a character's motivation; dialogue, action, or description; or even a scene).

When you read through the full manuscript, you'll still be using information from the checklists and the chapter questions and quick lists, but your approach will be different.

> With the second edit approach, you'll be reading the manuscript *as* story—not as parts of a whole but the whole itself.

In this way you'll be able to edit not only for individual elements and sections of the text but for the interplay and connections between the elements. You'll edit for continuity, pacing, clarity, rising tension, and the balance between elements. You'll still be searching for problems with the fiction elements as well as problems with technical issues (grammar and punctuation), yet you'll also read for flow and rhythm and the changing feel of the story.

In the first approach, you can start with the easiest steps—with what would be easiest for you, that is—but you could start with the toughest areas. Do whatever works for you, but don't grow so tired or frustrated that you stop before you get to the important stuff— big-picture elements or the writing areas that give you the most problems. Either get the hard stuff out of the way first or make sure you have time and the desire to deal with the difficult issues. The little details in your book may be perfect, but that won't matter if the major story elements have failed.

Use the second approach to root out remaining problems and the weaknesses that are difficult to see when you're editing and reworking only sections of text or a single fiction element. Use the second edit approach to push into the finest of the fine details.

Types of Editing

Relative to fiction, there are different types of editing: developmental, substantive (or content), copyediting, and proofreading.

Developmental editing has to do with developing text from the very beginning, putting the manuscript together, giving it a focus. A major thrust is determining what should be included before the first word is even written.

Developmental editing often features in nonfiction projects. This isn't what you'll be doing during a fiction manuscript's edit stage. Instead you'll be ensuring that events happen in the proper order with the right characters and just the right degree of drama. You'll be looking at the lengths of scenes, at the effectiveness of dialogue, at the usefulness of characters. You'll be editing to make sure that events make sense, that characters have sufficient and believable motivation, that events follow the pattern of cause and effect, action and reaction. You'll be editing for clarity and for effect, for pace, for emotional impact. You'll not only be looking for problems with what's in the story, but searching for fiction elements that have been left out or underutilized.

While you will add text during an edit, a major part of what you'll be doing is working with the text already on the page.

All this and more is the purview of substantive editing. And you'll definitely be operating as a substantive editor when you edit your novel. When you hire an editor to edit a fiction manuscript, substantive editing is typically what you'd want him or her to do.

Copyediting focuses on the technical issues of grammar, punctuation, and spelling as well as on word choice and style. Copyediting also includes fact-checking, searching for duplicate or missed words, inadvertent changes in verb tense, or problems with continuity. When you copyedit, you'll be looking for errors as well as omissions.

PROOFREADING

Proofreading is the final stage of getting a manuscript ready for publication or submission. Proofreading isn't actually editing, yet if you plan to edit your own work, proofreading will become part of your editing duties. You'll proofread to make sure errors haven't been overlooked or added during one of the other stages. For the writer who is self-editing, copyediting and proofreading duties will overlap. The final pass you make through your manuscript will typically be for punctuation, capitalization, formatting, and other errors visible to the eye. That is, this won't be the time to ensure you've given your protagonist sufficient motivation to step into his adventure.

Still, during any of these three stages—rewriting, editing, and proofreading—you *can* make changes to any story component. A professional proofreader wouldn't tackle rewriting and editing tasks, but a writer can and should. While these categories are separated for comparison's sake, that doesn't mean you can't address a problem, any problem, when you see it.

FORMATTING FOR PRINT AND E-BOOKS

This section is an example of text added during the formatting stage. Until I began formatting the print version of *The Magic of Fiction*, getting the book ready for printing, I didn't consider that a writer would still be adjusting text, even rewriting, as she formats a book. But it's true that you'll need to make adjustments for layout, for the look of text on a page, and for getting rid of orphans and widows (single lines of text at the bottoms and tops of pages that end up separated from the rest of a paragraph) *while you format.*

As you format (a necessity when you self-publish), you may need to adjust text for a better visual fit. That may mean adding, deleting, or rearranging words. Sometimes changing a single word to a longer or shorter one is all that's needed. Sometimes adding or deleting one word will be sufficient. But other times a change will mess up the format for other pages and you'll need to make additional changes.

With their multiple headers and font styles, nonfiction books may face more potential problems regarding formatting, yet all writers should be aware that they may be changing text while they format.

OUR APPROACH

Because my intention is to help you craft the best possible story you can put together, we'll look at the fiction elements and at the rules of writing for ways to strengthen your stories at any stage of the writing process. So, for example, I won't limit tips on writing strong scenes to only the rewriting stage. When you find a suggestion that mentions *working or reworking a scene*, assume that unless otherwise noted, this means that you could apply the suggestion at any stage, including those of writing the first draft and editing the final one.

So even though writing, rewriting, editing, and proofreading focus on different tasks, we're going to include each of them in our approach. Recognize, however, that some tasks *are* better suited to different stages—to the initial stage of creation or to rewriting, to editing, or to proofreading.

You'll want to include major changes to as many of the plot events and scenes as you think will be necessary before you start editing the fine-detail areas. You'll want to have finished adding, cutting, and rearranging text, for the most part, before you begin a proofing pass.

You'll want to complete most rewriting and editing tasks before allowing beta readers to read your manuscript, although if you have a critique partner, he or she may read sections of text before you've done a lot of polishing. Still, for betas you usually want the read to be as clean as possible so the readers don't trip over words or meaning.

Write and then work *major* revisions—especially the addition of scenes and large sections of text—with the writer's hat on. But once you've completed those major revisions, turn off the writer and think like an editor.

THE TAKEAWAY

We've seen that there's overlap in the stages of working and reworking a novel manuscript, but the typical broad order is:

- research and outline (the amount of detail in your outlines is solely up to you)
- write the first draft
- rewrite (create multiple drafts, changing major elements including characters, setting, and scenes)
- edit—first approach (focus on issues, fiction elements, and/or broad sections of text)
- edit—second approach (work through the manuscript from beginning to end)
- proofread
- format for print and e-books (if necessary)

Use the suggestions and tips in this guide to help with any stage, but put them to work specifically to change an early draft into a finished story ready for submission or publication.

Part Two

MAJOR ELEMENTS OF FICTION

5

VERIFYING VIEWPOINT: AFFIRMING POINT OF VIEW

I SPENT A LOT OF HOURS fussing over this chapter, trying to decide how to start it and what to include in it, before I finally reached a breakthrough that would allow us to cover issues with point of view without this chapter becoming a book itself.

Point of view (POV) is so important a topic that I can't highlight all the particulars in a few pages, can't point out all the ins and outs, the fine details, and all the variations in the limited time and space I have here, not in a book that also needs to cover every other major writing, fiction, and editing topic.

Yet because it's so important, I can't gloss over the subject either.

So what I concluded is to simply remind you (as if anything about point of view is simple) that you have choices in point of view and that you need to maintain a consistent point of view.

Consistency is the key to much in writing. Consistency doesn't absolve writing sins, but it does make them easier to put up with. For example, if you have to change every instance of one type of wrong usage, you can easily search and replace. But if you've experimented with half a dozen resolutions for the same problem, the fixes will take longer. So be consistent in both your approaches and your solutions.

I won't be delving into all the aspects of point of view, but I believe we can cover enough for you to be comfortable about your choices. And you can always research the topic; there are plenty of resources that cover POV.

IMPORTANCE OF POINT OF VIEW

This topic is a biggie, which is why I put it before reviews of the other elements of fiction. Point of view is a major component of stories and you want to get it right. Many other story elements are affected by POV, so make sure you've chosen the right one for your story and that you maintain it throughout the story (or scene or chapter if you're alternating POVs).

You'll also want to ensure that you maintain a consistent viewpoint character within a scene, a related issue.

If you're tempted to skip this chapter because it's not about the fun stuff and/or you find a discussion of POV tedious, may I suggest that you don't. Skip it, that is. This one's important. Poor handling of POV marks an author as an amateur. It can earn you a negative reputation. It can cost you fans and sales. It can make the writing process unnecessarily difficult or tedious.

Maybe readers can't pinpoint what's wrong with a story with wandering POV or a viewpoint that switches back and forth between characters like a tennis ball batted across a court, but they do *feel* the effects. A reader doesn't have to be able to pinpoint a problem to know there is one. It's not a reader's job to point out the flaws in your fiction; that's your job as both writer and editor. But readers will not enjoy one particular story, not as much as they'd enjoy others, if POV isn't consistent, clear, and without miscues.

The terms *viewpoint character* and *point of view* are often used interchangeably, though they aren't the same. They are related, however, and so we'll look at them together in this chapter.

Yet we'll be looking primarily at both issues from the editing side and not a writing one. So while you'll be able to pick up pointers for writing the different POVs, this will not be an in-depth discussion of the many permutations of the different points of view.

We want to instead talk about maintaining a viewpoint and viewpoint character, and decide whether you've chosen the correct ones for each scene and the story as a whole.

WHERE TO START WITH POINT OF VIEW

Choosing a story's point of view is one of the earliest decisions a writer makes. It's often an unconscious decision, yet it should be given more than passing consideration.

Let's say you just read three young adult (YA) novels told in first person. After that, of course you're going to write your YA novel in first person. Or maybe you've only read third-person narration, so that's the one option you're familiar with. Or you read a lot of romance, where third-person narration flips back and forth between hero and heroine, and even though your story is a mystery, you automatically follow the same format.

If you're reading this chapter before you start your novel, may I suggest you give thought to your options for POV and don't simply fall into the familiar. Yes, what has worked for others may be perfect for your story. But then again, there may be an option that produces a stronger story.

> If you've already written the manuscript, use this infor-mation to decide whether or not you've made the best choice. It's never too late to change even the foundations of a story. And POV is pretty much the most founda-tional of elements in a novel.

TIPS FOR POINT OF VIEW

Consider genre and reader expectations when you evaluate POV. Many mysteries and YA novels and some literary novels are told using first person. If your narrator has a quirky or fascinating inner thought life, one that readers will find captivating and *one they won't grow bored with*, first person may be your best choice.

Yet even the greatest of first-person narrators can grow cloying or annoying. Make sure you haven't filtered every action, event, and fragment of dialogue through the first-person narrator, making every story event connect to her.

You wouldn't want to keep saying *I heard, I saw, I felt, I read,* or *I noticed*, relating every action and bit of description to the narrator. Rather than write *I felt the sharp shards on the bottom of my feet*, try *dozens of shards slashed at my feet*. Rather than *I heard the heavy breathing of someone else in the shadowed room*, try *heavy breathing filled the shadowed room*.

Unless the character's sensory reaction is the important part of the sentence—*I heard, for the first time, the song of a violin through my right ear*—skip that part. Give us other details instead—*The pathos of a violin carried through the still autumn night.* Focus on more than the narrator so he doesn't come across as a narcissistic attention hog or a two-year-old who always says *mine, mine, mine.*

A simple editing tip? Cut uses of *I*. Definitely cut their use as sentence and paragraph openers.

You will want to take advantage of character thoughts, emotions, and reactions in first-person stories; that's one of the strengths of first-person narration. But you don't want the character talking non-stop about himself in the reader's ear for the entire book. Use the strengths of the first-person narrator—insights, unfiltered feelings and thoughts, and immediacy—while eliminating the weaknesses—too much time in the character's head and too much emphasis on him at the expense of story events and other characters.

Also, there are restrictions with first-person narration as well as with third person. Your narrator or viewpoint characters can only report what they know, so you'll be limited in the information you can convey.

Characters can't know what they'd never know. They can't dwell on it, report it, or use such information to make decisions. Unless they see an event or another character fills in the blanks, characters are ignorant.

But ignorance adds to conflict. And confusion. And disquiet. It's good that your characters can't know everything; just keep that in mind as you write. They don't know what's happened around the world unless someone tells them. They don't know what other characters are thinking—although they can *guess.* They don't know what their own facial expressions look like.

Using first- or third-person narration allows you to reveal the deep thoughts and motivations of characters in a way that brings readers close, so close that they can imagine themselves as those characters.

But at the same time, if you're not using an omniscient POV, neither characters nor readers can know everything.

Characters can reveal themselves from the inside out, showing how they relate to their worlds from inside their skin and minds and hearts, but they don't know what they look like to others at any given moment. They wouldn't report facts about themselves the same way an outsider would.

Except for narcissists and perhaps young teens, people typically don't describe their physical characteristics in a list or in a blatantly self-aware way. Not many would describe their own luxurious ebony tresses swaying with each movement of their bodies. And a woman couldn't know that a cold, predatory look had entered her eyes.

But a character might bemoan that she could never get all the gray out of her hair when she colored it at home in the tiny bathroom crowded with kids, husband, and two German shepherds.

A man might note that his shoulders tensed when he caught sight of the lowlife having an affair with his wife.

The key here, with both first- and third-person POVs, is to think *inside out* rather than *outside in*.

MULTIPLE VIEWPOINT CHARACTERS

To provide more information about what's going on in a story world, you can use multiple viewpoint characters, changing them each chapter or scene, but there are limitations to this option as well.

If a character is so strong that you want readers to live within his head, then why would you want to write *several* characters that way? Readers can't identify with all the characters in one story and you won't want them to; they can't pretend to be every character. Pulling readers out of one character's head only to drop them into another character will not help them bond with the first character. Instead, readers may feel resentful. Or they may just hold themselves at a distance, failing to identify closely with any character.

This doesn't mean that you can't use multiple viewpoint characters; you can and you should if doing so fits your story. But don't do it simply to give yourself a way to reveal more information. Find another way to do that if that's the only reason you need multiple narrators or viewpoint characters. And use as few viewpoint characters as you can make work. Stories are stronger when readers can bond with characters, but there's no way readers can bond with everyone. Be selective to make your stories more appealing.

Not every character deserves to be a viewpoint character. Not every character is fascinating enough. Not every character is important enough. Not every character is complete enough for the duty.

And, as I said, ignorance fuels conflict. So when a character doesn't know something yet knows there's something to be known, you've got strong conflict built in. Take advantage of what viewpoint characters don't know to power your scenes. To drive your story.

Instead of trying to share all knowledge with your readers, limit yourself in some way. Either you don't get to tell us everything that's going on in your story world or you do, but you don't get to do it all through one character.

Is it too late to change POV once the story's reached the end? Not at all—you can always rewrite. And once you've written more than a couple of novels, that option won't sound nearly as daunting as it sounds to the writer who has finished only one manuscript and thinks a quick proofreading pass of the first draft is all it needs to ready it for publication.

> Rewriting and editing are extensive and time-consuming tasks, but this is where the heavy work of writing gets done. It's fairly easy to throw characters and events together in a rough draft. The work comes in when you have to hide and reveal and use nuance and foreshadowing and link events and play with pace and decide on word choices and build conflict.

Rewriting is good for stories; approach your rewrites and edits with anticipation, knowing that it's in these stages that you'll create memorable fiction and stories that others will enjoy reading.

And lest you think that only first-person point of view holds traps for the unwary writer, think again. Third person and omniscient have problems of their own.

Any point of view can be wrong for a particular story; any viewpoint character may prove to be a bad choice.

THE BASICS

The *viewpoint character* is the one who lends his eyes and ears to a reader so a scene can be experienced through that character. He may also share his thoughts and emotions related to the events of the scene. The *point of view* prescribes how that sharing is accomplished.

So POV deals with *how* a story is told, and the viewpoint character is the one *who* allows us to experience the story through him.

VIEWPOINT CHARACTER

Events are presented through the viewpoint character, through his experiences and history and personality. Scenes are typically shown through the eyes of one character; that is, through one at a time. While readers see through a character's eyes, we can also hear through his ears, feel through his emotions, and react according to his experience and reactions. We can see how other characters react to events or dialogue, as noted by the viewpoint character, but we can only feel and know the inner reactions of the viewpoint character.

We know what's important in a scene because the viewpoint character notes the importance of object, speech, event, or setting detail. What the viewpoint character notices is what the reader sees.

> Stories are shaped through the viewpoint character.
> Stories are *made* by the viewpoint character. A story told
> through the eyes of a different viewpoint character
> becomes a different story.

Word choices reflect the viewpoint character and his background.

If a story follows Larry's viewpoint—his actions, the places he goes, the events he is part of—then that's a story different from one that follows Martin through his days. The right viewpoint character can make a story, can add the right amounts of emotion, distance, or empathy. The wrong viewpoint character can produce a flat story, an uninvolving or a confusing one that fails to draw readers close.

The wrong viewpoint character can sabotage a story.

Choose your viewpoint character or characters for what they can bring to a story or scene.

Do you need a character who can stand back and analyze? Is that the character you chose? Do you need someone readers can get close to and feel empathy for? If so, is that the character you chose to tell your story?

Have you played up those characteristics, the ones needed for your viewpoint character?

If you need a viewpoint character to be emotional, do you have him or her reacting emotionally? If the viewpoint character needs to notice his surroundings, have you made sure that he does? If you need a character who hears what others don't, have you shown his superior hearing at work in different ways and in a handful of scenes? And have you made sure he doesn't miss a sound or bit of dialogue that someone with his skills would never miss? If he did miss it, is there a reason for him overlooking, say, the screams of a neighbor? A booming thunderstorm? A race night at the local stock car track with lots of *vrooming* engines?

While you have almost limitless options, some genres favor a certain character as the viewpoint character.

In most romances written today, both hero and heroine get viewpoint duties. In mysteries, the sleuth is usually the viewpoint character, though John Watson did the job in most of the Sherlock Holmes stories. In some books the antagonist gets viewpoint scenes, though readers may not know the character's identity until the story's end.

We typically employ one viewpoint character per scene, though a number of authors have learned how to include thoughts and observations of multiple characters in a scene without driving readers mad.

Head-Hopping. Head-hopping occurs when the narration jumps from one viewpoint character to the next *in the same scene* and usually without warning.

You've noticed this in your own reading, I'm sure. The story's rolling along and suddenly you stop reading, wondering why Larry is admiring the way he walks. Then you find out he's not narcissistically admiring himself; *Margaret* is watching and admiring, and the readers are, without warning, treated to her thoughts. It's as if she's slipped into Larry's head.

The best way to prevent this problem is to use only one viewpoint character per scene. When you're ready to give another character the viewpoint duty, mark the page with a visual scene break.

Do some writers switch between characters in a single scene? Sure they do. And some do it well. They blithely pass off viewpoint duties from one character to the next with the touch of a hand, as if in a game of tag—*You're it. You're now the viewpoint character. Start sharing your thoughts and paying attention to those setting details, events, characters, and sections of dialogue that only you would notice.*

Other writers don't do this too well, however, leaving readers confused and yanking them straight out of the fiction the writer otherwise so carefully constructed.

> My advice? Don't head-hop. Don't vacillate between viewpoint characters in one scene. Mine a scene for the experiences and emotions of one character. Let him or her take on the scene in its fullness, appreciating every event and emotion the scene holds. Let the reader imagine himself as a character in the scene the same way characters experience events—through the eyes and heart of only one person.

Both new writers and very experienced writers head-hop. Yet the results can be vastly different. Bouncing between the heads (thoughts, emotions, and viewpoint) of multiple characters within a scene can drive readers batty. Or it can enrich a scene. But if you're a beginner, don't do it. If beta readers told you they couldn't keep the story straight because you bounced between characters, listen to them and fix the issue. Unless you're using the omniscient viewpoint—which involves much more than treating readers to the thoughts of all characters in a single scene—then don't change viewpoint characters midscene. Not until you understand the effect on the reader and learn to change viewpoint characters in a manageable way.

Never change viewpoint characters midparagraph.

Change viewpoint characters, if you need to, at the top of scenes. And use the first or second sentence of a scene to tell readers just who the viewpoint character is. This is especially important if you change viewpoint characters often. Mention the name of the character right away and give readers a thought or reaction, or maybe a line of dialogue, that only he could offer.

In your edits, make sure you've maintained a single viewpoint character per scene—no sudden shifts for just a single line or one paragraph midscene.

> There's a vast difference between switching between viewpoint characters once per scene—passing off viewpoint duties purposely—and bouncing willy-nilly from character to character or throwing in random thoughts from characters who aren't the viewpoint character.

Check your scenes. If you're randomly switching the viewpoint between characters, your scenes need work and your approach to viewpoint needs reevaluating. If you purposely and clearly switch viewpoint characters midscene, you may be able to make such scenes work. (But it's likely you could just as easily insert a scene break.)

OPTIONS FOR POINT OF VIEW

Almost any character could be the viewpoint character for a scene. Not everyone would be the best choice, but you could argue that any of them could do the work. But what of point of view?

The basic points of view are first person, second person, third person, and omniscient (a version of the third-person narrator according to some, a category of its own according to others).

There are shadings and levels and combinations of POV, but let's look at options at a basic level. I'll mention instances when a certain point of view might be expected or may work well, but don't consider yourself limited. Use the point of view that works for your story.

First person lets the narrator say:

> I was minding my own business, jogging through Central Park, when I tripped, most literally and embarrassingly, over a body. A dead body. Two bullet holes, head and chest. And one garish high heel posed elegantly upon the belly.

This option allows you to flavor the moment with the narrator's word choices and style and attitude. The first-person narrator can report what he wants to report and keep out what he wants to ignore. He can even tell lies without letting the reader know he's lying. To do so wouldn't be playing fair, but there's no law that says he must be fair.

First person can produce an immediacy that many readers enjoy, with the reader feeling that he's part of the action, that's more difficult to achieve in other POVs.

When to use it: with a quirky or funny character; when the character's thoughts and insights are needed to make sense of events; in detective stories, coming-of-age stories, in YA novels; in any story where the narrator is fascinating enough to handle the job.

Potential problems: readers can get tired of being in the character's head; overuse of the words *I, me, my,* and *mine*; too much is filtered through the character's thoughts and senses.

Second person narration, highly unusual and quite noticeable, might read this way:

> You were minding your own business, jogging through Central Park, when you tripped, most literally and embarrassingly, over a body.

This style purports to put the reader inside the story. Readers, however, may object to being told what they think or feel or what they're doing. It's a stylized narration that can feel quite false and improbable. On the other hand, it can feel edgy and innovative. Second person is used often in nonfiction but not nearly as often in fiction, though it's not completely rare either. If you're feeling bold, try it for a short story. My recommendation is that you not try it for a novel without a compelling reason that outweighs potential problems. Though you may use it well, readers may not be welcoming.

Second-person narration, rather than being about *you, the reader*, may actually be directed toward a part of one of the characters, addressed as if that individual part were human, extant on its own. The *you* may be the narrator's heart or soul or younger self.

When to use it: in experimental fiction, in short stories.

Potential problems: it can seem fake and can remind readers that they're reading fiction rather than participating in the story's adventure; it's unfamiliar to most readers; it can sound accusatory.

Third person narration might read:

> Kassim was minding his own business, jogging
> through Central Park, when he tripped, most literally,
> over a body.

Third-person is the most common POV. It's versatile and could present the same information multiple ways, depending on the tone or impact the writer wants to create and on the distance the writer intends to set up between events and characters on the one hand and readers on the other.

While some claim that the first-person POV offers the greatest sense of immediacy, others would argue that third-person also offers immediacy, that it can make the reader feel that the story is unfolding right before him, right now, with the reader, if not a part of the action, at least a witness to it.

Third person can be objective or subjective, an outsider's observational POV or one that allows readers into the thoughts and emotions of the viewpoint character.

When to use it: when you're going to use multiple viewpoint characters, when a story needs more distance than a first-person narrator allows, in almost any genre or story of any length.

Weaknesses: there aren't many; however, third person may not be the best POV for your story. If your main character has a new and unique voice, consider first person rather than third.

A more distanced third person point of view could read:

> Kassim was jogging through Central Park when he tripped over a body.

Third person with deep point of view (*less* distance) could read:

> He was picturing Lola waiting for him in their bed and just picking up his pace when he tripped and went skidding across the jogging path. Damned bums. He jumped up and turned. Holy crap. She was no bum, not in that getup.

Deep POV is a way to invite readers inside the third-person viewpoint character's head and heart to hear his thoughts and feel his emotions. Deep POV lessens distance between the viewpoint character and the reader. It does for third person what first person naturally does—keeps the reader inside the head of the viewpoint character.

When to use it: in romances; in much of contemporary fiction; when you want to immerse readers in the character's head and heart, his thoughts and emotions.

Omniscient might report:

> Kassim, grinning, had just picked up his pace when he sprawled headlong across a lump in the jogging path. He'd stumbled, quite literally, over the Park Strangler's fifth victim.

The omniscient narrator knows everything and can share part or all of what he knows. And I don't mean he only knows everything about one particular story. No, the omniscient narrator can know anything about any event or place or person in any time period and, theoretically, he could include any of that information as he tells your story.

His reports of story events can be impersonal, or he may share his opinion. He also has the option of showing the reader what characters are thinking or feeling, or of hiding that information from the reader. The omniscient narrator could, if he so chose, speak directly to the reader. The omniscient was used much more frequently in stories from the late nineteenth and early twentieth centuries than it's used now.

The omniscient POV (as does the objective third person) holds readers at a distance from story events and characters. Some omniscient stories read as less distancing than others, but in general, this POV is distancing. And it can often read as a report, cool and impersonal in tone.

The omniscient could also contain a lot of *telling* at the expense of showing events as they play out.

When to use it: in epics of any style—science fiction, historical, or fantasy—in political thrillers that cross the globe; in stories that feature large named casts; in stories that span long periods of time; when you need distance between story events and the reader.

Do note that the omniscient can be used briefly in third-person narration to introduce scenes. Typically this is done through wide-angle or large-picture views at the top of scenes, before the POV narrows in on a viewpoint character. This, however, doesn't work in first-person narration or when deep POV is used consistently in a third-person story. Readers can't remain inside a character's head and at the same time receive information that the character couldn't or wouldn't have.

These, then, are the most basic options for point of view. There are variations, most especially in terms of narrative distance, and each can be used in combination with other POVs if you want to use different POVs for each viewpoint character in your novel.

The options allow great variety, but always remember the reader on the other side of your pages. If he's confused by your story presentation, why would he read on? The choices of point of view and viewpoint character should make the read enjoyable and clear for the reader, not make it impossible to follow the story. Be daring with your choices if they allow you greater freedom in storytelling, but don't alienate readers. Stories are for them, after all. Help readers navigate the unfamiliar rather than hinder them as they explore your fictional worlds. Choose the POV and viewpoint characters that work best for your genre, setting, characters, plot, desired impact, mood, narrative distance, and tone.

MANIPULATING NARRATIVE DISTANCE

Narrative distance, that perceived distance between reader and viewpoint character or narrator, allows writers to create stories with intimacy or with cool distance. Readers can feel close to characters, as if inside them, or feel as if they're standing next to them, or feel as if they're watching them from a distance, as in a movie theatre or across even greater distances.

You create or change narrative distance through your choice of POV and the words you use. You can choose narrative distance from a range of distances. For some POVs, you can even move between points on the range in the same story.

First person and third person with deep (or close) POV both allow the reader to get up close with the viewpoint character. These POVs allow the reader to not only see what the viewpoint character sees, but to feel his feelings and hear his thoughts. For first person, this is true all the time. For deep third, you could have almost no narrative distance all the time, just like first person, or you could move in and out of the close POV. This is helpful when readers are caught in the head of the viewpoint character for too long and need a break. (This technique requires practice and a deft touch. You *can* move in and out of deep POV, but you don't want readers to feel that they're bouncing between POVs.) When you use a deep POV for third person and stay with it, it's very close to first-person narration.

In first person, of course, readers don't get a break from the character's thoughts unless you switch viewpoint characters.

The reader has no doubt about who the viewpoint character is in any scene when first person and deep third are used correctly. Every thought is obviously the viewpoint character's thought. Every emotion is hers. Every time we read about a sound or about an event glimpsed through a window, we know who heard the sound or saw the event. The writer doesn't have to use filtering words (*I/she heard, I/he felt*) with these POVs because the reader knows who heard and felt and saw.

This is the closest the reader can get to identifying with a character without actually being inside the story herself.

On the opposite end of the range is the wide distance created by the objective omniscient narrator. This point of view uses telling to a great degree. It reports what is happening or has happened from the view of someone watching. Consider this an outsider's viewpoint. The omniscient narrator knows all, but at the greatest narrative distance he doesn't allow any glimpses into the characters' minds or hearts, at least not directly. The writer can always show how a character feels or what he thinks through his speech, his expression and posture, and his actions.

Between these points—between virtually no narrative distance and the wide valley of a great distance—there are other options.

For example, the omniscient narrator might choose to show every character's thoughts, some characters' thoughts, the thoughts of only one character, or the thoughts of a single character per scene. When we get a character's thoughts, we move a bit closer to her, even with an omniscient point of view. Yet with omniscient, we can still get reports about what a character looks like, which is distinctly an outsider's viewpoint.

When an omniscient narrator shines a light into a character's head, highlighting his thoughts, we certainly don't enjoy the close narrative distance we get with first-person narration, but we're closer than we would be with other omniscient options, especially the camera view, the objective POV that's similar to a movie camera's all-knowing but outside-only eye.

To create distance in third-person POVs, pull away from the character's head and heart. Show the character's thoughts, yes, but at some distance from the thoughts. This is the time to use those filtering words (*he heard a car backfire down the street*). This is also the time to use thought tags (*he thought*) and to maybe use italics for the character's thoughts. The more of these devices you use and the more often you use them, the greater distance you put between reader and character.

In deep POV, you can skip the thought tags and slip thoughts directly into the text without pointing to them, without highlighting them in any way. In contrast, when you want distance in third-person POVs, you point out when a character is thinking and/or you use italics for her thoughts.

As you edit, look for consistency in narrative distance. Make sure that word choices fit your intended distance. Make sure that you don't bounce from one distance to another without a plan.

Always remember that except for first-person narration, you could show thoughts or knowledge from an omniscient narrator for all viewpoints in some circumstances.

For example, you can almost always open a story or a new scene with a bird's-eye view of setting or action and then move closer and step into your regular point of view. You don't have to do this, but it's an option. And you may not want to do it because it could have readers wondering who's telling them the information. But the device is successfully used in novel after novel.

THE QUICK LIST

- Make sure there's only one viewpoint character per scene unless you can switch between them without confusing the reader and without destroying the reader's connection to a character, an outcome that's not achieved effortlessly.

- If you've chosen unusual viewpoint characters—animal or object—make sure such a choice fits the genre and audience. While a child might enjoy a story from the viewpoint of a German shepherd, an adult may not be as accepting, especially if there's nothing else in the story that allows the reader to believe that a German shepherd can reason and deliberate the way humans can.

- If you use first-person narration or a deep third-person POV, remember to move outside the viewpoint character's head occasionally. Help readers focus on more than the viewpoint character. One way to do this is to remove self-references to the viewpoint character in first person. A second method is to reduce filter words in first and third person.

- Make sure not to give only a single line from a different character's viewpoint, popping readers into a second character's head in the middle of a scene. (Pay close attention to this one—it happens a lot, and it's sometimes hard to notice.)

- Use only as many viewpoint characters as you need and as few as possible while still telling the story you want to tell.

- If you plan to regularly switch between POVs or between viewpoint characters, do so early in the story to alert readers to the pattern. You wouldn't introduce a new POV or switch viewpoint characters for the first time in the final chapters. That's not playing fair with the readers, and they may wonder why you hadn't included scenes from the viewpoint of a particular character earlier. And if readers are wondering about the underpinnings of a story, they're not lost in the fiction.

- To choose a scene's viewpoint character, make sure you've chosen the character with the most at stake or the one who can stir up the most trouble and conflict. Maybe use the character who'll have the strongest emotional response or whose reaction is necessary to provoke a particular response from others. Don't be afraid to rewrite a scene from the viewpoint of a different character in order to produce a different, a more potent, effect.

- If you use multiple viewpoint characters, make sure they sound different, that they think differently. That their focus and interests are different.

- Be sure you've maintained the same POV throughout the story unless you change it on purpose.

Yes, you could have one chapter in the first-person POV of your protagonist and the next chapter in the third-person POV of your antagonist and then switch back and forth throughout the length of the story. But you could use a single POV (first, third, or omniscient) paired with either multiple viewpoint characters or only a single viewpoint character for the whole novel. No matter your viewpoint choices, do check for moments when you slip between POVs. I'm not talking purposely switching viewpoint characters here but making mistakes with POV, changing from third person to first (or vice versa) midparagraph or midscene.

6

NARRATIVE TENSE: WHAT HAPPENS WHEN?

WHILE THE TRADITIONAL narrative tense for novels has been past tense, some genres today favor present tense. You should recognize, however, that present tense is still somewhat unusual, especially in some genres. Some readers won't/don't like it. Still, you can use what works for you and your story no matter what others think or like. Just be aware that not all readers will agree with your choice.

While I'm limiting much of my explanation of the narrative tense in this chapter to either past and present—typically *simple past* and *simple present*—do note that you will mix verb tenses as well as verb *forms* in your narration. Much of the dialogue—for example, the words that are actually spoken—is written in the present tense, even if the rest of the narration is past tense.

> "I **need** to tell you something," Patrick said. "Your job **is** in trouble. Jonas **wants** to give it to his son."

Even dialogue, however, uses a mix of verb tenses. Because the rest of the story from our fictional example is past tense, the dialogue tag, *Patrick said*, is past tense also. And even in the spoken words, a character could refer to an event from the past or one in the future.

> "I need to tell you something," Patrick said. "When you **turned down** my proposal, I **wanted** to demand answers from you."

> "I **will tell** you everything tomorrow. I promise."

Not only might you mix *tenses* in this manner, but you'll also use a variety of verb *forms*. So even if story events are conveyed largely in the *simple past*, you'll still use other forms of the past tense. (The same holds true if you write in present tense.)

Because you want your characters to have the ability to look forward and back and have conditional actions—and because you'll need variety and flexibility as you write—you'll use more than the simple past or simple present. That's where the other verb forms come in.

You'll call on conditional verb forms and progressive, perfect, and perfect progressive forms.

Please don't think that you need to study these verb forms. This isn't a lesson in verbs and grammar, just a quick reminder of verb forms you no doubt know well and use often in your writing projects.

I just want to point out that when we say a story's written in the past tense, we're talking about most of the verbs, not all of them. And while most verbs might be the *simple* past, again, that's not true all the time. There are other forms of the past tense. The same is true for present tense. (True for the future tense, as well, but while you might use future tense occasionally as you write, it's not likely that your major narration will use the future tense.)

Have I confused you? Let's look at examples to get an idea of what we're talking about and the options you'll likely use in stories written in either the past or present tense.

Simple

She walks to the park, enjoying the sunshine. (Present)

She walked to the park, talking to herself all the way. (Past)

She will walk to the park to search for her brother. (Future)

Progressive (or continuous)

She is walking to the park to get an ice cream. (Present)

She was walking to the park to meet a friend. (Past)

She will be walking to the park this afternoon. (Future)

Perfect

She has walked to the park to look at the ducks. (Present)

She had walked to the park to find her lost hat. (Past)

She will have walked through the park before you find her. (Future)

Perfect Progressive (or continuous)

She has been walking to the park every day for years. (Present)

Until she broke her foot, she had been walking to the park for exercise. (Past)

Come June, she will have been walking to the park daily for three years. (Future)

Conditional

If he loves her, she will go with him to Paris. (Present)

If he loved her, she would go with him to Paris. (Past)

If he had loved her, she would have gone with him to Paris. (Past Perfect)

Note: The conditional is actually an example of a mood, yet since it's a common verb setup, it's likely you'll use it (as well as the imperative mood—*Finish it now!*) in your fiction.

If the events in your story have already happened, you'll be using the past tense. That means simple past much of the time, with other forms of the past used when necessary. It's likely, however, that you'll also use some future- and some present-tense verbs.

For editing purposes, you'll want to make sure you use the appropriate forms for your chosen narrative tense. There are always exceptions, so I'm not going to say you'd never find a present perfect verb form in a story told using the past tense, but for the most part, you'd be consistent.

These next examples—past first, then present, and then a combination of past and present—show the different forms using the same text. Fair warning that the writing is pretty stinky in order to highlight my point—that point being that you don't want to mix tenses accidentally. Also, to help you see the verb tenses and forms easily, I purposely didn't use contractions.

> Dar **thundered** across the plain, **searching** for Gia. He **had** already **searched** the nearby forest, but she **was hiding** from their attackers. She **was** smart and **had hidden** before. Yet **if she heard** Dar calling, she **would show** herself.

> Dar **thunders** across the plain, **searching** for Gia. He **has** already **searched** the nearby forest, but she **is hiding** from their attackers. She **is** smart and **has hidden** before. Yet **if she hears** Dar calling, she **will show** herself.

This next paragraph mixes past and present, an example of what you *don't* want. When you edit, look for an incorrect mix of verb tenses.

> Dar **thundered** across the plain, **searching** for Gia. He **has** already **searched** the nearby forest, but she **was hiding** from their attackers. She **was** smart and **has hidden** before. [This combination should have you cringing.] Yet **if she hears** Dar calling, she **would show** herself. [This one is just as bad.] **✗**

PROGRESSIVE VS. SIMPLE FORMS

The majority of your verbs will be simple past or simple present. While it's okay and occasionally necessary to use the progressive form, it shouldn't be your go-to choice. The impact is often stronger with the use of the simple past or simple present.

I'm not telling you that you can't use the progressive form of verbs when it's called for, because you will need it. Yet don't allow yourself fall into the habit of using it as a matter of course when it's not needed to convey a sense of continuous action.

You'll often use a combination of progressive and simple verb tenses in the same sentence to show what was going on when something else happened.

> Veronique **was peering** into the window of the village's premier antique shop when a rusted-out Toyota **jumped** the curb two feet from her.

Yet unless you need or truly want to stress the ongoing nature of all of a character's actions or movements, refrain from using the progressive for each of them.

> Veronique **was peering** into the window of the village's premier antique shop. She **was whistling** a happy tune. Her mother **was waiting** at the dress shop, **calling** Veronique every five minutes to remind her of that fact, but Veronique **was ignoring** her.

Can you imagine paragraph after paragraph with *was* after *was* after *was*? The following options make for less reader-annoying reading. The first takes advantage of the impact of the simple past, declaring what had taken place. The second, using one progressive verb, creates an emphasis the first paragraph doesn't have. (Note that the present participle *whistling* is the same in past and present.)

> Veronique **peered** into the window of the village's premier antique shop, **whistling** a happy tune. Her mother **waited** at the dress shop—and **called** Veronique every five minutes to remind her of that fact—but Veronique **ignored** her.

Veronique **peered** into the window of the village's premier antique shop, **whistling** a happy tune. Yes, her mother **was waiting** at the dress shop—she **called** Veronique every five minutes to remind her of that fact—but Veronique **ignored** her.

When you edit, look for an overuse of progressive verbs. They often jump out from the printed page, but you can do a word search for *is* (present tense) and *was* (past tense) and even *ing*, although not all *ing* words will be part of a progressive verb. Don't eliminate all uses of the progressive, yet work to limit them. Use the progressive deliberately, purposely, and not out of habit.

A writer may also choose the historical present (the use of present tense for events that took place in the past) for a scene or two, even in a novel that otherwise uses the past tense to tell the story.

What I'm most concerned about with narrative tense is having you know that you've chosen the best narrative tense for a particular story and then ensuring that you've maintained that tense throughout the novel, changing it only consciously and purposely.

If you find that the narrative tense you chose doesn't work for the story, you can always change your mind. Rewriting from beginning to end in a new tense may be the making of your novel. It will take a lot of time and a whole lot of reworking of scenes and sentences, but if you found that something as relatively simple as changing the narrative tense meant the difference between selling 100 books and 100,000, wouldn't you make the change?

Yet before you commit to a wholesale change, try changing the narrative tense in a few scenes or chapters and study the effect. Is the result worth changing the entire story? You should be able to tell.

THE BASICS

The most common storytelling tense is the simple past. You'll find the past in every length of story in every genre. It's the tense we use in our own lives when we tell of an event that happened earlier in the day or when we share events with a friend we haven't talked to in ages. Think *once upon a time*. Think of stories that relate events that have already happened. Think typical—traditional—fiction.

Once upon a time there was a boy who loved a girl.

* * *

Paloma, a princess by birth if not temperament, snatched off her stylish crown and tossed it across the audience chamber.

* * *

The sky hovered close, dark and ugly, not merely threatening a storm, but guaranteeing it. Was it a perfect day for a murder or should Gormley have stayed in bed? After all, even hit men deserved decent working conditions. He turned up the collar of his Burberry knockoff. Yeah, he'd put that in his next contract—no assassinations during inclement weather.

We're so used to the simple past that, as readers, we have no trouble jumping into stories that use it. We just go with the narrative.

Janelle **eased** between the trees as she **followed** the man who'd been following her earlier in the day. He **didn't** even know she **was** there.

In present tense, this would read—

Janelle **eases** between the trees as she **follows** the man who followed her earlier in the day. He **doesn't** even know **she's** there.

As I mentioned, present-tense stories have become quite popular in some genres, especially YA. But you can use present tense in most genres if you can make it work. Present tense is typically not used in today's romances or in epics, yet you'll find it in science fiction and mysteries. It's definitely a popular choice for literary fiction.

In terms of editing, what's most important is that you weed out mistakes in tense. If your story is present tense, there shouldn't be inadvertent switches to past tense. And the same is true in reverse.

When you edit, be alert for tense switching. If you typically write in past tense but your new manuscript is present tense, be especially vigilant. Switching tenses midparagraph or midscene is common when a writer is writing in a tense he's not used to writing in, and the practice often goes unnoticed by the writer. Reading from hard copy will help you spot this kind of error.

Also, if you've written a past-tense story, look for tense switches in simple words, such as *it's*. *It's* is a contraction of *it is* or *it has*, both present tense, and not *it was*, past tense. I come across this error often in stories written in past tense. Other contractions to watch for include *he's* or *she's*, *I'm*, *I'll*, *he'll*, and *she'll*.

Make sure the tense you choose works for the story. If beta reader after beta reader has a problem with the tense you choose, perhaps that choice deserves another look. While changing tenses would be time consuming and difficult once a story is complete, rewriting in a different tense is not impossible. Be open to the possibility that you may have to change your story's narrative tense.

FIRST PERSON AND PRESENT TENSE

I've already mentioned that first-person present-tense stories can create a particular problem with too many reports of *I'm doing this* and *I'm doing that* and too many references to *me*, *my*, and *mine*. Edit with an eye toward reducing these annoying repetitions. Think about getting outside the narrator's head and cutting back on the number of self-references. Readers need a break from relentless mentions of the first-person narrator.

Refuse to filter every event and object through the narrator and her senses. Write sentences that focus on other characters and objects, making them the subject of sentences and the recipient of the narrator's and the reader's attention. Since the story is told in first person, readers already know that they're getting the thoughts and focus of the narrator; they don't need to have every story element or event relayed through that narrator. Not with an obvious reference to the narrator. Readers don't need to see strings that reach from the narrator to every object, person, or event. The strings are a given—they don't need to be made visible.

You might be wondering about first-person past-tense narration—can't it also be heavy-handed with references to self? It can. But for some reason it's the mix of present tense and first-person narration that produces the worst examples of this kind of overwriting, at least in my experience. The reason may be due to most writers' deeper familiarity with the past tense and inexperience with writing present tense. Many writers seem to struggle with writing effectively, fluidly, in the present tense. But reading books written in the present tense and practicing writing in the present tense can help writers correct this problem.

No Play-by-Play

I've found that manuscripts of first-person stories, both present and past tense, include more simple actions of the character, more details of every step the character takes, than do third-person stories. I've surmised that writers feel the need to share every moment of the character's adventure in order to justify using first-person narration. But readers don't need that, not every common action. They want the good stuff, not a report of every move a character makes to get her from one location or one moment to the next.

If you discover that you've written—multiple times—something such as *I picked up my keys, walked to the door, opening it wide as I stepped through, and locked the door behind me*, then your manuscript probably needs major editing. An exception is possible if you're including such details for a reason, such as revealing a character quirk or if the character is recounting a sequence step by step to prove a point. If, however, your story reads like this all the way through, know that you'll annoy your readers. Don't share details of every event or action; share the necessary and fascinating details.

> You're not writing a play-by-play report; you're writing engaging fiction. Resist showing every movement your characters make. Resist assigning more importance to events than they deserve. Sometimes the mere mention of an action is sufficient, but sometimes a mention is more than is even necessary.

Give the reader credit for being able to connect dots and assume common actions. Readers are smart—they know that a car needs to be started before a character can drive it. There's no need to show your character getting in, putting the key into the ignition, turning the key, and putting the car into drive. Don't include these kinds of details with a driving sequence and don't include them for other commonplace action sequences.

LOOK WITHIN

Think about your own thoughts. While you see the world and its events as they relate to you, you're not always thinking *I, I, I.* You may seldom use the word *I* at all, at least not in your mind.

You think how hot the day is or how bad the burned eggs smell. You focus on the heat and the stench, not on yourself. You're not likely thinking *I feel that the day is hot* or *those eggs smell really bad to me.*

It's more likely that you'd think *it's blasted hot* or *those eggs smell nasty.*

In another instance you might think that an object looks intriguing or out of place and needs investigating, yet you're probably not thinking *I need to investigate* or *that padlocked building looks intriguing to me.*

The difference is the focus. The object, event, or other character—and not the person observing it or him—is the focal point.

Focus on the people, objects, and events that interest your character instead of highlighting the character's links to those objects and events. Use the narrator's background and personality to color the words she uses, of course, but direct attention outward, from the inside of the character to the outside, rather than presenting events as reports—*I ran, I smiled, I spoke.*

Consider these next examples. The first is not overly loaded with self-references to the narrator, but it still shows a heavy hand. The second and third are ways to shift the focus away from the narrator, to allow readers to see more than just that character. I include two examples to remind you that you're not limited when you make changes; there are always multiple ways to edit text.

The fourth example is an exaggeration of too many references to the first-person narrator and to too many action details involving that character. If the greater part of your manuscript reads like the fourth example, you've got major rewriting ahead of you.

> I walk toward the door, intent on discovering what's behind it. I hold my breath, then grasp the handle. It's cold in my hand. After I press my ear to the wood, hearing nothing, I yank the door open.

* * *

> The closed door draws me to discover what's behind it. I grasp the handle; it's cold, like the handle on a chilled beer mug. Yet no unusual sounds escape from the room beyond—no ghostly moans or clanking chains. Could it be a mere closet? The doorway to a forgotten attic? The threshold to a magic kingdom? Prepared for anything and open to everything, I turn the handle and push.

* * *

> The closed door is a beacon, drawing the curious. I grasp the handle; it's cold, as if it faces the snowstorm outside rather than the fireplace inside. No sound escapes the tightly fit jamb, no shadows shift between the lowest panel and the threshold. Invitation seems to pulse from the wood. Invitation, but not dread. I pull the door open.

* * *

I study the door, determined to understand why it calls to me. I approach, cautiously, and reach out my hand. The wood hums under my fingers, and I shift my attention to the handle. I grasp the ornate metal. I feel its chill against my skin. The unexpected coolness makes me shiver. I inhale a deep breath, filling my lungs, and I quiver again in anticipation of what I'll find. I yank on the handle and pull the door toward me.

You may not be bothered by the overuse of references to the speaker, yet it's likely that readers, at least some, would be. Consider rewriting to be a means of eliminating unwanted repetition and creating variety in word choice.

There are always multiple ways to say what needs to be said.

It may be hard to gauge the number of references to the narrator in each example, so I'll repeat them, highlighting those references.

I walk toward the door, intent on discovering what's behind it. **I** hold **my** breath, then grasp the handle. It's cold in **my** hand. After **I** press **my** ear to the wood, hearing nothing, **I** yank the door open.
(7 references)

* * *

The closed door draws **me** to discover what's behind it. **I** grasp the handle; it's cold, like the handle on a chilled beer mug. Yet no unusual sounds escape the room beyond—no ghostly moans or clanking chains. Could it be a mere closet? The doorway to a forgotten attic? The threshold to a magic kingdom? Prepared for anything and open to everything, **I** turn the handle and push.
(3 references)

* * *

The closed door is a beacon, drawing the curious. **I** grasp the handle; it's cold, as if it faces the snowstorm outside rather than the fireplace inside. No sound escapes the tightly fit jamb, no shadows shift between the lowest panel and the threshold. Invitation seems to pulse from the wood. Invitation, but not dread. **I** pull the door open.
(2 references)

* * *

I study the door, determined to understand why it calls to **me**. **I** approach, cautiously, and reach out **my** hand. The wood hums under **my** fingers, and **I** shift **my** attention to the handle. **I** grasp the ornate metal. **I** feel its chill against **my** skin. The unexpected coolness makes **me** shiver. **I** inhale a deep breath, filling **my** lungs, and **I** quiver again in anticipation of what **I'll** find. **I** yank on the handle and pull the door toward **me**.
(17 references)

Might you ever want to use something like the writing in the fourth example? I won't say you'd never use such an approach, but you certainly wouldn't want your whole novel to read this way. Readers, if they could get past the early pages, would likely tire of so many references to the viewpoint character.

In addition, these kinds of references come across as reporting or telling. We do need to tell at times, but to make stories inviting, we also need to show. Rather than only recite to readers what characters are doing and feeling, *show* them participating in their lives. Show them acting and reacting. Show and tell at the right times.

This is a simple fix to an annoying problem, but if repeated references to a first-person narrator plague your stories, this simple fix will make a major difference in the feel and rhythms of your scenes.

Make sure you don't run everything through your first-person narrator, as if all events and objects and observations first have to touch her hands, her thoughts, or her senses. And if you find yourself using the same approach with third-person narration, use the same kinds of fixes.

So . . . this section covered much more than present tense. But since this is an issue I see often with present-tense first-person narration, I thought this a good place to include references to and fixes for it.

HISTORICAL PRESENT

The historical present is not a different tense but a different use of the present tense. It makes use of present tense for events that took place before the current moment in your story's present.

The historical present is used in fiction for dreams or flashbacks that would normally be told with the past tense. You could use past tense, but to quickly identify dreams and flashbacks as something other than the normal narration, the historical present works well.

A character might also shift to the historical present when telling a story within your novel.

Readers notice right away that the feel of the narration is different, but they've seen the historical present before, and therefore switching to the present tense in such a situation shouldn't bother them or slow their read.

This use of the historical present in a story that otherwise uses the past tense frames the scene or section and identifies it as something *different* or *other*.

An example of the historical present—

> Mikey was still shaking when Nigella wrapped her arms around him.
>
> "Was it a dream, sweetie? That same dream? Tell me." She brushed his hair away from his eyes and pulled him close.

"Well . . . **I'm** in the woods, like behind Grandma's house. And **it's** dark. And this giant, **he's chasing** me. **He's got** this big knife. **I run**. **I run** real fast, Mommy. And **he yells** at me to stop. But **I'm afraid** he'll catch me. **I keep running** and **he keeps yelling** and then **I fall**. **I fall** really far into a black hole. And the giant just **laughs**, but **I can't see** him anymore. **He laughs** like **he's getting** me, like he made a trap and that's what I fell in. But before **he gets** me, before **I get** to the bottom of the hole, **I wake up**."

This use of the historical present is one way to add variety to your narration, to vary the tenses of sections of your story. Remember, however, to switch back to your regular tense once you've finished recounting the dream or story. If you've included such a scene, check the text that follows in one of your editing passes.

THE QUICK LIST

- Make sure you haven't switched from past to present or present to past partway through the story.

- Check your use of the progressive form of your verbs (*is walking, was walking, is running, was running*)—both past and present narration in novels should rely on the simple verb form (*walks, walked, runs, ran*) rather than the progressive. Yet do use the progressive when it's called for or to enhance the moment.

- Don't overuse the perfect forms. Again, much of a novel will be simple past or present.

- Give extra attention to verb forms used infrequently in your stories (conditional, perfect, and the progressive forms) to be sure you haven't used the wrong tense of the form.

- Change from past to present or present to past if doing so would create a stronger story.

7

SHAPING CHARACTERS

CHARACTERS, PLOT, AND SETTING are the three support legs your stories are built on. Consider this three-fold foundation to be a tripod for fiction.

A novel needs all three legs to be strong and steady; otherwise, your novel won't stand. Stories must take place somewhere, involve at least one character, and have a plot.

Even plot-first stories, as many genre novels are, need characters. And every character-first novel, as many literary novels are, needs events related by cause and effect, which is the plot. Both styles of stories must take place somewhere and that setting—place and time and all that goes with them—can have a dynamic effect on characters and plot. Setting can also influence tone, mood, and emotion.

Let's look at character as an editor might, to see if you've covered the relevant story issues relating to character.

CHARACTERS MUST HAVE A REASON TO LIVE

Characters are the drivers of action in story. They act and others react. They speak, and other characters respond. They have goals and agendas and want what *they* want, often uncaring of what others want or need as they pursue their desires.

Each must have a purpose in your story and in the scenes in which they find themselves.

If a character isn't needed to advance plot or to influence other characters or to be an important element of setting, why is he hanging around a scene?

> Make sure characters have overall purposes as well as scene purposes. Make sure they have enough to do to justify inclusion in your story.

Your main characters—protagonist(s), antagonist, hero and heroine, the protagonist's best friend, and anyone who appears on the page frequently—have to appeal to the reader. Not necessarily appeal in such a way that readers *like* them, but appeal enough that readers are eager—or willing—to spend a lot of time with them.

Readers typically root for the protagonist and hope to see the antagonist defeated. That's not always the case, but it happens much of the time. Have you given readers reasons to root for the protagonist? Is he or she sympathetic? Have you given readers reasons to care? Or not necessarily care for him but care that he gets what he's after?

Have you given readers reasons to hope the antagonist will be firmly defeated? Defeated but redeemed? Maybe simply redeemed?

Can you point to sections in the text where you've done this, where you've made a character's needs important to the reader? There should be multiple passages in the story where you've revealed a character's personality in such a way that he or she draws empathy or dislike from readers. Giving readers one line—*Ricky saved a drowning puppy when he was fifteen*—isn't sufficient to establish a baseline for sympathy or for dislike. Not in a 350-page novel.

You wouldn't want to overdo either, hammering a character's traits and quirks into the reader. But if you want readers to feel for your characters, positively or negatively, you've got to show those characters in action (action can include thinking and speaking), doing deeds that will draw or repulse readers, and you need to reveal character personality more than once.

You also need to allow readers to draw conclusions about characters, not have them merely read *Ricky was a good man*. Readers need to experience Ricky as a good man and Greg as a sneaky one and Tina as a penny-pincher. A character's personality will become real to a reader as personality characteristics are made real on the page, through action, dialogue, the thoughts of other characters, and the thoughts of the characters themselves. And when readers draw conclusions about a character, those conclusions will become a part of the reader's ties to the story. They'll become part of the reading experience. And then the story becomes real.

CHARACTERS MUST FIT

Your story people must fit your story world. That means a fit to genre and setting and plot. Characters must also fit one another.

If you've written a historical, do your characters treat one another as men and women of the era would? Do they know what people of that age would know? Characters of earlier ages may know a lot more about hunting or plants than many people do today. They may know something of the English court and its intricacies. They may know the stars.

They may have greater experience dealing with death—the violent and the everyday—than the people of today have.

On the other hand, they may know little of people from other lands, may have never heard of an ocean, and may have never traveled more than a few miles from their birthplaces.

Make sure your characters don't know more, or less, than they should. Make sure you haven't given them the sensibilities of a man or woman of a different age.

When editing, make changes if characters sound like people out of their era or if a character has knowledge he couldn't or wouldn't have. If a character's background and experiences don't give her a way to know how to hack a computer, she's not going to be able to break into a programmer's files in twenty seconds.

Make sure characters don't destroy the suspension of disbelief by displaying knowledge or skills they couldn't or don't possess.

CHARACTERS MUST BE DIFFERENT

Your characters should be different from one another in both major and minor ways.

They think differently and move differently. They approach problems from different perspectives. They have different life experiences and motivations.

Make characters sound different and act in ways that distinguish them from one another. If two characters can't be differentiated, one might need to be cut from the story. At the least, one needs to change enough that the two become clearly dissimilar.

(MAJOR) CHARACTERS MUST BE MOTIVATED

Give characters their own motivations. For example, the reason Burton wants to find the treasure—find it himself, not merely be on the team that discovers it—should be different from his brother's reason. What gets him involved in the hunt is different from what drives his brother.

While every character may give in on some matters, each may possess a single intractable issue. That place where a character takes a stand or draws a line in the sand—pick your cliché—is ideal for stirring up conflict. Give your major characters stands or opinions or motivations that will tangle with the stands of other characters and then make those differences work to raise conflict and lead to inevitable—and rousing—confrontations.

Characters should also have goals, goals that might prove incompatible with the goals of others, even others who are their friends.

Characters need to want something—want an object, want success, want to be left alone. Near the top of the story, you need to induce a want in your main character, a want that he can't help but go after. Chasing after this, whatever it is, may become his major story task or it may be only what leads to his major goal. But characters must want something and want it enough to act.

Characters may share related goals and wants.

Let's say that Patsy wants her sister Gertrude, a detective, to check out a guy she met. Gertrude, who wants only to be left alone to work, might have succeeded in putting Patsy off for weeks but when Patsy camps out in Gertrude's car on stakeouts and shows up in Gertrude's office—while clients are present—to declare she won't leave until Gertrude checks out Pierre Lightfoot, Gertrude gives in.

Gertrude now has a reason to check out Pierre. Her stated goal is to be left alone to work, but now she has another task. And you know this task, this goal, is the one that will direct the story.

In an edit, make sure the characters' motivations and goals are clear. Make sure they're different in some way from the goals and motivations of other characters. Make sure these are what push characters into the actions they undertake.

One character's goals might be similar to another's—both your main character and his nemesis want to find the treasure—but they won't go about seeking that goal in the same manner. Or they'll get into one another's way. Or there won't be enough treasure to go around, so not only will they each seek to reach the prize first, they'll also actively try to keep each other from getting it.

CHARACTERS MUST RESPOND

Characters are in stories to do things. So once the action starts, make sure your characters respond. This is especially important to remember if you've got multiple characters in a scene. When something eventful happens in that scene, everyone should react. Yes, you can include group responses, but it's the individual reactions that will keep the story moving forward. Reactions lead to responses which lead to more action and reaction, and the story wheel turns until you've got 300-some pages of active and involving fiction.

If an event takes place, even your secondary characters need to react. If it's a big event, even background characters should respond.

If you were making a movie, all you would have to do is show a wide shot that catches the reactions of everyone in the scene. If a new character comes into view—say a doctor with a report about a surgery—you'd see all the characters tracking the doctor's progress across the room. The characters don't necessarily need to talk, but if they've been waiting on the doctor, they wouldn't ignore his entrance.

In a book, *you* have to create the characters' responses. And those responses should fit the type of action and logical level of response needed. They should also fit the character's personality and should be directed by other events that have already transpired.

Don't leave characters without a response—without a fitting and *logical* response.

If there are too many characters to a scene and you don't want to include responses for all, write a few of them out of the scene. Either have them exit the scene before the event or don't include them in the first place.

Not every character is required to be in every scene.

Each scene should be asked to support only those characters necessary to make the scene work and to advance the plot to the next event or scene.

Beyond making sure that characters respond to the words and actions of other characters, make sure they respond to a new setting or a change in setting if it's important for them to note that change.

> Lack of character reaction is a shortcoming I find in many manuscripts. If characters, especially major characters, don't react to the words and actions of others—if they don't react to the degree that their characters should—it's as if the words haven't been spoken and the actions haven't taken place. In order for plot to move forward and tensions to build, characters must respond. Responses include thought, dialogue, and action.

Keep in mind that characters should experience different levels of response over the course of a story, so one character shouldn't always be shrieking or fainting or shooting someone who slights her.

Characters could also have different responses depending on whether they're present when an event takes places or they simply hear about the event.

When character A does something, make sure character B responds. Sometimes that will be it, one stimulus and one response. But at other times you'll want to include more. You'll want to push and escalate the action/reaction exchange. You'll want to drive your characters to extremes. So when character B responds, you'll want character A to push back. Then character B might back down or push back. You'll want to vary the response pattern and response levels—each confrontation shouldn't be just one reaction to one stimulus.

Nor should each go back and forth twice. Think variety. Think escalation, especially as you push toward the end of the story.

In terms of editing, you want to hone character responses to match the event that stimulates the response and make sure the response sets up another action or event.

MAJOR CHARACTERS CHANGE (OR DO THEY?)

While characters should act in ways consistent with their personalities, experiences, and backgrounds, major characters—typically the protagonist—will change in some way, perhaps multiple ways, by the end of the story. The character arc shows the path of this change. By the end of the story, the protagonist may think in a way different from the way she did at the beginning of the story. She may behave differently. She may speak differently and possess a new outlook.

Traditionally, the character who changes most is the story's protagonist. The events of story affect her more than they affect anyone else. And the changes are real, not temporary but long lasting.

Might some major characters not change? Sure. If you intend to highlight futility, want to show that no matter what a character does the result is the same, want to show that she can't change her world no matter what she tries, a character could end up the same as when the story began. It's an unusual direction for a story, to leave the protagonist unchanged, but it can be tried.

Still, if the character had tried hard to achieve her goals and failed, it's likely that she'd be affected by her failure. If she discovered that she couldn't fix the wrongs of her world, it's likely that such a discovery would affect her outlook.

If events occur that *should* change a person and yet don't, you're telling us that the character doesn't behave or respond as a normal person does. So maybe this reveals the character's inability to see reality or to think rationally. Maybe the inability to change shows a mental or personality disorder.

Such a story could work, but remember that to keep readers involved in a story's events, characters must also be involved in those events. A character who remains unchanged and uninvolved may not interest readers.

Also, a character who remains unaffected may subconsciously influence readers into thinking that the story is uninvolving or the story events are of little consequence. If events don't influence characters, it's likely that they aren't the right events for the story.

Exception: A character from a series—perhaps a detective—may show little change over the course of a story or even across the full series. In such stories the accent is on the plot, the solving of the mystery, and not on the growth of the protagonist. The protagonist might change from book to book, but that change may be slight.

Readers want series characters to be constant and consistent, and may read every book in the series counting on that consistency to be there.

CHARACTERS NEED CHALLENGES

If a character gets everything he wants beginning on page 1, you won't have a story.

You need to create barriers and challenges for your characters—different challenges for each character and different levels of challenge for different stages in the story.

One character might be challenged by a lack of finances. Another by a lack of brawn. Both protagonist and antagonist might by hampered by a lack of knowledge.

Even antagonists shouldn't get everything they want. Frustrate and anger them so that they'll lash out, driving both tension and conflict ever higher.

In your edits, make sure characters are plagued by challenges, valid and authentic challenges. Something must keep characters from simply taking what they want when they want it.

Also, make sure that when characters overcome challenges—and they should overcome some—new and more difficult challenges take their place. A character's story task—achieving his major goal—should become harder to attain as the story approaches the end, not easier. Easy doesn't happen until after the climax, when the character is either victorious or defeated.

Ensure that the story-long challenge or barrier that the protagonist can't smash before the story's end is sufficiently difficult to last the length of a novel. If a character should be able to defeat a challenge by page 70—because she's gained knowledge, experience, skills, and helpers—and yet hasn't done it by page 250, you need to rewrite.

THE EMOTION COMPONENT

Emotions come into story through characters; don't shy away from those emotions. Push for harder and deeper and varied emotional responses, especially when story events call for strong responses.

Show emotional responses through action, dialogue and thought, and use a variety of responses and response levels.

Characters shouldn't always break down. They shouldn't always laugh off pain or distress. They shouldn't always suck it up. Remember that while characters should have consistencies, they should also be changed by story events. While you don't want them acting out of character, their characters can evolve.

Characters can reveal emotion through what they *don't* do. Don't overlook restraint, a purposeful nonresponse, as a valid reaction.

Match emotional responses to a character's personality and experiences as well as to the stimulus. Allow the presence of other characters to influence the response level so that some characters encourage others toward exaggerated or reckless behavior while other characters restrict and constrain behavior.

CATEGORIES OF CHARACTERS

Protagonist

The protagonist is your lead. He or she is sometimes referred to as the main character (MC). In most mysteries, this is the detective. In romances, the heroine used to be the MC, but heroes share billing as main characters these days. Sometimes the story is the hero's, and sometimes hero and heroine are joint main characters.

In epics, hero duties may be shared over the course of years or major events.

No matter which character is your protagonist, make sure your story has one. Make sure he or she has goals. Makes sure the reader can tell what that main character wants. Make sure the MC has worthy opposition in the antagonist and other major characters.

Give the protagonist internal opposition as well.

Make sure the protagonist is introduced early in the story, so readers know who they're following, who they should become attached to. In epics and family sagas, you may have changing lead characters, perhaps as years pass and characters die. But while a character is the main character, treat her as such.

Make sure you've given the main character strengths and weaknesses. Make sure she's someone readers will want to spend time with. The MC doesn't have to be likeable, but she does need to be bearable enough that readers will follow her through the story.

The MC should be compelling and interesting.

Introduce the protagonist in a way that shows readers she's the protagonist. Make your major characters stand out from thousands of other fictional people, including the others in your story. Make them memorable. Make them vulnerable. Make them touch your readers in unexpected ways.

Make them matter.

Antagonist

The antagonist is typically a character who stands in opposition to your main character. He can be a "bad guy," but he doesn't have to be. He may be the hero or protagonist in a different story. He is the hero of his own story (and in his own mind).

The antagonist is a major character who may be the viewpoint character for some scenes. He has his own contacts and support systems. He may also be at the center of a secondary story thread.

Protagonist and antagonist may be after the same goal, with no personal animosity between them, or they may hate each other passionately. Their goals may be to deny the other what he or she wants, whether they actually want the thing itself or not.

They can be strangers when the story opens or well known to one another. They may share friends and/or enemies. They may be friends pulled apart by a disagreement. They may be kin. You can give protagonist and antagonist any kind of relationship, close or distant.

The antagonist, like your protagonist, should have strengths and weaknesses that help and hinder his passage through story events.

Secondary Characters

Major secondary characters appear again and again in a story. These could be a family member of protagonist or antagonist, a best friend or lover, a boss or co-worker.

Secondary characters have major duties in novels. They cause setbacks, create barriers that distract, delay, or discourage the main characters—whether the secondary characters think of them as barriers or not—provide assistance to main characters, and sometimes make great sacrifices, even up to losing their lives, when helping the protagonist or antagonist.

Plenty of sidekicks are put in the hospital or morgue, thus stirring the main character to avenge them. And an antagonist's number one henchman or buddy often winds up damaged or dead as he tries to secure some object or goal for his boss.

Secondary characters may be the featured players in their own plot threads—you see this in romances when the best friend of either the hero or heroine gets a romance of his or her own.

Like the protagonist and antagonist, secondary characters need goals, though theirs could very easily tie into the protagonist's or antagonist's goals. It's likely, however, that their motivations are different. A sidekick may travel on a quest with the protagonist because he owes him a favor or he vowed to always protect him. Maybe because he loves him. Though they might ultimately be seeking the same prize, main characters and secondary characters won't have the same motivation or the same drives. And these differences may well get in the way of friendship or duty (creating some lovely conflict).

Secondary characters might try to circumvent the main character's plans—for good or not so good reasons—causing new troubles.

In an edit, make sure that secondary characters have purpose and motivations, have skills and strengths that complement the main character's weaknesses. Make sure that the main character has a use for them and can be hurt by them or set off course by them. Give a main character a skill or strength that can help a secondary character.

Consider linking secondary characters to the protagonist and antagonist with emotions as well as through common backgrounds or histories. Give them sufficient ties so that when conflict arises between them, the pain is great for them both.

Support Characters

Support characters fall between secondary characters and background characters in terms of prominence in the story and amount of time and/or attention given them. *Support character* is not an official designation, but in my opinion they deserve a mention.

These characters get a decent amount of page time in novels, so they're more than background characters. They're usually named but don't often direct story events. They are co-workers, family members, and contacts of major characters. They may add to a major character's emotional woes, giving him grief and worry, more than they figure in the main plot.

Background Characters

Background characters are nameless, and most of the time they need to stay that way.

Characters used to fill in large scenes or who are necessary to conduct the normal business surrounding a major or secondary character should remain in the background, or they should be treated as walk-ons—there for a particular purpose and then gone, specifics about them unexplored and forgotten.

They need no history, no detailed description, very little dialogue. These are taxi drivers, delivery people, customers waiting in line in front of or behind a major character. They are nurses in an ER, a doorman, a flight attendant.

In most stories, characters move through settings where other people would normally congregate. If you fail to include people in such scenes, the scenes will feel unreal, like an empty, echoing stage.

On the other hand, if you give too much attention to background characters, readers might imagine that they'll play a major role in the story, and they'll be looking for them to do something meaningful.

You want neither of these outcomes.

In an edit, make sure that background characters haven't stepped into the foreground, taking the focus off another character or an event. Keep their parts small. And use as few as necessary. Use named characters, when possible, to keep story events unfolding. Yet don't ignore background characters. Use them as part of the setting and as a means of making major characters interact with others.

Viewpoint Characters

We looked at viewpoint characters in the chapter "Verifying Viewpoint," but I want to mention them here as well.

Any character can be a viewpoint character, yet you typically want the viewpoint character to be the one with the most at stake in a scene, and that usually means a major or a secondary character.

When events unfold, you want the viewpoint character to have a reason to care, to have an opinion about those events. To be affected by them.

In much of our fiction, the main character is often the primary viewpoint character, but he doesn't have to be.

The editing reminder here is to check viewpoint character scene by scene. Make sure you've chosen the best character to convey the scene's events. And if you change viewpoint characters fairly frequently, make sure you don't go too long before giving readers a scene from any *one* character (unless story events prevent it—for example, a character is in a coma).

QUESTIONS TO ASK ABOUT CHARACTERS

- Did you give characters enough to do? Could characters be combined? Do the right characters feature in major events? What would a change in character do to a scene's or the story's outcome?

- Do characters sound like they're giving reports to a supervisor rather than living their adventure without an awareness of performing for an audience? That is, do they go about their business without a recognition that an unseen audience watches them?

- Do characters react? Do they react as characters in their positions would be expected to react?

- Do too many characters have names that sound or look alike, that have the same number of letters? Make a chart—examine first and last names for similarities.

- Do characters tell everything rather than allow readers to make conclusions? Do characters tell too much?

- Are major characters fully fleshed out?

THE QUICK LIST

Make sure

- characters are different from one another and that each is necessary; cut out and/or combine characters if two are too much alike or there's not enough for each to do.
- character names don't sound the same, look the same, start with the same letter, or have the same number of letters. A cast that included even two of these would be tough to deal with: Mark, Mary, Marty, Marv, Merv, Mack, Max, Maria. The same for Jack, Jake, Jane, John, June, Jade, Jen, Jean, Jenna, or Jana.
- to give characters quirks—mannerisms or speech peculiarities, hobbies or habits—that make each character stand out.
- to give characters different and realistic occupations.

- you give major characters strengths and weaknesses, and reveal these traits primarily through actions rather than by exposition or direct report.
- to check character introductions—make sure each fits the character and the scene.
- characters who are emphasized actually play a role in the story; if they don't, de-emphasize their importance.
- characters are only in scenes they need to be in, make sure they add something to those scenes, and cut them out of scenes where they don't belong.
- the protagonist—and not some other character or outside source—solves his story problem.
- your main characters both act and react—they instigate and they respond to provocation.
- that necessary or featured characters aren't dropped from the plot without explanation—show what happens to characters who influence story events and other characters.
- you share the main character's thoughts, feelings, motivations, insights, and growth, especially for stories that are character driven.
- characters behave according to their nature except when events so challenge or move a character that he can't help but act contrary to his nature.
- your protagonist changes—he shouldn't be the same guy he was when the story opened. A protagonist unchanged by story events, the most unusual of his life, is an odd man. Maybe a wretched one. If he's unchanged by all you put him through, there's no hope for him. Yet a valid reason for leaving a protagonist unchanged would be to highlight his hopelessness, though you wouldn't reveal an inability to change too early in the story because readers likely wouldn't follow him; the protagonist must possess the possibility of changing. Another exception is the series mainstay who's expected to remain steady. A third exception is the protagonist who changes his story world more than it changes him.

- your protagonist has a goal to work toward, motivation to keep him on task, and increasingly tough obstacles to challenge, distract, or delay him.

- readers understand what's at stake for your protagonist and that they realize what, if anything, he's lost or gained by the end of the story.

- characters are identified by name and not by pronoun at the tops of chapters. This is especially important when you have multiple characters of the same sex or a great number of characters who could be the *he* or *she* referred to at the beginning of a chapter.

BONUS: CHARACTER RANTS‡

While we covered character emotions briefly, this section will give you more ideas about what to include and what to edit for as you consider characters and their emotions.

Consider giving your main character or antagonist, or even a secondary character, a tour-de-force emotional blowout that will shake up the story and shatter the reader.

Many of us were trained from an early age to hold in our emotions. We weren't permitted to yell at parents, we were told we must respect our siblings and playmates, and we didn't talk back to adults, not ever, ever, ever. So we spent much of our early years learning how to stifle emotion, honesty—because you couldn't tell a neighbor or a teacher that her dress was hideous—and our confusion.

There are individuals, of course, who ignored their parents' training or whose parents didn't encourage polite manners. Those children were the ones who pitched fits in the grocery store or who bullied other kids on the playground. We're not going to talk about these people, children whose emotions ran wild and who grew into adults whose emotions run wild. Or into adults who use their volatile emotions or the mere threat of them to control those around them.

No, I want to talk about people—in our case, characters—who *hold back* their responses.

- Women who've been trained to be polite, not assertive.
- Men who are told that tears—and the grief that prompts them—are unmanly.
- Family members cowed by more outspoken family members.
- Employees stifled by custom or workplace conventions.
- Teens who haven't yet found their own voices, who've instead been forced to keep opinions to themselves both at home and in the schoolroom.
- Men *and* women who don't speak their minds over matters either insignificant or noteworthy because to do so would be impolite or rude or an imposition.
- People who've been repressing their emotions or their thoughts, their preferences, dislikes, or their opinions, for years. For decades. For so long that they have no room for one more repressed thought or unvoiced emotion.
- Characters so close to letting loose and breaking down that one nudge more will send them over the edge.

Ah . . . can you see it? Feel the tension? Sense the volatility of the middle manager who's been forced to stand behind others his entire career, waiting to make his move, waiting for recognition. Never causing a fuss, never venting even when he was wronged.

Can you see him, pushing down and pushing deep his emotions? And can you see him at his moment of triumph, when he should finally be making his mark, can you see what happens when his grand idea is shot down or he's asked to once again support the plan of a lesser man? For the good of the company, of course. Maybe for the good of the industry or for the sake of the planet.

What happens when this man can't take any more, *won't* take any more? Does he go quietly into the night?

Not if he's a character in a novel.

No, our middle manager explodes at his wife, pre-empting the news of her promotion, her pregnancy, her cancer diagnosis.

He hits the tipping point, but it's the worst conceivable time for him to lose it. He gets a big scene—spewing his disappointment, spilling his rage—and the story tension soars. Then when his wife is sympathetic but also shares her news, and his needs must once again take the back seat to someone else's, they go at each other and conflict jumps.

Such conflict—and the resulting tension raised between characters and stirred within the reader—creates involving, absorbing, unforgettably powerful fiction.

Or is that involving, absorbing, powerfully unforgettable fiction?

Why not make it both? Why not make your characters' responses bold *and* powerful? Arresting *and* memorable? Shocking and haunting and potent?

Why not give your major characters a powerful moment to be completely human, completely real, fully engaged and completely—gloriously—exposed?

When a character rages, when he falls apart, lets go, and breaks down, then we've got a scene that engages readers. That rips at their own emotions. That touches and moves them. That breaks and shakes and shatters them.

When the reader has drawn close to that character, when he can empathize with him, the breakdown is even more disturbing or moving.

It can even be cathartic.

Catharsis is the purging of emotions, an event that often happens when those emotions have built to an explosion point. Catharsis is a cleansing, a washing clean and clear.

Characters who explode—in rage or grief or fear—give themselves a release as well as provide a release for the reader.

You've watched such scenes in movies when the star gets a chance for a tour-de-force moment, when he explodes with passion and reveals the true character he's been hiding for much of the story.

Such scenes can become unbearable to the point they're difficult to watch. The power of the released emotion—*the long-repressed emotion*—pushes every button of the audience. It batters at the other characters in the scene.

It most definitely pushes the character who's letting loose.

Pushes him to say what he's never said, what he'd been afraid to say, what he probably, in polite society, would never reveal. But when he gets to throw out and throw up the seething repressed words and feelings and truths he's been hiding, wow. The release changes him. Brings him peace or at least a little relief.

Maybe his response also brings him guilt. Maybe it brings healing. Maybe his rant leads to more trouble if his release comes at the expense of his boss or a foe or even a child who doesn't understand why Dad went wacko for a while.

You can include such moments in the lives of your characters, moments when the inner man comes to the surface and reveals himself without apology and without fear. Moments when the repressed is freed. Moments when characters let 'er rip with no thought to consequence or repercussions.

Consider giving your protagonist and maybe your antagonist—and *maybe* a major secondary character—such a scene. Let your lead character cast off society's rules and be honest with himself and those closest to him. Let him let loose and use his catharsis to send the story in a new direction.

What's needed for a satisfying character rant?

- reader identification with the character—be sure the rant doesn't occur too early in the story or before readers empathize with the character
- a character who has something to rant about, a topic that will engage other characters and/or the reader
- a character who hasn't already been ranting or breaking down throughout the story—a passionate catharsis will be most striking if it comes from a character who's been constantly repressing rather than venting
- a scene of sufficient duration that nevertheless doesn't go so far or drag on for so long that you lose the reader's attention or his ability to empathize

- consequences, negative and positive, to the character or those he loves as a result of the blowup
- a character and/or the story moving into a new direction as a result of a character's emotional release
- word choices that convey the emotion the character is feeling and word choices that elicit the emotion you're looking for from the reader

Recommendations

Strongly consider giving your main character his own tour-de-force scene, one that readers will remember because it not only *touched* their emotions, it pulled and twanged and stomped on them. Consider such a scene especially if your character hasn't done much emoting throughout the story. Consider an emotional cleansing if it's past time for a character to speak his mind.

Consider such a scene if the story doesn't need another action scene that arises from outside forces but could use one that's prompted by character needs.

Shake up your readers by shaking loose your characters. Make readers witnesses to the most personal moment of a character's life. Let them see, experience, and *know* a character at his most vulnerable.

Make a strong character human by allowing him to break down in a spectacular fashion, in a way that changes him. In a way that opens the eyes of those who thought they knew him.

Show your tough guy's emotions, your intellectual's heart, your timid mouse's backbone and passion.

> Let truth emerge through unrestrained words and unfiltered emotions. Let a character make himself foolish and not care, at least in the moment of his release. (Afterwards you can give him remorse and embarrassment and all sorts of painful fallout.) Push beyond your own limits to make yourself uncomfortable at the raw emotion you let spill out of your pen and your head and your heart.

Allow your characters to tell off the world and allow yourself to be impolite, to butt in where no one belongs, to tell secrets that shouldn't be brought to light.

Make characters bare their aching, battered hearts. Show readers what your characters are made of at the core, without benefit of the protection of lies, half-truths, and polite social responses.

Give your characters a catharsis. Give your readers a treat.

Write powerful rants.

Write memorable characters.

8

CREATING EMOTION
IN THE READER‡

SINCE WE'RE DISCUSSING EMOTION, let's talk more about creating emotion in the reader.

You want to capture the reader's attention and her mind, but you also want to tap into her emotions. Whether you're after fright or anxiety or empathy or humor, you need to be aware of what your scenes and events stir within the reader.

Making readers feel is one of the easiest ways to bind them to a story and its characters. When readers feel, they're involved and invested. They need to know what's going to happen with the characters whose lives move them. Readers will stay with a story when it touches them.

When you edit, check every chapter and scene for emotion-producing elements. Ensure that you've not only written in a way that touches readers, but that you've induced the right emotion at the right time. All scenes will not, should not, create the same feelings in the reader. Check your scenes to make sure what you've written and the way you've presented each scene and event will create a variety of emotions of differing levels.

While we want to determine whether or not you've succeeded at provoking emotional responses or at least created the conditions necessary for such responses in the reader, we also want to mention techniques that writers can use to create these responses. If the techniques and options and elements are absent, consider adding them, and their attendant emotional components, to your scenes.

Don't imagine that you need to use every technique in every scene, but play with combinations of techniques to discover which will produce the emotions you want to create in the measure you want the reader feeling them.

Ways to Stir Reader Emotions

Write in scenes rather than in reports

The topic of scenes gets a chapter of its own, yet even without delving into all the details concerning scenes, you no doubt understand why scenes are more engrossing for readers than reports would be. Make sure your story opens with a scene and that emotional events and the moments you want the reader to feel are conveyed by real-time scenes and not summary or exposition.

Make a character sympathetic

If a reader can identify with a character, he can also identify with his emotions. Make sure you've given readers opportunity to know characters, reasons to sympathize and empathize with them. Make sure you've invited readers into the intimate events of a character's life. Make sure you've given readers reasons to want to feel what a character feels.

Make a character *un*sympathetic

If you want readers to root against a character or feel repugnance for him, make sure he's unsympathetic. Make sure he's unlikeable. Don't be afraid to write a character who's not nice or good or kind. When you edit, tweak a character's personality or actions if he's bland or not as unpleasant, mean, or nasty as he needs to be in order to make readers feel antipathy for him.

Don't hold back

Don't fear writing an emotion-inducing scene. You want readers crying or shivering or laughing out loud, so give them reasons to cry, shiver, and laugh. If you find sections of text where you held back, rewrite. A scene that's restrained will not likely get at the emotions you want to tap. If you need to kill off a character, do it. If you need to make a character look foolish, do that.

Tease and foreshadow

While you don't want to give everything away too soon, teasing and foreshadowing can raise emotional levels in readers.

Romance readers like to be teased with the will-they/won't-they dance in romances. Suspense readers love trembling with anxiety, in fear of the events the story is building toward. And any story can foreshadow, hinting at what could happen if certain events do or don't play out.

Check your scenes for foreshadowing, for ways of creating anticipation in the reader. If you don't have any, look for places where you could place hints or elements of foreshadowing. Do this through an object that becomes a focal point for one or more characters. Do it through the (seemingly) innocent words of a character. Do it through changing weather. Choose words that influence the mood of a scene.

Or consider adding a story thread or subplot that will increase reader anticipation.

Use words linked to emotions

Some words on their own stir emotional responses in people. When you hook those words into your story events, you've got readers primed to respond.

Cuss words, passion words, words linked to evil, humorous or odd-sounding words, and words connected to religious or sexual ecstasy may instantly arouse a reader's emotions. You don't want these words where they don't belong but when you want to tap into an emotion shared by many, maybe tap into cultural triggers, such words may be the perfect sparks.

Also, make sure that *motion* verbs fit the emotion you're trying to create. If you're pushing for tension and fear, with characters fleeing a monster (human or other), characters wouldn't simply walk or stroll or amble across a room. They'd race or fly or sprint or haul ass.

Check your verbs as you edit. Decide whether they build, neutralize, or maintain emotion. If they don't fit your needs, change them. Play around with verbs until they fit a scene's events and mood, the characters, and the emotion you're trying to promote in the reader.

Create story events that are more than ho-hum

Make sure characters have something to risk. Events that don't matter, won't change the outcome of a story, or don't cause problems for characters need to be changed or cut. Readers won't get emotionally involved in non-events. If events don't matter to characters, they won't matter to readers. And if characters don't respond, readers won't either. If there's no reason for characters to care about the outcome of an event or scene, if nothing's at stake, readers will have no emotional response to that event or scene.

Set a clock ticking

To increase a reader's tension, put characters under time constraints. If something has to happen or not happen by a certain time or day and you keep readers aware of the approaching deadline, reader emotions will be enhanced.

Force characters into making a decision they'll regret or into one between a bad choice and a worse choice

Readers will feel bad for a character and the people he hurts when he's forced to choose between two bad choices or forced to act against his will and better judgment. Make sure that choices are inevitable and that there's no way out. If you do give a character wiggle room, make sure he takes advantage of it and that doing so creates even worse problems.

Keep the story moving

Dwelling too long on a scene or issue can drain a reader's emotions or dilute his empathy. Make sure you don't overplay an emotional scene. Move on before readers tire of the drama or humor or fright.

Give characters realistic problems

If readers feel a story problem is contrived or could be easily solved and yet you drag out the resolution, they won't engage. When you edit, make sure your characters' problems are true problems.

Adjust the pace

Fast-paced and breathless can keep readers biting their nails, but slow *could* have them leaning forward, anticipating when the next problem will pounce on the characters. Make sure you've varied the pace and used the correct one to agitate, soothe, or humor readers.

Blindside the reader

Turning a story in an unexpected direction, especially more than once, keeps readers unsettled and their emotions closer to the surface. Make sure you've written a couple of events that surprise the reader.

Include conflict in every scene

Conflict gets a chapter of its own in this guide, but the reminder here is that you ensure that every scene has some. Conflict keeps both characters and readers stirred up.

Adjust tone and mood

Both tone and mood affect the feel of a story. Make sure viewpoint characters use the right tone for every scene. Make sure the mood of each scene is the one you need. If a scene feels light and easy and you need dark and heavy, readers won't be feeling what you want them to feel. Check for words and sentence construction that doesn't fit or doesn't match the mood. Check for character focus in a scene that doesn't feel right—should the character focus on something else? Maybe there's not enough subtext in the dialogue or the subtext is wrong for the scene.

Help readers focus

Make sure readers focus where you need them to by including only the necessary details. Cut superfluous details that distract or introduce the wrong element or tone. If a scene tries to touch the reader in too many ways, decide on one purpose or one mood for the scene and cut other details and elements. Or split the scene into two scenes so you can direct the focus to one issue and one emotion in each.

Use setting to influence reader emotion

Take advantage of the power of setting to create a mood and influence readers. Use setting details to immediately touch readers and to prime them for events to come. If you find a scene that isn't strong enough to move readers, check the setting details. See what you can add to increase reader emotions or what needs to be taken away because it interferes with the buildup of emotion.

Appeal to readers' senses

Edit scenes for the sense elements. If you can get a reader imagining the taste or smell of food you've just described or have him feeling the searing heat of a desert on a cold and snowy day, you've touched him. Use the sound of a cackle in the dark to spook the reader, the squish of slimy guts between a character's toes to gross him out, or the scent of natural gas in a daycare to start his heart racing.

POWER IN EMOTION

If you can get a reader to laugh or smile, to cry or go teary-eyed, to gasp or shiver or moan, you've moved her. You've actually entered her three-dimensional world and touched her. Something fictional, something you created, has meshed with a living person and moved her in a meaningful way. You've created not only something memorable, but something real and tangible.

When you influence a reader's emotions, your words are no longer flat symbols on a page; they've crossed from the imaginary world into the material world.

> Touching a reader, sparking a response, is powerful. And humbling. And rare. It's an ability to be desired. It is creativity realized at the ultimate level.

Move your readers. Stir their emotions.
Touch their souls.

9

INSPECTING PLOT: DOES ANYTHING HAPPEN?

PLOT IS THE SERIES of events in a story, *events related in a causal way.* Events that transpire willy-nilly with no connection and no cause and effect are not a plot.

Plot isn't a grandmother getting a phone call in the morning, going shopping at noon, and picking up her grandson from daycare at five.

Plot *is* a grandmother getting a phone call in the morning, one from her cohorts telling her that their plan to extort millions from the city has begun, and her going to a source to pick up two AK-47s and ammo at noon, and then her going to the daycare where her grandson is and barricading herself, three employees, and a dozen kids inside.

Related events—events that *cause* other events which cause even more events—are the foundations of plot. And when you edit, you need to make sure that story events are related in a causal way and that there are enough of them to sustain your story.

Every story, even character-first literary novels, needs a plot. Something must happen and because of that event, other somethings must happen. (Exceptions for experimental fiction and deliberately plotless fiction.) We're talking events and not just actions here, so stories need more than characters stomping around a room or waving their arms. Events drive characters into a response and those events and responses move them, usually chronologically, through the story.

Events can create instant responses or delayed ones, grand responses or subdued ones, but something must happen from the very beginning of a story to the very end, and what happens must be related to other story events. And not only that, but events should influence the actions, thoughts, and emotions of the characters.

Plot events fuel the engine that keeps stories moving forward. If you run out of plot, the story stops. If you have an illogical or incomprehensible plot, the readers stop. Stop reading, that is.

> Plot, like character and setting, is one of the legs of the fiction tripod that supports a story. If one element is missing or isn't as strong as the others or doesn't extend to the same length, your story will not stand.

The main question regarding plot is not *does anything happen in your story* but *does anything of* consequence *happen in your story world*, something that affects the characters and has them reacting?

Another necessary plot question is *have you made the reader care about what happens or will she say, "So what?"* Events alone don't make plot work; readers have to be invested in characters before what happens to those characters is truly meaningful. (Thus the ties between plot and character are clear.)

Events that happen on page 1 may capture a reader's attention, but they likely won't stir her emotions. Be sure to include another event near the top of the story—yet after readers meet the major characters—to forge emotional connections between reader and story.

Not every story will have jump-off-the-page events, events such as explosions and kidnappings, murders and chases. But every story will have events that propel the story forward and touch characters' lives—a man arriving home early to catch another man sneaking out of his wife's bedroom, a woman's mind going completely blank on day two of the bar exam, a couple getting the news that they're going to have a baby.

BETWEEN MAJOR EVENTS

What happens between large or noteworthy story events? Do characters reflect on what's happened and then react to the proper degree to those events? If characters don't respond, an event hasn't done its job. It actually hasn't done anything. And it most likely won't lead to another event. The purpose of action and story events is to create responses and counter-responses leading to more events. Make sure events, big and small, produce reactions. Characters might react right away or after a bit of reflection, but they need to react.

And those reactions should become more significant as the story progresses. One way to direct character reactions is to raise the stakes. The protagonist and antagonist need to have reasons to do what they do and they need to have reasons for not turning back. And as the challenge of getting what they want becomes more difficult, they need to have even stronger reasons to persevere. One way to do that? Raise the stakes of failure for both of them.

You can also manipulate character reaction by raising the emotional level of story events. By the time the story is heading toward the climax, story events should have consequences with an emotional impact for both characters and readers. A character's frustration or rage or humiliation at story events should be clear and running hot.

PLOT THREADS

The main plot is the central story line.

For a murder mystery, for example, the plot is the linked events that take characters and readers from the early pages—often a murder happening onstage, right in front of the reader, or the discovery of a dead body—to the unmasking of the murderer. The plot deals with the sleuth's search for the murderer, and one plot event leads to the next and to the next until the sleuth catches and reveals the murderer.

Subplots are secondary plots, often featuring secondary characters, although protagonist or antagonist could feature in a subplot.

In a romance, the main plot is the growing relationship between hero and heroine. A subplot might be the solving of a mystery or the budding romance between secondary characters.

Subplots can touch the major plot at different places in the story. For example, a subplot could bring secondary characters into a scene where the main characters are already interacting. The subplot could track along with the main plot for a while, or even for the rest of the story, or it could veer off to intersect again at another point.

A key component of editing is to ensure that major *and* minor plot threads are resolved in believable and satisfying ways. You must also ensure that secondary plots don't overshadow the main plot. When you edit, compare the amount of page time given to your two plot threads. Examine character reactions to events from both the main plot and subplot—the subplot shouldn't produce stronger character reactions than the main plot does. The secondary plot shouldn't create stronger emotional responses in the readers.

The subplot should be subordinate to the main plot in every way.

Subplots can be resolved before the main plot finishes or you can tie them together and resolve both at the same time.

If you include subplots and make readers care about secondary characters and the events they're involved with, you need to follow through with them. The only reason not to conclude a plot thread would be to continue it into another book in a series. But even then you'd want to let readers know your intention. You wouldn't have to come out and say that was what you were doing, but you could intimate it. Let readers know that you didn't forget a character or plot line. You don't want the alert reader wondering what happened to a character or a side issue you introduced but then dropped.

Steer your characters and readers from event to event. Take longer trips between some events, shorter trips between others. Make sure events trigger character responses appropriate to the character—not every character would react as every other character would. And not every character reacts the same way in response to every event that hits him. Characters can also act against type, especially if they've been pretending to be something they aren't and circumstances now force them to reveal the kind of people they are under the pretense.

In an edit, follow each plot thread from beginning to end, ensuring that there *are* clear beginnings and ends. Cut out threads that were abandoned without resolution and smooth over the sections where you remove material.

Decide whether all secondary plots are truly necessary.

CONTRIVANCE, INEVITABILITY, AND COINCIDENCE

While stories can turn in any number of directions, you want the choices you make for plot to seem inevitable. Because of strengths and limitations, because of motivation and challenges, your characters will inevitably choose certain responses. And because they do, certain other events will take place.

Like dominoes falling one after another or a disease spreading from one person to the next, story events should arise out of what came before, from some source of initial action that causes reaction after plot-necessary reaction.

The first action can be rather simple, yet it can set chaos into motion. Make sure you show not only the inevitability of actions but also show that those actions make sense.

Actions and events produce consequences; make sure yours are natural and not contrived, not stretched to fit where they shouldn't be made to fit.

> If readers doubt your chain of actions and reactions, they're not going to buy your protagonist's motivation or his need to act or the danger you tell them is stalking your story world. While the connection between one event and the next is actually manufactured by you, it shouldn't feel to the reader as though it were created merely to fit the circumstances. That is, it *is* wholly contrived—created for impact and to move the story along. But to the reader it should feel natural, as if it arose organically out of the circumstances in the story world and not out of your need to make it work.

And please don't rely on coincidence to advance major plot threads or to resolve them.

Coincidences do show up in real life. When they show up in fiction, they come across as unbelievable and as poor planning on the writer's part. Readers don't buy coincidence and when they see it, they lose the suspension of disbelief. Remember that you want readers lost in your story, in the events and in your characters' problems. Coincidence is a knock on the head, a knock that allows reality to intrude, that wakes the reader from the fictional dream. You definitely don't want readers entertaining moments of disbelief and especially not at critical junctures. Make your plot tight and the events believable; erase any hint of farfetched coincidence.

STORY STRUCTURE

At this point we could delve into formal story structure: investigate three- and four- and five-act structures, cross our eyes at images of crisis points imposed on graphs, and examine the fascinating hero's journey and monomyth. Yet I'm going to leave most of those details to another book. (The chapter on story middles does contain a few specifics regarding one view of story structure.)

The study of story structure is actually pretty cool. Many fiction and story experts have shared their versions of what typically happens at particular points in stories—what *typically* happens because such components arranged in specific patterns work successfully to create entertaining stories—so you can find that information from a host of sources. I suggest you make the time to study narrative structure, at least to familiarize yourself with the knowledge that others have discovered, knowledge that helps them write stories (or produce films) that appeal to an audience that loves fiction.

But for our purposes, we'll boil story structure down to a dozen or so basics:

- An event must take place early in the story to change the status quo of the main character's world—this may or may not take place in a scene and in front of readers. So this event could be the offstage murder (reported but not shown) in a murder mystery or the kidnapping of a world leader in a techno-thriller.
- Something must happen (inciting incident) to start the main character on his adventure, journey, or voyage of discovery (through a physical world or the character's mind or both). This incident involves the main character directly. Think of the inciting incident as the character's kick-starter, the means of getting the protagonist involved in unfolding events.

- Because of what has happened, the main character must now want something so strongly that he'll turn from what is common and normal for him in order to pursue the uncommon. At least what is uncommon for him.

- The main character must have a goal which leads to or links with the main story goal.

- The story goal should create a story question in the reader's mind, a question that keeps the reader reading and that must be answered by story's end—*will* the protagonist reach his goal; *how* will the protagonist reach his goal; what happens *if* the protagonist reaches his goal, a success that will turn his entire family against him.

- The main character must face opposition from others who want the same thing he's now searching for or trying to achieve, from others who want to deny him victory, from others who don't want to see him hurt (friends and family), and from competing desires within himself.

- The main character should face a point of no return, the last moment where he could change his mind and turn around (but doesn't). Readers should be able to feel the character's renewed resolution to go forward no matter what.

- As the story progresses, other events must take place to keep the main character moving forward in pursuit of his goal despite challenges and increasing risks and setbacks (thus implying you must include challenges and risks and setbacks).

- Plot and characters must face turning points and *must* turn. Attention-grabbing stories don't move in a flat straight line.

- Events should build in terms of scope, effects, importance to the plot, and consequences.

- Tension should rise as story events lead ever closer to the black moment (the protagonist's low point) and the climax (the story's high point and showdown).

- The story must have a climax where forces collide or where tensions come to a head and where the protagonist either fails to reach his goal or succeeds at reaching his goal.

- Stories need to end with a resolution or denouement where necessary (and only necessary) explanations are laid out, where meaning is revealed, where the cost of seeking the goal is measured, and where the right blend of emotion and strong writing creates a resonance the reader can feel and carry away with him when he closes the book.

> In simple terms, stuff happens to your main character, stuff that, because of who she is and what she wants, makes her act and react. Her actions and reactions lead to more stuff happening until she's caught in something inevitable, unable to step away until the events have run their course, leaving her better or worse—or both—for what she's gone through.

Your task in an edit is to ensure that you included all the elements necessary for plot to advance *and* that you made those elements an appropriate fit for the characters. A related task is to make sure that events unfold in the best order to create the feel and effects that you want to create and that best fit the story as a whole.

As you edit for plot, search for the inciting incident, the major turning points, and the moments where risk is increased. Look for rising tension. Study the protagonist's point of no return. Make sure you've been thorough with each element. Make sure you've *included* each plot element. Make sure each does its job.

For example, decide whether turning points actually redirect the story and put characters on a different path. If they don't, rewrite to create turning points that actually turn the story and characters.

- Do turning points lead to new story locations and interactions with new characters? Do they allow (or force) characters to put the past behind them? Do they indicate a character's fresh understanding or show that his eyes have been opened?

- Does the new direction point to new possibilities for the story's climax and resolution?

- Does the new path require a character to solve problems in a fresh way, to rely on different friends, to call on skills and talents he didn't know he possessed or that he'd intentionally hidden away?

Whatever the plot element, examine it to see if it accomplishes all that it should and make sure it doesn't negatively interfere with other story elements. If there are problems, start making changes.

> Keep in mind that changes to plot will affect other story elements. Be prepared to follow changes through each element and to do so from the beginning of the manuscript to the end. (Or from end to the beginning if that makes more sense for the particular plot element.)

KEEPING THE PROTAGONIST ON TASK

As the story progresses and risk to the main character escalates—it does, doesn't it, and you can point to places in the text where it does?—determine whether or not you've given the main character sufficient reasons for not quitting, for not packing it in and going home. If the risk of loss—loss of status, loss of love, loss of job, loss of family, loss of self-respect—grows ever greater, the protagonist may need new reasons for staying the course. Or he may just need vivid reminders of why he can't turn his back.

Possible reasons for not quitting include a personal sense of duty or commitment, stubbornness, a promise made, determination not to be bested by the antagonist or by the forces arrayed against the character, curiosity about what lies ahead, a need to prove himself worthy, and a pathological need to never be bettered or never lose.

While you might imagine that a reader would need to see a combination of reasons that keep a protagonist moving forward as problems heat up and risk increases, in reality, a single strong reason should ultimately stand out. And that compelling reason that keeps the protagonist true to his course should be clear in the point-of-no-return moment.

The reader should understand in her bones why a character forges on instead of turning back. And she should know because at one memorable moment in the story you showed her why the protagonist had to stay on task. You convinced her of the reason why nothing will sway him from his path.

Now, the character can still have doubts, still doubt that he can see the task through no matter how committed he is, especially as the challenges grow tougher and exceed his skills and wisdom. And other characters can try to poke holes in the protagonist's resolve, not understanding why he must carry on. But after the protagonist resolves that he will push forward no matter what, the reader should be convinced and not need constant reminders of the character's determination. You don't need to keep reminding readers why the protagonist is staying the course, not after that key story moment. But you do have to give readers that moment in an emphatic and memorable fashion.

The reasons that characters keep pushing forward must be shown on the page, where readers see and absorb them, and not merely exist as fuzzy concepts in your mind.

QUESTIONS TO ASK ABOUT PLOT

- Does your plot stand out from other stories? How? What events make it different? Is it different enough? Does it sound too much like other books or like a popular movie?

- How far into the book does a reader have to get before she notices how different it is and before she reaches the good part? Hint: you've got to put the good part on page 1. And on page 2. And on every page through the one that finishes with *The End*.

- Do plot events follow logically from one to another and if they don't, is there a logical reason that they don't? Do events make sense?

- Do plot events follow the pattern of cause and effect?

- Is the inciting incident strong enough to incite? Is there rising tension? Have you included enough major plot events?

- Are there highs and lows? Are there enough true challenges for the protagonist and are they of varying levels? Can you actually point to those challenges in the text? (You wouldn't want either protagonist or antagonist to succeed too easily, too often, or too early.)

- Do major characters take part in major events? If not, make changes. Your main characters, typically protagonist and antagonist, should be directing events. Secondary characters can set a few events into motion, but your major characters should drive most story events and definitely direct the climax and resolution.

- Do events fit the genre? If not, consider changes.

- Have you given your main character sufficient reasons to commit to a course of action, to answer the call to action?

- Have you folded everyday events and actions into the main plot so that characters look like they have full lives, so they seem like real people? Keep in mind that realistic characters have many concerns, not only the critical one. At the same time, you don't want to distract with incidentals when a character should be concerned about the problems shaking up his life. Look for a realistic balance.

- Does your main character experience a dark moment when it looks as if failure is inevitable? Do you give that black moment enough attention, enough page time?

- Is there a climax? Is it suitable for the story type? Is it dramatic enough? Does it go on for too long? Is it predictable from page 1? If it's predictable, make changes.

- Does the resolution tie up loose ends? Does the end satisfy the story problem presented at the story's start?

- Does the end answer the reader's story question?

- Does the protagonist change by the end of the story—in the great majority of stories, he will—and if he does, in what ways? Have you shown both what the protagonist wins and what he loses?

- Does the protagonist change his world?

THE QUICK LIST

Make sure

- all plot threads are resolved—unless you're using unfinished business to set up a series or sequel.
- plot events are sufficiently different from one another—in type, in feel or weight, in consequence, in duration, and in characters involved.
- there aren't too many events or too few.
- plot events are causally related, not random.
- the problem introduced at the beginning is dealt with at the climax and resolution.
- there *is* a climax and a resolution, both sufficient in length, depth, and scope to fit the story.
- subplots are related to the main plot and/or the protagonist.
- plot events are possible and believable.
- events happen in a logical and compelling order. (Exceptions if they're out of order for a reason.)
- events produce character responses.
- events lead somewhere specific, particularly as the story approaches the climax.
- you've included several events that raise the intensity of the tension and take the story to new levels and turn the direction of the story.
- plot events are of sufficient interest to readers—chose your subject matter with an eye toward reader interest and make changes if the plot proves to be dull and insipid.
- events and character reactions to those events get more intense as the story advances.
- you cut out play-by-play reporting of unimportant actions—give readers only the good stuff.

10

SHOWCASING THE SETTING

SETTING DETAILS SET YOUR STORY APART, apart from every other story (including your own), apart from movies, apart from real locations. They establish place and time and can influence mood. Setting details can very quickly—even from page 1—set up reader expectations and influence reader emotions.

Setting showcases your characters, both their strengths and weaknesses. Setting can reveal character traits as well as shape characters.

A love story or mystery can take place anywhere and at any time. *Your* love story is different because it's set in Gallipoli just before the Crimean War. Or in pre-Civil War New Orleans. Or on Palzar, the fourth moon of Rak'ar in the year 2602.

Your mystery is unique because it takes place in Edwardian London or on a space station that's the last human outpost at the edge of a wormhole.

And the particulars of those places and times should influence, saturate, and even drive your story.

> Place, time, and cultural events should make stories different. They should influence characters. A setting should be so tied to a story that to change the setting would be to change the story.

And as you edit, you may need to do exactly that—change your setting. Your first choice of setting may not be the best one for your story. If you switched the year—to just before or during or just after a major event or upheaval—would you have a stronger story? Would you give protagonist and antagonist more ammunition?

What of the era in general? Have you used the one most beneficial to your fiction? Can enough happen in that time period? Do the characters of that age or era hold the proper opinions, the mindset, for what you need from them? Are they able to do what you need them to do? Do they have the knowledge they would need for the circumstances you write them into?

What of seasons or weather? Have you chosen the best for your needs? What would happen if you started the story three months earlier or six months later? Could you work in more challenges for the characters if the conditions were cold and snowy? Hot and humid? If it was the rainy season? The dry season? Hurricane season?

If you've featured holidays in your book, could you have benefitted from a more emotion-laden one if story events began earlier or later in the year?

What of the political climate? How are characters affected by local, national, or world events? Do national or international events speed up your fictional timelines and deadlines? Have you taken advantage of your locale and its singular elements?

Your broad setting may not change much—for example, every scene in your story may take place in a small Florida city. But characters move from one room to another, one building to another, from downtown to the beach. And the smaller settings should fit the larger setting as well as fit the events that take place within them.

The larger settings can also change, of course. The setting itself may be changed by story events, by something such as war or large-scale weather events. Or characters may leave one setting and enter another. Whatever the reason for changes in setting, make sure they don't pass unnoticed, not if characters should notice the change. On the other hand, don't overplay the change if it's not a big deal.

SETTING IN GENERAL

I can keep asking questions to help you focus on the particulars of your setting, help you determine if it's the best setting for your story's needs and whether you've used the strongest setting elements, but let's first look at the basics and the components of setting.

At least some setting details should show up in the opening pages. These details give readers a sense of time and place and give characters a stage on which to move and speak.

If the setting changes with a scene or chapter break, make sure readers know right away (this is critical if you change time or place). Unless you want to intentionally confuse readers, orient them to a new setting or to changes in an existing setting at the top of a scene.

You can also set up setting markers for one scene at the end of an earlier scene. All it takes are references to time, place, and a future event. When a subsequent scene opens at that event, readers already know when and where the scene takes place. So the end of one scene might include a line such as this: *"I'll see you Thursday afternoon at the lawyer's office."* And the beginning of the new scene might be: *I strolled into the offices of Dexter, Kelsey, and Pratt wearing my faux detachment.*

You'll also want to employ sense elements as part of your setting detail and have characters interact with setting props. And you'll want to make sure that setting fits genre. A mismatch between setting and genre will put the story off balance right from the start. If that's your intention, you have some leeway. But since setting is such an easy way to accentuate genre, get accentuating.

Determine whether characters fit the setting or stand out against it. If characters don't mesh with your setting, consider a new locale or different time period.

> A change in setting may be the answer to a ho-hum, predictable novel.

A different setting may help solve a lack of tension and conflict. Fish-out-of-water stories can set character and reader nerves jangling right from the story's start. Maybe you need to take your characters out of their fishpond and give them a highly unfamiliar place to play.

Make sure you've included details appropriate for the scene, the characters, and the action. When characters *can* notice more, let them notice more. When they're racing quickly from place to place, they won't be engaged in much noticing unless they're searching for something or a setting element stands out (or is tripped over).

When the location changes from scene to scene, include details that make the new locale different. Yet when characters return to a locale they've already been in, don't feel that you need to repaint the scene. When you edit, cut out setting description that's already been established, leaving only necessary reminders.

If setting details have changed, however, make sure those new details are made known. And point out details that one character might notice that others wouldn't, especially if that character is new to the details and is the viewpoint character for the scene.

But a character doesn't have to be the viewpoint character to notice setting details. Any character can react to setting components, responding with action or dialogue.

To get a sense of what can be included in setting, we'll look at a few broad categories of setting. Use this list to ensure that you've included setting details and done so in a variety of ways. Use the list to ensure that your story doesn't go too long without additional references to setting.

As you edit, keep in mind that some genres may lean more heavily on one setting component than on others. Make sure you've included the kinds of setting references that readers expect in your story's genre. At the same time, you'll want to cover all relevant details, not only the major ones. And remember that time and place are always significant since they frame characters and events, and orient the reader. If characters seem to float from event to event without touching the physical world, check references to setting.

MAJOR COMPONENTS OF SETTING

Locale

Locale may mean city or country or planet. It may mean a pasture, an office, or the kitchen of a home. It could be any building or a ballpark or the seashore, a movie set or an archaeological dig in Egypt. An alley. An aircraft carrier. The cab of an eighteen-wheeler. Any physical location is part of the setting. If you can put action and/or characters there, it's a valid location. Beyond the biggies of planet, country, or city, consider buildings (and rooms), fields, woods, vehicles, the seas, the skies, and outer space.

Era/Age

Era and age refer to a time period. The period may be characterized by years or by what happens during the period. Think the Roaring Twenties in Harlem, the Middle Ages in Europe, the Renaissance in Florence, the late sixties in San Francisco, the Old Kingdom in Egypt.

Architecture

Building styles can greatly affect setting and story and mood. The events you place in a sleek and modern skyscraper will be different from those in a bed and breakfast in the country with its comfy room and the fun nooks and crannies where characters can explore antiques and period furnishings. A story set in a tent city in a desert would differ greatly from one in a high-rise condominium complex in Paris. Both would differ from a story that takes place in the abbreviated buildings on the back lot of a Hollywood film studio.

Background Characters

Most stories have plenty of unnamed characters who bring the fictional world to life. Remember to include background characters so your main characters aren't walking through a people-free landscape. Unless your story world is absent other beings on purpose, remember to include them and put them into motion. They don't have to take over, they don't even have to talk, but they should show up. Unless you're going for a locale barren of humans—something like the setting in the video game Myst—include characters who bring depth to setting.

Culture

Culture includes typical practices as well as forbidden ones, items such as rules, laws, business procedures, and national holidays. Culture as setting includes a wide range of elements with numerous customs and traditions, with a variety of emphases regarding each. Cultural elements include the broad elements themselves plus the means of creation of those elements, the element's importance to a people group, purposes—intended and accidental—and differences in cultural elements that set one people group apart from all other groups, tribes, and communities.

Culture elements that can be mined for setting include:

agriculture	laws
arts and music	literature
business practices	means of transport
clothing and food	methods of production
commerce and trade	mores, traditions, and customs
communication methods	national identity
crime and punishment	political decrees
crops	politics and government forms
defense/military	religious practices
dissemination of news	societal expectations
education	societal taboos
entertainment/games	technology
family makeup	treaties and war
geography	value of life
history	value of money
holidays	competing or hierarchical social groups (including castes)

Consider cultural details at the world or national level, at a community level, or at a race, gender, or age level. Any of these can be included in setting and thus affect characters, mood, tension and conflict, and events. Cultural details may fill in the background for a fictional world or character, but they could feature in plot, as in dystopian fiction.

Geography

Geography can relate to the land, the way it rolls or juts from the earth, or it could be the layout of streets in a city or town. Consider water in all its guises, mountains and valleys, swamps, deserts, prairies, caves, and forests. Don't forget plant life. And remember that geography can influence both time and distance—how far and how difficult is it to move between towns, buildings, or other locales in your story?

Weather

Weather can be a strong influence on mood in your stories as well as a contributor to your characters' states of mind and their attitudes. Weather can also contribute directly to story events and action—slick roads can cause accidents, sunshine could blind someone at a critical moment, a storm might keep rescuers away. Think rain, snow, fog, sunshine, extremes (or norms) in temperatures, hurricanes, tornadoes, droughts, and so forth.

Time/Season

Time can include references to time of day, a specific day, the month, a season of the year (one tied to nature, such as planting, as well as those tied to society, such as a school term), or a holiday period. Time can also be mentioned in relation to upcoming events, those feared and those welcomed by characters.

Props

Props are the physical objects of setting. Imagine movies or the set of a play—what objects are used to dress a room or location? You'll want to make sure you dressed your settings properly. Surround your characters with the kinds of objects readers would expect for them to find in the locations where you plop them *and then put those objects, those props, into the characters' hands.* When characters interact in a setting with props, the setting comes to life. Don't overlook movable objects or the everyday items found in any home or office.

Props can be furniture, animals, food, tools, clothing, toys, vehicles, gadgets, home furnishings, and workplace paraphernalia—anything the characters can touch and use as they advance through a scene. I would argue that children could be considered props in some stories. Typically people wouldn't be considered props. Yet children that play no other role *might* serve as part of the stage dressing.

PUTTING SETTING TO WORK

Setting is quite obviously made up of both unrelated and interlocking elements. A writer can choose from thousands of combinations of setting details to bring authenticity to a story.

> One grouping of setting details can make a story unique while another combination of details could make story events unbelievable. One of your editing tasks is to make sure that events can actually happen *as you said they happened* given the parameters of your setting. If an element of your setting should prevent an event from unfolding in a particular manner but doesn't, or if a setting element should have kept a character from performing a particular act but didn't, you need to change that setting element, change the event or character action, or provide a reason for the exception.

What Setting Can Do

Setting details can help frame the story world, but once they're in place, characters (and you) have to abide by setting rules or you have to show which conditions would allow for exceptions and the reasons those exceptions would be permitted.

Many setting details can happily remain in the background, or they could step to the fore to be noticed. When you edit, make sure setting details aren't given too much attention if they're supposed to be part of the background. But if certain objects should be stressed, make sure they get that stress.

Setting details can drench scenes with not only rain but with political overtones, maybe the oppression of a hated regime. Setting can touch characters through ongoing background rumbling—literal or figurative rumbling. So the ground may shake with the rumbles from a volcano or the streets may shake with the rumblings of revolution. Either rumbling will cause characters to act in peculiar ways, will influence their emotions and decisions, will make what's about to transpire feel inevitable.

Your task in editing is to make sure you've used a variety of setting details, that each is the most effective for what you need it to accomplish, and that such details are consistent unless something changes them. You also want to make sure that setting components don't overwhelm action and dialogue, that they take their proper place.

Setting Can Play a Featured Role

A volcano on the verge of erupting or a dam threatening to give way can be used as a ticking clock. If a town needs to be evacuated, such setting details work to deepen the tension and influence characters to make rash decisions.

Or imagine the spooky old house in a moody historical or horror story. You could feature the house in a major way, treating it in much the same fashion that you treat characters.

Yet if the spooky old house is just part of the setting, even a major part, you don't have to give it special attention, don't have to treat it as anything other than setting. Some element of the setting *could* take on the feel of a mute character, but that would be rare.

For most stories, it's likely that any element of setting, even one that pushes story events, will still take a back seat to characters. So establish the complexities of the setting and then relegate setting to the background. You don't forget about it—you still use it to infuse scenes with tension. Yet you don't dwell on it to the detriment of character action.

So even though some aspects of setting may have a bigger part to play in select novels, setting isn't plot and setting isn't a character. At least not in the great majority of stories.

Put Setting in its Place

Once setting details are established and are set to work to influence characters and events, make sure they stay in their place. They're necessary, but they shouldn't overwhelm other story elements. They also shouldn't hide, as if they don't belong. Setting details of various types belong in your stories; give them their proper place.

> Setting is necessary to story, but it's not the story itself. It's part of the structure of a story that bleeds into events and character consciousness.

Setting elements are used, seen, touched, embraced, and discarded as a story plays out. Sometimes a setting element is even the focus of the characters. This is typically true of props such as a gun or an object of great worth, sentiment, or power. This is also true of that haunted house or a law that says no town can have more than 20 children under the age of ten at any one time.

Yet in some stories, setting remains largely in the background, a near-empty stage on which action plays out.

Whatever the breadth and depth of your settings, make sure you give thought to them. Make sure the types of setting details are varied and a fit for your story. Make sure they don't take over and they don't disappear completely.

Setting elements can be ready-made reasons for events to unfold. They can provide rationale that doesn't need a lot of explanation. If you need to get action started, see if one of your already-established setting details can't do some of the work.

THE SENSES IN SETTING

Including sense elements in every scene is a sure way to keep setting involved in those scenes.

When a character's shoes click and clack down a hallway, you reveal setting. When the smell of baking chocolate chip cookies meets a character at the front door, you reveal setting. When a character steps over a minefield of scattered toys, trying not to wake sleeping toddlers, you reveal setting.

To get setting right, imagine what should be present in your story locales. Imagine what a character new to a place might notice. Imagine what a place sounds like and what it smells like.

Picture setting from an unusual angle.

- Imagine what a building or room looks like from the viewpoint of a thief on the roof, to a man lying on the floor and looking up, to a person who'd been blind but now can see.
- Imagine what an office building sounds like at night, with no workers in it and no machines (including elevators) running.
- Imagine the smell of an electrical storm.
- Imagine the feel of the confines of a locked room to a woman used to open spaces or the uncluttered space of a prairie to a man used to a crowded city.
- Imagine the sway of a suspension bridge as a driver approaches it for the first time. For the first time after an accident. For the first time during a storm. During a hurricane.
- Imagine a character's feelings as she steps off a plane or train in a country where she doesn't know the language, where she can't read the signs or communicate with those next to her. How do unfamiliar sights, scents, and sounds affect her?
- Imagine a character on an island surrounded by a vast ocean. Does he feel overwhelmed? Cut off from the familiar? Safe? Trapped?
- Imagine a first-time flier crossing that vast ocean for hours. What does she feel? Anxiety? Dread? Freedom? What does she see? What sounds frighten her? Does she jump at every vibration of the plane?

Once you've imagined, make sure you've translated your imagination into a reality that readers will pick up on.

Allow characters to rely on one sense more than others so that Jane notes smells more often than Jack does and Jack notes sounds more often than Jane does.

> Use the senses, but don't allow character reactions to
> sense stimuli to take over; you don't have to make a big
> deal over every scent or sound. Give characters *realistic*
> responses. Have them pay attention to the unusual or
> what's important to them, not to every stimulus.

When you tap into the senses, consider color, music, flavor, shape, texture, size, movement, volume, weight, angles, dimensions, and temperature. Use common references to sense stimuli when necessary or when the reference shouldn't be overplayed, but don't hesitate to try the uncommon. For example, a character may feel an explosion in her chest more than hear it with her ears. When you describe her reaction, you could focus on the feeling rather than the sound.

ONE CAUTION REGARDING SETTING

Don't feel that characters must explain the unusual in their settings. That is, don't have them explain *what's unusual to you and your readers* if it's ordinary to the characters.

This isn't one of the major weaknesses I see in manuscripts, but it is fairly common. A writer is so keen to explain a fascinating technology or odd social practice to the reader that characters—who would find nothing at all unusual about the technology or practice—end up acting as if such things deserve their attention and wonderment.

But if an object or a practice is normal to your characters and their world, they wouldn't dwell on it, wouldn't talk about it, wouldn't explain it. The common in your settings shouldn't be brooded over by your characters.

A person of today wouldn't explain the workings of an internal combustion engine in his thoughts. A driver wouldn't travel down the road, marveling at the components of asphalt. We typically don't have conversations, in our minds, detailing how pencils are made.

Refrain from explaining the cool objects and the technologies and practices of your fiction that are common, therefore not issues of curiosity, to your characters. They can marvel over what's unfamiliar to them, but the familiar, no matter how fantastic-seeming to us, doesn't warrant awe or wonder from those familiar with it.

As you edit, if you find characters oohing and aahing over technology foreign to today's humans but common in your characters' world, change that behavior.

And while you're searching your manuscript concerning this matter, also root out specialized knowledge that characters couldn't or wouldn't have.

Your characters don't have to know how to explain the everyday workings of their world. As many today couldn't explain how a car runs, how radio broadcasts travel through the air, or how to build a rocket (or an artificial heart or even a bridge), characters in your era may not know the details of the technology of their day. Not every man and woman of every age knows farming or weaving or animal husbandry. Not everyone can explain the common in their environment. Some people are more curious, that's true. But most people are more caught up in the events of their days and the actions of others than in understanding every object or technology. It's okay for characters back in the past or forward in the future to be as ignorant of their surroundings as men and women are today.

It becomes *your* job to explain what needs to be explained in ways that fit the characters and story events without resorting to characters marveling over everyday items and common practices that typically wouldn't raise a brow for them.

THE REACH OF SETTING

The major problem with setting is that you have to come up with one for your characters and plot events. The second problem is maintaining consistency of your setting and remembering that your characters have to interact in physical locations. To make characters real, give them a real place to play out their stories.

Many writers want to get into the action or lay out the plot, create cool characters that readers can fall in love with or hate or admire. But setting? Setting, for many, isn't sexy. It's not story the same way action and dialogue and characters are story. But setting is the third leg of the fiction-element tripod on which other elements find their balance. Setting is vital for fiction.

- Setting gives you a stage where action plays out, where characters live through their traumatic and dramatic moments.

- Setting gives life to action and to character. Setting establishes mood. Setting conveys, in very few words, the feel of a story, scene, or fictional world.

- Setting details turn characters from hazy, ghostly forms to three-dimensional figures who have an impact on their stories.

- Setting allows characters to touch their world, to taste and smell it. It allows characters to be real, real people who don't only think and talk, but who move around and leave very real messes behind as they try to fix the problems you write them into.

- Setting brings veracity. Setting makes a story not only believable, but tangible. Lifelike.

- Full settings help make two-dimensional letters on a page, text printed on pieces of paper (or the zeros and ones of digital stories), seem real. *Be* real.

- Setting is frame and foundation. It's color and support. Setting is time and era and clothing and history. It makes up a major part of the story world, the place where your characters spend all their time and the place into which you've invited readers. It should be unique to your story. It should be a place where readers want to hang out.

If readers can't put a book down, if they cry or laugh over the adventures of imaginary people, then fiction is real. And lifelike and accurate setting detail is one of the surest methods for bringing authenticity to fiction.

When place and time and weather and props—all the elements of setting—come together to build the story world, magic strikes.

A world is created. And the reader is enthralled.

QUESTIONS TO ASK ABOUT SETTING

- Is setting established right away, within a few pages of the story's opening? If not, introduce setting detail in the early pages. If you don't want to (or can't) reveal much right away, make sure you don't forget to add details when possible.

- Does setting fit the story's or scene's mood? The characters? Events? If not, something should change.

- Did you use a variety of setting details, not just place but geography and culture?

- When scenes change, do you orient readers to place and time right away? Unless there's a strong or deliberate reason to not do this, make sure the opening of each scene contains setting markers.

- Do setting details overwhelm, seem overly stressed? If so, cut back on them.

- Do you play up the setting to manipulate mood and reader emotions? If not, consider doing so.

- Do you use setting to increase conflict? If not, why not? There's no reason not to use setting for exactly this purpose.

- Do you allow characters to interact, both positively and negatively, with setting and setting props? Do your characters even use props? If you put props into a setting, put them into a character's hand.

- Do you have different characters interact with different aspects of setting? Except for obvious objects and elements, characters wouldn't all notice the same setting components.

- Have you played with intensities in setting details, for example, escalating weather problems or building civil unrest over a period of time until it explodes into a city-wide riot?

- Are setting details introduced naturally, with the flow of the story? If not, make changes. Setting should almost never be lists of details thrown at the reader.

THE QUICK LIST

Make sure that

- setting fits genre and characters fit setting (by scene, by chapter, for the story as a whole).
- setting is clear, not ambiguous. (Exceptions for purposely ambiguous elements.)
- appropriate props are in place to be used and *are* then used.
- setting influences a scene's mood and/or a character's tone.
- setting is revisited throughout the story.
- unless setting details play a major role, they are kept in the background, not in the spotlight.
- setting description doesn't get in the way of action.
- setting description doesn't go on for too long. Weigh the other scene elements and provide a balance.
- rather than list details of setting like a grocery list, you've included details that mean something important to a scene, to the character, and to the plot.
- characters focus on details that you need readers to make note of (both everyday objects and objects necessary for plot and even setting details that you're using for red herrings).

11

CRAFTING CONFLICT

EVERY PIECE OF FICTION must contain conflict. Conflict is fuel for our stories. It's what keeps the plot churning and characters amped up. It makes events unfold and holds readers glued to the page.

At the most basic level, conflict is disagreement, typically disagreement that's not instantly resolved.

Each scene and chapter must have conflict at some level, perhaps multiple types at different levels. Conflict can stem from (or feature) a difference of opinion, an argument, a fight, or a war. Dialogue should increase conflict. Action should increase conflict. A look cast across a room should increase conflict. If characters are always agreeable, always in accord, there is no conflict. There is no story.

Conflict can play out in words, in body language, and in action.

If you're a novelist, you're not writing a business report, a document scrubbed clean of emotion or blame. Fiction is not emotionless or distancing—it's filled with highs and lows, pain and angst, joys and fears and expectation. Disagreements and emotion attract readers, pulling them close to the essence of story. Fiction, with its requisite discord, makes readers pay attention. They want to know what's going to happen, whether characters will work out their differences or come to blows. If your story is good enough, readers will *need* to know how story conflicts are settled. Characters who always get along have little to offer readers.

Characters should rub one another the wrong way and push each other's emotional buttons, and it's conflict that leads to this behavior. And, as with any cycle, emotional button-pushing should lead to increased conflict.

> As you edit, check every scene for conflict. Every single one. If conflict is absent, add it. No scene is only filler, free of tension or some kind of disagreement.

Set characters against one another, even against good friends and loved ones. Set a character against himself to struggle with competing needs—long-held beliefs pitted against the demands of a crisis.

Conflict doesn't mean someone is always throwing punches, though that might be necessary for some novels. Conflict might mean a difference of opinion. Or it might be a character offering the silent treatment when someone else is trying to elicit information or simply trying to have a civil conversation. Conflict may arise when one character ignores the advice of another and then the two have words about why the first character didn't follow the advice.

Conflict may be present even when characters are in seeming agreement. If business partners agree to pursue a project yet disagree on how to best carry out that project, you've got conflict.

Friends who can't decide what to do on a night out are in conflict.

Lovers who need love to be conveyed back to them in ways different from the way the loved one offers that love—through word, through affection, through gifts, or through service—are in conflict.

You can add conflict to a scene by giving a character competing choices. He may clearly want one choice, want both, or want neither. But when you make him have to choose, you've introduced conflict.

Readers feel conflict as tension; when you write conflict well, readers feel it. They may feel uncomfortable or antsy or fearful.

> While readers might feel good at the end of your story, the unfolding drama shouldn't be all hopscotch and lollipops. When all goes well and characters get along, readers will yawn. If you neglect conflict, readers will turn away. And you might have trouble wooing them back.

Keep readers involved by disrupting your characters' lives with conflict. Make readers wonder what might happen—no, make them anticipate what's bound to happen—given the degree of disagreement between characters.

Yes, give readers an enjoyable time and an engrossing read by making life disagreeable for your characters.

Types, Levels, and Duration

Conflict can be of different types, and you should use multiple types in a novel. So your protagonist might have conflict within herself when she finds that what she has to do is contrary to what she wants to do or runs contrary to her personal code.

She also may have conflict with a friend or loved one, either an emotional conflict or a difference of opinion that escalates over the course of the novel. This conflict—parents arguing over the way to treat a child or best friends differing dramatically over the direction a shared business venture should take—can prey on your protagonist, affecting her emotions and actions. It can set her off balance so that she has trouble making decisions, or it can make her miss clues about the behavior of her enemies, proving a distraction which in turn makes her angry at the cause of her distraction.

And of course she'll have conflict with the antagonist and his cronies. This can be all-out war, a physical fight, a battle of wills, or even a cat and mouse game of the mind.

A character can even fight against her physical environment, battling the elements as she tries to rescue someone or reach a destination. She may be in conflict with society or culture.

Arresting stories force major characters, especially protagonist and antagonist, into conflicts both internal and external. A character who battles outside forces while at the same time fighting inner battles— fear of success, fear of failure, doubt, indecision—is a character readers want to root for. If not that, they certainly want to see if she can survive all her conflicts.

A character in conflict has something to offer the reader—reasons to keep turning pages. Whether a reader wants to see a character succeed or fail, she'll keep reading until her curiosity is appeased.

Conflict shouldn't remain at the same level throughout the story. Think escalation, perhaps in measured steps or maybe as a series of emotional blowouts. Think resolution as well, so that conflict has an end point. Levels of conflict should change from scene to scene because different groups of characters are involved in each scene and the conflicts between and among them should be different, should reflect the different mixes.

Conflict levels should also be different at different points in the story since conflict should be high in key scenes (such as the climax).

A single point of conflict can escalate over the length of a story, coming to a head at the climax, or it may last only for a few chapters, until characters resolve their differences *concerning that issue*.

You'll want to make sure that the levels of conflicts vary and that characters don't always respond the same way—with low-key acceptance, for example. That may be the response the first couple of times that another character prods and pokes at a character, but by the third or fourth time, your character should be prodding and poking back or exploding or doing something underhanded to stop the other character's behavior.

Make sure that your characters don't always suck it up. They should sometimes get to explode. And if they've been holding back for a while, they can explode in a spectacular way, overcompensating for a minor disagreement.

Conflict levels can range from modest irritants, the proverbial pebble in the shoe, to war (both physical and emotional). And conflict levels should increase over the course of a story. Yet you must make sure characters have a logical—to them—reason for raising conflict levels.

As you edit, check each scene for conflict. Make sure it's not only present but that it's not the same type or level as in the prior couple of scenes. Make sure that not all conflicts are settled within one scene, as in an episodic TV show. See to it that some conflicts stretch over multiple scenes and chapters, maybe for the length of the story.

> Make sure you've included a character's response to conflict. Characters shouldn't be unaffected when they have major disagreements with friends or loved ones. They should blow up or apologize or forgive or carry grudges. Conflict should lead to bad decisions or missed opportunities. Conflict could lead to regret.

Conflict should make characters *feel* out of sorts and *behave* out of character. Or at least behave differently than they normally do.

Conflict should see them making stupid mistakes and taking reckless chances. On the other hand, having it out with a friend could bring a character to a realization of her own behavior, make her recognize that she'd been out of line.

Repeated conflict may ultimately prove to characters that they can't be together with someone with whom they always disagree. Thus the conflict may lead to a parting of the ways.

Conflict needs to be present in story. And it needs to make characters behave in ways they hadn't expected to behave. And that behavior needs a response from the character. She may regret what she did; she may be remorseful. She may regret her actions but not be remorseful, understanding she did what had to be done. She may be glad she finally acted on those impulses that goaded her.

Whatever the response, she should *have* a response. And characters around her should respond as well.

WAYS CHARACTERS EXPERIENCE AND INCREASE CONFLICT

Characters experience conflict in a variety of ways. When you edit, be sure your characters experience that variety. Make sure every scene has conflict, make sure that conflict isn't limited to one type (fist fight or silent treatment, for example), and make sure that conflict levels increase as the story approaches the climax.

Check your manuscript for the following ways to create and/or increase conflict. Any one story may not feature each, but every story should include several.

Have characters

- engage others in a verbal disagreement
- give another character the silent treatment
- spread rumors
- use body language and/or facial expressions in ways that rile other characters

- enlist the aid of mutual friends or set a friend against another
- betray a confidence
- pick a fight
- fight verbally or physically
- denigrate something/someone another character loves
- steal or destroy the possessions of others
- ask third parties (law enforcement or colleagues or even friends and family) to intervene
- tell themselves to not get involved
- turn away from or ignore problems, delaying confrontation

In dialogue specifically, introduce or increase conflict

- through miscommunication (a garbled message)
- through pretended miscommunication (*Oh, I thought you meant . . .*)
- when one character ignores another, speaks right over him, or holds the other character in contempt and so gives no attention to his words
- by having one character leave the room or hang up the phone, thus incensing the other
- by having one character use hot-button words and pursue hot-button issues that set off the other character
- by having one character goad another, just because the first character likes to see the reaction
- by having one character use sarcasm
- by having one character ignore another character's warnings to back off
- by having one character refuse to play the games another introduces and revels in

To introduce conflict in action

- have one character take something from another (make conflict worse by showing that the first character doesn't even care for the object or person he stole)

- allow a minor verbal disagreement to escalate to the physical and violent
- give a character new facts to ponder, facts that add a twist
- include spectators to the conflict so characters can't back down without losing face
- allow a bit of fun or teasing to go too far and lead to a true physical fight
- prick a character's ego so he has to defend himself
- make a character have to defend another character or creature (a kitten) or a choice or personal trait (his reputation)
- arrange for one character to set up two other characters—they won't know they've been set up by a third party and so attack one another (the setup must be convincing)
- use the body language of one character to show contempt
- make one character physically challenging—he gets in others' faces, pushes fingers into their chests, talks loudly, always offers an opposing opinion
- introduce your main character to another character, but one with an opposing viewpoint or a different method for approaching problems, and make your main character experience doubts about his own approach because he can now understand this new approach, one he might not have thought of before
- give a character conflict between what he thinks he knows and what he's learning from a wise counselor

To introduce conflict through setting

- set a character at odds with cultural norms, laws, public policies, religious practices, or family traditions
- drop a character into an unfamiliar setting, one that frightens or challenges her or one that she has trouble navigating
- include people groups with incompatible belief structures, politics, or social systems
- show how geography led to social developments that characters may not agree with but must partake of and/or enforce

WAYS WRITERS INTRODUCE OR RAISE CONFLICT

Characters are the ones in conflict, but it's the writer who must put them there. Make sure you've introduced conflict in multiple ways and raised the conflict level using a variety of methods.

- Choose emotion-loaded words for dialogue.

- Put characters into unfamiliar situations.

- Pile on character problems and challenges.

- Introduce characters with opposing viewpoints.

- Force characters to make a stand.

- Force characters with different outlooks, backgrounds, or morals to work together to achieve a shared goal.

- Raise the stakes for a character.

- Make characters disagree realistically.

- Give characters opposing goals.

- Give characters the same goals but different methods of achieving those goals.

- Make one character a go-getter who acts before thinking and one a planner who thinks before acting.

- Give characters vastly different backgrounds or outlooks so that what's significant to one is meaningless to the other.

- Make characters face their fears; make them face their fears in the presence of their foes; make them face their fears in the presence of those who love them.

- Make a character think she's the only one who cares about a particular outcome or issue.

- Make characters rely on weaknesses rather than strengths.

- Don't resolve or back away from conflict too soon.

- Give a character something worth fighting for; make the prize worthy of the fight.

- Deny a character what he wants and then deny him again and then deny someone else what he wants.

- Give readers conflict that satisfies by making your choice of conflict type fit character personalities, yet also surprise readers (and characters) with conflict they didn't expect.

- Put obstacles in a character's path—make him stop to deal with problems on his way to his main goal.

- Frustrate characters by making it hard to reach goals or distract them with necessary obligations that slow down their march toward their goals.

- Introduce uncertainty—is a friend really a friend? will the next action lead to the one that will bring about the desired goal, or is a character on the wrong track?

- Stir a character's emotions—make him care and then threaten what he cares about.

- Pile on conflict so your protagonist feels isolated and under attack from both friends and enemies, and even from himself.

THE QUICK LIST

Make sure

- each scene contains conflict.
- you use a variety of conflict types and intensities.
- you understand that a single conflict won't be sufficient for a full-length novel.
- conflict seems real, authentic.
- conflict escalates as the story approaches crisis points, especially the climax.
- conflict arises from multiple sources—from the story world, from within a character, between characters.

- conflict is appropriate for the genre, the characters, the plot, and the scene.
- conflict produces reactions.
- multiple characters are involved in multiple conflicts.
- you surprise main characters with conflict from trusted allies.
- conflict drives character action and reaction.
- conflict isn't so simple that it can and should be resolved with a conversation.
- conflict between characters isn't limited to that between protagonist and antagonist.
- conflicts are settled, concluded, and don't merely *stop* at the story's end; give conflicts proper resolutions.

If your story has conflicts that are unresolved on purpose—between protagonist and antagonist in a series or perhaps a deep cultural issue that doesn't change even when other story issues are resolved—make it clear that some conflicts may never be resolved. Don't merely drop the unresolved conflict—point out its ongoing nature.

12

Dialogue that Doesn't Stink

SOME WRITERS MAGICALLY spill golden dialogue from their fingertips, writing character-speak perfect for the character, the moment in the story, the book, the era and setting, and the genre.

And then there are writers who fumble through a writing task we figure all writers should excel at because we do it every day.

At least that's how it seems when we're examining dialogue.

We talk. We communicate. We express emotion. We convey information. We stir up family members and tick off our co-workers almost daily. And we do it all with our spoken words.

Yet often our characters struggle to speak, and we struggle to get them to do what we need them to do with their words.

Dialogue is a major component of fiction, a necessary component. And writers owe their readers engaging dialogue that achieves multiple story purposes at the same time.

The how-tos of writing dialogue deserve a book of their own, but since this book isn't that one, we'll cover the high points and some do's and don'ts. If you've never studied dialogue, now might be a perfect time to check out resources on this fiction element.

Because dialogue is so important to get right and so easy to get wrong, we're going to look at not only the editing of dialogue, but the writing of it as well. If you want to skip to the end of the chapter for the do's and don'ts and the quick list, feel free to jump ahead.

PURPOSES OF DIALOGUE

What *are* the purposes of dialogue?

- to introduce or exacerbate conflict
- to stir characters to action; to provoke reactions

- to provide cover for subtext or said another way, to reveal subtext that rumbles beneath the surface
- to push characters to a breaking point
- to reveal character, advance plot, and establish or change tone or mood
- to reveal theme
- to raise the tension level and stir up emotion in the reader
- to break up or balance description, action, and exposition
- to reveal back story (but not in long, boring, or slow-moving clumps known as info dumps)
- to misdirect both characters and readers
- to set one character against another
- to provide a forum to voice a character's thoughts
- to show character growth and development
- to reveal character relationships
- to secure agreement for one character's plans
- under certain circumstances, to purposely reveal information

Your dialogue needs to have a purpose, and typically one beyond *Wow, no one's talked for 20 pages—must be time for some dialogue*. That's a reason for *you* to include dialogue; your characters also need reasons to speak.

If you can work multiple purposes *for* dialogue into the same section *of* dialogue, that's a plus. The dialogue will be memorable and will feel indispensable. And not only indispensable, but full. Purposeful. Worth reading. If you can convey the building emotions between two characters and reveal a detail of the mystery *and* raise the conflict level with the same bit of dialogue, your dialogue is multitasking.

Dialogue isn't the same as real-world talk. Good dialogue doesn't contain all the *um*s and *uh*s of real speech, and it doesn't include mind-numbing talk about the weather, details of the trip to the office, or particulars of a phone call from Mom. Not unless such common topics are being used to mask subtext or build conflict.

No matter how cutesy or clever fictional conversations are, they must push the plot forward, reveal something new about characters, drive characters to react, influence a scene's mood, touch the reader's emotions, and/or increase conflict. They must achieve one or more of the major purposes required of all fiction elements.

Dialogue isn't filler, it's meat. A novel can't be constructed of only dialogue since we also need action and description and exposition, but the dialogue you do include shouldn't be fluff.

Not all sections of dialogue will be as full as others—as with any fiction element, you want to include different lengths and depths and degrees and varieties. But you can make even a two-line exchange meaningful, make a single line poignant or revealing or shocking.

So dialogue should work, but it also should resonate.

ATTRIBUTES OF DIALOGUE

Dialogue is allowed to be murky. Confusing to the other characters. Indirect, oblique, and incomplete.

It isn't real conversation. It should cause story problems, not solve them (at least not too many of them). Characters should lie, be heartlessly honest, abrupt, and rude, misdirect other characters, hold back (the truth), and let fly (with emotions).

If your dialogue is flat and all surfacy, add subtext.

What are characters tiptoeing around? What are they *really* talking about when they discuss an issue? What are they purposely ignoring? What are they saying about a volatile topic by talking about another topic instead? Subtext needs to run under the surface of dialogue.

One point to remember is that conveying accurate information is not always the primary purpose of dialogue. Often the main intent has nothing to do with clarity.

In fact, one intent of dialogue is to obscure, to cover over and make unclear. You don't want your characters telling everything they know to the fullest degree. If the characters all knew what was going on, what everyone's motives were, then there'd be no uncertainty and little tension. There'd be no reason to write the rest of the story.

Only rarely is the major purpose of dialogue to tell other characters something true and unambiguous, and being truthful and explicit often has a purpose of its own. When Ty dishes to Callie about Frank, Ty may actually be quite truthful. Yet at the same time he may be hiding other information, such as his own secrets or his purpose for spilling Frank's secrets. He's being truthful because he has an agenda, and his deliberate choice of words furthers that agenda.

Characters should go out of their way to *not* reveal complete information and the full truth, not unless it serves their purposes. If the truth would compel another character into a reaction desired by the speaker, that speaker will likely speak the truth to elicit the reaction.

But characters can speak some truth and still withhold information. So they're speaking factually, but lying by omission.

Some characters may withhold truth until they're forced to dump on someone. *Then* they should let the truth come flying out of their mouths. And that truth should be painful for both the speaker and the listener. Maybe uncomfortable for the reader too.

Bottled-up truth that is freed from its bottle can burn and sting. It can open characters' eyes. It can turn a story in a new direction.

And it is fun, fun, fun to write.

▪ Dialogue is used to misdirect and confuse other characters, to thwart and anger them. It's used to send them off in the wrong direction. It's used to stir character emotions.

▪ Dialogue can be used to speed or slow pace.

▪ Dialogue should give characters humanity, should erase the edges that separate characters from real people.

> Dialogue isn't a report of everything that characters say. It's the compelling and noteworthy real-time, purpose-filled talk that plays out in front of the reader. It's the words, the lies, and the truths that characters want to reveal, the emotionally charged words they can't help but reveal, the meaningful words their hearts long to share. Dialogue is the intentional words a character speaks to further his agenda *and* it's the self-censored words that eventually can't be suppressed any longer.

Talking about the weather, asking another character how she's doing, reporting what a character did that day . . . these details aren't necessary and shouldn't be included in dialogue *unless they serve a story purpose.* If one character is avoiding talking about the hit and run she had the night before by talking about the weather, that dialogue can build tension and tick off the person she's speaking with, *and such dialogue can work.* It's the filler talk of weather and greetings and nothing in particular that needs to be cut from dialogue.

Dialogue can also reveal how characters relate to one another— the protagonist speaks differently to his wife than he does to his best friend. And he speaks differently again with the antagonist.

THE VERY SPECIFIC SPECIFICS OF DIALOGUE

- As the climax nears (as any high point or emotional moment nears), the feel of dialogue should change. Sentences may get shorter, with characters getting to the point. Or, conversely, sentences may get longer, showing a character building up his rage or confusion. There may be fewer action beats and more straight dialogue.

- Word choices in dialogue should reflect the character (his emotions, his needs, his purposes) as well as the emotion of the scene, the setting, the era, and the genre. For example, the banter in a detective story of the 1930s shouldn't sound like the dialogue between pirates from 1790.

- Dialogue should never feature what characters already know purely as a way to convey information to readers. Such dialogue always sounds fake. It *is* fake.

> "You know, Bob, when we trolled the bars back in our college days, the girls never gave us their real phone numbers."

> "Yeah, they sometimes gave us the numbers for their boyfriends."

> "And a couple of times they had us calling the local police precinct. Things were tough back then."
>
> "Well, Bill, when we did this in college, we didn't have a pot to piss in."

Bob doesn't need reminding, and such reminders introduce phoniness to a scene. Don't include any *you know, Bob*s. And while we're mentioning Bob . . . keep names in dialogue to a minimum. People don't often call each other by name when they speak to them.

▪ Spell out numbers in dialogue except for years, for names—including product names and numbers used for identification (Highway 5, Channel 12)—and for numbers too long or complex to be spelled out, such as 10-digit phone numbers. Spell out symbols in dialogue. People speak words, not visual symbols. Let readers hear what's spoken and how it's spoken.

▪ Dialogue should sometimes be direct, sometimes indirect, often incomplete, and always effective. It should be felt by the reader as well as heard. And even though it's spoken, it should help readers *see* something new, some insight, about the characters. Even if information is withheld by the characters as they speak, readers should pick up a whole lot—information, emotional undercurrents, insights, character motivation, back story—from exchanges of dialogue.

▪ Dialogue is not a time for a writer, hiding behind a character, to preach or lecture. This is the characters' story, not yours. If you find characters getting carried away with your pet causes, stop them. If you've allowed them to preach or teach, start cutting.

▪ Interrupt dialogue through the words of others, with action or movement, even with description if that's appropriate. Dialogue shouldn't always be smooth and unhindered.

▪ Have characters cut off their own words. Not every character will be glib and articulate, able to get out what they need to say on the first try. Let a character stutter or begin again or change direction as she speaks. Let a character mangle names or other words.

SUBTEXT‡

Subtext can affect dialogue in a major way, so let's look at subtext in greater detail.

Subtext is what characters are saying, or not saying, in a coded way about one issue even as they speak plainly about other issues. Subtext is what's going on in your story below the surface. The inclusion of subtext adds depth to dialogue and fiction, giving it a layer that hums or rumbles below the obvious surface layer, a hum that's often felt before it's understood.

Subtext is unspoken but not unrecognized. It reveals truth, even when characters don't intend to divulge that truth.

Subtext deals with those topics and truths that characters don't want to talk about but which affect what they do or don't do, what they say or don't say, what they feel, what they want, what they fear, and what they dream about.

> Subtext identifies what's important to a character. If a character can't talk about a topic or won't talk about it but the subject and the character's feelings about it scream from the page anyway, that's subtext. It's not boldly spoken but it is clearly felt.

Subtext is what the reader sees when a character says one thing but obviously means something else.

It's the meaning hidden beneath spoken words or quick glances. It's the truth that characters are hesitant to speak. It's revelation of truth, but revelation that's veiled, even if the veil is thin, thin, thin. And the revealed truth is sensed, is experienced, by both characters and readers.

Subtext isn't used only in dialogue. Glances, body posture, and attitude can highlight subtext just as easily as dialogue can. Yet since we're considering dialogue, that's also our focus with subtext.

Subtext cuts deep, goes way beyond surface events and dialogue. It creates some of the most heartfelt moments in stories. Subtext is the unspoken but nevertheless exposed feelings, history, fears, and dreams of your characters.

Subtext is potent because it reveals truth—true emotions, true thoughts, and unfeigned motivation. It reveals characters at their very core, exposing the unadorned—the unprotected—man or woman.

Characters can lie—to others and to themselves—through their dialogue. But their thoughts and motivations are more honest. When readers see into a character's mind, they see what drives the character, what moves him, what keeps him at his duty way beyond the time that others would quit.

Subtext is the reality of a character's life that's seldom brought to the surface to be hashed out or examined. But what's revealed in subtext is central to who a character is and what he wants.

Subtext instantly identifies what's important for a character, what's on his mind, or what pushes him to act or speak as he does.

It's the emotions and thoughts hidden beneath dialogue and behind action.

It's what the reader sees when a character says one thing but obviously means something else.

Characters don't say what they mean for several reasons: doing so might hurt another character, or it might hurt them; they're unsure of what they're feeling; they don't know how to articulate what they're feeling; they fear what will happen, what they may lose, if they speak their minds.

Subtext that runs through a story brings depth and dimension. It ramps up tension and conflict. It's much deeper, more fundamental to a character's traits or personality, than is surface revelation. Yet because what underlies the text isn't explicitly stated, the reader might have to look harder and listen closer to understand.

When subtext flows under dialogue, readers might need help to realize that there's more to the moment, scene, altercation, or exchange than meets the eye. This means in turn that the writer must take special care with subtext to make sure that it's clear enough for readers to recognize. Yet at the same time, you never want to overplay subtext. Obvious subtext comes across as nudge nudge, wink

wink—the writer shining a spotlight on a story element that should remain in the shadows.

Subtext is marvelous for creating tension and escalating conflict.

For a couple who's lost a child or for a detective feeling out a suspect, what is unsaid may be more important than what the characters do say. Subtext allows you, the writer, to hint at emotions and events and relationships without actually spelling out all the details. Subtext can be conveyed through words (spoken and thought or even withheld), through actions, through looks, and through reactions.

An example of subtext in dialogue

A man who argues with his wife about the time she spends away from home, shopping, may actually be bringing up the affair she had two years earlier when she also spent time away from home.

The man may never mention the affair, the other man's name, or the fallout from when the man bragged of the affair to the husband, but that affair could be driving every word the couple share and the emotion behind them.

In this example, both husband and wife are talking about the affair even as they talk around it.

> Nate slammed the cabinet door and then opened and slammed another.
>
> "Geez, Leslie, you'd think with all the shopping you do every single day that there'd be something to eat in the house."
>
> "Not every day, Nate. Never every day."
>
> He flicked at a carton of cigarettes on the counter. "You got your cigarettes, I see. Always gotta make sure you've got cigarettes after an hour or two of shopping." He thrust the carton against the toaster. "Cigarettes always taste better after shopping, huh?"
>
> "You smoke too, Nate."

> He peered into the fridge, then crossed his arms, tapped his foot. "No beer? You'd think th—"

> "Beer's in the other refrigerator. As always."

> He closed the door, leaned against it. "You always have a ready answer, don't you, babe? Always ready with a logical answer."

There's much more to this exchange than what they're actually saying. The shopping, cigarettes, and beer aren't the true topics; they serve as an excuse to needle at old problems. Yet they don't provide a forum for the characters to truly face and resolve those problems.

Thus the conflict.

Check your scenes for subtext. Dialogue should hint at it. If it doesn't, all meaning will be above the surface, exposed too easily. If characters reveal their inner selves only through obvious action and speech, you've not used every tool available to create complex and compelling stories.

Not every dialogue exchange requires subtext—not every story needs it—but don't overlook its usefulness, especially as a means of deepening conflict or referring to past events.

Make readers have to push—at least a bit—to read between the lines. Make them want to read between the lines. Use at least a touch of subtext if you want readers to plumb a character's depths.

Subtext can be used to

- tell readers information that (some) characters don't know
- add tension and conflict
- reveal a character's true motivation or emotions
- reveal theme
- add depth to story

DIALOGUE TAGS AND ATTRIBUTIONS‡

Dialogue tags and attributions are simply the devices we use to let readers know who is speaking.

Not every line of dialogue needs a dialogue tag, not even every paragraph of dialogue needs one. Use tags only when necessary to help keep track of speakers or for rhythm or a particular feel to dialogue. Your style will have you using more or fewer tags than another writer uses, but don't ram attributions down your readers' throats. Readers can follow along easily if you've been clear.

On the other hand, don't think that you have to pull every dialogue tag from your fiction until you leave only bloody holes where they used to be. Dialogue tags are necessary, and you should include them. You simply shouldn't overdo their inclusion.

And not only do you not want to use them too often, you won't want to get too creative with them.

While fiction is creative writing, there's no need to get creative with dialogue tags; *said* and *asked* work perfectly well and almost invisibly most of the time. Yet not *all* the time. If you use *said* with every line of dialogue, readers will notice.

Still, while the general recommendation is to use *said* and *asked*, there are allowances for genre expectations.

Romance writers are allowed great leeway with dialogue tags. So are writers of YA and children's fiction. And an occasional tag other than *said* is accepted in almost every genre *if* the action of the tag can actually work for spoken words.

So while characters can't laugh dialogue, they could whisper it. They can't jeer it, but they can murmur it. Follow the allowances of your genre, but don't go crazy with dialogue tags. Their purpose is to identify the speaker, not draw attention to the tag itself. The purpose of a tag isn't to show off the writer's familiarity with a thesaurus.

> Writing dialogue tags is an exercise in restraint and in underplaying your creativity.

A caution for romance writers—

Please don't copy the practices of other writers, especially those who wrote 30 years ago, rather than write for your characters and the era in which they live. *Retort, query, question, opine, quip,* and *inquire* are all valid verbs, but they often don't fit the characters of today, and when they're used as dialogue tags, you're liable to stop your reader when instead you want the reader cruising along with the action.

I'm not picking on romance writers; I'm sure every genre has its overuse of particular words. But I do see these words used as dialogue tags again and again in romance manuscripts. These are examples of what I call *romance-ese*, words copied from one romance book to another, typically from books written more than a few years ago.

It's okay to borrow writing techniques that work, to twist them and make them your own, but don't borrow what doesn't work, including words that make your stories sound like every other romance or suspense or mystery or YA novel. And don't try to copy the styles of writers from years ago. They wrote for the readers of their era; you should do the same.

Words need to fit your characters, their situations, and their eras. Words should also fit narrative distance and POV.

How many real-world people do you know who regularly think the word *retort*, who claim that others retort? An omniscient narrator might use such a word, but most men and women of today wouldn't think that another person *retorted*. If you've given us a close-up of your viewpoint characters and their thoughts, make sure that their words reflect them. Use words they would be likely to use.

The advice for every genre is *write dialogue tags that make sense*.

But what of using other kinds of verbs as tags, something more than *said* and *asked?* Wouldn't those work?

We've all seen a variety of verbs used as dialogue tags, so it's not that they aren't accepted for the role. But just because they're allowed, that doesn't mean they're the best choice. People do *answer, claim, assure, explain, exclaim, question,* and so forth, and that's just some of what they're capable of. But they *speak* dialogue. They *ask* questions.

These types of verbs *are* used as tags, but they come across as more a description of the act of speaking, as a report, than as a simple identifier of the speaker. Someone is reporting to readers that Mike or Malik or Monique delivered their words a certain way. Some outsider is narrating what he or she sees, explaining what he sees.

Said or *asked* aren't reports; they've become near-invisible markers or guideposts, just like common punctuation and especially like the period. They don't get in the way of dialogue; they allow dialogue to be appreciated as spoken words delivered directly from the character, with no outsider's commentary attached.

With report-style dialogue tags, we may find ourselves asking who's reporting to the readers, who's intruding on the scene by declaring that a character *shouts, exclaims, bellows, declares,* or *proclaims* a particular bit of dialogue. Is it the viewpoint character taking the time to tell us how another character delivers his lines? Not usually. No, this report is typically straight from the writer.

This is author intrusion hiding behind supposed creativity.

I know, I'm trampling all over a few sacred cows. But rather than argue about the right to use any verb as a dialogue tag, why not try using *said* most of the time, *asked* some of the time, and other verbs rarely? Try this and see how stretches of dialogue read without the commentary regarding the way a line is delivered. See how your dialogue is kept in the moment, kept uninterrupted, when it's delivered without explanation.

Readers don't need the writer or a narrator calling out from the wings, explaining what's happening on the stage. Readers need only the characters themselves doing their thing.

Most of us pass over *said* and *asked* as easily as we do a period at the end of a sentence and a capital letter at the beginning. These tags are background, part of the mechanics of story; they meet their purpose but don't stand out. They let the dialogue take the spotlight.

Readers don't have to slow their read to make sense of *Nancy said.* Those two words convey the speaker as Nancy, but otherwise pass under the radar. The reader gets to hear Nancy speaking, almost as if the reader is in the room with her. The reader doesn't have to rely on someone else explaining exactly how Nancy delivered her lines.

Other speech verbs used as dialogue tags tend to stand out and demand attention, if only for the briefest moment. But that brief moment can be enough to distract the reader. And when it happens again and again, the reader can feel that she's no longer inside the fictional world but watching from the outside.

And what of other verbs, the even more creative ones that get used as dialogue tags? What about *smile*, *sneer*, and *laugh*? Can these be used as dialogue tags?

They shouldn't be. These verbs describe actions, not speech delivery methods.

We smile a smile, but we say our words. We laugh, but we don't laugh words. These are each separate actions that shouldn't be joined into one.

Don't assume that a verb can be used for a dialogue tag just because it's an action performed by the mouth or tongue, the throat or chest. We do more with our mouths than speak, and none of those other actions magically produce speech.

Do we use *kiss* as a dialogue tag? How about *lick*? What of *taste* or *chew*? *Gargle*, *gurgle*, *pant*, *sneeze*, or *hiccup*?

"You are precious to me," he kissed. **✗**

"My love for him has me all twisted up," she licked. **✗**

"I need to run to the store for eggs," she sneezed. **✗**

No, we'd never use these actions of the mouth as dialogue tags—thinking of doing so is laughable—so why use *smile*, *laugh*, or *hum*? Why insist on using *sneer*, *snort*, *smirk*, *grin*, or *snicker*? These actions are no more capable of producing speech than are *kiss*, *lick*, or *taste*. Don't conflate actions made by the mouth with speech. They are actions, just as jog, dance, clap, and jump are actions. Just because they're performed by the mouth doesn't mean they're involved with talking.

It's true that we can perform multiple actions at the same time, so just as we could clap while bungee jumping, we could both smile and speak. But we aren't smiling the spoken words. We are saying the words and smiling the smile. The actions may be related, but they're separate, and two discrete actions deserve two separate verbs.

> Think of the dialogue tag as a simple identifier. It shouldn't be used as explanation. Save that for the dialogue itself and for the actions surrounding it. The tag has one major function—to identify the speaker. (It may also be used for rhythm or balance.) It doesn't convey the way dialogue is spoken; it reveals who, not how.

When you edit, give thought to this issue. See if maybe a new view of dialogue tags might not prompt a change in your use of creative tags.

And if you're thinking about books from the past, wanting to use them as an argument for creative tags, I'll agree that writers of the past used great variety in dialogue tags. But I'll also point out that you don't live or write in the past. Your readers don't live there either.

And while other contemporary writers may use a wide variety of verbs in their dialogue tags, I'm challenging you to write differently. To use tags as near-invisible punctuation as a means of letting your dialogue—the spoken words themselves—take center stage. I'm challenging you to give as much thought to the true purpose of dialogue tags as you give to other fiction elements.

Use a different tag every so often for effect; I would never say you could use *only said* or *asked*. But now that you see the consequences of using unusual dialogue tags, see what you're actually conveying to the reader, you might want to make changes to your approach. After all, you'd never use a different punctuation mark at the end of a sentence when a period is called for. You have reasons to use question marks, exclamation points, the ellipsis, and the dash for certain sentences, but at all other times, you use the period. You wouldn't substitute a comma or an apostrophe just to be creative. The words of the sentence, not the terminal punctuation mark, should be the focus.

> You'd never want to use so many different dialogue tags that readers are more curious to discover which tag you'll use next than to find out what's going to happen to your characters in the next scene.

And please refrain from using tags that might have readers howling. You don't want readers laughing at your word choices unless that's the purpose of those choices. I strongly suggest that you not write something such as *"I love you," he husked.* Yes, his voice may well be husky, but if a character's husking dialogue, the poor guy needs help.

The takeaway?

When you edit, check your dialogue tags. Ask yourself if you really need something other than *said* or *asked* or perhaps occasionally *he told me* (although that too is a *report* of what was said). Ask if an outsider is reporting what your characters are saying when instead characters should be speaking directly to each other and being overheard directly by readers. (Exceptions when you actually want a distance-creating report of dialogue, perhaps from an omniscient narrator.) Ask if a particular dialogue tag is less a way to speak and more an action performed by mouth or lips or tongue.

Ask what is accepted *and* expected in the genre. And ask yourself if a tag is needed in a particular sentence or paragraph at all.

Action Beats

For variety and a different feel, use action beats in place of some dialogue tags. This accomplishes at least two goals—it puts characters in motion and identifies the speaker. It can also break up sections of text that contain too much straight dialogue.

Examples of action beats—

> **Tia brushed the crumbs from her lap**. "I'm sorry you feel that way."

* * *

> "Gotta run, Mom." **Adam jumped up from the table**. "I'll be late tonight."

* * *

> "I forgot to tell you"—**Jaden eased away from Wanda**—"that I ate all your chocolate."

As every line of dialogue doesn't need a tag, so too each won't need an action beat. But do use action beats for variety and to accomplish several objectives with a single line of text.

You can combine action with dialogue tags, yet remember to vary your format. You wouldn't want to repeat the same sentence constructions again and again. Any repetition in form, even more so with unusual constructions, can be more than annoying to the reader.

Here are a few options for pairing actions with dialogue and dialogue tags when you do need the combination:

—dialogue tag paired with participial phrase

> "I need you," Selma said, watching Walter in the mirror.

—participial phrase first

> Watching Walter in the mirror, Selma said, "I need you too, sweetheart."

—tag modified by prepositional phrase operating as an adverb

> "I hate you," Roxie said with a sneer.

—action only, no dialogue tag (some verbs, such as *sneer*, don't work as dialogue tags, so make sure they get a period, not a comma)

> "I hate you." Roxie sneered.

—tag paired with dependent clause (no comma after *said* except when the subordinating conjunction is *although* or *though*)

> "But you're my best friend," Bo Peep said as she reached out to Curly.

—tag as present participle

> Randall stomped his foot, saying, "But I wanted the blue one."

—tag paired with an action performed by the character who is speaking (no comma is required after *said*, though many writers do use commas in such a construction—your decision about a comma may come down to style and feel and the needs of the sentence)

"Your lips are turning blue," Pat said, and turned away.*

*See more about this construction in the chapter "Punctuation in Dialogue." There's some controversy about proper punctuation and whether it's acceptable to join an action to a dialogue tag this way.

—action of the character who is speaking paired with the dialogue tag and placed before the dialogue (no comma between the action and the tag)

Randall stomped his foot and said, "But I wanted the blue one."

—action of the speaker paired with tag, with the action included after the dialogue

Randall said, "But I wanted the blue one," and stomped his foot.

—tag paired with an independent clause (comma required between the tag and the independent clause)

"But her lips are red," Peter said, and he pivoted to watch her stride away.

—tag paired with absolute phrase (comma required between tag and absolute phrase)

"She would have been thirteen tomorrow," he said, his voice heavy with grief.

—absolute phrase before the tag (comma required after the absolute phrase)

His voice heavy with grief, he said, "She would have been thirteen tomorrow."

—tag and action interrupting a single line of dialogue (a comma is required before the tag and after the action)

"The dog jumped over the couch," Lance said, waving his hands over his head, "but the cat jumped over the dog."

—tag and action coming between two sentences (a period is required at the end of the first sentence and a capital letter is needed to begin the second sentence)

"The dog jumped over the couch," Lance said, waving his hands over his head. "But what was really funny was watching the cat jump over the dog."

—action beat with no tag interrupting a single sentence of dialogue (dashes are required)

"Rover leaped over the couch"—Johnny clapped with excitement—"but Daddy tripped over Rover."

You've got options for variety and to meet all sorts of needs and conditions, but sometimes dialogue should be all talk. Sometimes you want the speed and intensity of a strong back-and-forth conversation with no tags and no action beats.

"I'm sorry I introduced you to my father."

"But I like the old guy."

"That's what I'm sorry for."

When you edit, make sure you've not limited yourself to the same one or two sentence constructions throughout a scene or chapter or full book. Try multiple options for laying out dialogue.

Adverbs

Tags and adverbs are not a music group, not a must-have combo. My advice? Don't fall prey to their allure.

Adverbs—*slowly, happily, elegantly*—modify verbs, adjectives, and other adverbs. Writers are generally discouraged from using adverbs to modify dialogue tags. Actually, writers are discouraged from overusing adverbs for any reason.

> "I saw you do it," Mia said gleefully.
>
> "But I'm telling you it wasn't me," Kelly said angrily.
>
> "It was you," Mia said stubbornly.

Adverbs aren't evil and they have their place and they can be used selectively with dialogue tags just as they can be used for other purposes in your sentences. But you won't want to modify every dialogue tag with an adverb. As you gain experience writing dialogue, you'll discover that you don't need to modify most tags.

Adverbs, when added to dialogue tags, tell—*report*—information to the reader. To allow readers to experience story moments and character emotions for themselves, without reliance on a narrator or viewpoint character explaining to them, skip the adverbs and instead show how a character feels and behaves through action, posture, and facial expressions. And through the dialogue itself, of course.

Remember that the tag is used to identify the speaker and not to convey the manner in which dialogue is spoken, which is generally what an adverb paired with a tag will do. Can you sometimes use adverbs with dialogue tags? Of course you can. Should you use them often? No.

When you rewrite and edit, actively work at reducing the number of adverbs in your attributions, especially if you use a lot of them or use them in successive tags.

An exception to the recommendation for not pairing adverbs with dialogue tags would be children's fiction, though you still wouldn't want adverbs with each tag, except maybe to purposely create a particular feel or humorous effect.

Dialogue Tag Word Order

Unless you're writing for a specific effect or have set your story in the past and want it to sound as if it's from an earlier era, put the name or the pronoun (or noun that identifies the speaker) first in the tag itself. *He said* or *Max said* is just fine. *Said Max* or *said he* is old-fashioned and sounds odd to the modern reader. We don't say *walked Max*, not unless Max is the dog and someone else is walking him. And we don't share stories with our friends by saying *said he*. *Max walked* works well and so does *Max said*.

There *is* leeway for stories written for British audiences and those who follow writing rules geared to British English. Yet keep in mind the way your readers and your characters actually speak.

Another exception is to reverse the word order when the more common order would be awkward or the tag uses a string of words to identify the speaker. In the following examples, the speaker is unknown to the viewpoint character and information necessary to identify the speaker follows the tag. The same information could be presented other ways, yet this is an economical and clear way to do it.

> "The doctor will be here in a few minutes to answer your questions," said the tech who was fiddling with Stanley's IV and blood pressure cuff.

* * *

> "Put down your weapon," said a deep and unfamiliar voice from across the room.

The attribution can go before the dialogue itself, but more common is to put it after the spoken words. It's not that you can't put it first—and doing so might be great as a way to change up your sentences—but after is perfectly acceptable. The spoken words are the important part of dialogue, so it's quite all right to let the tag hide behind them instead of introducing them.

If you do put the tag before the dialogue, make sure you haven't also put effect before cause, reaction before action.

> A deep and unfamiliar voice from across the room
> said, "Put down your weapon."

This word order is usually not a problem, as long as the tag is part of the same sentence. But the possibility is there to have readers wondering or doing a double take. The problem? The viewpoint character can't recognize—and therefore can't report—a voice as being deep and unfamiliar until *after* the words are spoken.

If you're ever worried about effect coming before cause, put the dialogue before the tag.

If you forgo the dialogue tag and use only an action beat or a thought related to the dialogue, that beat or thought should follow the spoken words: a character can't respond to dialogue before he hears it.

> The voice whispering from across the room was deep
> and unfamiliar. "Put down your weapon." *X*

Instead, try—

> "Put down your weapon."
>
> The voice whispering from across the room was deep
> and unfamiliar.

In a paragraph of all dialogue (or of several sentences of dialogue), insert your dialogue tag at the end of the first sentence of dialogue or, even better for rhythm, at the first natural break in that sentence. There are exceptions, naturally, but since the main purpose of tags is to identify the speaker, do so early in the paragraph most of the time.

> "I told you I'd do it," Juan said to the rest of us. "I've
> got everything arranged, all the pieces in place. Please
> don't mess it up by sticking your noses in where they
> don't belong. I'd hate to see you in jail just because
> you couldn't resist poking around."

* * *

"The dogs," he said, turning to the kennel, "need to be set free. They don't belong in cages any more than we do. And your daughter would be in tears if she saw the conditions here. She'd free them herself if she could reach the locks."

* * *

"It's a tossup," Mary said, "a real tossup. I wanted the deep blue, but the aqua is a better match. You think you can help me decide?"

* * *

"It's a tossup, a real tossup," Mary said. "I wanted the deep blue, but the aqua is a better match. You think you can help me decide?"

There's no need for multiple dialogue tags in the same paragraph. If the reader doesn't know who's speaking after reading the first tag, the paragraph needs work, not another tag. There is an exception when the speaker addresses one character at the beginning of the dialogue and a second character later in the same paragraph. Use dialogue tags or action beats to show the change in the speaker's focus.

NAMES IN DIALOGUE

Unless you want to drive both characters and readers crazy, don't include names in every line of dialogue. People don't call each other by name often, not when they know the other person fairly well. If you need names—if the characters and readers need them because you've massed a group of characters into one scene—use them. But one fix is to write dialogue so that you don't need names. A second fix is to use the names in action beats, but again, only for clarity.

Now, if a character is purposely calling another character a name to annoy her, that's a different animal. Have fun annoying the snot out of your characters.

INTERNAL MONOLOGUE

Character thoughts can be conveyed in a number of ways, including ways that bring depth to a novel. But character thoughts can also smother the reader and stop a story's momentum as though it had stumbled into molasses.

Character thought, for all its strengths, shouldn't supplant action and dialogue as a way to reveal character, motivation, goals, back story, and a character's emotions. Thoughts *can* reveal all those things, yet sharing character thoughts shouldn't be the only method you use to show what's inside a character. Dip into a character's thoughts, by all means. But don't move into his head. Free the reader from the confines of a character's mind. The mind eventually becomes stuffy and limiting and dull. And yes, boring. And we don't want any part of a story to bore the reader.

We don't want to bore the characters either. Free readers and characters from overbearing internal monologue and thoughts that go on for too long.

And keep story events flowing. The forward motion of a story stops each time a character holds a conversation with herself. It's never a good idea to repeatedly stop a story's momentum. Readers read to find out what's coming next; don't frustrate their desires.

Even in first-person narration—where every observation comes from the narrator—make sure you've taken us out of a character's head and its limitations.

One way to do this is to remove filters and thus allow readers to directly experience what the character does at the time he does it. Besides bringing readers closer to the action or emotion, removing filters also reduces word count, definitely a plus when you get only so many words to tell your story. Use words that matter, those that serve multiple purposes if possible, and get rid of those that don't.

Check for common filters such as *felt, saw, heard, watched, knew, noticed,* and *noted.* Show what a character noticed without reporting *she saw, she heard, he recognized* or *he noticed.* (See the appendix for a longer list of filter words.)

For example, you wouldn't want to always frame a character's actions or observations in this manner—

> I watched as the snow fell, softly at first and then quicker and harder. I felt the cold rush through me, and I shivered. I noted that the cars crept through the neighborhood, but I saw kids racing down the shallowest of hills on sleds, plastic bags, and even cardboard boxes.

To free readers from the claustrophobia of a character's mind and an unrelenting focus on the character, you could write—

> The snow fell, softly at first and then quicker and harder. Cold rushed through me, and I shivered. Cars crept through the neighborhood, but kids raced down the shallowest of hills on sleds, plastic bags, and even cardboard boxes.

Give us the character's perspective—his words, emotions, and peculiarities—but don't continuously remind us that he's telling his own story. Allow the reader to pretend to be the character. That's difficult to do when a character is always saying *I, I, I* or *me, me, me*.

If you've got a first-person narrator, do one editing pass solely for the word *I*. Cut instances of the word by rewriting, as in the example shown above.

Read passages aloud to see how they sound when the character keeps mentioning herself. It's just as annoying as when real people talk about themselves, so limit the use of *I*.

DIALOGUE DO'S AND DON'TS

- Don't let characters repeatedly call other characters by name.

- Don't have characters answer questions fully, not with complete sentences and not with complete answers.

- Don't allow all characters to begin dialogue with *oh*, *well*, or *hey*.

- Don't have characters answer with a *yes* or *no and* also explain the answer. Drop *yes* or *no* from most answers.

- Do let characters be oblique.

- Do have characters lie.

- Don't have characters talk aloud to themselves just to fill in the reader. One character might do it once or twice; most wouldn't do it at all. Use other ways to report what characters are thinking.

- Don't give in to talking-head syndrome, where characters only talk and don't move through their setting. Do provide setting details and show where characters are and what they're doing while they talk.

- Don't explain how every line of dialogue is delivered; let most dialogue stand on its own.

- Don't forget background and secondary characters while two other characters are talking. If characters are in the scene, readers need to see what they're doing or need to hear from them. If they're in a scene, put characters to work.

- Do have your characters interrupt one another, talk over one another, misread one another.

- Don't have characters spill secrets too early.

- Do surprise readers by having a character reveal something readers never would have suspected the character would tell or even know.

- Don't overuse creative dialogue tags.

THE QUICK LIST

- Your novel should have abundant dialogue; characters do more than move or ponder.

- Look for white space that indicates dialogue; if too many pages are dense with action and exposition, add dialogue.

- Make sure that dialogue contains conflict.

- Dialogue shouldn't be an opportunity for characters to preach or for authors to lecture—save instruction for a nonfiction book and preaching for another occasion.

- Characters should have different speech patterns, use different words, and sound different.

- Dialogue can affect pace and conflict, and reveal back story and motivation—make sure yours accomplishes multiple tasks.

- Use dialogue that bounces from character to character, stripped of action beats and dialogue tags, if you need to speed the pace.

- Add dialogue tags and actions between lines of dialogue to slow a scene's pace.

- Substitute narrative for dialogue to slow pace.

- Keep in mind that dialogue should be much more than filler.

- If dialogue is flat, consider adding subtext.

- Make sure that subtext isn't too obvious.

- Make sure that internal monologue features consistent punctuation.

13

SETTING AND BREAKING THE PACE

LET'S PERFORM a quick review of pace.

Pace in fiction deals with the speed at which either the story or a scene moves. Consider the speed of unfolding events, particularly the amount of story time between them. When events are widely spaced, with a lot of time given to a character's thoughts or introspection between those events, the pace is slower. When events unroll nearly on top of one another, the pace is faster.

Scene lengths also influence pace. Long scenes placed back to back can make a story seem languid, unhurried. A series of short scenes makes a story move faster.

> When readers turn pages frequently, the story feels fast. Short chapters and ample white space, which usually means a lot of dialogue, lead to the feel of a fast pace.

Pace can be deliberately manipulated by the writer, but it's felt by the reader. *Feel* is a key word when discussing pace. Pace is one story element that has less to do with character, dialogue, or setting (keeping in mind that all story elements do ultimately affect one another), and more to do with reader perception.

TOUCHING THE READER

Pace can influence, direct, and change a reader's emotions.

The differing speeds of passages of dialogue or action scenes can create different feelings in the reader. So a slow or dreamy scene may feel comforting or lulling. A scene that gets its business done quickly, allowing characters and readers to race through it, may create anxiety and tension.

Scenes that move slowly allow a reader the chance to catch his breath; a slow scene might put him at ease when you want to set him up for an unsuspected event. A pace that's too slow, however, could put that same reader to sleep. Unrelenting sameness in pace and a story that goes nowhere are problems that need to be corrected. And you'll want to make your changes before readers or critics call you on the problem, telling the world that your stories are boring.

There's a true difference between leisurely moving stories and stories that don't move at all. One is a function of genre, the other often the writer's inability to know what to include and what to keep out and perhaps ignorance of what pace means for story. You should know what's expected for the genre and then make sure your stories meet those expectations.

Suspense and adventure will be faster paced than much literary fiction. For the most part, books for kids and young adults, no matter the subgenre and subject matter, will move fairly fast.

Romances can have unhurried beginnings and a slow build or can start fast and move faster with each chapter. The same is true for science fiction and mystery.

Some stories need a slow build before they take off, and the style or genre can handle the slower start. Other stories start fast on page 1 and pick up the pace as they unfold.

Yet whether your story is a fast-moving adventure or a leisurely character study, you'll want to change the pace at some point. Characters in in-your-face action novels need to slow down to breathe; the readers need them to slow down so they too can take a breath and relax. The break may not be long, but there should be breaks in the action before the story takes off at an even faster pace.

And leisurely reads need variety as well. The pace can't be so meandering and laid back that you put the reader to sleep or lose his attention to other pursuits from his own life. Some scenes must be faster paced. There must be changes to the rhythm of sentences, paragraphs, scenes, and chapters. There should be a change in dialogue, a change that's felt in increased tension for the reader, maybe in marked emotional highs and lows.

All stories should include a change of pace when the build toward the climax begins. The pace is likely to increase yet again just as the climax is unleashed.

VARY THE PACE

So what do you do regarding pace when you edit? You make sure the pace is varied and that it picks up as the story heads toward the dark moment and the climax.

Keep in mind that *fast* is relative—relative to what has come before, what's needed at the climax, and what's required for the genre.

In general, stories that start fast should not only maintain that fast pace but increase it. If your story starts out with a bang and then fizzles, rework the opening. Start a bit slower if necessary. Or rework everything after the opening.

You *could* deliberately start at a superfast pace and then bring the pace down to a less frenetic level, but readers will eventually expect pace—and the tension or other emotions generated by that original pace—to match or exceed that pace somewhere else in the story, especially just before the climax. You set the bar high if your story comes rushing out of the gate like a racehorse intent on winning a major derby. It's likely that readers will be disappointed if the story doesn't finish just as energetically.

Don't be hesitant about speeding up the pace to near frantic and then slowing it back down, even before the climax and resolution.

Your main character might need to step back and gather his thoughts once he accepts the story's call to adventure, and this would mean a slowing of pace as the story problem wraps itself around him.

The pace likely sped up when he was caught up in the story problem and needed to decide whether he'd commit to a course of action, but once he committed, the story's pace could slow a bit. With the decision made, he doesn't need you to pile on the tension and speed the clock to compel him to act. Not right away. At this, the beginning of the adventure, the main character is caught up in enough problems to make him miserable.

On the other hand, once a character commits to the call to action, he may take off running. That's a valid option. But keep in mind that he won't be able to sustain an unrelenting pace forever. And you'll still need to pick up the pace on the way to dramatic events.

Even if you slow the pace once the character commits to his course—and you've done so because the character no longer needs to be pushed to act—you don't want him to come to a full stop. Yet once you start the story clock going, that doesn't mean it has to go only faster. You can slow down every once in a while; both characters and readers will need that slowdown. Characters who go nonstop become cartoonish, their behaviors unreal and unbelievable. And readers who don't get a break from the author may take one of their own—putting the book down. Anything you can do to keep characters moving and readers reading is a good thing.

> Variety in every story element is desirable; you never
> want to serve your readers the same of anything for
> pages on end. A varied pace serves to freshen a story.

When you edit for pace, besides verifying that pace starts at the right level and then changes in the early scenes, also check for changes in pace leading up to anticipated events. Manipulate pace to build tension and suspense. Use pace to keep characters anxious or skittish. Use pace to keep readers on their toes.

Also check the story at about the two-thirds mark. If pace hasn't *started* picking up in a race toward the climax, then rewrite. For some stories we're not talking about super speed and lots of action, but we are talking about a different feel. Call it an expectation. You've got to weave in the anxiety of expectation.

The approach of a story's end is different from the opening pages and middle scenes. This isn't a function of genre but of story structure. The sections of a book have different purposes and should feel different to the reader moving through them.

If characters aren't under the gun or racing a clock but should be, correct for that. If the story's problem is coming to a head, readers should feel the tension. The writing should reflect the approaching showdown. For example, there should be less focus on description, unless that description has an immediate bearing on events unfolding at the moment the description is featured.

INCREASE THE PACE

What can you do to intentionally speed the pace?

Include shorter phrases in dialogue and more emotional dialogue. Characters who lose their tempers. Shorter sentences. More white space on the page. A *different* look and feel to the story. Yes, the end of a novel should feel different from the beginning.

The actions and simple movements you give your characters affect pace as well. Back-to-back action moves faster than a long scene of character thought and rumination. A scene featuring a man racing across rooftops will move faster than one of the same man sipping whiskey and remembering the first time he saw his wife.

Pace needs to change if you don't want to put readers to sleep with the monotony of sameness.

If a story's even tenor extends to the end, the story needs work. Even with a character-driven story, the reader should feel the end approaching; readers shouldn't be taking their cues only from the number of pages left to read. The story should be working toward a crisis point and resolution, and the pace should reflect that.

MANIPULATE PACE

Be deliberate in the ways you change the pace of individual scenes, a series of scenes, and the story as a whole. Use pace to alter the mood of scenes. Use it to keep readers involved in your story.

▪ Speed the pace by cutting words from sentences and paragraphs; slow it by adding words, by lengthening sentences.

▪ Include more description or description with a wider variety of details to slow pace.

- Use short summaries to speed the pace and jump ahead in story time; use longer or leisurely summaries to slow that forward speed.

- Jump from scene to scene to speed the pace; use longer scenes with fewer jumps within the same chapter to slow pace.

- Put action scenes back to back to speed the pace.

- Insert more dialogue scenes to increase pace; increase it even more by switching quickly from one speaker to the next. Cut out dialogue tags and action beats to speed the pace even more. Reverse these processes to slow the pace.

- Add back story and character thoughts to slow the pace; reduce both to speed the pace.

- Add a flashback to slow pace.

- Use short and common words to speed the pace, longer and more complex words to slow it.

- Include dramatic hooks at scene and chapter ends to keep the story moving and keep readers looking forward.

- Keep outcomes uncertain so the reader feels compelled to keep turning pages to find out what will happen.

- Give the reader reasons to care about characters so they'll want to keep reading, will *have* to keep reading.

WORD CHOICE AND PUNCTUATION

Since pace is about the feel of a scene or story, pace can be affected by word choice. Short or one-syllable words that are abrupt help speed pace. Longer, multisyllable words slow the pace. Sentences with a series of modifiers (adverbs and/or adjectives), multiple clauses, or strings of verbs can slow the pace. Shortening sentences to the basics can speed the pace.

Even punctuation can affect pace. A single sentence with sections joined by commas may not only sound different to the reader, it can feel slower than the same text broken by semicolons or periods. Or, conversely, it could speed the read.

A single long sentence with an easy flow unbroken by punctuation might give the impression of forward motion where a handful of shorter sentences punctuated by periods might serve to stop the reader or at least have her pausing. However, a *string* of long and complex sentences creates a slower pace. Experiment with punctuation to determine how changes affect pace.

> Jericho needed to reach Blood Highway before dawn, so he packed up his rifle and food stores, erased all trace of his presence, and headed west into the desert.

* * *

> Jericho needed to reach Blood Highway before dawn. He packed up his rifle and food stores. Then he erased all trace of his presence. He headed west. Into the desert.

THE DO'S OF PACE

- Use common words, words readers won't trip over, to keep a story moving. Use unusual words or use common words in unusual ways if you want readers to pause to think about what you're saying. Yet you want to be clear, and you don't want readers stumbling over words.

- Use strong hooks at the ends of chapters (and at the beginnings of chapters) to keep readers interested and turning pages. Check every chapter and scene ending to make sure they tug readers forward rather than give them an occasion to stop.

- Hold exposition to a minimum to keep a story moving. Write short transitions between scenes to maintain a speedy pace; write longer transitions to slow the pace or maintain a slower pace.

- Show the wide-angle view of a scene before focusing on the details to slow the scene's forward movement.

- Add character thoughts to slow a scene, cut them to speed it up.

- Cut description and modifiers to move a scene along.

- Use active action verbs to keep a scene moving.

- Slow the pace by writing long, flowing sentences. Use longer paragraphs as well.

- Introduce description or setting details to slow the pace.

- Lead a character into a place of solitude and let him pause to think to slow the pace.

- Insert a scene that includes back story to slow the pace.

- Vary sentence structure and length and rhythm. The same kinds of sentences—noun-verb-object or participial phrase first or sentence fragment—repeated again and again will bore the reader. Whether the pace is fast or slow, too much of the same construction will have readers howling for a change. Read passages aloud and listen to the rhythms and sounds. If too many sentences sound the same, it's time for variety.

- Decrease the time between events to speed up a story. Spend more time on each event or increase the time between them to slow a story.

Know what you need a sentence, passage, or scene to do and edit accordingly. Take out or add in words to create the effect you need. Manipulate pace. Use it as you do any other element of fiction to contribute to the feel of a scene and to influence the reader.

Use pace wisely. Don't bore the reader and don't kill him by snatching his breath away.

14

TONE AND MOOD: GETTING THEM RIGHT

TONE AND MOOD are at the heart of a how a story feels to the reader.

Tone is the attitude of the narrator (or viewpoint character) toward the events of story and the other characters. In first-person narration, tone can also be the narrator's attitude toward the reader. (In nonfiction, tone is the author's attitude toward his subject matter and/or his readers.)

A few words to describe tone—*snarky, indifferent, eager, disbelieving, cold, condescending*. Remember, this is the narrator's or the viewpoint character's *attitude*. Readers should be able to pick up on this as your narrator reveals a scene.

Mood is the atmosphere, the feeling, experienced by the reader.

A few words to describe mood—*dark, brooding, scary, ominous, light, buoyant*. Mood is what the reader feels from a scene or from the story as a whole. Mood is not the reader's emotions, but his take on the feel of a scene.

Both tone and mood are created and changed by diction (word choice) and syntax (word order and sentence structure). Both are also affected by the use of imagery and the inclusion of the sense elements. The use, non-use, or blend of literal and figurative language will also influence tone and mood. The use of devices we'd typically associate with poetry—similes and metaphors, rhyme, alliteration, and so forth—influence mood.

Words—the choice of words and the way they're used—are the major influences on mood and tone. The right word or string of words can nail the viewpoint character's attitude; a wrong word can make a scene *feel* wrong.

Characters should sound like the people you've described them to be. Their emotions should fit the circumstances and the events they're going through. Scenes should feel scary or victorious or depressing because of the words you use to describe them and because of the characters' reactions to the events that transpire during those scenes. Words need to fit every element of the scene.

Every scene and story will have a tone and a mood and yet, if you haven't consciously worked them, haven't tried to enhance them, you may have mismatched tones, with the narrator showing an attitude that doesn't match what's going on in a scene, or your narrator's attitude may change for no reason, or the mood you create may not match the events taking place on the page.

> If you can't pinpoint what's wrong with a scene or story and you find yourself saying *something just doesn't feel right*, check tone and mood for the story as a whole and for each scene. See if either or both might be off track.

Is a supposedly comical scene truly humorous? Does your viewpoint character have the right attitude for the dark mood you're shooting for? Does a secondary character have the right reaction to scene events, a reaction that will convince readers of the feel of the scene?

Does your viewpoint character's attitude—revealed through thought, action, and dialogue—match what you've told us about him?

What you're looking for when you edit is the match of tone and mood to the events of the scene and to the characters' responses and personality quirks.

For example, if the scene should be spooky, characters need to be spooked. They should sound and act afraid. One might whisper instead of speaking in a normal volume. One might have a shaky voice. One might have shaky hands.

If you fail to include character reactions that fit your intended scene mood, readers will have trouble picking up the mood. If you include character reactions contrary to the intended scene mood, you've created the wrong mood.

A character scurrying through spooky catacombs in the dead of night, tripping over bones and trying to outpace ravenous zombies, shouldn't be calmly swapping recipes with her companion who's also trying to escape the killer zombies. Exceptions for quirky characters who actually don't feel fear and for scenes where elements intentionally don't fit. But keep in mind that in such situations, it's likely that you wouldn't be *trying* to create a scary feel for the scene.

You want character speech and actions to match the scene's mood. You want those words and actions to help *create* the mood.

As another example, say that a character is supposed to be cruelly dismissive of a fellow character. If that's the case, the mood can't be light and playful. Mood must match what's happening in a scene.

You can correct problems with mood by changing what happens in the scene, by changing character action and reaction. Or you can change the mood to match what's happening in the scene. If the events are humorous and lighthearted but you tried to create an atmosphere of unease with your description of the setting, you can change the description to match the scene's events.

Tone and mood are greatly influenced by word choice.

If tone and mood aren't what they need to be, change words or word order. Or if the mood isn't deep enough, add a focus on the senses—try sounds—that deepen or emphasize mood.

If your viewpoint character is supposed to be wickedly sarcastic but you couldn't write sarcasm for her—or you included the sarcasm but diffused it with humor—changes are needed. If you need the character to be sarcastic, you must write her that way. If she needs to be likeable, make sure she's got endearing traits as well. But readers need to see her sarcastic side. They need to hear sarcasm in her words and see the effects of that sarcasm in other characters.

Don't let your desire to be nice or your sense of fair play keep you from writing characters as they need to be written. Give characters real weaknesses and flaws that get them into messes big and small, that make them less than perfect. That make them authentic. Endearing. Exasperating. That make them human.

If a scene should be suspenseful, include unexplained sounds and scents and events. Introduce the unexpected, including mysterious characters with murky backgrounds. Use foreshadowing and at the same time, surprise readers with the unexpected.

Introduce mood and tone right from the start. Don't wait until chapter 5 to introduce humor in a comedy or suspense in a thriller.

If your characters cuss a blue streak, don't play coy in the first couple of chapters and let loose on page 50. Make sure the story and the characters sound like what they are from the very first pages, with exceptions for characters pretending to be what they aren't and for characters who truly change because of story events.

Make sure the tone established by your viewpoint character or narrator fits story events and the character. Make sure the mood of each scene matches the events of the scene and influences the emotional impact you want to create in the reader.

Tone Should Fit

Tone can change as a story progresses, but it could remain fairly constant from scene to scene. Tone is, after all, an attitude, and attitudes wouldn't change on every page or with every event. Think consistency when you focus on tone until it's logical that event piled on event (or one big dramatic event) changes a character's attitude.

But if a character's attitude does change—and there must be a cause for such a change—then you need to reflect that change through word choice and the arrangement of your words. You could also show a changing attitude through a character's focus. If a character becomes concerned about something different as the story moves along—maybe a loved one rather than a job outcome—that reveals a shift in attitude.

If you use multiple viewpoint characters, each should have his or her own tone. Then when viewpoint characters change with scene breaks, readers should be able to pick up on the new viewpoint character because of the tone, because of the attitude she wears.

Once readers know the characters, they should anticipate what a character might do. That's part of what drives readers to turn pages—

they can imagine what might happen when two characters, characters they've come to know well, collide. This doesn't mean you write characters who are wholly predictable. It does mean that you've got character personality doing some of the work for you.

Have you ever said or heard it said of a character's behavior that a particular action doesn't sound like the character? If so, the writer likely didn't match word choices, thoughts, or actions of the character to the person he's purported to be. Or perhaps the character's attitude changed without reason or motivation. If that's the case, readers will be left shaking their heads.

Tone should fit the character and the circumstances.

Put Mood to Work

Mood might change more frequently than tone, yet a story as a whole should have a mood recognizable to readers. Still, you may have a dark scene followed by a light and comical one followed by a lushly romantic one. As long as the scenes are consistent within themselves and they fit the unfolding events and your aims for the story—and if they aren't jarring for the reader—then you can change mood as often *as is necessary.*

However, keep in mind that readers have to adjust when you change the mood. They may have been groovin' along with that dark vibe that you so cleverly infused into the last five scenes. If they're caught up in the story, they may have trouble switching to a new mood, especially a lighter mood, when you make a change.

That's not to say you can't do it and can't do it without warning— abruptly changing moods may make for a grand treat for the reader. Yet do remember that readers have to adjust. You don't want them stopped by a sudden change; you instead want them so intrigued that they just go on reading. Maybe you'll need to offer them something familiar at the same time you change the mood so that they don't feel blindsided. On the other hand, maybe a solid slap-of-a-change is exactly what the story and reader need. My caution for you is that you remain aware of the reader's possible reactions. You can overwhelm readers, of course. But you don't want to jolt them out of the fiction.

My advice is that you pay special attention to scene breaks where the mood change is strong.

You don't want your readers slamming the book closed or throwing it against the wall. You do want them pulled deeper into your story world and the problems you've caused for your characters. You want them determined to find answers to their questions—who will get what she wants, protagonist or antagonist? how will the climax play out? will the main character's world ever get back to normal?

As you edit, check each scene and the story as a whole for both mood and tone. Make sure they match your intentions and the needs of the scenes. Make sure viewpoint characters have different attitudes and their scenes have different tones.

Make sure mood heats up or deepens when the story hits the high points, when it descends into your characters' low points, and as it heads toward the climax. Think about a change in intensity to get the reader feeling whatever he should be feeling in each scene.

THE QUICK LIST

Make sure

- you check mentions of the senses—have you manipulated mood through sounds and scents, light and darkness, colors and tastes?
- character responses fit the character.
- characters have motivation to change.
- word choices fit the tone and mood you hope to create.
- scenes don't contain mixed or contrary or competing tone or mood elements—cut or change words that don't fit.
- you check uses of figurative and literary language to make sure they fit the scene, the character, and the genre—a supposed plain-talking man should not sound like a poet.
- you establish both tone and mood early in the story and in each scene.

15

EXPLORING EXPOSITION

IN THE WRITING of fiction, exposition can be considered the telling part of storytelling. Even though too much exposition is counseled against, exposition is a crucial component of stories.

While much of long fiction is made up of scenes, not every section of text is a scene. And not all scenes are limited to action and dialogue. Many contain exposition.

We need ways to connect scenes, ways to introduce scenes, and ways to skip a story forward. We need methods to introduce back story, sometimes through dialogue or action and sometimes through unvarnished and wide-open telling.

We need to establish setting and highlight changes in setting. We sometimes need to explain.

At times we need to relay information directly from character to character or to the reader. And sometimes we need to achieve these objectives quickly. Sometimes we need to starkly declare *it was a dark and stormy night*.

We use exposition for these purposes, for straight-out telling that conveys information succinctly and sometimes plainly.

When we use exposition to establish back story or setting, we typically frontload it in a novel. So you'd likely include more of this type of exposition in the early chapters of a book. Yet exposition as summary or transition can be used anywhere in a story.

Literary novels typically, though not always, feature more exposition than do most genre novels. But any one novel could use more or less exposition than another novel. Exposition meets different needs and can be used in dialogue, description, and narrative.

EXPOSITION USED TO REVEAL BACK STORY

Characters may be arrested by a thought or a memory and then travel to the past in their thoughts and/or their speech. In this way readers are clued in to pertinent events from a character's past, events that relay back story and some *pertinent* details of a character's history.

When you have characters remember events from their past, make sure that reminiscences are prompted by something the character sees or hears or does. Make a trip to the past a response to a specific stimulus in the character's present. You don't want characters arbitrarily sharing bits of their past.

> (stimulus)—I stared at the body in the coffin. She looked nothing like Tonie. The makeup was good, but the clothes were wrong. Tonie had worn the sky-blue flowered dress only three days ago.
>
> (memory)—Tonie's mother had been a seamstress. Her creations hadn't been particularly flamboyant, but her kids had always worn new clothes that aped the latest fashions. I'd been envious. While Tonie never wore the same outfit more than twice in a school year, I rotated a few shirts—sweaters in winter—and paired them with one of my two pairs of jeans.
>
> * * *
>
> (stimulus)—Tate's hands shook as he pulled cold cuts from the fridge. He dropped the jar of mayo and flipped the knife he'd been holding halfway across the room.
>
> He leaned both hands against the counter.
>
> (memory)—He'd felt the same drugging anxiety once before. Back then, more than two decades ago, he'd just left college. His buddies had taken an apartment together, but he'd wanted to strike out on his own.
>
> He'd achieved his desire. He'd been so alone that he'd taken to calling his brother once a month and his mother almost every week.

He found a job with a construction company, dutifully had a couple of beers every afternoon with the guys, and yet still stared at his TV into the early morning, never figuring out what had his heart racing and his mind churning.

And now the smothering loneliness was back.

EXPOSITION AS A SCENE TRANSITION

A major purpose of exposition is to create transitions between scenes and chapters. Transitions can be used to advance time or change locations from one scene to the next.

Transitions can be as short as one line, or they can be paragraphs or pages long. Short transitions can be used to eliminate the need for a scene break. So, for example, if you're advancing a party scene by a few minutes or even hours, you could use a short transition.

After they danced, Tom excused himself, and Jenny watched him hurry away to rejoin Cassandra.

Forty minutes later, Jenny was ordering her third Long Island Iced Tea. And still watching Tom and his wife.

If a lot of time passes between scenes and you need to advance story time by large jumps, consider giving readers longer transitions filled with more details of what happened during the time being skipped. This helps readers adjust to the time change and helps them feel that time actually has passed. Show that the time you say has passed—whether hours, days, or months—could have actually passed by including events or seasonal highlights or holidays.

Also remember that when readers have read a highly charged scene, they'll likely experience an emotional response for a time. Help bring them down from the emotional high with a longer transition.

Yet don't get so lost in summarizing events that the transition becomes a school report, something like *What I Did Last Month*. Provide details as necessary and then move on.

Also consider the amount of passing time in relation to your story. For a story that takes place over five days, a time leap of 12 hours might be big, might need some extra details in the transition. For a story that covers months, a leap of weeks may not be noteworthy.

Be sure to include scene or chapter breaks before transitions that cover a significant passage of time.

> The three weeks passed quickly. Kent and Eli locked themselves inside Kent's bedroom, coming out only for showers and food. They turned their phones off, demanded that Kent's mom hide all three gaming systems, and only left the house when Mrs. Lister insisted on fumigating the room.
>
> By the third Wednesday, their robot prototype was ready for real-world testing.

* * *

> Two hours later, Ed was already on the road, putting long miles and delicious thoughts of revenge between him and Joan.

EXPOSITION TO TELL WHAT HAPPENED OFFSTAGE

When readers hear a story secondhand, they don't get the particulars that make a scene dramatic—the actions and reactions of those involved, facial expressions, and posture. But you don't need to show every story event via scenes. Sometimes you need just the high points relayed to other characters through a character who was present during those events (or even through a character who heard about the events through others). Exposition is a necessary and effective method for conveying information regarding offstage events.

Because telling rather than showing these events separates readers from the action, you wouldn't want to use this technique again and again to relay information, but you certainly should explore opportunities for using it in your fiction.

Exposition that's used to convey details of offstage events can be brief—a single line—or it can contain a series of details or events. When deciding how much detail to include, keep in mind the information needs of characters and readers as well as the number of times the story's forward motion stops. If the story is stopping often for revelations of back story or other exposition, perhaps only a brief explanation of offstage events is called for.

Fox rushed into Rictor's tent and pushed the commander's counselors aside.

"Damn, Fox, where've you been? The offensive ramped up two hours ago. We need—"

"Listen, you gotta hear this. Wilbur Jenssen Matthews came into the bar while I was there. The Darlassian's *general* strode right into Bobby's bar, sat down, and ordered a beer."

"What?"

(exposition) "I didn't even have to sneak around or anything. He and some other guy sat at the table next to me while their aides waited at the door. Rictor, I heard it all. At least enough to know that this incursion is a ruse. He said the target is the dam. Well, not in so many words. But that's what they were saying by not saying it. They spoke old Darlassian, so I had to do some extrapolating, but I'm sure what I heard."

(also exposition) Rictor had never figured out how anyone understood what anyone else was saying in that language, but he took Fox's word for it since Fox spoke old Darlassian better than most contemporary Darlassians did.

"And they made it clear that the water source was their primary target. Damn, Commander, you were right."

Rictor waved his men closer. "Highlights first, Fox. When are they going after the dam?"

"The general said . . ."

The paragraph with Fox telling what he saw and observed is exposition. It's not a lot and it may be sufficient for your needs. But you may need to tell more. If you include the rest of what he saw and overheard, sentences or paragraphs that continue from the *general said* line, then you'll have added much more exposition. And you may need more. But often less is better.

Even when you need to use exposition, don't let a character talk uninterrupted for too long when he reports offstage events. Break up long sections of a character's report with the dialogue or movements of other characters. Give listening characters appropriate responses that prevent tension from lapsing into tranquility.

EXPOSITION TO FILL IN READERS AND CHARACTERS

It's okay to use dialogue for explanations when the dialogue makes sense for the characters and characters don't sound as though they're sharing information solely as a means of filling in the reader; it's important not to have characters exchanging information that they both already know You don't want those silly *you know, Bob*s.

But sharing info in a direct manner is sometimes necessary.

"Why didn't you tell me?"

"Why would I? I didn't want you to know my mother was a pro."

Katie frowned. "There's something else." She crossed her arms and added, "I see it in the way your shoulders are pushed up into your ears."

She wouldn't look away, so he did. "Drop it. There's nothing else."

"Of course there is. And I need to hear it."

The woman was relentless. More than a minute passed, but she didn't move. After another minute of her unchanging silence, he couldn't take any more.

"My father was a senator when I was conceived, the vice president when I graduated from high school, and is now the President of the United States. Satisfied?"

EXPOSITION AS DESCRIPTION

Some stories can handle more exposition as description while others need leaner descriptions. Literary novels, epics, some mysteries, and science fiction (when the accent is on an unknown world) and any story that moves at a fairly slow pace can handle more description that exists solely as description.

A fast-paced adventure, on the other hand, doesn't need the action-stopping insertion of long stretches of description (unless you include them to slow the pace on purpose). For such stories, description may work better folded into dialogue and into a character's thoughts and actions than set up as paragraphs of straight detail.

The following is an example of exposition as description.

Santa Cristina stood above the town and valley. Not hovering, not brooding, the mountain was simply there, independent of what happened far below.

When the sun shone on her, the townspeople imagined they could see into her heart. But Santa Cristina revealed her secrets reluctantly, and those determined to know them had to brave the climb, had to peer into the chasms and scale the crags.

Cristina wasn't an unwilling partner, she just wanted her lovers to come to her, to boldly display their daring. To court her with confidence.

She shared her secrets. But only with the worthy.

THE TAKEAWAY

Because of its structure and purposes, exposition can stop the forward motion of a story. It can shift focus to the distant past, it can detail events that recently took place offstage, and it can propel readers and characters forward through time.

Since readers want to watch important events and not only hear about them, you don't want exposition to replace scenes with their action taking place in real time. Yet exposition is necessary.

When you edit, check the story in places where the forward motion slows or stops. If there's too much exposition, such as an info dump, cut back on the details. Decide which info is truly necessary. See if details can't be broken up and inserted in several places rather than in one clump. If details aren't necessary, cut away.

THE QUICK LIST

- When you edit, look for long stretches of exposition that can be shortened. Reconsider sections of exposition that are arranged back to back or close together without being relieved by a scene.

- Make sure that major events are shown through scenes rather than as summary. Never summarize the inciting incident or climax.

- Make sure that scene transitions don't go on too long.

- Check to see if minor events or low-conflict scenes might not be better relayed as summary, told as exposition. Or told as a half scene, with a mix of scene and exposition elements.

- Make sure that the revelation of back story doesn't delay the forward movement of a story, at least not for long. And make sure that back story doesn't serve as an info dump.

- Decide whether the story's genre and style can support long passages of exposition used in description. While a full page of description might work for a literary novel, your political thriller might be able to handle one short paragraph at a time at the most.

16

REFINING STYLE

ALL WRITERS HAVE a style. That style may not be clear until a writer has written several manuscripts or many, many articles and short stories, but writers do have favorite sentence constructions, favorite words, even favorite punctuation choices.

A fiction writer's style is revealed in the way he presents his story. It includes everything from the use of literary devices—alliteration, amplification, euphony, personification, and so forth—to the tone he uses for his narrators to the lengths of sentences and paragraphs.

All the dozens of choices a writer consciously or unconsciously makes regarding presentation are what give his stories a particular feel and sound. Even a distinctive look. The collected choices make the writer's works recognizable.

The good thing about style is that you have one—you don't have to worry over creating one for yourself.

What is tough, however, is knowing that you'll likely want to refine your style over time and that you'll need to make changes to style for particular stories or for certain characters. The hardest part of making changes may lie in determining how to accomplish those changes.

When you write, you make many style choices unconsciously, out of habit. You may personally think in similes, so your characters end up using them. You like short sentences, so many of your sentences are naturally short. Therefore you may have to consciously work at changing habits and usual choices in order to create different effects, to create a feel or rhythm different for one story or character.

Yet writers don't necessarily recognize the components of their own style. To know your style, you've got to examine the elements that go into style and evaluate your writing relative to those elements.

To strengthen your writing, you don't need to create a style out of nothing—you have to discover and refine the style you already possess. You have to put the distinctions of your style to work for genre and the types of stories you write.

STYLE ELEMENTS

I'm going to list a wide variety of style elements, yet without going into much detail about them. My purpose here is to make you aware of these elements so you can in turn learn which you rely on and which you never use. Once you have an idea of the style elements and your go-to choices, you'll be able to enhance your writing by playing up some elements and decreasing your reliance on others. You'll be able to adjust style elements to change the feel and sound of a story.

> Style is one of the major differentiators of writers; no writers have the same natural style. Given an assignment to write a science fiction dystopian novel set on Earth two centuries from now—featuring a 16-year-old female protagonist who grew up on a space station and only recently arrived on Earth—a dozen writers would produce widely different stories.

Writers leave traces of themselves in their stories through the many choices they make. They leave their mark through style.

Once you're aware of the possibilities for style and of your own style habits, you can consciously choose to change your patterns as you write and, more importantly, as you edit.

An analysis of your writing style probably shouldn't take place when you're actively writing, but it could happen when you edit. Or you may want to tackle an analysis between writing projects. If you've written for a long time or have a couple of novel manuscripts completed, you've got plenty of material to analyze. If you're just starting out, you may want to wait until you've got more text to work with. But even if you're a new writer, knowledge of the factors that constitute style will be helpful as you create, if only to spark awareness of style's components and influences.

Exposure to style elements can give you an awareness of options you've never considered. An analysis of style elements may introduce you to the missing style ingredient you've been searching for.

A list of style elements and choices that affect style

- diction—word choice
- syntax—word order
- sentence, paragraph, and scene length
- variety in sentence construction—subject/verb/object, dependent clause/independent clause, independent clause/dependent clause, independent clause/independent clause, starting with a gerund or participial phrase
- sentence fragments
- sentence rhythms
- creation of neologisms—coining new words
- use or nonuse of one or combinations of literary devices— rhyme, simile, metaphor, assonance, alliteration, etc.
- use or nonuse of foreshadowing and symbolism
- a particular balance of fiction elements, such as amount of dialogue to exposition or description to action
- tone of the narrator or viewpoint character
- use of flashbacks or flash forwards
- the ways clauses, phrases, and words are joined or separated—*He was a bore and a genius. He was a bore, and he was a genius. He was a bore. A genius. He was a bore; he was a genius.*
- use and nonuse of punctuation marks, especially commas, dashes, colons, and semicolons
- number of characters, number of viewpoint characters
- type of person featured as protagonist or antagonist—age, sex, profession, personality
- speech styles of major characters—terse, chatty, hesitant, etc.
- character use of slang
- number of scenes
- use of modifiers (adjectives and adverbs)—used sparingly, paired often, clumped together in a series
- use of dialogue tags other than *said* and *asked*
- use of adverbs in dialogue tags
- use of common verbs, use of unusual verbs

- use of Anglo-Saxon words in comparison to Latin-based words—ask/inquire, begin/commence, belly/abdomen, job/profession
- favorite point of view
- flow—do sentences flow smoothly or is there a lot of starting and stopping, the feel of events or dialogue too often sputtering or stuttering and jerking to a stop?
- amount and types of description
- type of chapter-ending hooks—do they hint at what's to come or are they all-out cliffhangers?
- character-driven or plot-driven stories?
- use of subtext, use of humor
- choice of genre
- use of few words or use of many?
- narrow narrative distance or wide narrative distance?
- method used to vary your customary choices—when you do change your normal patterns, do you always use the same type of change?

THE TAKEAWAY

Style is already part of your stories, your body of writing, and with little conscious input from you. But style can be modified. It can be accentuated or muted.

When you edit, take time to examine the style elements you favor. Then ask yourself a few questions: Should you tone one style element down? Should you shift the balance of style elements? Should you change your dependence on one or more elements for a particular story? Should you reduce the use of one element because you've used it too many times? Should you consciously make a character unique through the use of unusual literary devices, word choices, and/or sentence patterns?

Should you exaggerate a style element?

To deliberately shake up your style, you could reduce the use of any one element, such as similes or a particular sentence pattern. Or you could try a different style element to see if emphasizing it might not add power or resonance to a story. (Reducing the *over*use of any element should be a regular part of your editing process.)

Learn how changing one or several style choices can create different effects, and don't hesitate to change or play up style elements for any one story or character.

Rather than merely accept your instinctive style choices, put style to work for your stories.

17

DEALING WITH DESCRIPTION‡

ALTHOUGH I'VE TOUCHED on description in discussions of the other fiction elements, description deserves attention of its own.

Description is used to provide information about the setting and characters and even a series of actions. For setting we describe how it looks, how it makes characters feel, how objects in it are arranged and used. For characters we describe what they look and sound like, how they move, and their characteristics, both physical and emotional. In action sequences, we describe what happens and who does what.

Description allows the reader to see and imagine your story world, to picture characters and events in motion in that world.

Authors writing for earlier generations spent a lot more time on passages of description than do writers today. In general, that is. As with anything to do with writing, there are exceptions. Some writers in the past included less description than their contemporaries did, and some writers today work in much more description than others do. But in the main, we're treated to less description, or maybe shorter sections of description, than readers were in the past.

A quick check of Internet resources at the time I began this chapter showed very little in terms of *how-tos* for description. Even though setting description is generally used less now than in the past, it's still important for fiction and deserves to be covered.

Editing for description may be one of the easier editing tasks. If a scene lacks description details, the lack is obvious if you're looking for it (and you need to look for it when you edit). An overabundance of details should also jump out at you as you edit.

> If you find yourself skipping ahead as you read, looking
> for action or dialogue, you've probably got a section with
> too much unrelieved description. Or maybe it comes
> across as seemingly pointless description.

While it's true that some novels will have more description than others—maybe to fulfill genre expectations or to match the writer's style—you don't want readers feeling the weight of description at the expense of other elements. You can add description to slow the pace of a scene, but there's little reason to stop a story completely in order to introduce a long section of description or to force readers to skip sections to look for more meaningful text.

On the other hand, don't exclude description. Readers need some sense of your story world and your characters.

WORKING WITH DESCRIPTION

Description can be included as just description, a stand-alone element with no purpose other than to give readers a sense of setting, character, the sequence of events, or mood. Or description can be folded into action or dialogue so that it becomes a part of other elements, not a separate story component unrelated to character or action.

Description typically comes into a novel right away, helping to orient the reader to the setting and characters. Description also helps to establish a scene's or story's mood from the start.

For example, a description of the weather can quickly establish mood and set readers on edge. Yet using weather to *start* a story, as a featured opening element, is usually a poor choice. Readers need more than weather reports to tempt them into exploring a fictional world. If you do use weather in your story's opening, make it earn its place. Make it influence mood and character behavior. Give a description of the weather a purpose that supersedes its perceived weakness as a story opener.

Description is usually given in the words and through the focus of the viewpoint character, but since any story other than one with first-person narration allows a touch of the omniscient in the introduction of setting details with a new scene or chapter, some description can be neutral, outside the impressions of the viewpoint character.

Thus almost any novel can open with a long-distance or wide-angle view of a location, and a description of the setting and the characters moving through it—including their attitudes—can be shared before the reader is introduced to the viewpoint character.

This technique works well at the beginning of a book and at the beginnings of chapters more than at the tops of midchapter scenes. While scene breaks allow for changes in setting and viewpoint character, pulling out so far from the story that an omniscient narrator takes over narration duties from one of the characters is likely too strong a change within a chapter. Readers are rolling along with the viewpoint character, often identifying deeply with him or her. To be pulled so far away at a scene break may be disconcerting. Not that it can't be done, of course, since you can try anything. Yet see if a chapter break isn't a more logical place for such a drastic change.

You don't want to lose readers.

> Unless one character needs to describe something to another character because the second character wasn't there to see an event or person for himself—or wasn't capable of seeing or hearing for himself—description in fiction is pretty much solely for the benefit of the reader. Characters have no need to describe objects, setting, events, or other characters to themselves.

Description establishes or changes mood—for the reader.

Description creates a sense of place—for the reader.

Description fills in setting details and character details for the reader who would otherwise be unable to see or hear them. For all our efforts at making a story real, efforts at putting readers inside the fictional world, the readers aren't actually there. We have to re-create that story world for them *in their minds*.

Description helps the writer do this.

Description fires a reader's imagination, primes it to picture places and characters and events.

Description isn't needed for the character who actually lives in the story world. The character who lives and works and plays there, who loves and hates and fears in the fictional world, knows what it looks like and smells like and tastes like. It's all right in front of him—under his feet and in his nostrils and over his head. He touches and experiences the world in the same ways we experience our own—through personal encounters and through the senses.

Characters, except for the reasons I already mentioned, don't need description. *Readers* do.

So keep readers in mind when you write description, but even more so when you edit it. When you choose what to include. When you choose what to *ex*clude.

ASK QUESTIONS

To decide which description details are needed, ask questions.

- What does the reader need to see and feel of your world, of your characters' world? What does the reader need to know to make sense of the events of that world? What would the reader like to know? What is she likely wondering about?
- Which details will make the reader feel like a native, as comfortable with that world as your characters are? Which details create boundaries that hold the world together, contained, and keep everything that's *other* outside the story?
- Which details would make the reader feel like an alien, just like the character who finds himself in a world new to him?
- How can you lead readers through that world, encouraging them to make note of the noteworthy, while assuring them that some objects and people, while *there*, taking up space, are part of the background only and will have little impact on major story events?

Remember that unless a book is part of an ongoing series, readers are new to every story world and its characters, new to its laws (natural and character-made) and social practices, new to its special locales and terrain.

Introduce readers to the incomparable places in your story world. Share the cool stuff with them. Show them the sights.

Description, your description, paints in the story world just as a reader is walking through it. For the reader, the story world doesn't exist before the moment she encounters it. Yet if you've done your job right, she'll feel that the world has always been there, that she's coming upon it with the elements of that world already in motion.

Readers can't step into nothingness, so some description has to come early in a story. A reader shouldn't stand around in a fog, hearing characters speak or feeling events explode around her, not knowing where she and the characters are. *Not unless you're purposely creating such a fog.* Until you include the first bit of description, typically of setting but sometimes of character, a reader is caught in a void, a blinding vacuum absent markers of any kind.

▪ Description of setting allows the reader to see where events are taking place.

▪ Description of characters allows the reader to see who's involved in the unfolding events and to draw conclusions about the characters.

▪ Description of events engages the reader, draws her into the story, and provokes her curiosity.

Reading a description of a character, getting a sense of a character right off, can orient the reader and give her someone and something to identify with. It can provide a sense of what's happening in this new world. The character's behavior, both action and reaction, can immediately hint at problems.

If the *character* is in his normal world, he has no need to have that world described for him. The reader, however, needs initial description. And if she's to travel this unfamiliar world, she needs more description, especially of the unfamiliar, as she follows your characters around.

If you intend for readers to be able to move easily through your story, especially in the early pages, give them a sense of setting and a sense of which characters are important; if readers are worried that they're going to trip over objects or places or characters or misunder-standings, they'll read slower. They'll hold back. They'll approach story events with a tentative air.

But when they start to feel comfortable in the story world because you've filled in the description, they can move through it as if they were born to that world. They can feel as if they belong.

Now, if you want the world to seem alien to the reader *because it's also alien to the main (or viewpoint) character*, then you'll approach description differently. You may end up spending a lot of time, at least at first, on unimportant objects because a character in a place unfamiliar to him has no idea what's important and what's meaningless. You wouldn't keep up this practice of the character focusing on every new object or event for the length of a novel since the character will learn along the way, but in the beginning, for a character new to the story world, you can make him and the reader notice everything. In such a case, you'd need to describe many objects and places and charac-ters—whatever strikes the character as unusual.

However you convey description, remember to put it in the words and experiences of the character. Show the world through the eyes and senses of your viewpoint character—show what he notices and use his words to describe what he sees and what unfolds around him.

Even though characters move through their worlds, for the most part you want to keep *readers* in the forefront of your mind both when you write description and when you edit it. Yet tell readers only what's necessary for them to make sense of the story world.

> The longer the reader is in the fictional world, the less description she'll need. Once she knows what's around every corner, you don't need to tell her again. Once she can correctly *guess* what's around every corner, you don't need to describe setting or character in as much detail as you did early in the story.

You will, however, almost always describe new characters (or changes in existing characters), setting details that have changed, or unfolding events, since by their nature they're unfamiliar. But established setting and characters may need only a brief word of description to spark the reader's recollection.

HOW TO USE DESCRIPTION

Readers don't need a description of Captain Ralston's limp every time they encounter him. They don't need a mention of the scent of the astrenth flower each time they pass one. And as they wouldn't need to hear the click of a dog's claws against the kitchen tile each time the animal ran through a house, they also don't need to hear the *click-clappy-crack* of a tingel beast every time it runs. A reminder now and again, especially if another character gets to experience these things for the first time, can be helpful. But too much stress on description, especially familiar details, becomes tedious for the reader.

Using one character's descriptions of other characters, places, and events to reveal his own personality is a great tool that accomplishes several story goals at the same time. You can reveal viewpoint characters through their descriptions of others, the setting, and events—what they say, what they exclude, the words they use. So when the viewpoint character notes the clenching jaw of another character and thinks that it reminds him of a dam under too much pressure or that the man's face looks like the Frankenstein monster held together with inferior parts, that description reveals both the personality (or current emotional status) of the viewpoint character *and* details about the second character. The reader learns something about both characters with the same line of description.

A viewpoint character who describes events not only lets readers know what's going on, but the character's word choices and focus reveal what interests the viewpoint character. Those details can give readers insight into her mind and thought processes, maybe her fears and expectations. Her worries. Her attitude and emotions.

One important reminder is that you don't want to drop description details into action scenes when characters would never notice them. When a character is caught up in action, he's not going to notice the fluffy white clouds, the flowering crape myrtles, or the scent of perfume on the woman sitting next to him in his fleeing car.

If noticing such details *is* important and a quirk of the character is to notice them, do include them. But make sure they make sense and that the character doesn't come across as nonsensical for paying attention to such details under demanding circumstances.

When you edit, look for full scenes and moments in scenes when characters should be too busy to note description. Take out description that the character wouldn't notice given the circumstances.

> In all scenes, consider what a character should or would notice. If you haven't included logical details and description, add them. If you've used excessive or unnecessary description, cut it from the scene. Or adjust the description. Many times editing isn't all or nothing but a matter of degree.

When action moves rapidly, that's a great time to weave description details into the action and not simply let loose with a paragraph of description about a character or place.

No matter how artistically written the description is, it must work with all other scene elements. Would a character notice the object or person or setting detail? How would a character describe it? Does the description pull the reader deeper into the scene or point off into some unrelated place?

You'll want to make description fit.

So rather than—

> I raced after them, straight down the street. The cobblestones were uneven and multicolored—red and brown and rust—reminding me of lanes in reconstructed colonial towns like Williamsburg. When a nearby transformer blew, I slowed, guessing that men in colonial days probably moved fairly slowly in the dark. Or they suffered a lot of broken ankles.

try—

> I raced after them, straight down the street. My feet
> slowed when a nearby transformer blew and blanked
> the streetlights. Now shadows played across the al-
> ready uneven cobblestones, making my passage a
> study in trust.

or—

> I raced down the street after them, slowing only when
> a transformer blew, shutting down the streetlights. I
> couldn't see the uneven cobblestones and had no de-
> sire to break an ankle.

The incidentals about colonial life and Williamsburg are a stretch for
our character at such a time. You may say this is a character quirk, but
if it is, this character needs to show such thinking at other times too.
A quirk, to work correctly, must show up more than once.

APPROACH THE EDITING OF DESCRIPTION AS A READER

When you edit for description, imagine yourself as a reader unfamiliar
with your story world and characters.

Look for scenes where you know description information is necessary, where description of the setting or a character would erase
confusion. If you haven't included the necessary description, add it.

- Check to see how you described major characters and major scene
locations. Have you made them intriguing to the reader who's never
come across them before? Do your descriptions overwhelm or do
they tantalize? Do they paint clear pictures? Do they make your
stories feel and look different from other stories, or are descriptions
common, the same as those in any other book?

- Make sure description—of places *and* characters—is sufficient
without being overwhelming, unique to just one story (or series), and
a fit for genre and style.

- Check to see if the story world in your head made it to the page. If you never described a central location—perhaps the *in* spot of your story, the place where characters hang out or where major scenes take place—find a scene where you can include details. If one setting location is different from every other place in your story, reread to see if you've made the differences apparent and different in the way you'd intended them to be different.

- Make sure description is easily understood, that making sense of it doesn't require a double take from the reader.

- Check to see if you've given characters quirks and habits and scars that differentiate them one from the other. Make sure a quirk or habit is brought up more than once but also make sure that readers don't see habits mentioned every time the character enters a scene. Blend habits into the action so they don't only sit atop the story as description unattached to events or characters. If a guy's a whistler, let his whistling get him into and out of trouble. If a woman rubs at her wedding ring, let that action give her away.

- Make sure to allow room for the reader's imagination while providing a framework of the story world and the characters who inhabit it.

- Make sure the way description is portrayed is consistent over the length of the story while giving consideration to pacing, events, and evolving (perhaps maturing) viewpoint characters.

- Review the specifics of character and location descriptions. Make sure a blonde in chapter 2 isn't a redhead in chapter 5. Make sure the diner on the east side of a highway in one scene doesn't migrate to the west side in another scene. Make sure that loud places are filled with sound and quiet places are actually quiet. Edit for consistency and common sense.

- Make sure that description is evenhanded, not too much in one chapter, too little in another, except as dictated by the needs of the story's events and characters. In other words, include description in ways that fit the ebb and flow of the story, but don't go without description for 100 pages merely because you forgot to include it.

Consider creating both a character and a setting bible, cheat sheets in which you note all descriptive details of your characters and setting locales, *whether you write those details into the story or not.* You can even include details that will show up in later books of a series. Note which details, settings, and characters appear in which books.

When you change description in a rewrite, make sure those changes get carried forward and backward through the story. Readers *will* notice if you get details wrong, even if you don't.

SUGGESTIONS FOR DESCRIPTION

▪ Describe setting or characters when the reader meets them for the first time, but don't go overboard with description. Make it interesting and useful, productive for the reader. Make description create, deepen, or change a scene's mood.

▪ Keep in mind that details can be more than visual—incorporate all the senses into your descriptions.

▪ Remember that the way a character behaves and what he says may reveal more of him to the reader than a physical description ever would. Choose the best descriptive details for the genre, the scene, the action, and the characters, both the character doing the describing and the character being described. Give the reader what she needs to know. Give her details that allow her to flow through scenes as a real person in such a situation would. Help readers feel, *experience*, the world in the same way the viewpoint character does.

▪ If you want the character and reader both to feel like outsiders, write description differently than if you wanted the reader to be as comfortable in the world as the characters are.

▪ Don't resort to a play-by-play for the description of action sequences; not every step is important. Allow readers to assume that common or everyday actions take place between noteworthy actions.

- Resist stringing together details as lists if you expect readers to remember individual details. A man with a pointed goatee, silver-gray hair, narrow dark eyes, and a sickle-shaped scar on his left cheek, who walks with a stately gait, nodding enigmatically, can come across as a man with a goatee. This is especially true if the reader has just read long or involved place descriptions or an action sequence reported step by step.

Too many lists fatigue the reader. Too many items in a list fatigue the reader.

> Instead of writing description as a list, reveal description details to highlight a character's personality or as needed for the unfolding events. Don't try to reveal *every-thing* about a character at a reader's first meeting with her—reveal only what's important at that moment or what makes sense for the story moment. Reveal what stands out. Reveal what's different. Reveal what the reader needs to know to remember that character and to differentiate between her and other characters. Reveal major event details. Reveal the unique. Reveal what strikes the viewpoint character.

- *Do* fold description details into a list if you need to include them but at the same time need to hide one or more of them. Mystery clues can be hidden in plain sight if they're included with other seemingly unimportant or general details.

- *Do* fold description details into a list to create an effect.

- Don't allow description to interrupt action unless you do so for a purpose, perhaps to slow pace or to introduce a new character or other element. Characters won't always be in a position to note the clothing another character wears or what everyone was doing at a critical moment. If characters are too busy to notice objects or the actions of others, they won't be describing those objects or actions, either through dialogue or in their thoughts. If your characters do describe something, give them a logical reason to do so. Make description fit the other elements of a scene.

▪ Make sure characters don't report description with details that they can't or wouldn't know.

For example, not everyone knows the formal architectural names for the parts of a building, can identify every bird species, will recognize the make of every car, or can name the maker of a man's suit. *You* might know these details but if your viewpoint character doesn't, he can't report such details. He may be curious and ask for information about objects he knows nothing about, but many characters wouldn't. Some details can (and should) remain vague or unmentioned or should be noted in only the most general terms.

For one character, a car might be *a green Aston Martin DB4GT Zagato.* Another character might describe the same car as *a two-door piece of junk* or *an old, sputtering sports car.* Make sure description matches character knowledge, experience, personality, and current emotional temperament. Characters will note more, or fewer, details under some circumstances than others.

In contrast, an omniscient narrator could know anything.

▪ Make your characters' descriptions relevant for the scene—it's not likely that characters will willy-nilly describe objects, other characters, their own feelings, or every move they make.

> Give characters logical and legitimate reasons to launch into description.

While description is ultimately for the reader, it comes through the viewpoint character's thoughts or a character's words, so characters need to have a reason to both pay attention and report descriptions of other characters, objects, and events. (An omniscient narrator can supply description as he wants to, but description should still have purpose and direct the reader's focus.)

▪ Have characters describe what they *see* in other characters and not merely *conclude* what another character is feeling or thinking, at least not all the time. So rather than have Bob note that Lisette was enraged, show Lisette's rage through Bob's eyes.

What does Lisette do or look like that has Bob concluding she's enraged? Show that to the reader. If you describe how she looks or behaves, then the reader can be the one to conclude she's enraged. In this way the reader becomes more involved with the actions and events of the story as well as more closely attuned to the characters, both the one doing the describing and the one being described.

When you edit, pay attention to description, especially what it means to the reader new to your story world. Give readers what they need to help them navigate that world as easily as your characters do.

Put description to work for your novels. Put description to work for the reader.

DO'S AND DON'TS OF DESCRIPTION

- Don't overwrite description or detail—don't give readers more than they need. This means you don't want to go on for too long, you don't want to provide too many competing details, and you don't want to share details too soon. Give readers description as needed.

- Be choosy. Decide what should be described and what shouldn't. Does description fit the scene? The viewpoint character? Would the viewpoint character even notice a person, object, or setting element that you're describing in such detail?

- Be specific rather than general. This doesn't mean you have to name-drop brands every other line—that can be annoying. But if a brand name can convey meaningful information to the reader, use it. Yet if *hulking SUV* works just as well as *Suburban*, try it, especially if the character doesn't know a Suburban from a suburbanite.

- Don't be overly specific. I know, I just suggested that you be specific. But you also want to refrain from being so descriptive that you shut down the reader's imagination. Give readers enough to run with and let them run. Don't hobble them with nitpicky details unless focusing on details is a quirk of your viewpoint character.

- Describe special objects in ways that declare their significance.

- Don't give your characters detailed knowledge that they couldn't have. If a character doesn't know diddly about castles, don't have him naming the features of a castle beyond those most commonly known. If a woman wouldn't know plants or flowers or birds, she can't call them by name. If characters know little about cars, it's not likely they could supply a model number or year of a car that races past. If a man knows nothing of fashion, it's likely he couldn't name a dress style or the material that a dress was made of.

  There are exceptions for general knowledge, of course. But be mindful of giving characters *your* knowledge or specialized knowledge that they shouldn't or couldn't have. An omniscient narrator knows all; Tim Carson, space jockey, does not.

- Don't describe an everyday object or place except to establish the ordinariness of the object or place.

- Don't allow description to stop a story's forward motion. This is another reason that straightforward description, outside of that used in action and dialogue, should come at the tops of chapters and not deep inside action scenes. It's less intrusive to action and the forward thrust of the story.

- Use a mix of the literal and figurative if both work for the characters, the genre, and the emotion of the moment.

- Don't let description overwhelm action and dialogue and never let it substitute for either. Each has its own purpose.

- Don't describe every step of common activities such as showering or driving to work unless there's something unusual about them.

- If you do use figurative language—similes, metaphors, alliteration, and so forth—make sure it's understandable. You don't want readers having to guess what you mean.

- *Do* include description. There are lots of don'ts, but readers need to see characters and story settings and objects. Fill in the blanks of your story world.

- Put description in words your viewpoint character or the speaker would use.

- Weave description into action and dialogue when possible so that rather than a character needing to stop to note a setting detail or object or person, that detail is folded into ongoing action or dialogue.

So instead of interrupting dialogue to write—*Already ticked off, Charlene noticed Jack's smirk*—try a line of dialogue—*"Don't push me, Jack. I'll slap that inane smirk off your face, I swear I will."*

As always, there are exceptions. Just understand your options and what each option does for the feel and the forward motion of events and scenes.

- Write fresh description that fits your story and your characters in their current circumstances and only them.

- Make use of the senses. At the same time, don't include all five senses for every bit of description. Use the sense elements that *your* viewpoint character would use or those that fit the emotion or action of the moment particularly well.

If a character notes odors, make sure he notices the odd ones. If sounds are important because it's the middle of the night and a house or office should be silent, include sounds or the lack of them in your description. Use what makes sense for the conditions and the character and the setting.

- Skip irrelevant details that mean nothing for plot or mood or character revelation.

18

GENRE EXPECTATIONS

I DON'T WANT to overemphasize genre considerations, but I also don't want to underplay their importance.

For all novels, you need to make sure you've included the hallmarks of the genre and included them in the right proportions, order, and places in your story.

To get a clear idea of what this means, let's consider the importance of genre elements in romance.

Romances need to show attraction between the couple. They need to include conflict strong enough to keep the couple apart and attraction strong enough to pull them together despite the conflict. Readers need to understand what the couple see in each other that ultimately leads to love. Declaring that hero and heroine fall in love isn't enough—there must be reasons for them to fall for each other, and readers must watch the love unfold.

Readers expect to see betrayal, apologies, and the realization that each of the pair loves and needs the other. Readers want to see a dramatic and emotional climax. They want to see the start of the happily ever after (or for some romances, the happy for now).

Maybe you don't write or read romance and can't quite see what I'm getting at in terms of genre expectations, so how about we look at the genre considerations for a mystery?

In mysteries, readers expect a puzzle to solve. In a murder whodunit, that means readers need to be presented with a murder right at the top of the story. They need clues, a pool of suspects to choose from, red herrings, false accusations, and suspicious characters who are hiding their own secrets, secrets that have nothing whatsoever to do with killing the victim. Some mysteries need a sense of suspense or danger. All need a murderer wily enough (not only lucky enough) to hide his tracks and/or deflect suspicion for most of the book.

Readers expect the detective or sleuth—amateur or pro—to have skills useful for ferreting out clues and for identifying the culprit.

Readers don't expect the sleuth to trip over the murderer by accident but to deduce who he is through purposeful thought and pursuit. (Exceptions for a bumbler like Inspector Clouseau.)

Or how about exploring the needs of literary novels?

Even literary novels are genre novels, the genre being literary fiction. Key components of literary fiction include high-quality prose, literary and poetic devices, a delving into the main character's psyche, an emphasis on character over plot (to some degree), and often a slower pace than you'd find in other genres.

Learn the hallmarks of your book's genre and use rewrites and edits to ensure that you've met the reader's expectations for the genre. Use those expectations to fashion a story that readers will find satisfying. Use twists on genre expectations to make your stories both appropriate for the genre and unique.

Whatever your book's genre, spend part of your edit time making sure you've included genre specifics.

Part Three

MAJOR STORY SECTIONS

19

MORE THAN HUMBLE BEGINNINGS‡

THE NEXT FIVE TOPICS are related, after a fashion, so I'm arranging them back to back to stress that connection. But there's too much to include in one chapter without overwhelming, so each topic gets its own chapter. We'll start with story beginnings and move to endings, introductions, sagging middles, and notable story moments.

We won't be looking at only the story's first page with introductions since there are many introductory moments in a novel, but we will largely restrict the chapters on beginnings and endings to a story's actual opening and closing pages, the two most important sections of a novel. Not single pages, necessarily, but the starting and finishing scenes and moments.

Your novel's opening is the hardest-working single section of your book (followed closely by the ending). It's a multitasker and it needs to be near perfect at each task.

> If readers aren't captured by the first chapter, it's likely that they won't read a second. And if they don't like the ending, it's likely they won't be back for another book. Not one with your name on it. The beginning and end of your novel have to deliver.

Beginnings introduce tone and mood, the main character and/or the antagonist, the plot and setting, and maybe a subplot. Beginnings establish and convey genre, introducing the necessary genre elements.

Openings must extend a hard-to-resist invitation, nab the reader's attention, and hold it long enough for the reader to decide to read on.

In an edit, your task is to ensure you've included not only all the introductory elements that will start your story engine and set your characters on their adventure, but those that will draw the reader in as well. Edit to make every element with a part to play in the opening both as strong and as convincing as possible.

HOOKS

A hook is vital for your story's opening.

Hooks tug at you, pulling you in a particular direction. They compel you to follow. This is as true for story hooks and readers as it is for fishhooks and fish.

Hooks are attention-getters that cause the hooked one to turn from what he was doing and go where the one controlling the hook wants him to go.

If the hook is well made and hits the target right, that target won't slip free. Instead, the target will follow the line wherever it leads. Objects and activities that had once held the target's attention won't have it any longer. Something more compelling will have taken over.

What have you used for a hook and as a lure to capture your reader's attention? Did you give the reader enough to snare her, or is your hook attractive for only a moment, too weak to grab the reader, too mild to pull her away from other interests?

Is your hook strong enough to pull a reader into your story, or does she watch as the lure passes by, not intrigued enough to follow?

Is your hook alluring? Does it have enough to capture readers of your genre? Is your hook designed to catch your intended audience?

Not every lure will capture every fish, and not every reader will want to read your story. But you can capture some readers. To do so, you have to know your audience and choose your hooks accordingly.

Let's look at a couple of general ways to hook readers. When you edit, see if you've made use of these methods. If you haven't, make changes necessary to attract and hold readers in the first few pages.

Genre appeal

What does *appeal* mean in terms of your books and their genres? What do readers expect to find within the first pages of your stories?

A murder mystery should open with a murder.

Suspense, thrillers, and horror should set the reader on edge, get his emotions churning. These books, even from the start, should make the reader uneasy or fearful or expectant.

Romance should introduce hero and/or heroine in an appealing or amusing or lustful way.

Literary novels should introduce an intriguing or troubled character, someone readers will be eager to know.

YA fiction should introduce a teenage protagonist.

Have you written your story opening to appeal to genre lovers?

Contrast

Consider writing an opening different from those in every story you've read or heard about. Let your story openings stand in contrast to others. Take a risk—be different.

Does your story sound like every other story out there? Readers do like commonalities within genre, but they don't want to read the same story again and again. Be sure your hook is a fresh one. Use a hook that tells readers that this is a story they've never read before.

Compare

Consider using the framework from a story you love. Don't copy all the opening elements, but analyze something that appeals to *you*, twist it, and make it work for your story opening. What works for others can work for you.

This contrast and compare can be a balancing act. Don't be afraid to use something that works for other stories—as long as you're not plagiarizing—but make it your own.

Engage the reader

Purposely engage readers from the first words, first image, first emotion, first bit of dialogue. You want the reader to bite? Give him something tasty to nibble on.

Story openings, our hook and bait, should not only look good, they should taste good too.

Check your first pages one more time. Have you engaged the reader who knows nothing about your story world and characters?

What is the very first hook—can you identify it? Is it in the first line, first paragraph, first page? If you can't pinpoint it, add one.

Compete

Write with the knowledge that your book competes with other entertainments in the reader's life and with the reader's life itself. This means you must make the opening intriguing. Evocative. Maybe humorous. Maybe mysterious.

How about hot?

Shocking?

What about quirky or sad? Flashy or tragic or compelling?

Different. Make it different.

Make your opening arresting, with some part standing out. Make one word or element demand attention.

NO HOOK

We've all opened a book to find an opening that doesn't grab us. Why? What's wrong? Have we chosen a book that doesn't meet our mood of the moment?

Possibly. Our emotions and the events of our lives can get in the way of our reading enjoyment. But when a reader fails to connect with a story, the fault doesn't always lie with the reader.

Sometimes the book has failed. Sometimes the writer has failed.

A story without an opening hook will not catch reader interest the way a story with a stronger opening will. Story openings without barbs have little power to keep readers interested.

So what doesn't work? Which openings fail to hook readers?

A woman lying in bed—daydreaming about her lack of a love life—stretching, yawning, getting comfy, yawning again. She's pulling the reader into . . . *yawn* . . . slumber.

Be honest—did you yawn at least once just now? Reading about yawning makes people yawn. It will make your readers yawn.

That's not what you want for your novel's opening, because you can't hook a reader with a yawn.

Scenes of characters going to sleep don't make good hooks, not for story beginnings and not for chapter endings. You want to keep readers engaged and eager to read more, not remind them it's time for a nap.

FAILURE TO HOOK

Other openings or elements of openings that fail to hook readers? There are plenty. When you edit, look for these problems in your story's opening and correct them.

Mismatched mood and tone

Do you open with humor in a book about death? Or is the opening too heavy for your light-hearted hero? Check tone and mood. A reader can turn away if a story's tone or mood doesn't match the promise of the genre or the story's description.

Poor grammar

Bad grammar also turns away readers. How can you hook readers when they don't understand what's happening? Grammar mistakes somewhere deep within an otherwise well-written book are forgiven. Such mistakes at the story's opening don't get the same leeway. Make sure your grammar is clean.

No obvious story problem

If you've failed to introduce a story problem, you won't hook readers. If you fail to follow through with the *main story problem* for the length of the novel, readers may slip off the hook.

The story problem is what draws the protagonist into the story's events and troubles. She's compelled to act because of an event that disturbs the status quo of her life. Something changes, requiring action on her part to restore stability. She must resolve a problem.

The catch is, the main story problem is not always the most obvious one. So if the protagonist has to rescue the kidnapped Supreme Court Justice, that's probably only one of a series of problems she'll face. Yet the true story problem might be that the protagonist has to finally face her fear of failing when others are counting on her.

Yes, rescuing the justice is a story problem, one that needs solving. But it's likely that the true story problem, the one that actually drives the character and proves meaningful to the reader, is the more personal one. The true problem is often the one that deals with the inner workings—psyche and emotions—of the protagonist.

> The protagonist may not know until partway through the story—maybe not until close to the end—that she's actually facing more than one problem.

The inciting incident and the story problem created by it become the impetus that compels the protagonist to act, to solve the problem so that her world will get back to normal.

When readers see the problem, a question is raised in them—*will* the main character solve the problem? *how* will she solve the problem? how will solving or not solving the problem change her? will she overcome her tendency to fail or give up when the stakes are high? When readers care about knowing the answer to some version of this question, however they word it, they're hooked.

One of the writer's jobs in writing the opening is to include a major story problem. One of the jobs in editing the story opening is to make sure that the problem is compelling enough that readers ask a story question that will keep them reading.

The writer's job for the remainder of the story is to keep readers sufficiently interested in discovering the answer to their question.

Annoyingly repetitive rhythm

Rhythm, sound, and patterns are important in fiction. Readers will elude your hook if the rhythm of your sentences is unvaried.

> The boys stared at the old house with awe. It had sat there abandoned for years. Not one of them wanted to go in. The property was scary and dark. Trees towered over the house and yard.

Not very enticing, is it, with that repetitive and plodding rhythm?

Combine sentences for variety and try both very long and very short sentences. Vary the number of syllables in words and sentences; play with sounds and inflections too. Accent words in the middle of some sentences and at the ends of others. Try words with different letter combinations and sounds.

> Readers will expect a book's opening strengths and weaknesses to carry through the book. If they find problems in the early pages, they'll assume the rest of the book has the same problems. Fix problems with your opening pages. Purposely search for them when you edit.

Repetitive sentence construction

In a way similar to repetitive rhythm, unvaried sentence construction also can repel rather than hook readers.

> Hoping to win for the first time, Annie faced down her boss. Dreaming of victory, she leaned across his desk. Fearing his denial, she nonetheless pressed her point. Moving in for the kill, she smiled; defeating her old nemesis would be marvelous.

Confusion

Characters can be confused—the reader shouldn't be. That is, the reader might not know how to *account* for everything that's happening, but he should have a fairly clear picture of *what's* happening in the story opening. You can't hook a reader who keeps rereading paragraphs because he has no idea what the words are saying.

Don't lose or confuse readers in the early pages.

Repugnant character

You may have trouble hooking readers if your story opens with a character who's too repulsive too soon. On the other hand, such a character just might appeal. Know your audience and genre.

Saccharine character

You might have a weak hook if you introduce a too-nice character too soon. The same holds true for a character without problems. Readers want to read about characters dealing with conflicts, not about perfect people whose every day is heavenly perfection.

> Polly's afternoon had been picture-perfect. The boys had done their homework without fighting, the cable guy arrived exactly when he said he would, and her neighbor not only returned the two cups of sugar she'd borrowed, she gave Polly a five-pound bag.

> Polly had no doubt that the rest of the day [and the week and her life and forever] would be just as perfect and uneventful.

Now, if this is a setup for a tragedy, that first paragraph could work. But if this is actually how the story plays out, changes are called for.

Character out of time

A sure way to turn off readers is by giving a character from another era the sensibilities and thoughts of a twenty-first century individual.

Can you write characters any way you want to? Within reason, yes. But the smart writer will remember that a medieval European peasant wouldn't have the same thoughts of national pride that a British military officer of 1812 would have. A woman who was a child in 1905 wouldn't have the same understanding of the world as a woman born in 2005.

People's interests differ from era to era. Outlooks are different. Our modern sensibilities wouldn't fit the people of another era, not the people of the past or the future.

When you introduce characters in your opening, make sure they fit your story time and place. After all, isn't that one reason you chose a particular setting, to give characters reasons to think and behave in certain ways, ways unique to the setting?

Too many plot threads

The introduction of a dozen major plot threads in the first three pages of your novel is not a surefire way to hook readers. In fact, you're more likely to lose them. Too many options means there's no single plot thread that can capture the reader's attention.

Keep plot threads manageable in your opening. Focus rather than scatter the reader's attention.

Too many characters

Introducing too many characters in a novel's opening is another way to keep readers from going after the bait and hook you've prepared for them. How can readers know who's important? How can readers keep up, especially if you name a couple of dozen characters and give them physical descriptions *and* titles?

Readers are meeting your characters for the first time when your story unfolds, so everyone's a stranger. Help readers by keeping the numbers down at the start.

Failure to identify lead characters

Readers may resist your lure if you fail to identify the protagonist, the antagonist, the hero or heroine, or other essential characters in the opening pages.

You don't have to tell readers everything or introduce every character in the early pages, but tell readers something. Give them someone important to follow. Encourage them to get involved in the story by giving them a character to become involved with.

Lack of action/event

A story opening in which nothing happens has no hook.

Novels are stories of the events happening to a particular character or group of characters. Something's got to occur in your opening; otherwise, you're writing something other than a novel.

Must there be an explosion on page 1? Of course not. But something does have to happen in *chapter* 1. And preferably before the point where the reader regrets picking up the book.

> Remember that story is primarily about characters and events. An opening without them isn't much of an opening. And such an opening may discourage even your most loyal fans.

Give readers something they can latch on to. They want to like your book; give them a story opening with a hook.

Too much dialogue

An overabundance of dialogue is a turn-off, but how much is too much in the early pages?

If your novel opens with dialogue and your characters don't pause to take a breath or to interact with the setting, if you haven't given a description of that setting because the characters are too busy talking and readers go pages without knowing where the characters are or what they're doing, you've got too much dialogue.

For the opening.

Characters *can* talk and talk—of course they can—but they should also react to what other characters are saying. Give readers visuals of what characters are doing and where they're doing it.

Dialogue *is* action, but your characters will do more than talk. People in motion can reveal a lot about their inner lives.

I'm not going to tell you what you can try as a writer. If you want to open with dialogue and only dialogue for three pages, try it. See what it does for your story. Yet remember your readers. If they're bored with talk unrelieved by action or exposition, you can't blame them for not being attracted by your style. *You* have to please them; they don't have to like your work.

Imagine yourself in a restaurant where the couple seated in the booth behind you is having a fascinating discussion about their latest murder. You hear the sound of their voices—the inflections—as well as the sounds of the restaurant. You smell the aromas from the kitchen, feel the bustle of the waiters as they pass by, taste the too-salty chicken on your plate. You even feel the emphasis when the couple pauses between revelations.

If you faced them, you'd get even more information—their looks, facial expressions, posture, gestures. You'd know if they were leaning toward one another or pulling away. You'd know if they gave thought to others in the restaurant or watched only each other.

But if you couldn't see the couple, didn't know where they were, couldn't hear their voices as they spoke, you wouldn't know if they were serious or joking. You wouldn't have any context for their discussion. If the words of the dialogue were projected on a white wall in your living room with no explanation or accompanying video, you wouldn't have the same reaction to those words, no matter how compelling they were in themselves.

> Dialogue without supporting information is insufficient for conveying the multiple elements necessary for creating good stories and intriguing hooks.

Readers need more than dialogue in the early pages. Remember to include setting and character details.

Not enough dialogue

Include in your story opening a character who either thinks or speaks so that readers get a sense of who he is or what he wants.

People relate to other people, and readers relate to characters that they can know.

An opening without dialogue might be utterly marvelous, but insight into a character's thoughts would assure the reader that the world he's entering is peopled with beings similar to himself, beings who reason within themselves and communicate with others.

How long can you go in a story's opening before the reader needs to hear thoughts or dialogue? Quite probably a lot farther than you can go with straight dialogue.

One way to decrease the need for dialogue early in a story? Show a character's thoughts, emotions, or intentions through action—an arsonist grinning as his tiny flame grows into a conflagration or a widow smiling through her tears as she runs fingers over her husband's headstone and reads the humorous epitaph there. Dialogue can be withheld without boring or confusing the reader if information about a character is revealed another way.

Note, however, that the visual of dense paragraphs of narrative without breaks for dialogue can turn off readers. Readers need white space on their pages, and dialogue provides that.

Too much description or setting

Swamping the reader with setting description before introducing a character or action event can underwhelm rather than hook.

How important is the setting? Is it the most important element of your plot? Does it set the mood? Is it almost a character in itself?

If setting is of special importance to your story, feel free to open with setting and emphasize it. Just keep in mind that readers will be looking for characters and events. How long do you want to keep them from what *they* want?

If setting is *not* key to your story, why give it the place of honor in your story's opening? Use setting, but put it in its proper place.

When you edit, see if the opening is a setting opening, elevating time and place or other setting elements over character and action. If the story has a setting opening but that's not your intent, rewrite the opening with a different focus.

If the whole first chapter is description of the setting, the balance is off. Include setting details, but don't include *only* setting details.

And if you open with weather, be sure there's a reason for doing so. If the night *is* dark and stormy and you've shared that with readers, make use of the dark and the storm. Make sure weather elements add to the scene and aren't simply fillers.

Does weather cause characters to wear raincoats and carry umbrellas? Maybe they wear hats that end up hiding their faces. Do slick roads lead to accidents? Do thunderstorms frighten the protagonist's children? Does unrelenting rain after a drought cause flooding?

Weather *can* be put to work in a story's opening, yet if the weather isn't of significance, why highlight it at a story's beginning? How many readers will you entice with weather words? Not many, I'm guessing. Not unless the weather has relevance.

It's okay to use weather in your story's opening if it's not a placeholder for the true opening. That is, don't use weather only because you haven't thought of a stronger opening. Open with a weather event if it sets the mood and causes characters to act and react.

Be deliberate about your opening scene—the words, the events, the characters involved, the mood you set.

Bait your hook in an appealing way.

FINAL WORDS

Make sure the story starts on page 1, not page 50. Even for literary fiction, where you can ease into the plot, something must capture the reader in the early pages. Today's readers aren't like those in the age before TV, movies, video games, and the Internet. They want something to happen. They want to be assured that something *will* happen. Give them assurance early, even if you only set a disquieting tone. A hint of something dark to come is sufficient to snare the reader.

Keep in mind the purpose of the hook—to draw readers *away* from outside influences and *toward* your story events and characters.

Make the hook appealing. Attract. Cajole. *Entice.*

Remember that you can't force the hook into the reader; he's got to come to it. Attract his attention and then beguile him. Make your hook tempting enough to draw him *to* your story and then *into* it to be tugged along by the power of your characters and their challenges.

Use the right bait. Lure the reader.

And keep the tension just tight enough that the reader not only can't struggle free, but won't want that freedom.

20

SIGNIFICANT INTRODUCTIONS‡

WE ALL KNOW that the adage is true, that you get only one chance to make a good first impression.

That's true for our stories as well.

Sort of.

It's true that a reader may decide to pick up our books because of the cover or because of a recommendation, and the way they feel about the book at that time is the first impression. But it's what happens between the covers that will keep the reader involved with our stories.

Readers often check out first lines, first pages, even first chapters before they decide to buy a book. So that first line, first page, and first chapter need to accomplish a whole lot in very little time.

Yet readers delving into our stories get more than one chance to meet the story, to form attachments and a liking for our book. They may get an overall impression from a quick read of the first pages, but their impressions won't stop there. And neither will the introductions.

What *firsts*—what impressions and introductions—can a reader find in a story? And what should a writer do to make sure firsts accomplish all that they should and could? This collection of tips for creating notable introductions and firsts will help you focus on major story events as you write, rewrite, and edit.

WHY INTRODUCTIONS ARE IMPORTANT

Introductions can be related to notable moments—the topic of another chapter—but we're going to look at them for other purposes in this chapter.

You want to make sure that every significant introduction in your story, every first of any element, every *story* first, accomplishes what it needs to in order to have readers feeling particular emotions or following certain paths or thinking specific thoughts.

Every first in your story allows you to direct your characters, the plot, and readers in the direction you want them to go.

Firsts do this well simply because they *are* firsts. When a reader sees one of these firsts, she will think *Ah, this means . . .*

Without depending on other issues, without even trying hard, these firsts establish the baselines for emotions, events, character personalities, and reader expectations.

> Until you lead story and reader off in a new direction, whatever you establish with these introductions is what stands. What you create with your firsts is the reality, the only reality, for the reader. When you edit, you want to make sure that your introductions present exactly what you want them to and in the necessary measure.

The first dialogue can set tone and reveal subtext. The first setting details can establish mood. The first action conveys what the story will be about and what's ahead for the characters.

Every *first* tells the reader something new or solidifies something that you've told them before via some other first or introduction.

So you want to put story firsts to work and give them the attention they deserve.

In your edits, make sure that these introductions and firsts don't work at cross-purposes, such as the first description reading like a tender love story and the first dialogue reading as hard-core erotica.

Yes, a story can progress. But make sure progressions are logical according to the genre, the plot, and the parameters you've set for your story world.

I'll cover a few common story firsts and introductions, but consider any introduction to be a segment of text that deserves special attention and give it that attention.

I'm going to ask a lot of questions in this chapter, but I'm not looking for answers in general terms, as if we were studying fiction as a classroom exercise. Consider your answers as they relate to elements in your story in particular.

For example, when I ask *what emotions can setting details generate in a reader*, I want you to find out which emotions you tried to stir in the reader with your setting details. Examine your text to see what you've done and then go a step farther—determine if you've chosen the best details to accomplish your aims. If not, change the details or the approach. Or change the emotion you want to create in the reader.

How can you make sure introductions stand out but at the same time fit perfectly into the story? Check them. See what they do. See what other story elements they affect. See what they include and what's been excluded. Make sure you've included what you needed to include without inadvertently creating a feel or impression you hadn't intended to create.

Make sure introductions are sufficiently moving or shocking or developed or convincing.

Don't limit yourself to the firsts I list here. Instead, make up your own list of firsts and check each one when you edit. See if they fit the rest of the story. See if they do all that they can to advance plot, reveal character, establish tone and mood, and increase conflict. And yes, make sure they do all that they can to pull the reader in and keep him reading. You wouldn't want to lose a reader over a mishandled introduction, especially now that I've reminded you about the importance of introductions.

MAJOR FIRSTS AND INTRODUCTIONS

At the minimum, these are the firsts you should examine when you edit. (Not all genres will contain each of these firsts.)

- opening hook and first chapter-ending hook
- first words of chapters, scenes, paragraphs, and sentences
- first conflict
- first image, action, section of dialogue, thought, and description of setting

- introduction of the first prop(s)
- first description using a sense other than sight
- first sound
- first kiss
- first murder or death
- first mention of a symbol
- first betrayal
- first challenge to the protagonist's conviction to act
- first abandonment by the protagonist's friends or allies
- first foreshadowing, first section of back story
- introductions of protagonist and antagonist to the reader
- first meet of protagonist and antagonist (or hero and hero-ine) with one another
- introduction of the protagonist's quirks
- introduction of subplot(s)
- inciting incident
- first crossroads or turning point for protagonist and plot
- first emotional blowout

Each of these firsts and introductions deserves attention when you edit. Look for ways to make them more engaging and more meaning-ful while at the same time ensuring they don't stand out too much. We'll look at a few of these story moments in detail in just a moment. First, a few general questions and tips.

FIRSTS IN GENERAL

Check the timing of your firsts—are they introduced at the right time? in the right order? through the right character?

Understand what you reveal with every first and each introduction. Determine whether what's revealed is precisely what you want to reveal. If the revelation isn't what you intended, rewrite.

Pump up the impact if you haven't provided enough emphasis.

Make sure firsts link into later moments of the story so they do double or triple duty. That is, don't waste them. Put them to use where they appear and then revisit them later to remind readers of those early evocative moments.

> Any anticipated element presented well can draw the reader to the writer's corner. Any anticipated element presented poorly can give the reader a bad taste about the story and/or the author.

Writers, then, need to make sure that they anticipate the elements their readers will anticipate and write to satisfy that anticipation.

Readers are drawn to enticing openings—make yours enticing.

Readers look forward to the introductions of both protagonist and antagonist—introduce them in memorable ways.

Wherever reader anticipation is likely to be high, be sure to give the reader something memorable—

- actions fitting the character
- a word or words that define the character's motivation
- an arresting meet between major characters

For each introduction, write a scene or scene snippet or single line that the reader will welcome and remember, something that fits the story, something fitting to an introduction.

In terms of structure, consider the first

- word
- sentence
- paragraph
- page
- scene
- chapter
- chapter ending

Every story first—all these introductions, the inciting incident, the first showdown between characters, the first event that raises the stakes for the protagonist—is a special moment and often a turning point, so be aware of what you include at these story points. Work them until the impression they leave with the reader satisfies your purposes for them. Make these sections of your story memorable. Apt. Strong.

The reader is always evaluating. When he meets one of these elements in your story, give him a reason to find it entertaining and a good fit for the rest of the story.

Leave him with a good impression. Use these story firsts to snare the reader and keep him involved in the fiction.

Caution: Don't overplay any story element or moment, including introductions and firsts. Just as other fiction elements should fit the scene and story, the setting and genre, firsts should also fit.

BEYOND FIRST WORDS

Beyond first words, scenes, and chapters, there are the other kinds of firsts that I mentioned. Consider them plot firsts. They can take place anywhere in a story where readers are introduced to something new.

Each first gives the writer even more opportunity for creating strong ties between story and reader. When readers anticipate these elements—and never doubt that they're anticipating them—they're silently demanding what they want the writer to emphasize.

INTRODUCTION OF THE PROTAGONIST

The introduction of your lead character is one of the highlights of your story. Make it memorable. Make each word count. Paint the picture of your main character that you want the reader to carry with him or her into your story.

How is the protagonist introduced? In what setting? With what action or dialogue? How do you describe him? What does the protagonist care about at the moment the reader first sees him?

What the protagonist says, does, and thinks at his introduction will stay with the reader for quite a while. Give your protagonist the words, actions, and thoughts that say exactly what you want to reveal about your main character at his introduction. What emotion does he show at that first introduction? What does that emotion say about him? Is that what you want to reveal? If not, make changes. If it's the right emotion but not the right level of emotion, make changes.

INTRODUCTION OF THE ANTAGONIST

The introduction of the antagonist is just as important and for the same reasons as the introduction of the protagonist.

Who is this character? What first impression do you want readers to have of him or her?

Whatever introduction, whatever *presentation* you give of the antagonist is the one that readers will use to evaluate him, to measure him, against the protagonist. Be mindful of every word you use in your staging of him. The elements you choose are the only guide the reader has to form opinions. What you omit will remain unknown.

INTRODUCTION OF SETTING

Given the right attention, setting can greatly influence story. Writers need to be aware of the effects of setting on characters *and* readers.

Consider what a particular location, era, social milieu, time of day, season, or weather event does to the mood of a scene, to the events taking place in that scene. Imagine the emotions that setting details can generate in the reader even as you explore the range of events that could unfold in any one setting. Ask yourself what expectations are raised by the choice of setting, especially the first setting.

Consider the effects that can be created by a change in setting, not only a change of place but changes in cultural practices, laws, geographic stability, and weather conditions.

What does the first image of the setting do for the reader? Do you need to make it more appealing? Moodier? Does your introduction to setting accomplish all that it could?

Write setting with keen awareness of where it can take the reader. Know what impression your setting is creating for readers.

Time the appearance of setting details—of each of these fiction elements—to best fit the story and to give the reader the impression you intend for him to have. Switch the order of introductions to see if moving a few of them will create a stronger impact and a more involving story.

INTRODUCTION OF TONE AND MOOD

Use words, from the very first one, to create the tone and mood you want a scene or story to have. Is the story light and loose, humorous, dark, elegant, wise-cracking, or highbrow? What's the viewpoint character's attitude? Whatever tone and mood you're going for, choose words to match. And get them right, right at the start.

The tone and mood you establish at the opening sets up what readers feel right away and what they'll expect to find throughout the story until they encounter a change. Make tone and mood fit and make sure they are the ones you want.

What mood do you want in those first pages, when the world is topsy-turvy for the protagonist and alien to the reader?

INTRODUCTION OF GOAL AND MOTIVATION

The goals and motivations of the protagonist, accompanied to some degree by the goals of the antagonist, drive the story. Make sure they're sufficient to do that driving, strong enough to compel the actions of the character, and of interest to the reader.

A lame motivation won't propel a character or the story far, and a weak goal will have the reader yawning. Make sure motivations and goals are logical and strong enough to power your characters.

OTHER STORY FIRSTS

How about other story firsts that aren't necessarily introductions for the reader?

First Meet Between Protagonist and Antagonist

Have you thought about this one, about what happens the first time these two characters meet? Is there instant antagonism? False friendship? Fireworks? Attraction that ultimately leads to betrayal?

Give thought to this first meet. It can send your story off into a new direction or solidify elements you've already introduced. It's definitely a principal moment in your story and deserves a second and third look when you edit.

Keep in mind, however, that the first meet might be no meet at all. In some stories the protagonist and antagonist don't meet in person or don't meet until the black moment or climax.

Consider other ways they could be introduced to one another.

One method is through the reports of other characters. The protagonist's reaction to the deeds of his nemesis should be clear and strong. And the antagonist, upon discovering he's been thwarted, should have a marked reaction, one the reader can see and feel.

First Meet of Romance Hero and Heroine

If you write romance, this first should be a story moment that you give great thought to. How do they meet, your hero and heroine? Where? Under what circumstances? What character traits do they reveal to each other at that first meet? What do they reveal to the reader? How does their first meet steer the story?

Is the meet funny, sweet, embarrassing, accidental? Make a deliberate choice and use it to propel your story.

First Hook

Typically the first hook is in the story opening; it's what you use to pull readers into the story. You have to decide what that hook will be and whether it's achieved through action, emotion, or dialogue.

Most writers know they need to do something to draw the reader in, but they often consider only one or two options. Take some time and play with your first hook—see how many different ways you can open your story and find the one that best fits not only the characters, but the tone and impact you want for the story opening. Use the first hook to make an irresistible first impression.

A great time to mess with your opening hook is while you're editing, after the other story elements are in place.

Draw the hint of an image or maybe the pre-echo of a line of dialogue from the ending or some other place in the story. Link—very lightly—to a special story moment. You don't want to dilute the impact of that special moment by giving too much away, but if you link very lightly to it, the discerning reader may pick up on it, creating for him a solid tie between story parts.

First Description

Where does it go, that first description? Before action or the introduction of characters? Or do you dribble it slowly through the opening scene? Maybe you don't even use description right off, content to let action and dialogue open the story.

Yet at some time you'll be writing description of place and characters. Choose the timing of that first description wisely. Choose the words of that description wisely.

What do you want to accomplish with your description? If you want to influence a scene's mood through description, focus on the mood you want and the words necessary to create it. Since we're talking the first description, you may need to be more explicit than you'd need to be later in the story.

How does your first description fit with other elements? How can you combine description with something else so a single bit of text does twice the work?

When you edit, find the first descriptions of both setting and character. Determine whether or not they accomplish what they should.

First Dialogue

The first spoken words are significant in any story. What is said? Who speaks those first words and how? To whom and in what tone? What impression do the words create? Where is the story steered by those first words? What emotion is stirred by the first dialogue? What kind of conflict is revealed?

The first dialogue may be spoken not by protagonist or antagonist but by another character, so when these two *do* speak for the first time, what is revealed then? What do they set into motion by their first words? What tone is established, what emotion sought?

What is changed by first dialogue? What is unleashed?

Use an edit to tweak these first moments of dialogue.

First Action/Event

Writers should deliberately craft the first action, the first major event, to realize specific goals. What is set into motion? Who is affected? Who is the character behind the action and who else is involved?

What would happen if a different character instigated or observed the first action moment? How would the story be changed? When you edit, you can always try a change in character to see what effect the change would create.

Yet if you do make changes that then affect other parts of the story, follow those changes through the other scenes and chapters. That is, once you start making changes, be prepared for the domino effect. Changes do beget other changes.

What intensity should you go for in the first event? Should action come before description? Physical action before dialogue? Does the first action establish the mood you want to establish?

If neither protagonist nor antagonist is involved with the first action or event, what do *their* first actions entail? How are both of their first actions introduced?

First Challenge and/or First Setback for Protagonist

What is the first challenge you set up for your lead character? How do you write his first setback? What is the result of that setback? How is the story changed?

A novel follows your protagonist through increasingly difficult situations, situations in which he meets a few successes but even more defeats. The first defeat may not outline all that will follow, but it should hint at the kind of problems the protagonist will deal with. Be sure to consider the setup to, the action of, and the consequences of that first setback. That moment, when the lead is first faced with something he can't conquer, will reveal a lot about him and the story.

Make it memorable.

And give the antagonist a worthy first setback as well. He should face some of the same tribulations the protagonist faces. If he plays a major role in your story, give him enough significant actions and reactions to fulfill his role.

First Victory of the Antagonist

The antagonist may be defeated at story's end (or he may not be), but he's going to enjoy victories over the protagonist before that point. If he doesn't, he's not a worthy adversary for your lead character.

How does that first victory play out? Is the antagonist jubilant? Does he crow, making the protagonist even madder? Does he plan even more mayhem for your lead?

In terms of actions, thoughts, and dialogue, how does the protagonist react to the antagonist's victory?

Make sure that the antagonist's first victory is a worthy one. If it's not time for the protagonist to get too mad, don't go overboard with the strength or importance of his loss. If you *do* want to make a statement with this first victory of the antagonist, go all out. Just be sure you have room to escalate later.

Remember that the first setback for the protagonist and the first victory for the antagonist are not the same. That is, they *can* be flip sides of the same coin—if they arise from the same event. But they create different results. One buoys a character, one discourages a character. Once can cause a character to relax his guard, the other could spur a character to new strengths.

First Kiss

The first kiss is significant in a romance and could be important in other genres. Don't allow your characters to fall into that first kiss; be deliberate in your choice of location and intensity. Consider options for place and time of the first kiss. Consider humor or anger or playfulness in lieu of passion.

Don't forget buildup and anticipation. Readers in some genres are looking for that kiss—make sure it satisfies them and sends your characters in a new direction.

DON'T STOP WITH THESE FIRSTS

We could look at other firsts, other introductions that create a strong impact on the reader and in turn direct our stories, but I'll leave those to you. Don't let this list limit those other possibilities. Instead, examine all the moments in your novel where you can make an impression on the reader, where what you write will influence the reader until you write something else to change that first impression.

Make the most of story firsts and use them to steer the story and influence readers.

The Takeaway

When you edit, check firsts and introductions. Because they're a natural part of stories, they'll be present whether you give them extra attention or not. Your task in an edit is to make sure they accomplish enough for the needs of the story.

21

Shore Up Sagging, Soggy Middles

THE GREATER PART of a story takes place after the arresting opening and before the even more exciting climax and conclusion. Yet writers often spend the greater part of their writing and editing time, their focus and effort, on the relatively few first and final chapters.

This makes sense in some ways since, if a story's opening doesn't entice, readers won't read the book, and if the ending doesn't satisfy, readers may not pick up another by the same author.

But none of this is a reason to shortchange either the writing or the editing of the middle, which typically turns out to be more than half the total page count, covering many more events than either the beginning or the end. If the middle is ignored, you can bet it sags in a not-so-pretty way, with bloat and confusion and boring passages. Middle chapters can easily wander, leading both character and reader into places neither belongs, perhaps abandoning them in murky places for far too long.

Middles can and should be strengthened, fashioned into taut powerhouses of sharp writing and engrossing fiction.

Middles should contain not only necessary back story but riveting front story, the current action of events unfolding even as readers press close to feel the danger, revel in the romance, or tremble with eagerness at what may be waiting at the turn of the next page.

Can you make your middle chapters just as spellbinding as your opening, as gripping as your climax, as rewarding as your conclusion? You can and you should.

I could no doubt write a book on the importance of middle chapters and why, even if a writer is pressed for time, he shouldn't focus on openings and endings to the detriment of middle chapters. But this isn't that book. I can only advise you to pay attention to your middle chapters, those that bridge story beginnings and ends. Those chapters that entrance readers as they follow your characters from their introduction to the inevitable conclusion of their adventure.

Middle chapters are the heart of story, the place where a story's lifeblood is pumped, the place where the story's essence is sustained. Without a strong and healthy middle, the opening and ending, no matter how attractive, ultimately have no life and therefore no impact on the reader.

Give your readers more than words. Give them riveting story.

If the middle doesn't hold together, if it's not able to support everything you hang on it, then the entire structure risks collapse.

Make your stories not only attractive on the surface, but also make them robust by giving proper attention to middle chapters. Fill those chapters with meat, with scenes and events with more substance than marshmallow fluff and more taste than dusty, dry sawdust.

> Examining every scene and every chapter as if they'll one day stand under the spotlight to be scrutinized by readers, critics, reviewers, and even students of literature will keep you on track as you edit long stretches in the middle of your stories.

Slogging through middle chapters can be tough, but look at editing those middles from another point of view: if *you* can't stand spending time with them, imagine how your readers will feel. If your middle chapters aren't compelling, there's definitely something wrong with them. If even *you* want to hurry through them, that's an indictment on the bulk of your story.

FOCUS ON MIDDLE CHAPTERS (WITH HELP FROM STORY STRUCTURE)

On one of your edit passes, focus solely on the middle chapters. To help you stay focused and keep yourself from compulsively returning to the first and last chapters, imagine the middle chapters to be the only chapters in your story. Separate your middle chapters into a beginning, a middle, and an end and edit with that mindset. Give each section a high point and fill each with fascinating characters getting into all sorts of trouble.

Treat the beginning and ending of the middle chapters just like the beginning and ending of the story—make every element work. Make each fit without gaps.

Try using the standards of story structure to guide you through the story's middle. There are multiple approaches to story structure; we're going to briefly touch on one as it applies to middle chapters. Although this is just one option, it's a good one to give you a sense of what needs to be included in middle chapters.

Begin the middle with your protagonist stepping into his idea of the solution for the story problem. The bridge between the story's early chapters and the middle is the protagonist's decision to accept the challenge before him, and it includes the first steps he takes to turn away from his normal world and move into the unfamiliar one where the problem can be solved.

On his way to fix the problem, your character will naturally run into characters who help or hinder him and he'll face challenges to his intention to solve the story problem.

Make sure you give him differing types of challenges that come from a variety of characters and problems. That is, make sure that your main character doesn't face the same challenge posed again and again by the same character. Give him and your readers variety. You don't want readers thinking that story events or situations from different chapters feel similar.

Not every challenge to the main character's progress has to come from the antagonist or a foe; friends and family can stand in the way. Loved ones can batter at your character's heart, tempting him away from his convictions. Challenges from characters that the protagonist loves and respects can have him doubting himself *or* have him doubling down on his commitment. Such challenges can definitely lead to tension and raise the conflict level.

Have the protagonist learn as he progresses through the story—knowledge he gains may be needed when he faces the antagonist or story problem head on, especially at the climax.

At the same time, test him with new challenges so that what he learns won't solve all his problems.

At the story's midpoint—which is also the midpoint of the middle chapters—the protagonist should be hit with a new problem, something that blocks him from pursuing his intended path toward the original problem's solution. He can try to work his way around this roadblock, as he did with earlier challenges and setbacks, but this setback should be greater in both scope and impact than the others, impossible to move around, through, under, or over.

This setback should not only be seemingly insurmountable, it should also be personal, hitting the protagonist in a way that promises significant consequences to him or to those he loves.

The middle-of-the-book setback can arise from one of a variety of sources, maybe from a twist or from the revelation of information that was previously hidden. Whatever the source of this new wrinkle, the protagonist should discover that his original course will no longer solve his problem.

Reasons his original plan is no longer viable? He was on the wrong path to get where he *really* needed to go and now discovers that the true path has hellish risks he hadn't anticipated; the real problem wasn't the problem he thought it was, and he's no longer sure he would've taken on the problem had he known its true underpinnings; the guy he was after turns out to be someone he knows, loves or respects, or someone he never knew existed, someone like a brother; he discovers something about himself that prevents him from following the original path to the solution of the original problem; he discovers someone he trusted withheld information and he was misled in order to secure his help and commitment.

This setback/moment of discovery should set your character on a different course, maybe with him nursing resentment or questioning his commitment, maybe angered at friends who withheld information. Whatever the midpoint event is, the change in circumstances or in the protagonist's understanding of the circumstances creates the need for a new approach and thus turns the story in a new direction.

The midpoint should feature a dramatic scene featuring the protagonist. When you edit, make sure your story has such a scene. Make sure it's sufficiently dramatic and that it highlights the protagonist's emotions. (Revisit the Character Rants section of the chapter "Shaping Characters" for tips on creating an emotionally charged scene for a main character.)

After this point, the stakes should be higher, the risks greater. The protagonist is usually more committed and relentless. If the problem and the solution weren't personal to the protagonist before, they are beginning with the midpoint. He not only wants to solve a problem, he wants to get to the bottom of the lies or the hidden information.

After the midpoint, the character shows renewed vigor and determination. Personality traits he's tried to keep tempered—rage, impatience, short-temperedness, single-mindedness—rise to the surface. The character is often determined that nothing will stop him now. The pace starts to pick up.

With his new attitude working for him, your character may make great progress.

Until he suddenly no longer does.

It's at this next point in a typical three-act story, just before the end of the middle and the beginning of the end, that the protagonist should face an additional setback, one even more shattering than the last one.

This event should trigger a true crisis, one that may devastate the character, leading him into his darkest moment of doubt, confusion, or even fear.

This juncture in fiction is known as the black moment.

The protagonist feels like a failure. Or in some permutations of story structure, this is not only where he fails but where he dies.

Death isn't (usually) literal. A character's death at this point may mean he's lost his innocence, his hope, or his certainty in himself. He may have lost trust in his friends or in all of humanity. Think of this black moment as a mortal blow to the protagonist's core—not only an assault on the inner man but a vanquishing of his very essence, a defeat of that which makes him who he is.

Now is the time he may honestly consider giving up and going home. Going back. He may reminisce on how good his life had been before he shunted it aside to pursue the problem that had prompted him to action.

He may suffer feelings of worthlessness or embarrassment.

This is a great time for a scene that plumbs the depths of the character's emotions. If you didn't include one at the midpoint, consider using one at the black moment. Or give your character two different emotional scenes, maybe one that focuses on anger or indignation (at the midpoint) and the other focusing on despair (at the black moment). If you include two such scenes, make sure they differ in cause, intensity, length, and character responses. The second should be bigger or deeper or louder in comparison to the one at the midpoint.

Of course, your character *will* pull himself out of his thoughts and doubts and rekindle his commitment to finish the course. Otherwise your story would end there, without him facing the antagonist in the climax, a feature of the ending chapters.

After the protagonist's dark moment, the plot again turns in a new direction as it pushes toward the climax, carrying characters and readers out of the middle and into the final chapters.

Working the Middle

Make readers want to get lost in the middle of your books. Make readers want them never to end. Make them wish there were more, not fewer, scenes and pages.

Write powerful, enticing, moving, motivating, captivating middle chapters. Keep the interest high for yourself and your readers. Cut out the boring stuff, the repetitious events and character responses, and make your middles soar.

Every writer gets tired of working through a scene *just one more time*. See if changing your attitude or your approach to those middle scenes and chapters helps.

If the edit of all that stuff in the middle is daunting, devise ways to divvy up the edit over time. Or reward yourself when you complete the edit of a predetermined number of pages or scenes or when you cover a certain number of story issues.

Do a systematic edit of the middles of your books. Don't let them sag between two well-written and well-edited ends.

Just as you edit the early and final chapters looking for problems with the fiction elements, writing and rewriting until each scene in every chapter is dramatic and serves multiple story purposes, you also need to check every middle chapter for every possible problem. Be especially mindful of problems you already know are in the text, but don't skip any issue. You may be tempted to focus on the first and last chapters when you edit, but you don't want any chapter to be a weak link. Reminding yourself that every scene and chapter is critical will help ensure that middle chapters get as much attention as opening and ending chapters.

If writing dialogue is one of your weak skills, check every section of dialogue. If you typically forget to write for the senses, check scenes for sense references. If you know your scene transitions and sections of narrative summary run too long, make sure you check transitions and summary *in every scene and chapter.*

I'll list suggestions that touch on common problem areas for story middles, but don't limit yourself to these issues as you edit. And while you're working on these issues, see if they cause problems for your openings and endings as well. Once you get this middle stuff down and your middle chapters soar, there's no reason that your openings and endings should suffer in comparison.

SUGGESTIONS FOR EDITING MIDDLE CHAPTERS

There is no rank or order for these suggestions; none is more important than another except as they affect your stories. Some deal with mechanics of writing, some with peculiarities of fiction and novels. I've grouped the suggestions under the major elements of fiction, yet there is overlap.

If certain of these speak to you more than others, perhaps because you have a weakness in one area, start with those suggestions. But unless you're absolutely certain you don't have problems in any one area, do consider each suggestion for every manuscript before you publish or send in a submission.

Edit middle chapters and scenes one at a time, the same way you do the opening and closing chapters. That is, don't lump middle chapters and scenes into one big section. Give each element of each chapter your full attention.

Plot

- Include only events essential to the story. Cut events and actions that don't fit or don't belong, no matter how well they're written.

- Reduce or cut out unnecessary back story. Reveal history and the characters' pasts through dialogue and action and sometimes through a character's thoughts, but don't let your middles sag under the weight of too much back story and explanation. You can even use flashbacks to divulge back story, but don't rely on flashbacks to explain everything. No matter how exciting the past is, current story events are always of greater interest to the reader.

If you've got back story in dialogue and then in character thoughts and then in a flashback, that stretch of text has essentially ground to a halt as characters and readers peer into the past. If the back story goes on for too long, readers may feel that they've moved into the past, into a different story.

Flavor with morsels from the past, but don't dwell there.

> Remember that readers always need much less back story than you do. You need to know what's happened in the characters' pasts to give them believable motivations and personalities that fit each other and your story events. Readers only need to know enough to make sense of present events and character behaviors.

▪ Reduce or cut digressions. Does the reader really need to follow your rabbit trails? Unless digressions have a purpose—maybe as a red herring in a mystery or to reveal character motivation—get rid of them. At least shorten them.

If digressions are included as a means of incorporating really cool knowledge you gained from long hours of research, have no qualms about deleting every last one.

If you just have to share the fabulous information you discovered as you researched your story, include it on your website. If it doesn't fit the story, it doesn't belong in the story.

▪ Cut out flashbacks whose purposes aren't worth the disruption of the story timeline.

Flashbacks, even necessary flashbacks, stop the forward motion of a story. If that happens too often or for pointless reasons, readers will notice. And they might be bothered. And if they're bothered by something you've done, they aren't enjoying the fiction. If they're thinking about you rather than your characters, that's a problem.

Do everything you can to keep your reader inside the fiction and oblivious to you and your machinations.

▪ If nothing new is revealed for pages at a time, either cut out those pages or rewrite to make something happen. If there's nothing new that can be done with the characters you have, introduce a new character. Or kill a character who means something special to either protagonist or antagonist. Maybe do both.

If middle chapter after middle chapter feels the same, introduce something new.

▪ Be sure that something worth reading about actually happens in each scene and chapter. Even if story events and dialogue fit and meet the requirements of good storytelling, if they're not engaging, not something that will interest your readers, cut or rework those events and dialogue.

All events, however, shouldn't be rendered at the same intensity or for the same length of time. Consider variety from event to event and scene to scene.

- Make sure the story builds toward a climax. If there's no sense of movement toward a showdown, rewrite. If there's no sense of pace speeding up, rewrite.

Character

- Cut back on explanations. By necessity, middle scenes and chapters get the bulk of back story and character history and justifications for character motivation. Yet that doesn't mean that every chapter should overflow with explanations for why something has happened or reasons that characters do what they do.

Characters need motivations so their actions make sense, but not every individual action needs to be explained *as it happens*. And bald explanations—delivered without finesse and without fitting smoothly into a scene or into a section of dialogue—come across as the worst kind of *telling*. (Exceptions for emotional explanations that burst from characters.) Convey back story and motivation, yes. But don't always or don't only simply explain. Let the reader draw conclusions about motivation and purpose without having to be told outright what that motivation and those purposes are.

To make motivation seem natural for character behavior in later chapters, plant motivational seeds earlier in the story so that when a motivation is required, it's already there, made obvious by what has already unfolded.

- While we're talking motivation, make sure characters have sufficient reasons—motivations—for all their actions. If they don't have a reason to react, they shouldn't be reacting. Motivations don't have to be spelled out in the same scene, tied directly to the action. But actions shouldn't come from nowhere. Keep in mind that motivations common to humans don't need to be spelled out, but if a character *fails* to react in an expected way, that would be cause for a reaction from another character.

- Make sure that your main character or protagonist initiates action. He shouldn't always be the one acted on or against. Put him to work doing something, even if it's often the wrong something.

- Combine characters when possible. Cut characters who serve little or no story purpose. Characters can't just take up page and story space—they have to do something: cause trouble, spur on protagonist or antagonist, get caught in the crossfire, or prove to be the reason another character does what he does.

   If you give characters multiple purposes, the story is strengthened. Lace purposes and story threads together and then start tightening the ties.

- Don't lose sight of characters in a scene. If you've got wallflowers hanging around, you need to activate them—they can offer snide comments, irritate other characters with their quirks, or interrupt the intended actions of protagonist or antagonist.

   If two characters go at it with words or fists, don't forget other characters you brought to the scene. If they're present, give them a purpose and a reaction. If there is no purpose for them in the scene, write them out of the scene and give them something to do offstage.

   And speaking of offstage . . .

   Keep in mind that not all the action of your story takes place in scenes in front of the reader. Characters who aren't featured in a scene aren't hiding out in some backstage room, waiting for their entrances; they're living their lives. Or they should be. Remember to have characters share what they were doing while readers were caught up with other characters.

- Give characters more to do, to care about, than one story issue. Make sure characters come across as real, with multiple concerns.

   On the other hand, don't dilute the thrust of your story by including too many unrelated issues and character interests. Give your characters full lives, but in a way that links their interests to the plot and other characters.

   Add if you have to, cut out side issues that don't belong.

- Cut out evidence of a character's tendency to preach or teach. Tell a story, don't share a philosophy. Especially not your own.

   This doesn't mean that characters can't be themselves. But they shouldn't be you.

- Ensure that characters have sufficient reactions to events, dialogue, and the antics of other characters. Action must produce reaction.

> Readers respond when characters do. Make sure that characters, especially the main ones, react when events happen. So add in reactions or cut out events that fail to elicit reactions. Don't allow the center of your story to become a quagmire of inconsequential events.

- Cut back on character thoughts, especially if they're at the expense of dialogue and action. Don't trap readers in a character's head with either first- or third-person narration. Allow readers to experience action and motion and dialogue.

- Be sure you've raised the stakes for both protagonist and antagonist at intervals throughout the middle of the story. What gets the protagonist moving at the beginning probably isn't enough to see him through each time someone challenges him or pushes him back. Give him new reasons to follow through.

- Make sure you've presented the emotions of your characters. People think and act, but they also feel. Be sure you've given your characters a range of emotions and a range of levels as they express those emotions. Make sure emotions are revealed in multiple ways—via thought, dialogue, and action.

- Make sure that you've given major characters quirks, habits, tics, or idiosyncrasies. If these quirks or tics show up when a character is nervous, make sure we see them when she's nervous. Yet if you've overplayed a habit, cut out some references to it. A character shouldn't constantly bite her nails or check her phone. Consider giving characters multiple habits. Use habits that have a bearing on the plot. Link habits to a character's emotions so that different habits show up at different times in the story.

- Verify that the character emotion you needed or wanted to convey was presented through both word choice and character reaction.

Dialogue

▪ Cut or edit dialogue that goes nowhere. If dialogue isn't advancing plot, revealing character, upping the conflict level (and reader tension), stirring the reader's emotions, or affecting mood, what's it doing in your story?

If you can use the same bit of dialogue to accomplish multiple purposes, that's even better. And if you can build subtext into dialogue as well, you've got dialogue that serves the story.

▪ Don't let any character talk uninterrupted. Break up character monologues, whether the monologue is in spoken words or thoughts.

Use an event, the dialogue of another character, an object in the setting, or the character himself to interrupt his talk. No one should get to talk unimpeded for too long.

You can even use action beats or thoughts to break up talk.

Any one element that's used too much or too often is boring, even snappy or dramatic dialogue. Don't make your readers' eyes glaze over at the speech of your characters.

▪ In dialogue, make characters look forward more often than they look back. This will keep readers looking forward too.

▪ Check every scene for talking-head syndrome. If characters come across as disembodied minds communicating via dialogue or thought, make changes. Add setting details. Show characters in motion or interacting with props.

Scenes

▪ Remove or rewrite scenes that serve no purpose or duplicate the purpose of other scenes. Like dialogue, scenes should advance plot and reveal character. They should change the conflict level and change or establish mood.

> Scenes should change the status quo. If characters and conditions remain the same after a scene plays out, the scene didn't serve its main purpose.

Think change, even small changes, when you compare one scene to the next. If a scene doesn't force changes to plot or character, if it doesn't send the story in a new direction, consider cutting the scene. Or consider combining it with another scene. Or reworking it until it accomplishes a necessary story purpose.

- Make sure middle chapters and scenes are of different lengths, feature different combinations of characters, take place in different settings, and reveal new and different information.

There are exceptions here. If your story features only two characters, your scenes will always include both or only one of them. But you understand what I'm suggesting—mix it up by grouping different characters together. Change group dynamics by changing the group.

And change the feel of the story by using a short scene after a couple of long ones, maybe a couple of short chapters rather than three or four average ones. Break up patterns that lull the reader, no matter where those patterns are found.

- Make sure that each scene carries tension for the reader and conflict for a character (or for multiple characters). If everyone gets along, you don't have a novel, you have a sweet and pretty lullaby that will put readers to sleep.

Always remember that conflict doesn't have to mean characters coming to blows or yelling themselves hoarse. Conflict covers a range of activities and reactions, and there are plenty of options to fit any genre and any style of story.

Genre

- Make sure that all story elements conform to your intended genre if that's important for the genre. If your self-labeled suspense has no suspense and no sense of danger, you need to rewrite or consider a different approach, maybe a different genre.

If you're writing science fiction and featuring a new world, make sure your world building is first-rate. Make sure you've highlighted the setting, as is common for science fiction. Make sure setting affects a scene's mood and character behavior.

Romances written today typically require a happily ever after or a happy for now. If your story doesn't have one, you either need to change the story, making it conform to expectations (genre requirements), or recognize that you're not writing in the genre you thought you were and make changes to adapt to the actual genre of the story.

- If you've overplayed genre conventions, remove some or tone them down.

Description/Setting

- Cut out unnecessary description or add missing description. As your story nears the end, description is usually reduced—characters tend to be too busy to smell the flowers as they're aiming for the showdown. But in other places, characters would notice what's going on around them, especially if elements of the setting have changed.

Make sure characters note differences or oddities in the setting.

- Make sure that characters interact with setting. This may mean handling props or noticing setting details or commenting on scents or sounds. Once a story gets going, writers sometimes forget to have characters relate to the setting. Check scenes to see if your characters act as if they're in a real location made with walls and floors, dirt and trees, water, or any other location identifiers.

Exposition

- Reduce the overuse of narrative summary and exposition. Make sure the bulk of your story takes place as scenes. Summary and exposition are necessary—especially to provide back story or to introduce new scenes and/or indicate a change in time or setting. But too much exposition turns a story into a report. By its very nature, exposition is low in conflict, and if it goes on for too long or there's too much in comparison to active scenes, you risk losing the reader.

If you can't identify setting or action for pages at a time or if your narrator is doing a whole lot of telling about the way he used to do something, start cutting. Keep necessary and useful exposition—cut out everything else.

Mechanics

- Cut out common wording and replace it with story-specific words.

> Because writers tend to spend far more time on openings
> and endings, those sections often pop with vibrant verbs
> and strong nouns. Yet the middle of the story can be
> subjected to common and inexact wording, to phrases
> that can be found in any story. Don't tire of writing well
> in your middle chapters.

Don't rush through the middle chapters. Give them the same consideration you give first and last chapters. And that means attention to word choices.

Cut out words that do nothing to indicate genre or era or a character's personality or emotions. Replace with words peculiar to your story, words that wouldn't be found in those combinations in any other book. Use words that highlight a character's personality and background and experience and desires. Replace the vague or imprecise with the particular and pointed.

- Review chapter and scene endings; make sure each concludes with a hook that compels readers to turn the page.

Hooks can be of different intensities, so don't think they must always be outrageously compelling. But do include them. At the same time, make sure chapter endings also conclude elements of an issue introduced earlier.

- Check the middle for balance. You won't want too much of any one element—dialogue, action, description, or exposition.

- Make sure that scenes include appropriate sense elements. Unless your characters are deaf and blind and have no taste buds or odor and touch receptors, include the senses. Bring readers into your story world by showing them how it sounds and tastes and what it smells like. Yet don't overplay the senses. If every scene contains a character's reaction to an odor, cut some of those reactions from the story.

- Reduce the number of uses of *I* in first-person narration.

- Reduce instances of character names, especially in dialogue.

- Cut back on uses of favorite words, whatever those are for you, as well as words common to many stories: *just, only, seem, stand, really, look, glance,* and *walk.*

- Make sure sentence structure and length are varied. Make sure paragraph lengths are varied.

- Check scenes and paragraphs for sing-song rhythms or monotonously boring sameness in rhythm and sound and feel. Change up any pattern that goes on for too long, any wording or structure that lulls or that sets your mind wandering. Change patterns that distract.

> If you find your eyes glazing over as you read the middle chapters or you don't remember what happened in the last paragraphs or pages you read, stop. Go back to the top of the scene and begin reading again. If nothing stands out, rewrite or cut.

FINAL WORDS

Most of what I mentioned here is valid for openings and endings as well as middles, but you probably already attend to these issues in first and last chapters as a matter of course. Now you'll want to extend that same persnickety attention to detail to the middles of your stories.

Think about streamlining and making every story moment a memorable one. Or at least one that doesn't put readers to sleep.

You've spent hours perfecting your characters and their story problems. Don't let characters down with soggy middles that suck the passion from their stories. Give your characters story events worthy of the greatest fictional characters. And give readers memorable stories that they can't put down and want never to end.

22

ENDINGS THAT ROCK

EVERY STORY HAS TO STOP somewhere, but deciding where and how stories stop isn't simple. Stopping a story isn't the same as *completing* a story, tying up the loose ends and sending readers away with a sense of satisfaction and the feeling that the end was inevitable.

Some endings are circular, with characters returning to the place they started. The characters are different, of course, mature or wiser or battered. Maybe triumphant. Sometimes defeated.

Other endings may take place far from a story's beginnings, with the main character in a new physical locale or experiencing a new mental or emotional state.

What you want to do with endings as you edit is make sure they satisfy, that they resolve the story problem introduced 300 pages earlier, and that they conclude the episode in the main character's life that you immersed the reader into.

You'll want to check the climax—is there one? Is it big enough for the story and the challenges that led up to it? Is it the right length, neither too short nor too long?

You'll also want to look at what happens after the big moment, at the way story threads are resolved. Did you account for what happens to major characters? Did you set up teasers for the next book in the series if that applies? Did you give the reader something to ponder in the final page, when she'll be disheartened that the adventure is over? Did you leave the reader with a resonating emotion that she can carry away from the book, one that will influence her for the rest of the day or that will encourage her to buy another of your books?

In this chapter we're going to look at story endings, a critical component of all fiction.

A great story can be ruined by a weak or inappropriate ending. And I'm not overstating that, simply acknowledging the profound power of a story's last events, images, dialogue, thoughts, emotions, and even rhythms.

You want to leave the reader with your best—your best words, images, and emotions—not only what you have left after giving your all for the rest of the book. Use your editing skills to craft solid and satisfying endings.

SATISFY THE READER‡

What do you owe your reader? A fast read? A world of escape? Adventure or thrills or beauty he can't experience at home?

Do you guarantee 300 flawless pages with characters who overcome odds or solve the mystery or promise to love forever?

Maybe your stories teach a lesson, open eyes, spark conversations over late-night coffees or breakfast-table cereal.

No matter where you take the reader, what you drag him through or under or around, you must see that he's satisfied, ensure that at the moment he reads the final page, he feels the satisfaction that yes, *this* story could end only *this* way.

When the hero limps home with a prize many times more valuable than the one he sought, when the amateur sleuth cracks the case that stumped professionals, when love succeeds where animosity failed, then the reader feels that the world is back in balance. The ride is over, true, but if all has gone well, it was a rewarding one.

You want the reader to feel that his foray into your fictional world was worth every minute that he spent with your characters. That it was worth passing up every other activity he missed or put off in order to read your book.

But a satisfying ending isn't easy to write.

You must write a climax worthy of the story. You must answer major plot questions without rehashing every event. You must remember to account for characters who were left behind when only your major characters clashed in the climax. You must answer the story question.

You must fill in the blanks.

For each problem you introduced, you must provide a solution.

You must conclude the series of events you unleashed on page 1.

Authors don't owe their readers a happy ending (unless it's an expectation of the genre). They don't owe annihilation of all evil. They don't owe restitution for every injustice bedeviling their characters. But they do owe readers satisfaction, a completion of the contract entered into when the reader laid out money and time to live in the writer's world for a couple of hours. It's justice of a sort, fair dealing between writer and reader. And if it's done well, this completion of the author/reader contract, the writer has reason to hope the reader will both recommend the novel *and* read more from the same author.

Authors do owe their readers a good read, and a satisfying ending is one way to ensure that good read. A reader will forgive and maybe forget a saggy middle *if* the end sings. But there's no remedy for a bad ending. The bad taste remains in the reader's mouth with nothing good to wash it away except a different novel with a more satisfying ending. But what writer wants to send his readers from his worlds to those of another writer?

Please your readers. Pay them back for their investment in your book by delivering a believable, entertaining ending. And invite them into your next story by giving them the expectation that each novel will not only take them on an adventure, but will return them to their world fulfilled and rewarded for having lost themselves in yours.

CHECKLIST FOR READER SATISFACTION

Ask yourself a few questions about your book's final events and the last quarter or so of the book. Let your answers guide your editing.

- Is the end inevitable? (Or would another ending suit better?)
- Was the end hard won? (Or did the protagonist fall into his triumph or his defeat?)
- Does it make sense by every measure? (Or were vital steps glossed over?)

- Is the end long enough—deep enough—for the length and breadth of the novel? (Or does a 400-page novel get a two-paragraph resolution?)
- Are major plot points addressed without being overemphasized? (Or does the ending drag?)
- Are burning questions answered? (Or are they relegated to nothing status by the end?)

SET UP A SATISFYING ENDING

To create a satisfying ending, the pieces need to be arranged well before characters play out the final events. Verify that you've included the right mix of elements that will ensure the ending you want.

- Create a main character the reader can identify with.

- Make sure conflict and tension are present and dynamic throughout the story.

- Engage reader emotions regularly.

- Vary the pace.

- Make sure action is seen, not only talked about.

- Create a layered story so that the reader must be satisfied by several outcomes on several levels.

- Make sure the ending grows out of earlier events.

- Make sure the climax takes place in real time, unfolds in front of the reader, and isn't relayed via summary.

- Make sure the details of endings can't be guessed easily. Foreshadowing that gives critical specifics or clues that are too straightforward produce a feeling of letdown in the reader.

- Make sure the ending isn't resolved through coincidence or the old deus ex machina solution—the main characters need to solve their own problems and can't rely on the cavalry riding in to save them. Characters need to be the cavalry themselves.

> *Deus ex machina* means god from a machine or device. In early Greek plays, an actor playing one of the gods often swooped down from the sky by means of some contraption to save characters who had no other possible escape from the danger they faced. The only answer for those in trouble was the intervention of a god.

What this meant in practical terms was that the play's writer didn't have to figure out a means of saving the character in a way that arose from story events and character skills and strengths.

Don't let an outside force save your characters; build the story in such a way that if characters need to be victorious (they could lose instead), you provide them with what they need to win that victory themselves. This may mean a particular skill set, friends, an attitude of ruthlessness, or even simple pigheadedness that keeps them from quitting and helps them outlast their foes.

In order to create an ending in which the characters succeed because of their own skills and traits, you've got to set up the skills and traits much earlier in the story. You can't introduce necessary components in the final chapter. In an edit, search for such components throughout the story. If they're too light, beef them up. If they're absent altogether, add them.

DELIVER THE PAYOFF‡

Have you ever read a book, a great book, only to get to the end and find it fell apart?

I don't encounter this often, but when I do, I'm thoroughly disappointed. Sometimes more than disappointed. I'm ticked off.

This last happened to me several years ago. I was enjoying the book, looking for the payoff, and then, not a bam. Not a wow. Just nothing. An ending of underwhelming proportion.

No payoff. No climax. No sparks or excitement or fireworks. No final race toward the big moment.

No big moment at all.

The book was a mystery, but a mystery literally without a climax. What kind of mystery has no climax, no high point? No moment the story has been building toward?

> An ending that doesn't pay off for the reader, that doesn't meet genre expectation or satisfy reader anticipation, is a problem ending.

This doesn't mean that an ending must be predictable. But it does need to be inevitable. And logical. And it needs to satisfy the reader on at least one level and preferably several.

Endings Serve Purposes

In terms of basics, the ending must rise out of the story opening; it must answer the question posed at the beginning. It must resolve the protagonist's dilemma. The ending doesn't have to be a positive resolution, but it must provide an answer.

No is an answer. *Failure* is an answer. *Death* is the ultimate unequivocal answer.

There are exceptions for experimental fiction, but you need to keep in mind how readers will feel if you cheat them out of an ending after they invest time in your book. They expect the whole story. And they expect endings to fit what has come before.

A story that in the opening asks what a man's life purpose is before delving into the intricacies of his spirit and soul for 300 pages can't be resolved by the man learning who stole his neighbor's dog.

A romance, in the modern sense of romance novels, can't end with the couple hating one another and uttering death threats. It can't because the story question for most romances isn't only *will the couple get together* but *how will they get together; how will they overcome their differences in order to be together.*

A suspense thriller can't end without the source of the suspense— person or situation—being identified and neutralized or being identified and succeeding in spite of the protagonist. (Yes, sometimes the bad guys win.)

I remember only three books that disappointed me at the very end and only at the end. But I remember each quite vividly.

One was the mystery without a climax. And not only was there no climax, but the identity of the murderer and the motive for the murder didn't satisfy. The murderer was introduced late in the story and given almost no attention. And the motive for the murder carried no weight; it meant nothing to the events of story. So little, in fact, that it seemed tacked on, an afterthought. No threads relating to the motive had been pulled through the narrative. No threads relating to the *murderer* had been pulled through the narrative.

Another story that didn't satisfy was a romance in which the author killed off the heroine in the final chapter. No, she hadn't been sick. No, there had been no foreshadowing. The heroine was simply killed off in the last chapter of a contemporary romance.

I never read that author again.

My genre expectations were shattered at the last moment, and that was what was so disappointing. Contemporary romance promises the chance of a happily ever after for the couple. The couple in that story had no chance for such an outcome.

I wouldn't have been disappointed had I not picked that particular book with genre expectations firmly in mind.

Also, the character's death achieved nothing for the ongoing story. A character's death midstory could be mined for tension and conflict and used to give other characters motivation to react. An unprovoked and unanticipated death at the end of a story, perhaps included only for shock value, indicates that the writer failed to plan the ending and needed to create an emotional impact by other means.

> Endings should feel inevitable, a result of what has come
> before. An ending that comes from out of the blue
> doesn't fit other story elements. An ending that's merely
> tacked on, with no connections to other story events and
> motivations, an ending that isn't intrinsic to your story,
> doesn't belong in your story.

The third book that disappointed me with its ending was one in which one of the main characters—who'd appeared in all the other books of the series—was killed off. I also never read this author again. I couldn't. I couldn't trust that he would play fair. I would always be looking for the sucker punch rather than allowing myself to get lost in the fiction.

This death *was* put to work for the story, so that wasn't the problem. My reaction was simply my very personal response to the reader/writer contract. In my opinion, the writer didn't keep his end of the contract. And so in turn I chose not to engage in any other business with him.

I'm not telling you that writers are wrong to choose the unexpected. I am letting you know that readers, of which I am one, may not agree with your choices. Does this mean you have to anticipate every possible reader reaction? No. But how about I suggest that you should be aware of possible reader reactions? Write what works for your stories, even if that means killing off favorite characters. Yet be aware that one option might be more successful than another option would be, especially in terms of reader satisfaction.

Kill away if doing so fits the story and advances the plot. Keep in mind, however, the other purposes of endings. A book that takes a left turn or spirals out of control in the final pages—especially when the writer didn't plan sufficiently or went off track solely to set up the next book in a series—hasn't fulfilled its own premise. And its author has broken faith with readers.

You don't want to turn off your readers, you *do* want to entertain. You want to surprise the reader *within the boundaries of the contract* that writers and readers share.

Series vs. Single Books

Each book in a series must stand on its own. If you can complete one story *and* introduce the following story of a series at the same time, go for it. But the key here is *completing the first story*. Don't deny the reader the ending that completes that first story. Finish what you start. Come to a resolution. Tie up story threads.

Answer the story questions and fulfill your promises.

When you edit, verify that you've successfully accomplished each of these goals.

There are methods you can use to ensure that readers are treated to a fulfilling ending rather than to disappointment. They require that you direct the ending to make sure it brings story elements to a true conclusion, not merely a stopping point.

Consider the following suggestions as you edit—and maybe even earlier in the revision process, as you rewrite.

Stay true to genre and to genre expectations

If you begin with a murder mystery, write the ending to a mystery and not the ending to a coming-of-age novel or romance. This means telling who did it, how, and why.

You can't please every possible reader simply by mixing genres. You can actually turn off readers when you promise one genre but include hallmarks of half a dozen others, creating a mess that doesn't offer enough of any one genre for readers to enjoy.

Stick to a single genre. (Exceptions for subgenres, of course.)

Every genre has accepted essentials and elements, essentials that readers expect to find in a novel, elements that appeal to readers' tastes. Readers pick up books of a particular genre because they want to read stories that feature those elements. If you don't include them, the reader may be disappointed. If you violate expectations, you may turn off readers.

Instead of angering or disappointing readers, honor their genre expectations.

- A mystery's conclusion must arise from the clues provided. You can't hold out on the mystery reader; they need to be able to solve the mystery from the information you've shared. The killer or perpetrator can't be introduced on the last page in the next-to-the-last chapter. You can't "forget" to include critical clues.
- Although there's great variety in subgenres, today's romances require either a happily ever after or a happy for now.

- A literary novel heavy on character development will need character growth or will need to show a character facing revelations about himself.
- A suspense story must end with the source of the danger being neutralized or victorious.

These are only a few examples. Each genre has expectations that need attention both throughout the story and at its end.

Remember characters

Make sure the ending fits the person your lead character has become while not ignoring the person she was to start with. Write an ending that fits your protagonist and your antagonist as well.

Give your characters a fitting send-off.

Maintain tone and style

Don't adapt a different style of presentation at the end. For example, don't suddenly shift to a teaching or preaching style to hammer home your theme. Don't switch to a humorous voice in the final pages if you've not used that voice in the rest of the story.

Maintain consistency.

Provide sufficient strength and balance

An ending must be able to support the weight of a story. It can't be too insubstantial or too short. It can't be weak, but must instead be strong enough to contain resolutions to all major plots and problems.

The ending doesn't have to answer every question, but it should address the vital ones, especially those that sent the protagonist on his adventure or trek or quest.

The ending, while it echoes memorable story moments, definitely shouldn't recap every event.

The reader has invested a number of hours in your fiction. Give him an ending worth his investment. Give him a meaty conclusion.

Don't skimp on your ending.

And while you're at it, keep your reputation secure.

If you give your story an ending that could happen no other way, that satisfies the story elements that have come before, your readers aren't likely to remember you in a negative light, as a writer who betrays their expectations. They won't be likely, more than 20 years later, to still remember the story that turned them away from your writing forever, something like the story and author that became an example in a chapter on what not to do in a novel's ending.

Be a writer who delivers on the promise you made at your story's opening. Write the ending that satisfies story needs, the story question, genre requirements, and reader expectations.

Deliver the payoff.

Keep the reader.

CLIMAX

The climax is the dramatic and emotional high point of your novel—make sure you've included one.

This is where protagonist and antagonist have their final show-down (at least in terms of the one novel—the two can tangle again in other stories). This is the moment story events have been leading to, where your protagonist makes the final push, stands his last stand, tackles the might and wiles of his enemy.

The climax is where your antagonist unleashes his most powerful weapons, where the fight is on and stays on until a clear winner emerges. This is conflict at its ultimate stage, whatever that means for your story.

The climax is one of a novel's defining moments. It's often the most memorable one.

When you edit, check the climax for essential elements.

- Your protagonist must be directly involved in the climax. This is no time for stand-ins.
- The action of the climax must take place on stage, in a scene. This isn't the time for summary.
- The length of the climax should match the story—you don't want to shortchange the reader.

- The climax must contain an emotional component and must create an emotional response—or deepen an existing emotional response—in the reader.
- The fight can't be too easily won or lost—those involved in the climax should have comparable skills, knowledge, strengths, and weaknesses.
- The characters involved in the confrontation can't use skills unknown to readers or tools that readers have never seen used by the character before. I'm not talking about general skills or a knife that a character picks up from the ground in a brawl, but knowledge or specialized weapons training or paranormal abilities. At the end, characters can use only the mental and physical abilities that readers know they possess, that readers have seen in action or have heard mentioned. Anything else would be unbelievable. Any skill *conveniently* made known at the climax but not before weakens the plot. If writers can introduce anything they can think of at the end, careful plotting is pointless.
- The climax must be more than a disagreement. Something critical must be at stake for both parties involved.
- Except for rare stories (almost exclusively literary novels), the climax ends with clear success or clear failure. (Exceptions for stories in which protagonists succeed at their goal but at great personal cost beyond the norm.)

RESOLUTION—TYING UP THE ENDS‡

We've all read perfect stories, novels that end on a high note with satisfying action and just the right amount of explanation and with a punch to our emotional centers. The kinds of stories that satisfy our minds as well as our emotions.

We've also read novels that ended too soon, without allowing us a moment of reflection to appreciate all that had happened, or that went on for too long and dragged out a satisfying ending until we lost all the good feeling the story had stirred in us.

How can writers craft their final pages to be just enough without either under- or overwhelming the plot and without deflating the bubble of satisfaction the reader enjoys after a great read?

We're talking resolution here, the final few pages that follow the climax of a story.

A resolution can either highlight how truly enjoyable a story is or it can so ruin a good story that readers forget how much they enjoyed everything up to that point.

At story's end, the warrior protagonist has found victory or defeat, hero and heroine have declared their love, the detective has caught his murderer, the time traveler has stopped popping in and out of time, and the lone wolf of an agent has saved the world.

But what happens next?

Whether they win or lose, we don't usually leave our warriors on the battlefield, bloodied swords in hand, feet mired in gore, with no moment to consider all that has happened. And lovers need a moment to reflect on their love and on the trials they overcame to reach that love. The detective ruminates on what his latest case cost him and whether or not he can face another when the stakes grow ever higher. The time traveler reflects on what he left behind and imagines what lies ahead. The spy needs a moment to catch his breath after his near-impossible quest to defeat the world's nastiest villain.

So how do you move characters from the battlefield or the declaration of undying love or the unmasking of the murderer or the saving of the world to *The End?*

You use your resolution.

You tie up loose ends and bring completion to the threads you so carefully laid out for the reader's entertainment. You finish the story. You give the reader enough explanation that he'll be fully satisfied by your tale.

Because each story is different in terms of length, tone, intensity of final scenes, genre, and number of subplots and story threads, there is no one way to bring stories to the final page. The resolution must fit the story, each *element* of the story. And as no stories are alike, no resolutions will be alike. Not in every way.

You'll come closest to conformity within genres. Thus series romance may recommend a two-to-five-page chapter for the resolution, and a political thriller might rely on a longer resolution in order to tie up multiple story threads featuring a large cast of characters.

Yet even with multiple options for resolutions, writers can learn skills necessary for writing strong resolutions that complete the story puzzle and answer the vital questions.

Resolve the Issues

No one wants story gaps in the final pages. Readers want to know what happened and how and why. And they want those answers for each of the major plot threads and characters, for anyone they've come to care for or developed an interest in.

If the writer has done her job, readers will care about the characters. Readers will *need* to know how the characters' lives play out, how all that they've faced will change them.

On the other hand, readers don't need to know *every*thing about *every*one; with solid hints and a clear presentation of what happens to major characters, readers will be able to fill in a lot of blanks. But you do need to show how major characters have been changed by what they've faced and done, activities far outside what they're accustomed to in their normal lives.

Let's look at elements to consider as you work your resolution.

Length

A novella doesn't need a resolution 30 pages long. A few pages should be sufficient to create a balanced ending.

A short novel with few secondary plots also won't need a complex, detailed, or long resolution.

A story with a complex plot, however, requires a longer and more detailed resolution in order to satisfy the reader. You want readers to know what happened as a result of story events and the climax without them having to guess.

Yet resolutions shouldn't be so long that they leach the emotion from the ending.

> It's better to leave readers wanting more than to undo a
> good story by boring readers right at the end. But better
> still is giving readers exactly enough in the resolution.

Resolutions should be sufficiently full relative to the novel. It's
jarring, almost a slap to the reader, to come to the end of a novel only
to be denied the complete ending. The protagonist might have
succeeded at his quest, but what does that mean for him and those
close to him? If you don't show the impact of story events and a
character's choices, both character and reader are cheated.

That bears repeating.

> If you don't show the impact of story events and the
> main character's choices *on* that character, both character
> and reader are cheated.

If you don't include consequences, readers won't know how story
events, including the climax, will affect your main character. They
won't know how what happened to him will influence him long term.

Ask and answer a few questions when you try to decide what's
necessary for a resolution. And include the answers *in* the resolution.

- What has the main character learned?
- How will his life be different?
- In what ways have his adventures changed his outlook?
- How did giving up possessions, friends and family, and his
  dreams affect him? Does he feel that the risk was worth-
  while? How does he feel about actions he was forced to take,
  actions that in his normal life he'd never have considered?
- How did his quest change those around him?

The answers to these questions don't need to be addressed directly—
you could show the cost of a hero's quest when the protagonist
returns home victorious only to find that home burned to the foundations, his family dead at the command of the very men he defeated.

Or an explorer could return from her voyage of discovery—ready to take up where she left off, a woman better equipped to handle her personal problems—only to discover her fiancé married her best friend in her three-year absence.

Or you could actually spell out what the protagonist learned, allowing the reader to hear her thoughts, understand what her actions and the actions of others mean for her life and future.

Breathing Room

The reader gains an opportunity to come down from the high of the climax by reading an appropriate resolution, so include one. Provide a few moments of reflection so the reader can ponder all that's happened and what those events mean for the characters and for the reader herself.

> Use the resolution to give both characters and readers a moment to breathe, to relax, to adjust to what's taken place. Characters need a break from the emotional ups and downs of the climax. And readers will need a moment of reflection and adjustment before stepping back into their own lives.

Emotions

Readers will come away from your novels feeling something. And that something is created in great part by your resolution.

Readers may feel relief that your main character succeeded at his goals. But they also may feel a sense of vindication or that justice has been done. If your hero has lost a lot, even if he ultimately wins, they may feel his pain. They may feel pure jubilation or a bittersweet joy.

When you edit your resolution, make sure you included the impact of choices on your protagonist and antagonist. Make sure that the impact is strong enough to match the story's events, strong enough to reflect the price the character paid for those choices. This impact, the realization of what happened to the characters because of their actions, can stir strong emotions in the reader. Control your resolution by steering reader emotion in the direction you want it to go.

Direct the emotion by your word choices, by character reaction and thought, and by the choice of issues to focus on at the end of the story. Whatever you turn the reader's attention toward is what you're declaring important. Be sure to direct reader focus at the end. Decide on what you want the reader to remember, the emotion you want her feeling when she closes the book, and make sure that your resolution achieves your intent.

Balance

Resolutions should be in balance with the rest of the story—not too long, not too short, not overly detailed, not overly cryptic, humorous if the story has been humorous, short on humor if the story hasn't been funny.

Epilogue

Use your editing time to decide whether or not you should include an epilogue detailing what happens over the next few days, months, or years in the life of the protagonist.

Some readers will love knowing what happens down the road, but others won't want to know; some readers don't like to imagine characters changing or growing older. Some want to remember characters as they've been presented in your story, in their moments of glory and fear, at those times most meaningful to their lives.

Decide how much of the future to include in your resolution. If you want to go beyond a brief mention, use an epilogue.

You may give readers a summary of the hours or days following the climax, but you *could* tell readers what a character will be doing 60 years into the future. You could paint a full picture of the protagonist's life as a result of his actions during his adventure.

When you edit, try your ending with and without an epilogue that reveals the future. Decide which option produces the effect you want to leave with the reader. Choose the more striking option if it fits genre and the other elements of your story.

Tips for the Resolution

The style of a resolution should match the other parts of the story, yet by its very nature, a resolution is different.

Most novel resolutions are written not in the dynamic phrasing of unfolding events and vibrant scenes but in exposition. And the resolution is typically summary.

You'll have used exposition in your story in other places, but you'll have followed it in those places with increased tension and conflict. With the resolution, you're purposely reducing tension. Think of resolution as a means of settling the reader after making him undergo the drama of your story.

You resolved the characters' conflicts and the characters stood down and eased back, and now the reader can relax as well.

Give resolution the right balance and cherry-pick the words and images you want to stay with readers after they turn the final page.

Take one last opportunity to focus the reader's attention exactly where you want it. Spotlight the key elements from the story. Spotlight the lead character's realizations and conclusions, maybe his new goals and his personal resolutions.

Harken back to the opening line or the inciting incident or a poignant moment from midstory. But don't only look back. You can use mentions of these story highlights to show a character looking to the future.

> Ease back on conflict, but use word choices to keep summary active. Resolutions contain the last words and images readers will see, so make them count. Choose those words and images with care and with an eye toward impact. Be deliberate in what you include and in what you exclude.

Think in terms of resonance—what do you want your readers feeling as they read your final words? What do you want them to hear echoing through their thoughts when they think about your story?

When you edit, make sure you've written endings and resolutions worthy of your stories and characters, worthy of the 90,000 words that precede them.

THE QUICK LIST

- Plan your endings. Make sure that major plot threads and story questions have been resolved.

- Cut out a deus ex machina ending and replace it with an ending that relies on the main characters to resolve story issues.

- Set up the next book in a series if that's appropriate.

- Don't drag the ending on forever.

Make sure

- you've included both climax and resolution.
- protagonist and antagonist feature in the story's climax. The antagonist doesn't have to be featured in resolution or epilogue, although he could be.
- endings arise from what has come before. Plant the solution, at least a hint of it, inside the problem.
- the ending is of sufficient length and depth and breadth to fit the story that came before.
- you satisfy genre expectations if that's a necessity.
- you deliver a complete story.

23
NOTABLE STORY MOMENTS

READERS CAN BE TOUCHED by a variety of story elements. They may be caught up in an action event, may become enraptured by an emotional scene, or may laugh along with the characters at a fabulously humorous bit of dialogue.

Readers can be moved emotionally as well as intellectually, and you can and should purposely touch your readers at multiple moments in your stories, giving them something special to remember your story by.

But how do you know how and where to touch your readers? How do you know what will move them? How do you know when to be humorous, when to be tender, when to be tough?

Genre provides some answers.

Literary novels appeal for their phrasings and word choices. They also often delve into a character's psyche and motivations. To touch readers of literary novels, give them notable story moments that take advantage of beautiful writing and characters who discover something earth-shattering about themselves.

For suspense novels, provide uncertainty, anticipation, and an urgent sense of danger or menace.

For mysteries, provide puzzles that readers can try to solve.

For romances, include highly emotional scenes.

For horror, provide something frightening, something unexpected.

For science fiction, include a fascinating story world.

For time travel, make your protagonist a true fish out of water.

As you edit, make sure your story has the expected genre high and low points. You can always include more expectations than the genre demands, but you don't want to include fewer. At least not many. Read up on your genre or get a cheat-sheet going and then make sure you've included the required story elements.

Not all notable story moments are related to genre, of course; some are foundational elements of all stories. Many have to do with characters, but some are plot related, events that jump-start the story or steer it in a new direction.

I included many notable story moments in the chapter "Significant Introductions," but not all notable moments are introductions. Let's look at a few general notable moments.

When you edit, your job is to ensure that you've included these moments and that they're in the right place, that they're given the right amount of setup and introduction, and that they're introduced at the proper time and by the character best suited to introduce them. You'll also want to be sure that repercussions of notable moments are felt throughout the story. Make sure you put them to work not only for the scene in which they're featured, but later in the story as well.

Notable moments include

- a creative opening
- a worthy ending
- the inciting incident
- climax *and* resolution
- the protagonist's tipping point/surrender to the call
- events that raise the stakes for protagonist and antagonist
- the protagonist's support being cut off
- incidents of betrayal
- moments of sacrifice
- death—of a loved one, an enemy, a company, a job, a dream
- recognition or acceptance of maturity—becoming a man or woman, accepting responsibility (and blame), taking control; taking responsibility back from others
- making a grave mistake, betraying others, being betrayed
- having a secret uncovered, uncovering someone else's secret
- emotional high and low points for characters *and* readers, the story's black moment, the story's redemptive moment
- chapter-opening and chapter-ending hooks
- tour-de-force moments for protagonist and/or antagonist
- the moment a major characters realizes a truth about another character that changes how the first character looks at that person or at the world or even at themselves

FINAL WORDS

Make sure your stories have these notable moments. Make sure they accomplish a purpose or have meaning for characters—they redirect the story or the characters, create or change emotions, cut the character off from his past, show the character he has no choice but to move forward, raise the stakes.

Decide if these story moments get enough attention from characters who should be paying attention. Are they meaty enough for what you've asked them to accomplish? Did you provide enough setup? Enough follow-through? Enough character reaction? Do characters look back on these moments for inspiration, or are such moments quickly forgotten?

Do you overplay notable moments? If so, dial it back. Don't overemphasize what should be meaningful by pointing neon lights at it. Make sure notable moments fit the story and make sure they produce logical and *noticeable* consequences, but don't stuff them down the reader's craw, saying, "Pay attention to this."

Make the notable fit your story.

Give readers something to remember.

24

VERIFY THE PRESENCE OF SCENES

UNDERSTANDING SCENES and their importance to novels is difficult for some writers, especially beginning writers. Yet as you edit, you need to ensure that the majority of your novel is relayed via scene and not by report, not through summary or exposition.

As with the differences between showing and telling, you either get scenes or you don't, and yet once you grasp what a scene is, what it contains and how it should play out, you'll never forget. And you'll understand why scenes and not reports should make up the majority of your novel.

A report tells the reader what happened. It's an account described from the outside looking in. A scene, on the other hand, invites readers into the events as they unfold. Scenes put readers inside story to experience it.

A report is *just the facts, ma'am*. A scene is the moving, breathing reality of unfolding story events.

> Scenes feature characters in action in a certain location during or over a particular period of time. Scenes have recognizable beginnings, middles, and ends. Scenes have purpose; they advance plot, reveal character, create conflict, and deepen or establish mood. Scenes show, they include references to the senses. But they don't only show, they encourage reader immersion into the characters' lives and undertakings.

A report is telling, even if that telling is dolled up with pretty words.

A scene is the ultimate showing, events played out on the page.

A report is a reporter standing outside a home destroyed by fire, informing a TV audience what has happened *after the event is over.*

A scene is a multi-sense camera inside the house as it burns, a camera catching the ignition of the curtains and the collapse of the ceiling, the crackle of books being devoured and the oppressive heat bearing down. Scenes capture character thought, emotion, speech, and behavior *as they happen* and in response to other events.

A scene allows readers to enter the setting, imagining themselves as characters inside the story while events play out. Think of scenes as immersion for readers and as real life for characters. A report is an account, a statement of facts. A novel isn't a news report. It's the events portrayed from within the fictional world as they unfold.

An example from a scene already in progress—

Tedesco ran wildly, dodging trash cans and assailants and bullets. He tripped over a box, went sprawling, and jumped up again, hands raw and ankle throbbing. Yet behind him, his pursuers never slowed.

"This way, Ted. Run, you fool."

The muted command came from his right, and Tedesco zigged and zagged his way across the street. He raced blindly into an alley and four strides later was jerked through a doorway.

The door eased closed behind him, and a muffled clang sounded in the darkness.

Tedesco bent forward and dropped his hands to his knees, panting.

Vanilla. Over the stink of rotted food and who knew what else, he smelled vanilla. And vanilla meant . . .

"Madison."

"You were expecting the Boston PD?"

A report—

> Tedesco had long imagined what he'd do when his adversaries caught up with him. He had plenty of practice to put his plan into action that summer when they came after him not once but half a dozen times. He escaped each attack, running through the dark streets ahead of his assailants.
>
> He used his wits, the confusing one-way streets, and the darkness to confound them. Madison had even played a part. One night, when Tedesco thought he'd run out of luck, Madison showed up to save his butt.
>
> She'd told him she'd heard he was in danger and couldn't let him be killed in the streets by nameless thugs when she'd denied herself the pleasure, hundreds of times, of killing him herself.
>
> But he'd always been lucky, and he'd take luck in any form, even that of his ex.
>
> By August, he thought himself sufficiently safe to show his face in his regular haunts. When he did so, visiting one after another, alert for attacks, he proved convincingly to himself that the men chasing him had given up, at least for the present. He returned to his regular routine, and by early September, he was back in business, a healing ankle the only souvenir of his adventurous summer.

The differences between the two examples should be clear. The first puts a character into an identifiable location for a period of time *at* a recognizable time. It incorporates setting, action, and dialogue in real time, as if the events were taking place just as the reader is reading. It shows a character interacting with setting and other characters.

The second example is summary, and it highlights the general rather than the specific. It tells what *typically* happened rather than what happened in a particular moment. It reports what was said instead of showing the moment of dialogue as it played out.

There is a time for reporting, a need for summary and a glossing over of events. But whole novels shouldn't read the way the second example does. Save that style of writing for necessary summary and to transition between scenes. Connect scenes with summary, but write scenes as scenes.

I'm stressing this difference between scenes and reports because I often receive submissions for edits that read like the second example for page after page and chapter after chapter. Every once in a while the writer throws in a line of dialogue, yet afterward immediately returns to reporting. My suggestion is that you make sure you understand the differences between scene and summary, and understand when each is useful or required.

WHAT TO LOOK FOR

If you find words such as *always, used to,* and *would* used often, if characters relay the gist of conversations but those conversations don't play out in real time as dialogue—with quotation marks and dialogue tags and action beats—you may have written reports rather than scenes. If a character lives in his head and simply tells us what has gone on before, describing events from his life and sharing his emotions, only popping out of his thoughts every so often to take a walk or order a cup of coffee or tell off a co-worker, you've not given us scenes but have reduced your story to reports, a recounting of events rather than the experience of the events themselves.

In an edit (or preferably in a rewrite), the task is to shift those reports to scenes. Use summary to advance time or to move to a different location—use summary at the top of scenes to orient the reader to a new time or place or viewpoint character—but use scenes to tell the story.

Use exposition for necessary explanations, for back story, but don't let it take over. Make scenes do the heavy lifting of storytelling duties in your long fiction.

There are exceptions for certain literary novels that shift the balance from scenes to a character's thoughts and memories. Such stories still contain traditional scenes, just not to the degree that other novels feature them.

If you're not quite sure what a scene is or how to write one, start researching. Pull out a novel, pick up a highlighter, and mark the sections that you imagine are scenes. Highlight summary and exposition in different colors. Develop a sense for what scenes include and how they're constructed.

Scenes typically don't begin and then continue for pages with text such as this:

> When I was a girl, my father took us out for ice cream every Friday over the summers. We would ponder our choices for long minutes, always choosing the same favorites in the end, and then skip along the canal. Daddy would always finish before me and Dinah, and then he'd try to steal our cones. ✗

This paragraph gives us details, true. But it's not a scene.

A scene might begin with something like this:

> I stopped by Cool and Tastee on the way home. The parking lot was empty, but I had to wait at the door for customers to leave before I could ease inside. The no-frills white tile, on the floor and halfway up the walls, echoed the squeals and delight of a gaggle of Little Leaguers celebrating their division championship. I turned around, intending to pick up a box of cones from the grocery store, only to whirl again at the sound of a piercing whistle and my name being called.
>
> "Yo, Cassidy." Maurice stood behind the counter, waving an overflowing waffle cone. "I saw you get out of your car."

Heat rose to my cheeks. Maurice had a crush on me, which I actively discouraged. But it did get me out of waiting in line, a perk I often took advantage of.

Big Mike, Maurice's father, waved at me, already pushing Maurice aside when I squeezed up to the counter.

Big Mike had a crush on me too.

In the second example, events are happening right now. A character is moving through a location in real time (or what passes for real time in stories). Dialogue isn't remembered, it's spoken.

Scenes contain events that you can picture, with events playing out right now. (Exceptions for flashbacks and flash-forwards, which are scenes from the past and of the future.) Think in terms of movie scenes. Imagine where your viewpoint character is as he undergoes the events playing out on the page; is he outside the event, looking back on it and narrating, or is he inside it, living the events?

For scenes, you want the viewpoint character inside story events as they play out.

> Scenes can be of varying lengths. Several scenes can be included in a single chapter, one scene can stretch across multiple chapters, or all scene breaks can sync with chapter breaks, creating one scene per chapter.

When you rewrite and edit, ensure that you've included scenes.

SCENE GOALS

As a novel has an overarching goal—the detective wants to find the murderer, the government analyst seeks to save the world, the teen protagonist needs to change the dystopian society—so do scenes have goals. At least they should. At least most scenes should.

A character featured in the scene—typically the viewpoint character—sets out to do or achieve something at the beginning of a scene and by the end should have accomplished it, accomplished it and created a new problem (or made her other problems worse), not accomplished it, or not accomplished it and created a new problem or made her other problems worse.

Scene goals don't have to be big the way story goals are big. In a scene, a character may simply be looking for information. She may try to find an object that will help her toward the next step on her path to meeting the story goal. She may try to learn details about her quarry's personal life or ferret out connections between characters.

If the character is absurdly successful at meeting her scene goals every time, the story will have no tension. Yet if the character is never successful, the story fails to move forward. Characters need to gain information and advance, even if advance means forcing a way over or around an obstruction. They need to find some success.

The best options for scene goals are often to either temporarily deny the character success and at the same time make things worse for her, or satisfy the scene goal and still make things worse.

Introducing complications and increasing problems for major characters are hallmarks of many scenes. The character should be more deeply mired in problems as a story, and as scenes, progress. Meaning that the outlook for success should grow more doubtful even as characters find some success with scene goals.

So the character looking for transportation across the country finds it, only to discover she'll be traveling with a hated ex-husband. Or the amateur sleuth finds a clue to the murderer, only to realize her best friend is the one implicated.

By the end of a scene, the status quo should have changed. Scenes that don't provoke characters to look or move in a new direction, thinking of new possibilities, eager to try different options to reach their goals, haven't achieved one of their purposes.

Something must be different at the end of a scene. Some component in the story world must have changed, if only in the character's understanding of it. That is, the world may actually be no different, but the character may see that world in a different way once the scene plays out because she's gained new information or insight.

However, what the character learns doesn't have to be true or accurate. What the character discovers just has to change her outlook and direct her behavior.

ADVICE

If you discover you've written summaries rather than scenes, don't throw away all those summaries. Although novels are made of connected scenes, they also need exposition and narrative summary, the first to set up and conclude a story and to weave in back story when necessary, and the second for scene transitions, to quickly and efficiently move the story forward in time or to another location or both. Neither should take over the story or replace action and dialogue unfolding in real time, but they have their place.

Novels need narration—telling—at some points because not every event can be shown as a full scene. Not every event *needs* to play out as a scene. Sometimes readers need only the quick down-and-dirty of fact-filled summary.

A character thinking out a problem while sitting out on a back porch and watching the stars *can* be a scene. Yet pages of character thoughts on their own, with no action and no dialogue and no sense of setting and no passage of time, do not makes scenes. Think of the combination of characters, setting, action/event, and passage of time when you need a scene.

Make sure scenes have a purpose, preferably several.

Scenes, chapters, and individual fiction elements (setting, dialogue, action/event, and so on) should each accomplish a goal. Each is successful if it does what you intend for it to do. If it accomplishes multiple goals, even better.

There's no room for filler in a novel. Yes, novels may seem big and sprawling, but they shouldn't be unwieldy or feature trailing threads or pointless issues and useless elements. The parts should connect so that tugging or tightening one part creates a reaction in all the other parts, more in some than in others, depending on which thread you're tugging.

Use scenes to accomplish your story goals and to create a place for the other fiction elements to do their work. Use linked scenes to move your story from start to finish, to draw readers into the life of your characters. To give your characters a full life and a voice.

MORE THAN SCENES

I'm stressing scenes in this chapter, but novels need more than scenes in order to be fully fleshed out.

We've already seen that summary is important, but character contemplation is another ingredient necessary to balance out scenes and to help move a story forward.

Both scene snippets (a partial scene or a section of summary with scene details blended into it) and a transition between major scenes can show a character thinking about events that just happened (the last scene) or show her contemplating everything that's happened since a particular moment. This contemplation, while it may have the hallmarks of a scene—time, place, action—may have a purpose different from what happens in most full scenes.

This time of reflection is often referred to as a sequel.

Characters may need time to appreciate what happened in the most recent scene. That is, sometimes characters jump from event to event, reacting quickly to the unfolding events. But at other times characters need to think before they act.

Characters should always react to events—and large-scale events should produce fairly large reactions—but sometimes characters need to ponder and plan before they respond.

And sometimes characters simply need to feel. Feel the disappointment when what they expected didn't come to pass. Feel when they're betrayed. Feel when they're overwhelmed.

They even need to enjoy the feeling when something they attempt actually works out the way they hoped it would. Both failure and success should create emotional responses in characters.

Say that what a character tries in one scene doesn't accomplish what she expects to accomplish—what does she do next?

She may try something new. She may try the same approach again, perhaps from a different angle. Or she may go to another character known for his or her wisdom.

What's important at this point is knowing that you may have to include a line or two—even half a page or more—showing the character thinking and planning her response. You need to include the sequel to the scene.

Characters shouldn't always simply respond blindly, though that's a legitimate response at times. But at other times they need to experience an emotional response, rethink their plan because of recent events and their emotional response to them, and only then act on a decision or decisions made as they were thinking.

My point here is that while scenes make up a great percentage of a novel, there are other elements as well. And those other elements shouldn't include only action events but contemplation and response.

THE QUICK LIST

Make sure

- you've included true scenes and make sure those scenes serve a purpose, preferably multiple purposes.
- each scene contains conflict.
- that scenes don't all begin or end the same way—with the same words, in the same location, with the same character engaged in the same activity.
- you change scene order if doing so would create more conflict or a more engaging story.
- that you take the story out of a character's head, out of his memories, and show it unfolding in real time.
- scenes are of different lengths.
- scenes feature different combinations of characters (when possible).
- the major character in the scene is in a different place—mentally or emotionally—at the end of the scene.
- scenes have purpose and goals.

Part Four

GETTING SPECIFIC: A FEW DETAILED DETAILS

25

PUNCTUATION IN DIALOGUE‡

GIVEN THE ATTENTION this topic gets on my blog, I assume that writers are keen to punctuate dialogue correctly. Yet apparently punctuation in dialogue is one of the major bugaboos for writers. Still, if you'll be the copyeditor for your books, yours is the task to check dialogue punctuation. Unfortunately, corrections aren't self-generating—someone's got to go through the text line by line. If you know the rules ahead of time, however, it's likely you'll merely be looking for typos or for options for odd situations rather than trying to correct egregious errors.

I've provided examples of common rules and practices and recommend that you read through them before you begin editing. Give yourself an idea of what the rules are and what you should be looking for as you edit. And keep in mind the power of consistency. You may get a rule wrong, but it's better if you get it wrong in the same way throughout a story. If you don't know how to punctuate a particular condition, look for the information you lack. If you can't find the pertinent rule, at least be consistent with what you decide to use. That is, don't try a comma in one case and a semicolon in another and a period in another, not if the cases all meet the same conditions.

While some writers might say that punctuation isn't as important as plot or character development, most recognize that punctuation does affect the reader's impression of a story and his ease in getting through it.

Many readers follow punctuation just as easily as they do words and if the punctuation says something other than what you intend for it to say, you can confuse the reader or pull him out of the fiction.

> The punctuation rules and suggestions in this chapter are specifically for dialogue; the same rules may not apply for other text.

In general, these are rules for the use of both American
English (AmE) and British English (BrE). Where the
two differ, I point out the differences.

The rules are fairly straightforward, and the examples should serve
most of the situations you'll write.

IN GENERAL

Dialogue has its own rules for punctuation. Commas go in particular
places, as do terminal marks such as periods and question marks.

Only what is spoken is placed within quotation marks. Other parts
of the same sentence—dialogue tags and action or thought—go
outside the quotation marks.

Dialogue begins with a capitalized word, no matter where in the
sentence it starts. (Interrupted dialogue, when it resumes in the same
sentence, however, is not capped.)

Only direct dialogue requires quotation marks. Direct dialogue is
someone speaking; indirect dialogue is a report that someone spoke.
The word *that* is included or implied in indirect dialogue.

Direct: "She was a bore," he said.

Indirect: He said [that] she was a bore.

You need quotation marks around the spoken words—always double
quotation marks in AmE; usually singles but sometimes doubles in
BrE. Text quoted within a line of dialogue is set off by single quotation marks in AmE and doubles in BrE (or singles if the surrounding
dialogue uses double quotation marks).

Commas are necessary with dialogue tags. When the dialogue tag
comes before the dialogue, the comma that separates the tag from the
spoken words is outside the quotation marks. When the dialogue
comes first, the comma is inside the quotation marks. Other common
punctuation used in dialogue are the em dash and the ellipsis.

And that's it for the basics.

Let's look at examples that cover both common and unusual punctuation requirements in dialogue. The examples should address most situations you'll encounter with dialogue in fiction. If you can't find an example to match your text, see if one option doesn't come close to the general format of your dialogue.

SINGLE LINE OF DIALOGUE, NO DIALOGUE TAG, NO ACTION BEAT

The entire sentence, including the period (or question mark or exclamation point) is within the quotation marks.

> "He loved you."

> "He loved you!"

> "He loved *you*?"

SINGLE LINE WITH DIALOGUE TAG FOLLOWING

The dialogue is enclosed in quotation marks. A comma follows the dialogue and comes before the closing quotation mark. A period ends the sentence. The punctuation midsentence serves to separate the spoken words from other parts of the sentence.

Because the dialogue tag—*she said*—is part of the same sentence, it isn't capped.

> "He loved you," she said.

Some BrE style guides may suggest putting the comma *outside* the quotation mark if there's no comma in the quote itself before the dialogue tag is added, but that practice isn't always adhered to and is typically *not* followed with dialogue in modern fiction. So even when you follow BrE rules, keep this comma inside the closing quotation mark.

SINGLE LINE WITH DIALOGUE TAG FIRST

The comma still separates the dialogue tag from the spoken words, but it's outside the quotation marks, and the period at the end of the sentence is inside the quotation marks.

> She said, "He loved you."

SINGLE LINE OF DIALOGUE WITH DIALOGUE TAG AND ACTION FOLLOWING

The dialogue is enclosed in quotation marks. A comma follows the dialogue and comes before the closing quotation mark. The dialogue tag is next and the action follows the tag—no capital letter because this is part of the same sentence—with a period to end the sentence.

> "He loved you," she said, hoping Sue didn't hear her.
>
> "He loved you," she said, but she hoped Sue didn't hear her.
>
> "He loved you," she said, and hoped Sue didn't hear her.*
>
> "He loved you," she said and hoped Sue didn't hear her.*

The action and dialogue tag can also come first.

> Hoping Sue wouldn't hear, she said, "He loved you."

Or you can put just the tag first and the action after the dialogue.

> She said, "He loved you," and hoped Sue didn't hear her.

* In *Lapsing into a Comma*, Bill Walsh counsels against this construction. Yet Neal Whitman, a linguist, notes in an article at Grammar Girl that although this format creates a problem with parallelism, writers can still make use of it. I've noticed that fiction writers do use both versions freely. Still, you have options, as shown here.

MULTIPLE LINES OF DIALOGUE SEPARATED BY NON-DIALOGUE WORDS

Full sentences of thought, action, or description can come between two complete lines of dialogue. Treat each line of dialogue and the element that comes between them as separate sentences. Each begins with a capital letter and ends with a terminal punctuation mark.

> "He loved you." It was a truth my sister never understood. "I remember your excitement the first time he said the words."

> "He loved you." I shook my head, knowing Annie felt bad already. "I remember when he first told you."

A dialogue tag can be attached to one of the lines of dialogue. (There would be no need for both to contain a dialogue tag.) The tag is separated from its dialogue by a comma. The three sentences are still three full and separate sentences.

> "He loved you," I said. It was a truth Annie never understood. "I remember your reaction when he first told you."

DIALOGUE INTERRUPTED BY DIALOGUE TAG

Dialogue can be interrupted by a tag and then resume in the same sentence. Commas go inside the first set of quotation marks and after the dialogue tag (or action following the tag).

> "He loved you," she said, "but you didn't care."

> "He loved you," she said, hoping to provoke a reaction, "but you didn't care."

Separating this dialogue into two sentences also works. The first sentence will end with a period and the second will begin with a capital letter.

"He loved you," she said, hoping to provoke a reaction. "But you didn't care."

When a dialogue tag falls between two sections of dialogue, use the needs of the text to decide on the proper punctuation. If there's only one sentence without the tag, there should be only one sentence with the tag. If there are two sentences without the tag, there should still be two sentences when a tag is used.

"My dog ran away last night. We finally found him at Grandma's house."

"My dog ran away last night," Ellie said. "We finally found him at Grandma's house." √

"My dog ran away last night," Ellie said, "we finally found him at Grandma's house." ✗

* * *

"After Rover had a bath, he ran away."

"After Rover had a bath," Ellie said, "he ran away." √

"After Rover had a bath," Ellie said. "He ran away." ✗

QUESTIONS/EXCLAMATIONS, NO DIALOGUE TAG

Question marks and exclamation points go inside the quotation marks for questions and exclamations in dialogue.

"He loved you?"

"He loved you!"

QUESTIONS/EXCLAMATIONS WITH DIALOGUE TAG

Question marks and exclamation points go inside the quotation marks *when the dialogue itself is a question or exclamation.* They replace the comma when the dialogue tag follows the spoken words. Even when the question mark or exclamation point sits in the middle of the sentence, the dialogue tag that follows doesn't begin with a capital letter since it's part of the same sentence.

"He loved *you?*" she asked, the loathing clear in her voice and posture.

"He loved you!" she said, pointing a finger at Sally.

He asked, "What are you talking about?"

Pointing a finger at Sally, she said, "He loved you!"

QUESTIONS AND EXCLAMATIONS IN THE SENTENCE BUT NOT THE DIALOGUE

When a sentence is a question or exclamation but the dialogue (a quotation) within the sentence is not, the question mark and exclamation point go outside the quotation marks.

Can you believe he had the nerve to say, "I paid for your schooling, so you owe me alimony"?

* See *quote within dialogue paired with a question mark* (page 316) for a related construction.

DIALOGUE INTERRUPTED BY ACTION OR THOUGHT BUT NO DIALOGUE TAG

Characters can pause in their words to do something and then resume the dialogue. If there is no dialogue tag, special punctuation is required to set off the action or thought.

Enclose the first part of the dialogue in quotation marks (opening and closing) but omit the comma. Follow the end quotation mark with an em dash and then the action or thought and then another em dash. Resume the dialogue with another opening quotation mark, complete the dialogue (the first word is not capped when interrupted dialogue resumes), and end with a period and a closing quotation mark. There are no spaces between the quotation marks and the dashes or between the dashes and the action/thought.

The spoken words are within quotation marks and the action or thought is set off by the dashes.

> "He loved you"—she pounded the wall with a heavy fist—"but you never cared."

> "He loved you"—at least she thought he had—"but you never cared."

Compare this construction to a similar one without dialogue:

> He'd forgotten all about me—my heart ached at the thought—but I'd never forgotten him.

Be sure to interrupt at a logical/grammatical break point.

> "He loved"—at least she thought he had—"you, but you never cared." *X*

ACTION OR THOUGHT INTERRUPTED BY DIALOGUE

Admittedly, this format is rare. And in a full career of writing, you might never use it. Still, you *might* find you need it.

Enclose the dialogue in quotation marks and separate the spoken words from the rest of the sentence with em dashes.

> She crouched in front of the bottom cabinet—"It's in here somewhere, I think"—and began pulling out handfuls of junk.

QUOTE WITHIN DIALOGUE

In the same sentence, a character may speak his own dialogue and also quote what someone else has said. Punctuation is necessary to show which words belong to the speaker and which belong to the person the speaker is quoting.

The entirety of what a character says is enclosed by double quotation marks. The part the character is quoting from another person is enclosed by single quotation marks. (BrE may use this format or may reverse the quotation marks, singles for dialogue and doubles for the quote within the dialogue.)

When single and double quotation marks are side by side, put a space between them. (This *thin space* is typically a smaller space than a character space.)

> "He said, and I quote, 'The mailman loves you.'"

> "He said, 'The mailman loves you.' I heard it with my own ears."

If the character is quoting someone else but not speaking any of his or her own words, you don't need both sets of quotation marks; use only the outer ones. But for clarity's sake, make sure readers and other characters know that the character is quoting someone else.

> "What exactly did Monroe tell you? I need to know what he said without your snide commentary."

> Patty studied Lila's expression. Then she crossed her arms, took on Monroe's slouch, and said, "Lila wants more than I want. She's okay to hang around with, but I can feel the noose tightening."

Compare to

> Patty studied Lila's expression. Then she crossed her arms and took on Monroe's slouch. "He said, 'Lila wants more than I want. She's okay to hang around with, but I can feel the noose tightening.'"

Indirect dialogue for a character quoting someone else would also work. Don't use quotation marks for an indirect quote.

"He said the mailman loves you. I heard it with my
own ears."

Direct and indirect dialogue emphasize different elements, so choose
the one that works best for what you want to convey.

*QUOTE WITHIN DIALOGUE PAIRED WITH A QUESTION MARK

Quotes within dialogue—with the quote, the dialogue, or both as a
question—have their own rules. (You'll have two sets of quotation
marks, and you must open and close both of them.)

Only the quotation is a question

Put the question mark for the quotation inside all quotation marks.
Use a thin space between the single and double quotation marks.

"He asked my name. And then he asked, 'Do you
think your mother would go out with me?' "

Only the dialogue is a question

Put the question mark between the sets of closing quotation marks.

"Do you think he was lying when he said, 'I lost my
key and my wallet'?"

Both the quotation and the dialogue are questions

Put the question mark (just one) inside all quotation marks. Use a thin
space between the single and double quotation marks.

"Do you think he was serious when he said, 'Would
you be upset if I asked your mother for a date?' "

Some sources allow for two question marks in BrE in this last
example. Yet one question mark is sufficient.

DIALOGUE ABRUPTLY CUT OFF

When dialogue is cut off—the character can no longer speak, something suddenly diverts his attention, another character interrupts him, or he interrupts himself—use an em dash before the closing quotation mark. Dialogue can be interrupted midword or at the end of a word. Consider the sounds of words and syllables before deciding where to break the interrupted word: you wouldn't break the word *there* after the *T* (t—), because the first sound comes from the combined *th* (th—).

> "He loved y—"

> "He loved you—"

> "How did it hap—"

> "How did it hap—?"

> "But I didn't tell Maisie—" she began.

These are all acceptable ways to punctuate interrupted dialogue. Personally, I don't like the question mark because the question is unfinished. We don't include a period for interrupted dialogue, so why include a question mark? The fact that the line of dialogue would have been a question is quite clear.

I also don't particularly care for the explanation tacked on to the final example (*she began*). It's a legitimate option, yet readers can tell that the character's speech was interrupted; there's no need to point out that fact. Still, this construction is used often and you might have a need for it.

Dialogue abruptly cut off by another speaker

When a second speaker interrupts the first, one option is to use the em dash where the first speaker's words are interrupted and again where they resume.

"He loved you—"

"As if I could believe that."

"—for such a long, long time."

But this isn't the only option. The first speaker might resume speaking at the same point, but she might not.

"He loved you—"

"As if I could believe that."

"Why do you always do that, jump in before I finish?"

Dialogue abruptly cut off by the character himself

When a character isn't interrupted but cuts himself off, you have several options for what follows.

He can cut himself off and then begin doing something else, including thinking.

"I told you I needed to s—" He slammed both fists to the table.

"I told you I needed to s—" He suddenly remembered his sons were listening.

He can cut himself off and then resume speaking without showing what interrupted him. This construction is fairly uncommon.

"I told you I needed to s—Never mind."

DIALOGUE THAT TRAILS OFF

When dialogue trails off—the character has lost his train of thought, is overcome with emotion, doesn't know what to say, or the writer wants to indicate hesitation—use the ellipsis. (Note that there is no space between the final ellipsis point and the closing quotation mark in the first and fourth examples and no space after the second opening quotation mark in the fourth example. Note too the capitalization of some words immediately after the ellipsis. A capital letter indicates the beginning of a new sentence.)

"He loved you . . ." A long time ago, she thought.

"He loved you . . . He loves you still."

"He was lost in the . . . lost in the mine."

"I'd really wanted to be the one to do it, you know. To reach out and . . ." She wiped away a tear. ". . . tell her what an angel her mother was."

Dialogue that trails off and is followed by the dialogue of another character before it resumes

Try something like this when you want a dreamy quality to the first character's dialogue, as though she's unaware of the other character even speaking.

"She wanted to tell you, but she . . ."

"I know. She didn't want to break my heart."

". . . she thought it would kill you."

Dialogue completed or continued by other characters

"It was too bad, 'cause I really liked Mookie. The punk was . . ."

". . . a lost soul . . ."

". . . a squealer . . ."

". . . a rat . . ."

". . . a punky, squealing, rat," the boss said, summing up the group's take on their former cohort.

Note[1]: In AmE, an ellipsis begins with a space, ends with a space, and has spaces between each of the three points (. . .). However, an ellipsis that butts up against a quotation mark loses the space closest to the quotation mark.

In BrE, there are typically no spaces between the ellipsis points, though there are still spaces on both ends (...)

Note[2]: Use nonbreaking spaces in an ellipsis so the ellipsis doesn't break at the ends of lines. In MS Word, use CTRL+SHIFT+SPACEBAR to create nonbreaking spaces. (You can use Autocorrect to create an ellipsis with the proper spacing.)

SHOWING ONE-SIDED DIALOGUE

To show that a character is speaking and listening to another when you don't want to show the spoken words of both characters, use an ellipsis to indicate when the second character is speaking.

This construction can make a sentence look like it contains a four-point ellipsis, but the first point is actually the period at the end of the first character's words. Because the first point is a period, it goes next to the last letter of the final word of the sentence (no space).

> Markie ran to answer the phone, but she sighed when she saw her mother's name in the display.
>
> "Hi, Mom. . . . Just finishing breakfast. . . . No, he left a long time ago. He had to take his car to the stupid shop. . . . I wish you'd told me before so I could've asked him. . . . No, I won't. If I ask now, he'll know you told me, so that's not gonna happen. . . . No, Mom. . . . But I can't. . . . Okay, okay. I'll make it happen. Gotta go."

NAMES IN DIALOGUE

Always use a comma before and/or after the name (if a terminal punctuation mark doesn't follow the name) when directly addressing someone in dialogue (even if the name isn't a proper name). This doesn't mean you need a comma before or after *every* name. Just the name of the character being addressed.

"He loved you, Emma."

"Emma, he loved you."

"He loved you, honey."

"He loved you, Emma, more than he loved Sally."

"He loved you more than he loved, Sally." ✗

MULTIPLE LINES OF DIALOGUE

Multiple lines of *uninterrupted* dialogue go within the same set of quotation marks. Don't use separate quotation marks for each.

> "You know she isn't one to spill her guts. But after three beers, she told me all about her breakup with John. After a fourth beer, she told me about her first marriage. After the fifth beer, she told me about the body in the cellar."

> "You know she isn't one to spill her guts." "But after three beers, she told me all about her breakup with John." "After a fifth beer, she told me about the body in the cellar." ✗

For a paragraph with several sentences of dialogue, put the dialogue tag, if you use one, at the end of the first sentence or at the end of a logical break within the first sentence. The tags are for readers, to help them keep track of the speaker. A tag lost in the middle or hiding at the end of the paragraph doesn't help the reader at the top of the paragraph.

This isn't an absolute rule, of course. Sometimes the feel or rhythm requires a different construction. But you can use this rule to keep your readers on track. If a group of guys is talking, the reader might guess who's speaking, but there's nothing wrong with helping out the reader.

> "I wanted to know if James had planned to go to the game. He wasn't sure, said he had to ask his wife. Thank God I don't have to ask permission of a wife. None of that ball and chain stuff for me, no sir. I go where I want, when I want. Yep, freedom," Maxwell said. "Nothing beats freedom."

> "I wanted to know if James had planned to go to the game," Maxwell said. "He wasn't sure, said he had to ask his wife. Thank God I don't have to ask permission of a wife. None of that ball and chain stuff for me, no sir. I go where I want, when I want. Yep, freedom. Nothing beats freedom."

If the speaker addresses two people at different times in the same paragraph of dialogue, you can add a second dialogue tag or action beat if necessary to show that the speaker is talking to someone else. If you can make the change of focus clear in the dialogue itself, try that first.

> "I wanted to know if James had planned to go to the game," Maxwell said to me, finger pointing. "He wasn't sure, said he had to ask his wife. Thank God I don't have to ask permission of a wife. None of that ball and chain stuff for me, no sir. I go where I want, when I want. Ain't that right, Lucius?" He turned to the cabbie. "You and me don't have to put up with that crap. Yep, freedom. Nothing beats freedom."

MULTIPLE PARAGRAPHS OF DIALOGUE

Dialogue may stretch across paragraphs without pause. To punctuate, put a terminal punctuation mark—period, exclamation point, or question mark—at the end of the first paragraph. There is no closing quotation mark at the end of this paragraph.

Begin the next paragraph with an opening quotation mark.

Follow this pattern for as long as the dialogue and paragraphs continue. At the last paragraph, use a closing quotation mark at the end of the dialogue.

> "He was my best friend. I told you that, didn't I? And then he stabbed me in the back. Stole my wife and my future. I hated him for that. Still do. Hate him bad.
>
> "But he's been punished, yes he has. He went to jail for embezzling thousands. Not even millions, just thousands. Serves him right, the petty crook. He's just a petty man."

CHANGING SPEAKERS

Begin a new paragraph each time the speaker changes.

> She looked up at the man hovering over her. "I'd wanted to tell you for years. I just didn't know how."
>
> "We've been married for thirty-four years, Alice. You couldn't find a way, in *thirty-four* years of living together and seeing each other sixteen hours a day, to tell me you were already married?"
>
> "I'm sorry."

> Exception: You could include a back-and-forth dialogue between characters in a single paragraph as a style choice, but each speaker's sentences would typically be brief and you wouldn't want the paragraph to go on for too long. Keep in mind your readers' expectations—they expect to find only one character's words in a paragraph.

Another exception is dialogue from unnamed characters in a group or a crowd. Comments from these characters could go in the same paragraph or even the same sentence.

> The most strident voices could be heard shouting their disapproval. "Fire the bum!" "Take back his bonus." "Buy the loser some glasses."

MIXING DIALOGUE WITH NARRATION IN THE SAME PARAGRAPH

Dialogue and narration *can* be placed into the same paragraph. If the narration refers to the speaker or is in his or her point of view, simply add the dialogue. Dialogue can go at the beginning, in the middle, or at the end of the paragraph.

If the narration refers to several characters or you can't tell which character is the focus of the narration, begin the dialogue with a new paragraph and a dialogue tag. That is, don't make the reader guess who's speaking.

If the paragraph opens with a wide view of a group of people but then the focus narrows to a single character, you could introduce that character's dialogue into the end of that same paragraph. Or you could begin a new paragraph with the dialogue. What's important is keeping the reader in the flow of the story. Confusion over dialogue will pull the reader out of the fictional world.

> Rachael was a beautiful woman; she'd been told so since the day she turned sixteen. And at forty-two, she decided she was just entering her prime. She stared at herself in the mirror, patted her hair, and grinned at the man watching her reflection with her. "I still got it, don't I, baby?"
>
> He reached for her shoulders. "And I love every inch of the it you've got."

* * *

Rachael was a beautiful woman; she'd been told so since the day she turned sixteen. At forty-two, she was determined to see herself as the ingénue. Carl wanted to tell her she was now more femme fatale than ingénue, and that was all right by him.

"I still got it, don't I, baby?" she asked his reflection.

"More than ever, honey."

* * *

Rachael was a beautiful woman; she'd been told so since the day she turned sixteen. At forty-two, she was determined to see herself as the ingénue. "You're stunning, sweetheart," Carl said, pausing by the dressing table. He wanted to tell her she was now more femme fatale than ingénue, that she turned him on more than she had as a younger version of herself. But Rachael was not only beautiful, she was touchy. And being reminded of her age wouldn't keep her happy.

Carl was all about keeping Rachael happy.

"Simply stunning," he said again.

Dialogue tags *can* come before the spoken part of the dialogue itself, especially if you want the dialogue tag to be noticed. While acceptable, this construction is used less frequently. To hide tags, put them in the middle or at the end of sentences. You will typically—but not always—want the dialogue and not the tag to stand out.

INTERNAL MONOLOGUE

Characters both think and talk to themselves. To differentiate between spoken words and thoughts, we put only spoken words inside quotation marks. For thoughts, there are a couple of options.

At one time almost all thought and inner monologue—with characters in third-person narratives directing words to themselves—was written in italics. Yet with the use of deep POV, we have less need for italics. Readers know that the character is thinking or speaking to herself, so there's no reason to use italics or punctuation to highlight that fact. As is true for first-person narration, thoughts are attributed to the viewpoint character. With first-person narration and deep POV in third, italics can be overkill.

How about a couple of examples?

> Denise pushed her way through the bolts of hideous cloth. **Geez, whoever chose those fabrics had a serious problem matching colors**.

> I pushed my way through the bolts of hideous cloth. **Geez, whoever chose those fabrics had a serious problem matching colors**.

This thought, in both first and third person, obviously belongs to the viewpoint character/narrator. The thought requires no additional punctuation for clarity.

Use this construction in a story with a close narrative distance or to help create that close distance.

Add a thought tag to create a greater narrative distance. (There's no reason to include a thought tag in first-person narration. Do use a thought tag for omniscient to signal that readers are now getting a thought from a character rather than from the omniscient narrator.)

> Denise weaved her way through the bolts of ugly cloth. Whoever chose those fabrics, **she thought,** had a serious problem matching colors.

In a story with even greater narrative distance, you could use italics for thoughts. Note, however, that the use of italics can become obtrusive. You may want to limit italics to thought-talk directed *at* the character, when she's actually talking to herself, not simply thinking to herself.

You *can* switch to present tense and to first person for thoughts and internal monologue in stories that use the past tense and third-person narration. This can create a true feel of a character speaking to himself. Let's look at a few options.

> **#1** Nan studied the statue that couldn't have moved. She must have lost her mind.

This first example uses a close narrative distance. It's a common construction and used often with deep POV.

> **#2** Nan studied the statue that couldn't have moved. She must have lost her mind, she thought.

Example #2, by using the thought tag, creates a greater narrative distance than #1. It's also a common construction. The problem with this construction is that if the viewpoint character really was thinking to herself, she wouldn't refer to herself as *she* but as *I*.

> **#3** Nan studied the statue that couldn't have moved. *I must have lost my mind*, she thought.

It's not as common to pair past tense and italics for thoughts (since one reason to include thoughts is to show what the character is currently thinking), but a character can refer to something from her past using this construction.

> **#4** Nan studied the statue that couldn't have moved. *I must be losing my mind*, she thought.

Example #4 creates greater narrative distance than example #1. Still, this is a common construction.

> **#5** Nan studied the statue that couldn't have moved. *I must have lost my mind.*

Because this example uses past tense for the thought, it's not as common a construction as some others, but it's not unheard of.

#6 Nan studied the statue that couldn't have moved. *I must be losing my mind.*

Using italics without a thought tag is common, maybe increasingly so. This construction is not as distancing as is #4 with its thought tag.

#7 Nan studied the statue that couldn't have moved. I must be losing my mind, she thought.

Using the thought tag without italics for a first-person present-tense thought in a third-person POV used to be an uncommon construction, but it's being used more often. Still, that switch to first person without the visual of italics could be jarring for readers, at least the first couple of times it happens.

#8 Nan studied the statue that couldn't have moved. I must be losing my mind.

This first-person present-tense thought—no italics *or* thought tag—is still fairly uncommon when paired with a third-person POV, but I have seen it used. Still, this is a construction that could definitely confuse readers. Most writers would never use this construction.

#9 Nan studied the statue that couldn't have moved on its own. She'd lost her mind. Knew it would happen one day.

This last example is a variation of #1.

The switch to present tense and first person for thoughts or self-directed dialogue in third-person present-tense stories is most often paired with italics and/or with a thought tag (#s 4, 6, and 7) so readers aren't confused by the switch from third to first or the switch from past to present.

Yet there is that seeming trend—or maybe it's just experimentation—that allows for no tag and no italics while switching to first person present tense in a character's thoughts (#8). But readers could easily become confused when narration switches from past to present or a third-person story suddenly seems to flip to first person.

For a tight narrative distance, try option #1. Allow thoughts (in third-person narration) to flow with the rest of the text without you pausing those thoughts to tell readers that the character is thinking or talking to herself. This helps the reader to hear the thought as a thought rather than as a report about a thought.

If you're using or want to create a wider narrative distance, use italics or thought tags or both.

If you're game to try them, give #7 or #8 a shot. Just make sure that you set up the unusual style right from the beginning of the story so readers get used to it. You may want to limit this option to stories with only a single viewpoint character (or perhaps two).

Talking Mind to Mind

If you've got characters who can mind-talk, that's one more twist to add to the dialogue mix.

Try italics and thought tags for dialogue between minds. Yet if you use italics for this purpose, don't also use italics for a character's regular thoughts unless readers will be able to differentiate between the two. Instead, use thoughts folded into the text, as in examples #1 and #9, for the standard thoughts. Or if the distance created by a thought tag doesn't matter, try pairing regular thoughts using the pattern in examples #2 or #7 with your italicized mind-talk.

The point here is that you want readers to instantly know whether they're hearing a character's thoughts directed to himself or to others who can also hear him. And that means that you have to create different setups for each scenario.

We won't explore the conundrum of how characters can refrain from broadcasting all their thoughts to all other characters who can hear them. We won't wonder what mechanism they use to shut off their thoughts so others don't hear everything they're thinking rather than only the thoughts directed toward the other character. (Although this is an issue you may realistically need to deal with in your fiction.)

And we won't figure out the mechanism mind-talkers use to broadcast thoughts at the same time to all others who can mind-talk, similar to an old-fashioned telephone party line.

Other topics we won't be able to explore in this book? If multiple characters can mind-talk, how does a character send thoughts to only one of them, without others overhearing? And just how far can a mind-talker send his thoughts? Does the other character have to be in the same room? The same building? The same time period?

And can the character receiving the thoughts block them, or must he interrupt what he's already doing, thinking, or saying to listen to the thoughts being beamed his way?

And how does the one sending the thoughts know that the other character received them? How does that first character even know where to send the thoughts? How does mind-talk travel to one particular mind-talker but not another? Are we assuming something like IP addresses for each mind?

Definitely some issues to explore. But for now let's turn to a topic with more certainty—writing numbers in fiction.

26

NUMBERS IN FICTION‡

WE'VE GOT RULES and standards for everything in our novels and short stories—how to start those stories, how to increase tension, how to introduce characters, how to format, what to include in dialogue, how to punctuate dialogue, what to exclude from the first chapter, what to include in the ending, what to always include, and what to never include. And we have rules for numbers. Or maybe we should call these rules *conventions*.

This chapter covers specifics for using numbers and numerals in fiction. I'm going to list the conventions without much explanation, laying out those that you'll typically make use of in a novel. Keep in mind that there are always exceptions, yet for the most part, you'll want to stick to the standards to make the read smooth and easy for the reader *and* to create consistency within the manuscript.

Still, we're talking fiction here, not a treatise or dissertation. You have choices. And style choices sometimes get to stomp all over the rules. If you want to flout the rules, do so for a reason and do so consistently every time that same reason is applicable.

For a comprehensive list of the rules concerning numbers, check out *The Chicago Manual of Style* or another style guide.

GENERAL RULES

> Spell out numbers from zero through one hundred.

You could argue for spelling numbers from zero through nine, as is recommended for AP style (see the *Associated Press Stylebook*), but note that AP style is primarily for newspapers, magazines, and nonfiction works (such as this book). Rules are different for fiction.

You could also make a style choice to spell out almost all numbers, even if that choice conflicts with other rules. If you spell most numbers, be consistent with your exceptions.

Use numerals for most numbers beyond one hundred. While this is the standard, there are definitely exceptions to this one. But first, a few examples of this two-part basic rule—

The witch offered Snow White one crisp, dewy apple.

Suzie sang thirty-five songs before her voice gave out.

The rock-a-thon lasted for just over 113 hours.

The witch offered Snow White 1 crisp, dewy apple. *X*

Spell out whole numbers from 0 to 100 even if they're followed by hundred, thousand, hundred thousand, million, billion, and trillion. (See the money section for an exception.)

Your characters may have reason to say or think all manner of odd numbers, so yes, something like *zero thousand* might be needed.

The forces at Wilmington were bolstered by the arrival of ten thousand fresh soldiers.

The knight had died four hundred years earlier.

[but] The knight had died 418 years earlier.

* * *

"How many thousands of lies have you told?"

"I've told *zero* thousand, you fool."

Spell out ordinal numbers through one hundred as well.

That was the fiftieth time the phone rang.

Use full-size letters, not superscript (st), to mark ordinal numbers (st, nd, rd, th) written as numerals.

We follow these two rules about ordinals even for military units and street names.

So we write the 101st Airborne Division but the Eighty-second Airborne Division. Note that newspapers and military publications may have different conventions.

A restaurant would be on Fifth Avenue, not 5th Avenue. Or the restaurant is on 129th Street, not One Hundred Twenty-ninth Street.

Use *first*, *second*, *third* and so on rather than *firstly*, *secondly*, *thirdly* unless your character would use this odd construction as part of her style.

Spell out numbers that start a sentence. If spelling creates awkward wording, rewrite.

> One hundred and fifteen [not 115] waiters applied for the job.

> Although a traditional rule tells us not to use *and* with whole numbers (especially dollar amounts) that are spelled out, keep your characters in mind. Many people add the *and* in both thought and speech, especially after *hundred* or *thousand*. Once again, fiction allows us different rules. Use wording your characters would use.

Hyphenate compound numbers from twenty-one to ninety-nine. Do this when the number is used alone or in combination with other numbers. (But only when the number should be spelled out.)

> Louise owned forty-one cars.

> "I heard that Sasha bought one hundred and thirty-five diamond rings."

> Sasha bought 135 diamond rings.

> For an easier read when numbers are written side by side, write one as a numeral and the other as a word.

He made 5 one-hundred-pound cakes.

We lashed twelve 6-foot ladders together.

> When two numbers in a sentence refer to the same category, spell out both or use numerals for both, even if one is equal to or less than 100 and the other greater than.

One of his dogs weighed thirty pounds and another weighed one twenty.

The first company had been in business for over 130 years and the second for 75 years.

One of his dogs weighed thirty pounds and another weighed 120. *X*

> Spell out simple fractions and hyphenate them.

He took only one-half of yesterday's vote.

He needed a two-thirds majority to win the election.

> Use numerals for percent (except in dialogue and at the beginning of sentences). *Per cent* is the usual BrE spelling, but *percent* is often used.

The technician checked the stats; 62 percent of the members hadn't responded.

He told me he added 12 percent to the total.

"He told me he added twelve percent to the total."

Twelve percent seemed a lot to me, and I told him so.

Use words rather than symbols in dialogue and in most narrative. Symbols are a visual representation, a type of shorthand. But characters need to think and speak the words.

Use the words rather than the symbols for degree (°) and percent (%) and number (#), both in dialogue and narrative. Use the word *dollar* rather than the dollar sign ($) in dialogue. Don't abbreviate the words *pounds* or *ounces, feet* or *inches* (or *yards*), *hours* or *minutes* or *seconds*, or *miles per hour* (or similar words) in dialogue or narrative.

An exception might include something like stretches of text where you note the changing speeds of a car but don't want to repeat *miles per hour* again and again. Your use of *mph* becomes a style choice. Yet you wouldn't use *mph* in dialogue unless the character was saying the letters *m-p-h* and not *miles per hour*.

You can, of course, use symbols in titles and datelines. (Datelines are akin to scene or chapter subheadings. They contain details of date and place: Jakarta, October 25; New Jupiter, 20 hours after initial terraforming.) In geopolitical thrillers, datelines might include longitude and latitude, and the degree symbol might be a useful shortcut.

If you include full compass coordinates in the narrative, using numerals and the symbols for degrees, minutes, and seconds could be the best choice in terms of clarity and ease of reading, but try words first. Not every reader will understand the symbols.

"But I don't have a million dollars."

"Nobody gave a hundred percent."

"The baby weighed seven pounds eleven ounces."

"It's fourteen degrees out there!"

The # of crimes he'd committed kept rising. ✗

The chasm looked at least 40 ft. wide. ✗

The roadster crept along at no more than 28 mph. ✗

You're writing fiction, so consider visual flow along with the flow of words and sentences. Use options that will make sense to readers and keep them from tripping over your style choices.

TIME

> Except in dialogue, use numerals when you include a.m. and p.m. But you don't *have* to use a.m. and p.m.

> Use lower case letters with periods or small caps without periods for a.m. and p.m. (a.m. and p.m. or AM and PM).

> Include a space between the numbers and a.m. or p.m., but no space within a.m. or p.m.

It was 5:43 a.m. when he got me out of bed.

It was five forty-three a.m. ✗

[but] "It's five forty-three *A-bleeping-M!*"

> Spell out numbers when you include *o'clock*.

But he did wait until after five o'clock to call.

> Use noon and midnight rather than 12:00.

It's too easy to introduce confusion by using 12:00. If you need straight up twelve o'clock, say noon or midnight.

> Use numerals to emphasize exact-to-the-minute times, except in dialogue.

She pointed out that it was still 5:43 in the morning.

"It's four forty-three." She looked out into the darkness. "In the morning!"

The robbery took place at 2:22 a.m.

> Spell out words for the hour, quarter hour, and half hour.

The hall clock was wrong; it showed eight thirty. No, it showed eight forty-five.

> Don't use a hyphen to join hours and minutes.

I've seen advice on a few internet sites that suggests you use a hyphen to join hours and minutes except when the minutes are already hyphenated. So they'd have you write *two-twenty* but *two twenty-five,* which makes no sense. Skip the hyphen between the hour and the minutes. (And always check multiple forums and sites for advice.)

It was four-forty-five. ✗

It was four forty-five.

The bomb went off at eleven-thirty. ✗

The bomb went off at eleven thirty.

While we normally would never use both *o'clock* and *a.m.* or *p.m.* and typically don't use o*'clock* with anything other than the hour, fiction has needs other writing doesn't, and you may have to adapt the rules to fit your circumstances. The following might very well come out of a character's mouth or thoughts—

It was five o'clock in the a.m.

"Mommy, is it four thirty o'clock yet?"

DATES

Dates can be written a number of ways.

The twenty-fifth of December, 25 December (BrE), December 25 (AmE), 25 December 2019 (BrE), December 25, 2019 (AmE), and the twenty-fifth are all valid options. December 25th and December 25th, 2019, are incorrect—see the first rule listed here. (Note that a comma follows the year when a date falls midsentence.)

> Don't include an ordinal indicator (*st, nd, rd,* or *th,*) for dates that use the month in the format of the last two of the previous examples.

You can, however, write the twenty-fifth of December.

December 25 and December 25, 2015, would both be pronounced as the ordinal, even though the *th* is not written.

There is an exception for dialogue.

"Your kids can't wait for December twenty-fifth."

> Don't use a hyphen (actually, we use an en dash between numbers) for a range of dates that begins with the words *from* or *between.*

This rule is true of all numbers, not just dates, arranged this way. Use the words *to, through* or *until* with *from,* and pair *and* with *between.*

He'll be out of town **from** April 15-May 5. ✗

He'll be out of town **from** April 15 **to** May 5.

He'll be out of town **between** April 15-May 5. ✗

He'll be out of town **between** April 15 **and** May 5.

He'll be out of town April 15-May 5.

> Use numerals for years in both dialogue and narration.

Had Carter been born in 1909? "I think it was 1909."

Decades can be written as words or numbers (four- or two-digit years). Unless a reference is to a named era or age—the Roaring Twenties—don't capitalize the decade.

The cars from the thirties are more than classics.

Cars of the 1930s were my dad's favorites.

The teacher played songs from the '60s and '70s to get the crowd in the right mood. (The punctuation is an apostrophe, not an opening quotation mark.)

For decades, don't use an apostrophe between the year and the letter *S* except for a possessive.

The doctor gave up smoking back in the 1980's. *X*

The doctor gave up smoking back in the 1980s.

The doctor gave up smoking back in the '80's. *X*

The doctor gave up smoking back in the '80s.

[but] She claimed that her uncle was the '20s' [or the twenties'] most notorious mobster.

Spell out century references.

He wanted to know if the uprising had happened in the eighteenth or the nineteenth century. When the guide reminded him it had been the seventeen hundreds, he was even more confused.

Adding *mid* to date terms can be confusing. The general rule is that *mid*, as a prefix, doesn't get a hyphen. The same rules apply for other prefixes, such as *pre* or *post*, that can be used with date words.

So midyear, midcentury, midterm, midmonth, and midthirties are all correct. There are, however, exceptions.

Include a hyphen before a capital letter. Thus, mid-October.

Include a hyphen before a numeral. Thus, mid-1880s.

Include a hyphen before compounds (hyphenated or open). Thus, mid-nineteenth century and mid-fourteenth-century lore.

The Chicago Manual of Style has a comprehensive section on hyphenation. I recommend it without reservation.

Broad eras include BC (before Christ) and AD (in the year of the Lord), or BCE (before the Common Era) and CE (of the Common Era). All era abbreviations follow the numeral except for AD, which precedes it.

The notation said the tomb had first been opened in 36 BC. Reynolds opened it again in AD 324.

DIALOGUE

Spell out numbers in dialogue.

When a character speaks, the reader should hear what he says. A reminder: Although a traditional rule tells us not to use *and* with whole numbers that are spelled out, keep your character in mind. Many people add the *and* in both words and thoughts. Once again, the rules are different for fiction.

"I collect candlesticks. At last count I had more than a hundred and forty."

"At last count I had more than one forty."

"She gave her all, 24/7." ✗

"She gave her all, twenty-four seven."

One exception to this rule is years. You *can* spell out years, and you'd definitely want to if your character has an unusual pronunciation of them. But using numerals for years in dialogue is a common practice.

"He said the land passed out of the family in 1942."

"I thought it was fifty-two?"

"I thought it was '52?"

A second exception would be for a confusing number or a long series of numbers. Again, if you want readers to *hear* the character saying the number, spell it out; even common numbers might be spoken differently. One character might say *eleven hundred dollars* while another says *one thousand one hundred dollars*.

If you must include a full telephone number—maybe because a detail about the digits is vital for the plot—use numerals, even in dialogue. (But if you want to emphasize the way the numbers are spoken, spell out the numbers.)

You'd use numerals rather than words because writing seven or ten words for the numbers would be cumbersome. But most of the time there would be no reason to write out a full phone number.

> Write product and brand names as well as titles as they're spelled, even if they contain numbers. For example, 7-Eleven, Super 8 (the hotel chain), 7UP.

HEIGHTS

> Heights can be written in a variety of ways.

He was six feet two inches tall.

He was six feet two.

He was six foot two.

He was six two.

He was six-two. ✗ (This is a recommendation from some sources, although not one I'd make.)

MONEY

For the most part, treat money amounts the same way you do other numbers.

He needed sixty dollars for the bar tab.

He needed $59.28 for the bar tab.

I gave him the twenty-eight cents.

She owed her mother fifteen hundred.

Libby handed over $475 for her share of the rent.

"He told me the pizza cost him thirty-two dollars and nineteen cents."

For dollar amounts of a million or more that would otherwise be written as numerals rather than words, pair the numerals with the words *million*, *billion*, and *trillion* rather than writing the full number as a numeral.

Writing out large money amounts with a mix of numerals and words keeps the numbers easy to read. An amount written as $118 billion is easier to grasp at a glance than $118,000,000,000 would be.

The state's debt would soon exceed $120 billion.

Money and currencies have changed over time. Be sure to check facts about money if your story is set in a time period other than the present or in a country other than those you're familiar with.

WEAPONS AND GUNS

For the most part, stick with the rules governing numbers when you write about weapons. Keep in mind your speaker's or viewpoint character's familiarity with weapons. One character might know every detail about a weapon while another calls every weapon a gun.

Use only the necessary detail. For example, in fiction you might not often have cause to write *The AH-64D Apache Longbow was the team's first choice.* Instead, you might write, *The Longbow was the team's first choice.* Yet before this moment in the story, you might have needed to list the equipment available to the characters, writing out the full name of several helicopters.

As with any detail, use only what the viewpoint character or the character who is speaking would know. If the character wouldn't know make or model, use other details to describe weapons and guns.

> In both narrative and dialogue, if you use the name of the gun or ammo, spell it as the manufacturer does, including numerals and capital letters. Do the same for military weapons and tanks. Spell out the word *caliber.*

If you don't use the full name, still capitalize brands and manufacturers. The designation *mm* is accepted in narrative but not dialogue.

> He eyed the .357 Magnum in the loser's shaky hand.

> Anderson's Colt .38 was under his pillow, two rooms down the hall.

> Both the Browning 9mm, his favorite, and his stacked salami sub, another favorite, were flattened by the junkyard's car crusher.

> I knew she'd lied when she told me the M1 Abrams had been named for her dad; he was much too young.

In dialogue, if the character is saying a variation of the name but not the name itself, you have options. Use words when doing so isn't convoluted or cumbersome or unclear.

> "Dirty Harry always used a forty-four, never a three fifty-seven."

* * *

> "How would I know? Thirty-aught-six, thirty-aught-seven. What's the difference anyway?"

* * *

> "What was it? A nine millimeter?"
>
> "A Glock 17 Compensated. New and shiny."

NUMBERS USED FOR IDENTIFICATION

Numbers used for identification—for rooms, floors, buildings, TV channels, dorms, interstates/routes, districts, versions, episodes, sessions, (TV) seasons, chapters, pages, and the like—are typically written as numerals rather than words.

We write building 17, room 415, chapter 4, Lassiter 122 [dorm room], page 13, Route 66, and Channel 12. These become names, of a sort.

So what about dialogue? Does the rule for writing out numbers in dialogue trump this rule? You could argue that it does, at least in some cases. Maybe in most. We'd write Route 66 in dialogue, but for building or page numbers, you have leeway. Most people aren't going to consider a version number a name the same way they'd consider Route 66 or Channel 4 a name.

You could argue for spelling out certain of these—rooms, floors, buildings, episodes, chapter and page numbers, and even versions—in dialogue (as a style choice) if you like the way the spelling looks and especially if you're using multiples of them.

Consider the following.

"What were you doing?"

"Nothing important. Just checking out chapters ten and eleven again."

* * *

"Taking the device apart invalidates the warranty on versions two, five, and six. But you can get a replacement for versions three and four."

But

"He pulled onto Route 1, and I lost him."

"I know. Channel 5 showed the whole thing."

Whether you use numerals or you spell out the words as a style choice, you'll want to be consistent. Not necessarily consistent for the identification category as a whole, but at least for your exceptions.

So if you decided that only TV channels and route numbers had to adhere to the rule but all other numbers could be written as words, that's a valid choice. You may also want to consider spelling some identification numbers—chapter five, page two—in narrative as well.

PUNCTUATION

No commas or hyphens between hours and minutes, feet and inches, pounds and ounces, and dollars and cents when they're spelled out. If the meaning is unclear, rewrite.

Ben promised to be there at four thirty, but it was six twenty when he pulled into the driveway.

At seven feet three inches, he was the shortest of the Marchesa giants.

The piece of salmon weighed one pound eleven ounces, but they charged the rude customer the price for three pounds.

"He owed his boss forty-two dollars and fifty cents."

> Use hyphens for compound adjectives containing numbers the same way other compounds are created; they're hyphenated as an adjective before a noun. In addition, they're usually hyphenated as nouns.

A two-inch hole in the street became a six-by-six-foot car-swallowing crater.

My two-year-old loves puppies.

My son has a two-year-old puppy.

[but] My puppy is two years old.

> No hyphen between numbers and *percent*.

He claimed to give 125 percent of his salary to charity.

The drink was 20-percent beer. ✗

"The drink was sixty percent beer. The rest was nasty tap water."

> For multiple hyphenated numbers sharing a noun, include a hyphen and a space after the first number and hyphenate the last as usual.

This is not an inclusive range but two (or more) discrete groups.

Our Johnny couldn't wait to tell us about the ten- and twenty-foot-tall monsters in the yard.

His sister shared details about the two-, three-, and four-headed versions that lived under her bed.

For the words *half* and *quarter*, use the hyphen for adjectives but not for noun forms. (Some words with *half* are closed compounds—halfway, halfwit—so check a dictionary.)

"Join me in a half hour if you want your car back."

Join me half an hour from now.

The half-price items were poorly made.

For compound words made with *odd*, always use a hyphen.

Thirty-odd hours later, my son finally returned home.

He'd saved some 150-odd comic books.

For dollar amounts written as numerals, use the period as a decimal point to separate dollars and cents, and include the dollar sign (or other currency symbol). For amounts less than one dollar, spell out the number and the word *cents*. Don't include the decimal point and zeroes for whole number amounts.

The little girl asked for $12.19 exactly.

I wondered what the nineteen cents was for.

The check amount was $175.00. ✗

Don't hyphenate dollar amounts except for the numbers between twenty-one and ninety-nine that require them. Don't use a hyphen between the number and the word *dollar(s)* (except as noted below, when the number joined to the word *dollar* becomes a compound adjective). Note the absence of commas.

two dollars

twenty-two dollars

two hundred dollars

two hundred twenty-two dollars or two hundred and twenty-two dollars (when spelled out in dialogue, but otherwise written as numerals—$222)

two thousand two hundred and two dollars (in dialogue, but otherwise written as numerals—$2,202)

But

a two-dollar bill

a twenty-dollar fine

a two-hundred-dollar fine

Don't add a second period to end a sentence if a.m. or p.m. comes at the end. Do use a comma midsentence if necessary.

The fire alarm was pulled at 11:58 a.m.. ✗

The fire alarm was pulled at 11:58 a.m.

The alarm was pulled at 11:58 a.m., just before lunch.

CONTRADICTORY RULES

If you've got rules that conflict, you have options.

- Rewrite.

- Choose the option that gives greatest clarity to the reader. For example, if you end up with sentence after sentence of numbers written out as words, try switching them, or at least some category of them, to numerals. You are allowed to wield creative license as a style choice, especially if doing so serves the reader, follows the rules you establish, and isn't merely a whim.

▪ Remember that in fiction, words can almost always be substituted for numerals. When in doubt, write it out. Yeah, corny and elementary, I know. But as advice, it's easy to remember.

▪ Be consistent with your exceptions. Choices you make concerning numbers are a great addition for your style sheet.

THE TAKEAWAY

Keep in mind that characters don't all speak or think the same way, with the same words. Let your choices reflect your characters and not only the rules. That is, sometimes the rules are less important than the way the characters express themselves.

Be consistent. Create a style sheet and stick with it. Know what choice you made for your numbers in chapter 6 and make the same choice in chapter 15.

Fiction is different from other writing styles; we use words rather than the shorthand of symbols. If you're unsure, spell out numbers. Put it into words.

27

GRAMMAR AND PUNCTUATION AND SPELLING, OH MY!

NO NOVEL-LENGTH STORY will be published without errors, including technical errors. It's just not going to happen.

I hope that admission doesn't shock you. I hope you're not expecting perfection out of a 400-page manuscript written and edited by fallible humans and sent through software programs devised by other fallible humans.

Not only will you find errors—often just right after you publish—but not every critic or editor or reader will agree which errors are really errors and which are a matter of interpretation or style.

But you still owe your readers and your reputation the cleanest story possible. And that means you've got to learn the rules *and* take the time to look for errors.

This isn't a grammar book, so we can't cover every rule and all the exceptions to those rules. (And I certainly can't claim to know every grammar rule.) I can advise you to study grammar books, noting rules unfamiliar to you, and then take another editing pass through your manuscript, correcting for obvious grammar violations. Then do the same for punctuation. You could do a pass for both at the same time, of course. *If* you're not trying to juggle a zillion rules new to you.

We can look at grammar tips, and I can make general suggestions, but a few minutes of quick reading won't substitute for true study or knowledge. You're writing novels and maybe even editing and publishing them yourself, so you need to learn the rules for punctuation and grammar. That's part of the job. Don't try to get by. Don't settle for a cursory proofing pass regarding these issues.

Get yourself a couple of good dictionaries and a half dozen reference books that detail the rules of grammar and punctuation.

But don't just learn the rules—learn what happens when you break the rules. Sometimes rule-breaking leads to honeyed prose. Other times it leads to plain horror.

If you know next to nothing about grammar and/or punctuation, you still have time to learn before you publish or submit.

Buy a couple of grammar and punctuation guides. This isn't the time to be frugal and borrow from friends or the library—you need your own copies of good reference books.

Take notes if you have to. Highlight and flag important rules. Look for more information on areas that confuse you.

As is true with every writing element, there are always exceptions to grammar and punctuation rules. Always. I can point out a rule, and immediately someone will point out an exception. So learn the rules and the exceptions. Grammar and punctuation are tools of the craft; put in the time to learn how to use the tools. And allow me to goad you into thinking about rules and options and possibilities you haven't yet imagined.

> And remember that not only are there exceptions built into the rules, there are also allowances for style and effect and impact. Yes, you can choose to add a comma or omit one solely to create a certain effect or feel. To head off reader confusion. Or maybe simply because a paragraph is cluttered with punctuation.

This is where I admit that I had planned to include vital rules for both grammar and punctuation. I even wrote what turned into 70 pages and two chapters filled with rules and tips. Yet as I was editing, I concluded that covering grammar and punctuation in a way broad and deep enough to help fiction writers was beyond the scope of a book on writing and editing.

I will address punctuation and grammar in general, and I want to mention a few rules that will help with common mistakes, but as for in-depth rules, those will have to wait for another book. One that I've got a 70-page start on.

ONE APPROACH TO EDITING THE MECHANICS

I recommend that you proof for grammar, punctuation, and spelling without getting caught up in the events and feel of the story. Is that difficult? Perhaps. But try it. You're looking for errors, not reading to get lost in the fiction. Look for out-of-place or missing punctuation, changes in verb tense, subject-verb number disagreement, and wrong choices out of a heterograph pair or group (*there, they're, their; canvas* and *canvass; do, dew, due, doo; discreet* and *discrete*).

Take a close look at *your* problem areas. If comma use or some particular rule about grammar isn't your forte, make time to check those items in your story.

If you're prone to certain typos—maybe you add letters or routinely hit the wrong keys—typing *not* for *now* or *note*, *know* for *now*, *droop* for *drop*, *best* for *beast*—then check each instance of your problem words. Or maybe you frequently type one word in place of another. I often do this with *reader, character,* and *writer.* When I'm using two or all three of the words in a section of text, I sometimes write the wrong word. This is especially true if I'm thinking ahead and using one of the other words later in the sentence or in the next line.

Because you end up typing valid words, a spellchecker won't catch these errors, so you need to find them yourself.

A spellchecker also won't find missing words. Noticing where words have been dropped can be difficult since our minds fill in the blanks. And if you know your stories well, it's likely you won't easily see that words are missing. Reading from hard copy, using a different color paper or ink, and allowing the story to go cold before proofreading are ways to help you see where words are missing. These methods may also make other errors more noticeable.

Be sensitive to subject-verb agreement, particularly where you've changed text. It's easy to create a disagreement between singular and plural subjects and verbs once you start changing the words.

Don't rush to publish, even if fans are clamoring and you're tired of looking at the manuscript, if you haven't first proofed for grammar, punctuation, and spelling.

Consistency

One key to creating clean text is to be consistent with grammar, punctuation, and spelling. If you use the serial comma sometimes, use it all the time *unless* you've specified situations when you won't use it or you make allowances for clarity. Capitalize words always or never, again including exceptions if you standardize those exceptions. For example, will you capitalize God? Heaven? Earth?

Decide whether *cellphone* is one word or two and whether your characters send *email* or *e-mail*.

This is where a style sheet comes in handy. You know a publisher uses one—if you're going to be the publisher, get one going. Note unusual spellings, special allowances for handling numbers, and exceptions to rules.

If you're writing a series, start your style sheet from book one; you'll definitely want consistency across your books. When readers read them back to back, you know that differences will jump out at them, spoiling a bit of their enjoyment. No, little problems don't necessarily turn into big problems. But if you change the spelling of character names from book to book, don't think your readers won't notice. They often notice much more than the writer remembers putting into a book.

Quick Tips

There are so many areas to consider when editing, that you might not know where to start or what to include. We'll look at a few tips to get you started.

▪ Capitalize nouns that should be capitalized, typically names and titles, not every noun.

▪ Capitalize trademarked products—Coke, Jell-O, Dumpster.

▪ Capitalize adjectives when they're based on a national name, personal name, or people group—Italian bread, French onion soup, Mohawk (hair style). Note, however, that even with this seemingly straightforward rule, there are exceptions and allowances.

Some reference sources suggest capitalizing words such as *French* in *French fries* while others suggest that *French* doesn't need to be capitalized in *french fries* because the reference is not to fries that are French. You can see this allowance in phrases such as *roman numerals* and *manila envelopes*.

Yet there is disagreement concerning this issue. For editing purposes, check adjectives derived from proper and national names with a dictionary or style book. Make your choice and then be consistent.

▪ Decide whether you'll use British English (BrE) or American English (AmE) for spelling and punctuation. Some rules are different.

And once you decide on BrE or AmE, decide if there are allowances for using particular rules from the other style. Will you allow the use of *which* in place of *that* in restrictive (essential) clauses for American English? American English recommends *that* for restrictive, *which* for nonrestrictive. But if you're going to be both editor and publisher, this is something you might allow. (BrE allows the use of both *that* and *which* in restrictive clauses.)

I admit that I like the option to use either *that* or *which* in restrictive clauses. I also regularly use *dialogue* (BrE) rather than *dialog* (AmE). *Dialog* looks like an incomplete word to me.

Even though we won't press deep into specifics, let's look at a few general editing tips for spelling, punctuation, and grammar.

SPELLING

I won't cover much on spelling other than to suggest you get it right.

Check spelling multiple times, but always after you make changes to the text and just before you're ready to format for printing. Listen to beta readers if they tell you that you've used the wrong word (not a spelling error, but a related problem and one that a spellchecker won't find).

Most words have one spelling, and that spelling can be found in a dictionary. Don't rely on an internet search or on Google's Ngram viewer results to decide that the most popular spelling is the correct one. Check a dictionary.

Be especially attentive to the ends of words; it's easy to omit a *d* for the past tense of a word (*endorse/endorsed*) or an *s* for a plural (*girl/girls*). Look also for *ing* in place of *ed* or the problem in reverse. It's easy to make typos, especially once you begin editing text and moving it around.

Compound Words

The spelling of compound words can be tricky, and you might not find a compound word in a dictionary. Also, you may need to create your own compounds and choose their spellings. *And* some words are in flux and may be changing from two words to a hyphenated compound to a single-word (closed) compound even as you're writing and rewriting. Still, there are rules to help with the spelling of compound words.

Compound words can be open (two or more separate words, such as *swimming pool* and *vice president*), hyphenated (two or more words joined with hyphens, such as *sister-in-law* and *weak-kneed*), or closed (single words, such as *toothache* and *makeshift*). A comprehensive and *current* dictionary can verify closed and hyphenated compounds.

When you need to create your own compound words or need to know how to hyphenate compounds for temporary purposes (such as for compound adjectives before a noun), check out the rules in a style manual. *The Chicago Manual of Style* has a detailed section on compound words and the rules for hyphenating them. *New Hart's Rules* has a brief section as well.

Let's consider a few general rules regarding compounds (although there are many more) helpful to fiction writers. You'll likely need most of these rules for your current project.

> Many compound modifiers are hyphenated before a noun.

    coffee-flavored candy

    ice-cold fingers

    slow-moving train

> Compound adjectives are often open after a noun.

The candy was **coffee flavored**.

Tammy's fingers were **ice cold**.

The train was **slow moving**.

Note: A rule for BrE recommends that compound adjectives made by joining an adjective with a participle should also be hyphenated after the noun. So for BrE write—

The candy was **coffee-flavored**.

The train was **slow-moving**.

> Compound modifiers that begin with an adverb ending with *ly* are not hyphenated.

The **fussily attired** businessman looked uptight.

But not all words ending in *ly* are adverbs.

The **surly-sounding** stranger asked for Janice. (*surly* is an adjective)

Both **family-controlled** companies have seen profits since their founders started them. (*family* is a noun)

And note that there are even exceptions to exceptions. If the compound adjective contains an adverb ending in *ly* and is three or more words long, hyphenate it.

Ernest, contrary to appearances, was a **not-so-happily-married** man.

The **oh-so-blissfully-ignorant** optimist lost all his money on the first roll of the dice.

Compounds with prefixes are usually closed, but there are exceptions for when they should hyphenated, as when they come before a numeral or capitalized word.

Prefixes include bi, mid, non, over, under, pre, post, re, sub, and un.

> The **midday** sun was hot, but it was **mid-August**, wasn't it?

> In the **post-1929** years, William's family didn't trust banks or the bankers who managed them.

You can make a style choice for exceptions as well, especially for clarity. For example, I've used *non-event* and *non-use* in this book. In my opinion, without hyphens they look like confusion waiting to strike. Some words, such as *non-stop/nonstop*, can be found in dictionaries with and without the hyphen. Make a choice and stick with it.

Phrases with multiple hyphens are acceptable and often reveal a character's personality, but if the phrase is extremely long, using italics rather than connecting the words with hyphens is acceptable. Or you can rewrite the sentence.

> His second trip to Klaxon Five was a **by-God-too-fantastic-to-be-believed** adventure.

> His second trip to Klaxon Five was a *by God too fantastic to be believed* adventure.

Compound colors are hyphenated before nouns, open after nouns.

> Her **blue-green** scarf drew the color from her eyes.

> Her scarf is **blue green**.

> The wound dripped **pinkish-red** blood.

> His blood was **pinkish red**.

British or American Spelling

Choose BrE or AmE spellings based on your needs and audience. Stick to one format throughout a story, but know that you can make exceptions for certain words if you choose to.

One word I consistently find misspelled? The color gray. It's *ay* in AmE and *ey* in BrE. The name *Grey* is usually spelled with an *E*.

In a related issue, when making word choices, consider character backgrounds as well as reader needs. If one character is British and another American, they may not use the same words. Not only might they call objects by different names—*torch* vs. *flashlight*, *nappy* vs. *diaper*—but they might use different forms of the same verbs. So one might say *spoilt*, the other *spoiled*. One might say *leapt*, and the other *leaped*. Using words that reflect a character's speech and thought is an excellent way to make that character's background clear.

Match your spelling choices (BrE or AmE) to the intended audience but your word choices to the character. So your characters' words should always reflect their backgrounds, but the spelling should reflect your audience's expectations.

GRAMMAR

There are dozens and dozens of rules concerning grammar useful to writers and editors, each with permutations and exceptions. We'll look at just a few that are often overlooked or followed inconsistently by fiction writers, rules that you'll want to be aware of as you edit.

Parallelism

Parallelism in grammar has to do with joining items of like grammatical form. A sentence has faulty parallelism (something you don't want) when the joined items (words or phrases or clauses) have different forms. The sentence with faulty parallelism is unbalanced and may have readers stumbling through the words.

Faulty parallelism can be common in items in a series of three or more, but even two items can have faulty parallelism.

There are typically multiple ways to correct faulty parallelism.

Ellie wanted to climb the stairs, climb into a tub, and wanted to sleep. *X*

Ellie wanted to climb the stairs, ease into the tub, and drop into a dream.

Ellie wanted to climb the stairs, she wanted to see her husband, and she wanted to start the day over.

* * *

The professor had several specialties: teaching undergrads, writing white papers, Greek plays, and solving mysteries. *X*

The professor had several specialties: teaching undergrads, writing white papers, translating Greek plays, and solving mysteries.

* * *

The professor had varied interests: undergrads, white papers, Greek plays, and solving mysteries. *X*

The professor had varied interests: undergrads, white papers, Greek plays, and mysteries.

* * *

Charlie preferred to ride buses to walking to work. *X*

Charlie preferred riding on buses to walking to work.

Dangling Modifiers

We'll touch on dangling modifiers again in the next chapter when we look at common mistakes, but let's look at some details now.

Modifiers dangle when they refer to a word that's not in the sentence or when they seem to refer to the wrong word, creating nonsense sentences. Dangling modifiers can be corrected in multiple ways. When you edit, look closely at participles that begin sentences. Dangling modifiers don't show up only at the beginning of a sentence, but that's a common place to find them.

In the following examples, the subject should follow the comma.

> Having worn her heavy coat, the heat of the day made Jessica too hot. **✗**

Jessica, not the heat of the day, wore the coat, so try

> Having worn her heavy coat, Jessica was too hot once the sun came out.

> Jessica was too hot in her heavy coat once the day heated up.

* * *

> Prepared to scream, the baby's face was red. **✗**

The baby and not her face was prepared to scream, so try

> Prepared to scream, the baby, her face red, opened her mouth wide.

> The baby, her face red, prepared to scream.

> The baby's face was red as the sweet little thing prepared to scream.

Pronoun Errors

Using the wrong pronoun, confusion about which noun a pronoun refers to, and using *it* to refer to something never named are problems that can hide in stories.

Everyone. *Everyone* is singular, so we say *everyone is happy* rather than *everyone are happy*. But what about using a possessive pronoun in relation to *everyone*? This causes problems.

Everyone drives his own car.

This works if all the everyones are male, but if they aren't or the sex is unknown, this can be taken as sexist. Yet if a character would think or say *his*, don't think that you must change such a construction.

Unless all the drivers are female, *everyone drives her own car* creates problems too.

Everyone drives his or her own car.

This works, but sounds fussy, too correct for fiction. Are your characters going to think or say this? If they do, this wording works. But if this doesn't sound like your character, don't think you have to use wording that sounds so stiff.

Everyone drives their own cars.

This wording is used often in speech, but experts argue against its use for the written word. Yet once again, if this is what a character would say, use it. Don't let rules keep you from writing realistic characters.

For an omniscient narrator, however, you may want to rewrite to avoid possible problems.

Car owners drive their own cars.

Pronoun, contractions, and verb tense. Problems with contracted pronouns and verb tense are tough to root out because they're hard to see. The words are legitimate words—they're just used incorrectly for the narrative tense. Which means if this is a particular problem for you, you should examine each use of the problem words.

It's close to midnight.

It's in this sentence is a contraction of *it is*, present tense, not *it was*, past tense. If this is a sentence of dialogue or a sentence in a present-tense story, it works. But if it's nestled inside a paragraph in a story written using past tense, it's wrong. I find this construction used often and slipped into past-tense narration. The same problem happens with *I'm, he's,* and *she's. We're* and *they're* are also present tense and can't be used for *we were* or *they were.*

> We waited until the moon was covered by clouds before we took our positions. **It's close** to midnight before we saw the man scurrying toward us. ✗

> We waited until the moon was covered by clouds before we took our positions. **It was** close to midnight before we saw the man scurrying toward us.

The same problem arises from contractions using *will—it'll, I'll, he'll, she'll, we'll, they'll*—and *would—I'd, he'd, she'd, we'd, they'd. It'd* is a legitimate contraction, if maybe not a common one. Use the contraction if it fits the character, but consider other options too.

Use *will* for present tense and *would* for past tense. (*Will* and *would* both have additional uses outside of this one—the discussion here pertains only to this particular use of the words.)

> As Tamara runs out of the office, she **says she'll** be back before three.

> Tamara ran out of the office. She **said she'll** be back before three. ✗

> Tamara ran out of the office. She **said she'd** be back before three.

Pronoun confusion. Pronouns sometimes refer to the wrong noun, and sometimes there's confusion about which noun is being referred to. Rewriting can clear up or head off confusion.

> Andy and Jethro carried their hiking boots to their cars. **They** were covered in itchy, drying mud.

You can see how readers might be confused about what's covered in mud. Rewrite to prevent confusion.

> Andy and Jethro carried their hiking boots to their cars. **The teens** (or boots or cars) were covered in itchy, drying mud.

> Andy and Jethro carried their hiking boots to their cars. **Boots, SUVs, and boys** were covered in itchy, drying mud.

> Andy and Jethro carried their hiking boots to their cars. **The guys were tired out after the long hike. They** were covered in itchy, drying mud.

Pronouns that could refer to one of two (or more) characters of the same gender can also cause confusion.

> Mac told Brian that Mrs. Jones wanted **him** to work on her yard.

Which *him* is meant here, Mac or Brian? Rewriting will clear up the confusing text.

> Mac told Brian that Mrs. Jones asked him to work on her yard from now on since Brian had burned the grass three times.

> Mac told Brian that Mrs. Jones wanted him to work on her yard while Mac was gone for the summer.

> Mac told Brian that Mrs. Jones wanted Brian to work on her yard while Mac was gone for the summer.

Pronouns and possessive antecedents. There's an interesting rule about a possessive noun not being allowed to be the antecedent for an objective or subjective pronoun. (Don't worry about the names of these grammar elements—there's no test at the end of the chapter.) What this means is that a possessive noun—Marley's ghost, Jane's car, Matthew's beer—can't be followed by a pronoun linking to the implied but unstated noun—Marley, Jane, or Matthew.

Some say that this rule must be followed while others say to follow it only when there's a chance for misunderstanding. I suggest that you stay alert for this setup and rewrite at least the worst sentences.

In an example used earlier for dangling modifiers, we used this poorly constructed sentence:

Prepared to scream, the baby's face was red. *X*

One obvious correction for the dangling modifier would seem to be

The baby's face was red as she prepared to scream.

This construction is commonly used, yet it actually pairs the pronoun *she* with the baby's face rather than with the baby herself, which doesn't make sense. She, the baby, hasn't been mentioned.

So a better option would be to use a noun rather than a pronoun, maybe with a twist to avoid repetition.

The baby's face was red as the sweet little thing pre-pared to scream.

Or you could mention the baby in the sentence before this one and then use a possessive pronoun or possessive noun to introduce the second sentence. In this way you're pairing the pronoun (*she*) of the second sentence to the noun in the first sentence (Marisa).

Marisa was sitting up in her crib. Her face was red as she prepared to scream.

Marisa was sitting up in her crib. The little darling's face was red as she prepared to scream.

Using a noun or name in the prior sentence will often fix the prob-lem. Still, if there's a chance for confusion, including a noun—not a possessive noun—in the sentence with the pronoun is always correct.

The setup in this next example is a bit different, but we're still looking at a possessive noun as an antecedent for a pronoun. The problem is clear.

> Half a dozen fire trucks raced down Ashbury Street.
> The gang hurried out of Mick's pub. He was the last
> one out. *X*

He is probably a reference to Mick, but Mick hasn't been mentioned. You'd definitely want to rewrite in this case.

> Half a dozen fire trucks raced down Ashbury Street.
> The gang hurried out of Mick's pub. Mick was the last
> one out.

It. *It* is a marvelously versatile workhorse word, able to accomplish multiple tasks with only two small letters. It can be used in a variety of ways.

There's the *impersonal it—it was a dark and stormy night.*

There's the *anticipatory it—it will be great to get away for a while.*

And there's the use of *it* in cleft sentences—*it's my love of money that stands in my way.*

But in fiction there's a problem with *it* when it's used again and again to substitute for nouns that have never been stated or when the writer relies on it to fill a gap instead of searching for a more specific word or phrase.

> I'd dreamed of Breckenridge College all my life. *It* was
> at the top of my wish list.

What was at the top of the list? Dreaming of the college? That doesn't make sense since she'd done just that all her life. Going to school there? Visiting? Seeing it? Walking the same paths her mother walked? Nothing was specified.

The word *it* tells us nothing here. Readers need more. And when writers include specifics, they can guide a reader's experience through a story. They can change ho-hum into fascinating.

Study the following example. Consider the different effects created by changing *it* to something specific, something that reveals more about the characters. And when you edit, look for ways of changing the imprecise *it* to something that draws readers deeper.

She couldn't wait to join him. **It** spurred her to drive like Mario Andretti in pursuit of a championship.

She couldn't wait to join him. The anticipation of his embrace spurred her to drive like Mario Andretti in pursuit of a championship.

She couldn't wait to join him. The delight she expected to find spurred her to drive like . . .

She couldn't wait to join him. The shock she knew he'd feel at seeing her spurred her to drive like . . .

She couldn't wait to join him. The knowledge that she'd kill him this time spurred her to drive like . . .

She couldn't wait to join him. Knowing she'd find peace spurred her to drive like . . .

Subject-Verb Agreement

For the most part, writers don't have trouble matching singular or plural subjects with the correct verb forms.

Problems do arise, however, when the subject is ambiguous.

Modifiers that confuse. Confusion might arise over a subject modifier that comes between the subject and the verb—does the modifier change the subject? No, subject modifiers don't change the number of a subject.

> **The mechanic**, who together with his brothers stole over a dozen cars, **was** sentenced to seven years.

No matter what the brothers have done, the mechanic (singular) is the subject of this sentence. In the next sentence, the subject is plural.

> **The doctor's brothers**, who'd written their brother off ten years earlier even though he'd never intentionally harmed them, **were** waiting outside his office.

Special cases. A few phrases that look like they create plurals can be especially problematic. Recognize that these particular phrases don't create plurals. That is, they're not a substitute for *and*. They're typically subject modifiers or parentheticals that don't change a single subject to a plural one.

The phrases include *accompanied by, added to, along with, as well as, coupled with, in addition to, no less than, not to mention, on top of,* and *together with*. Other phrases begin with the words *except, including, like,* and *with*.

Pam, no less than her sisters, **wants** justice done.

Pam, like her sisters, **wants** justice done.

The thief, together with his cohorts, **need** a lawyer. *X*

The thief, together with his cohorts, **needs** a lawyer.

The book, except for the covers, **is** made of onion-skin paper.

The book, with its onion-skin pages, **smells** old.

[but] The onion-skin **pages smell** old.

The most recent test score, coupled with those from the past five years, **tell** me that I'm still no master at test taking. *X*

The most recent test score, coupled with those from the past five years, **tells** me that I'm still no master at test taking.

The full season, including the finale and previews of the next season, **is** available on DVD.

David, not to mention his team, **wants** to win the contract.

[but] **David and his team want** to win the contract.

Collective nouns. Collective nouns refer to groups of people or things—*company, team, staff, band, troupe, gang, board, flock, audience*. But are collective nouns singular or plural? The answer is, it depends.

Typically in AmE, collective nouns are treated as singular.

> **The team needs** to practice in the restored arena at least once before the tournament starts.

> **The panel hopes** to come to agreement soon.

In BrE, however, collective nouns can be either singular or plural, depending on whether you intend to refer to the group as a singular entity or you want to consider group members as individuals, thus a plural collection of people.

> **The band are getting** their gear together. (referring to individuals in the band, so a plural)

> **The band is getting** its gear together. (referring to the group, so singular)

> **The company's board are** avid for change. (referring to the individuals, so a plural)

> **The company's board is** avid for change. (referring to the singular group)

To switch collective nouns to plurals in AmE, you can rewrite. Including a plural noun is a common practice.

> The **members** of the team need to practice in the restored arena at least once before the game starts.

> The company's **directors** are avid for change.

And allowances *can* be made for collective nouns to be plural in AmE. If you can argue that you're referring to the individuals—that you're emphasizing them as individuals—then you can try using a collective noun as a plural, just as BrE allows.

The staff have arrived earlier than expected.

The audience boo loudly when he fumbles his lines.

Such wording may sound odd to the ear used to AmE, but you do have options.

PUNCTUATION AND FONT STYLE

Punctuation allows readers to make sense of words, sentences, and paragraphs. Punctuation marks can separate sections of text or join them. Punctuation and font style (roman, italics, and bold) allow us to give shadings and exaggerated meanings to our words.

Let's consider a few rules for font style and punctuation.

Italicize unfamiliar foreign-language words the first time they're used; however, there's no need to italicize foreign words that most readers will understand. Never italicize foreign-language place names or proper names.

Vaut mieux prévenir que guérir was my great-grandfather's family motto.

They served both hot and cold hors d'oeuvres.

The Kurfürstendamm, in Berlin, is on my list of must-visit shopping sites.

Italicize words used as words and letters used as letters. (Don't italicize letters for school grades.)

He said the actual word was *victualler*, but I didn't believe him.

"Her name starts with a *b*, not *p*."

Elsa got an A in biology, but Bertie got a C.

Italicize sound words that you want readers to hear—*buzz* and *zoom* and *creak*.

The limb broke off with a stuttered *crack*.

Don't overuse unusual punctuation such as the ellipsis, the em dash, the colon, or the semicolon.

Even if you use these punctuation marks correctly, they shouldn't feature in every other sentence. Tell the story with words rather than through punctuation. Use punctuation as support, not in a featured role. Readers should feel punctuation at work, not make note of it.

If you set off a phrase beginning with an em dash, be sure to close it with another dash, not a comma or parenthesis. If the text doesn't end the sentence, use pairs of dashes, commas, or parentheses.

The box I was looking for—the heavy one painted with red stripes—was a treasure box.

The box I was looking for—the heavy one painted with red stripes, was a treasure box. *X*

Victoria found the treasure box under bags of old clothes in her grandmother's attic—just where she remembered seeing it when she was a child.

Use a consistent format for dashes.

Whether used midsentence or at the end of a sentence, the em dash in AmE touches the letters or punctuation that surrounds it—there are no spaces.

For British English, the punctuation used midsentence is usually an en dash – as seen in this pair – a dash shorter than the em dash but longer than a hyphen. It's preceded and followed by spaces. For dialogue or sentences that are cut off, BrE uses the closed em dash. (Some followers of BrE rules use the closed em dash for all cases, the same as in AmE.)

To prevent confusion, include only one set of dashes in the same sentence. (Exceptions when you're creating an effect on purpose.)

Dashes and parentheses draw attention to themselves and can be noticed for the punctuation that they are. Thus they stand out. Make use of them, but don't have them slapping at readers and reminding them that they're reading.

As always, do what you can to keep readers involved in the story events without being distracted by the mechanics. Readers can receive mixed visual signals if multiple pairs of dashes or parentheses are used in the same sentence.

The use of parentheses in writing is legitimate, but in fiction, the artifice is blatant—readers understand that a character is sharing an aside with them. Reduce the use of attention-getting punctuation.

Some experts suggest that parentheses don't belong in fiction. You may find you never have a reason to use them.

Dashes and parentheses (and even commas) can break the flow of sentences and paragraphs. Use them purposely and only when necessary, recognizing how they change the feel, rhythm, and sound of sentences.

> Gwendolyn got lost—as Ian knew she would—on her way to Timberley.

> The boy's dog—in truth, a wolf—followed him past the schoolyard and had the youngest kids—Toni included—screaming in fear. *X*

Maybe this last example could work. But you certainly wouldn't want a lot of this type of choppy sentence.

Use an apostrophe, not a single quotation mark, for contractions and omitted letters.

> He told her she couldn't do it 'cause she was too young and too short. *X*

He told her she couldn't do it 'cause she was too young and too short.

> **Be consistent in the use of the serial (or Oxford) comma.**

You don't have to use it, but if you do use the serial comma—a comma before the coordinating conjunction in a series of three items or more—use it consistently. If you don't use it, omit it consistently. There are allowances, however, for using or not using a serial comma in order to create or maintain clarity. The following are both correct.

Janice walked to the park, ran to the playground, sat on a swing, and cried.

Janice walked to the park, ran to the playground, sat on a swing and cried.

> **Use only one terminal punctuation mark at the ends of sentences, so no *?!* or *!?* or *!!!.***

If you're writing children's lit, you might be able to sneak in one or two question marks backed by an exclamation point (creating an interrobang), but most of the time, choose one mark only.

And unless you're writing melodrama—and maybe children's adventure—keep the exclamation points to a minimum. Use word choice and sentence construction, not an exclamation point, to convey emotion. Use exclamation points only for true exclamations, typically in dialogue. And see if you can't keep them to a very small number in a full-length adult novel.

To reduce unnecessary exclamation points, delete them before printing for an editing pass, and then, as you read from hard copy, add back those you must have. You'll have far fewer than you began with and ideally only those that are necessary. (I wish I could credit a source for this useful tip, but if I knew it, I forget it years ago.)

> Use question marks at ends of sentences that contain tag questions.

You wanted to sing karaoke, didn't you?

"The sky is really black, isn't it, with all those clouds?"

"You aren't the man kidnapped as a child, are you?"

> Use periods, not question marks, in sentences that begin with someone wondering.

"I was wondering if you'd like to go out with me?" *X*

"I was wondering if you'd like to go out with me."

Denny wondered who was at the door.

"I wonder who that could be."

But

Who was calling at three in the morning? she wondered as she picked up the phone.

> Don't use quotation marks for indirect dialogue or speech.

He told me "he wouldn't be able to surf the bay." *X*

He told me he wouldn't be able to surf the bay.

> In AmE, use double quotation marks for dialogue and to set off individual words.

Use single quotation marks only within doubles, as in a quote within a quote or for a title used inside dialogue.

For BrE, use single quotation marks for dialogue, with doubles inside for quotes within quotes.

Some users of BrE allow for the reverse, double quotes for dialogue and singles for quotes within quotes. But AmE never allows for the reverse and would never permit single quotation marks for dialogue except in nested quotations within quotations.

"He needs me," Anna said. (AmE)

'He needs me,' Anna said. (BrE)

TITLES AND NAMES (CAPITALIZATION, ITALICS, AND QUOTATION MARKS)

Most of us don't have trouble with capitalizing titles and names; it's choosing between italics and quotation marks that gives us fits. Let's look at a few rules.

> Proper nouns (think *names*) are capitalized. Titles are capitalized, though not all words in a title are necessarily capitalized.

Names

Capitalize names of people, places, and things. This means names of individuals and animals (pet names, not breeds), stores, restaurants, museums, municipalities (towns, cities, etc.), businesses, products and brands (Oreos, Cokes, Mustang), schools, books of the Bible, religious books (the Bible, the Koran).

Names need nothing more than capitalization—no quotation marks or italics. I've italicized the examples to highlight the names.

- *Sally* is capitalized, *Aunt Sally* is capitalized, *my aunt* is not capitalized, and only the name itself in *my aunt Sally* is capitalized.

- *Franklin Roosevelt* is capitalized, *President Roosevelt* is capitalized, *the president* is not capitalized, and only the name itself is capitalized in *our current president, James Millington.*

- *The doctor, the chairman, the general, the pope,* and so forth—nouns, not names—are not capitalized.

Use abbreviations for doctor, missus, and mister when paired with names—Dr. Johnson, Mrs. Rosewood, and Mr. Black. (No full stop/period in BrE—Dr Johnson, Mrs Rosewood, Mr Black)

▪ Capitalize nicknames when they are names, but don't capitalize endearments. So *Suzie* (short for *Suzanne*) is capitalized, but *sweetie* and *darlin'* aren't. *Doc* used once or twice to tease someone wouldn't be capitalized. But if a character is regularly called *Doc*, capitalize it.

▪ Capitalize *doctor, professor,* and *captain* (and other military ranks) when they're used in direct address in dialogue.

"I fell down two flights of stairs, Doctor."

"Two flights, Captain?"

▪ Capitalize compass directions when they're used to refer to a region (consider them names of the region)—the South, the Pacific Northwest, the West Coast, Northern Virginia, the Northern Tablelands.

▪ Capitalize compass directions when they're used to describe people of a region—*Those Southerners know how to make sweet tea and cornbread.*

▪ Don't capitalize compass directions when they refer to a direction or a general description of a place—we were heading north, the property is in the western part of the state.

Titles

In fiction we typically use *title case* or *headline style* and capitalize the first and last words of titles as well as most other major words—nouns, pronouns, verbs, adjectives, adverbs, and subordinating conjunctions. We typically don't capitalize articles, coordinating conjunctions, or prepositions. (There are exceptions for prepositions used as adverbs—*Stand Up for Pets.*)

If you're including a real title of a book or movie, you could check a jacket cover or other reliable source, but you could just as easily follow title case. Follow the same conventions for fictional titles. So if your characters refer to books or movies you've made up for your story world, treat those books and movies as real.

> *Gone with the Wind* and *Gone With the Wind* (from the original cover) are both acceptable.

> Capitalize *and* italicize big-picture titles.

Think big picture when deciding about italics with titles. If the work can be broken into smaller units that can also be titled (although they don't *have* to be titled), the large unit is italicized and the smaller units are put in quotation marks. For example, an album title is put in italics, and the songs on the album are put in quotation marks.

These are all italicized:

- book titles
- newspaper, journal, and magazine titles (don't italicize or capitalize the word *the* for a newspaper title, even if *the* is part of the title)
- titles of TV shows, radio shows, albums, movies, operas, ballets, musicals, plays, and long poems
- titles of works of art
- video game titles
- titles of pamphlets and reports
- podcast and blog titles (but not the names of regular websites or the titles of podcast episodes or blog posts)
- titles of cartoons and comic strips (*Peanuts, Pearls Before Swine*)
- titles of museum exhibitions

Shortened titles, like full titles, are italicized. So *Fried Green Tomatoes* (from *Fried Green Tomatoes at the Whistle Stop Café*) is italicized.

> Capitalize *and* put in quotation marks (doubles in AmE) titles for units that are part of (a subset of) a big-picture item. (BrE permits the use of single or double quotation marks—be consistent.)

The following are put in quotation marks:

- song titles
- chapter titles (this is in reference to chapter titles mentioned in a story; this doesn't mean that you put your own chapter titles in quotation marks in your table of contents or at the top of the chapter)
- episode titles from TV and radio shows
- blog articles and podcast episodes
- newspaper, journal, and magazine article titles (titles of regular newspaper and magazine columns are not put in quotation marks, e.g., Dear Abby, At Wit's End)
- short poems (most poems) and titles of short stories (or other works found in a book or magazine)
- essay titles
- long poems that are part of the contents of a book
- unpublished works (dissertations, manuscripts in collections)

Odds and Ends

Signs. Text on signs and other notices is capitalized but not italicized or put in quotation marks. And hyphens aren't necessary for compound modifiers on signs.

> Brandon forgot to put out Wet Floor signs.

> Brandon forgot to put out Wet-Floor signs. *X*

> The local garden club put up dozens of Don't Walk on the Grass signs.

There is an exception when the message on a sign is particularly long—say, sentence length or longer. Put the text from such signs in quotation marks.

> The sign was explicit. "No dogs, no cats, no birds, no gerbils, and no pet alligators."

Mottoes. Use the rule about quotation marks for long messages for mottoes as well.

> Their club's motto was Live Free and Don't Die.

> My sister's club's motto is a doozy. "Do it right the first time so you don't have to do it twice and won't have to listen to your parents complain."

T-shirts. Use quotation marks for T-shirt messages, especially for long messages or those you introduce with say or said. For short messages, you could try just capitalizing the major words instead.

> His T-shirt said, "I ain't no snitch, but I'll take a bribe if I have to."

Italicize the names of ships (on water, in the air, or in space).

Italicize the name but not the abbreviated prefix, such as USS or HMS. And don't use punctuation in the prefix (USS, not U.S.S.). Keep in mind that ships have names, not titles. It's not necessary to include *the*—the *Constellation* or the *Endeavor*—unless that's how the character would think or say it.

OTHER STYLE CONSIDERATIONS

Underlining

Don't underline in fiction. There's no longer a reason to underline in either a manuscript or your published work.

All Caps

Use all caps for a product name if necessary (although a better choice would be small caps), but don't use all caps to emphasize words in your story. One exception would be children's fiction, where you could use all caps *infrequently* for emphasis or to show excitement.

Contractions

Use contractions in your fiction, even in historical fiction. People have shortened and combined words for years and years and will do so in the foreseeable future. Allow your characters to think and speak in contractions.

Contractions allow for a quicker read. To slow the pace, you could allow one character to speak without contracting his words, but readers will notice. If there are too many instances when contractions should've been used and yet weren't, you may make the read unnecessarily burdensome for the reader.

You may skip contractions as a style choice, to convey a character's personality, or to make a point, but while nonfiction often foregoes contractions, fiction takes advantage of them.

The keys here are correctness and consistency.

THE QUICK LIST

- Make sure verbs and nouns agree in number.

- Check capitalization of nouns—most are not capitalized.

- Edit for faulty parallelism.

- Make sure nonrestrictive (nonessential) phrases are surrounded by commas and remove commas from restrictive (essential) phrases.

- Unless your story is for children or is melodrama, restrict uses of exclamation points.

- Maintain the narrative tense—don't switch verb tense of the story from past to present or present to past.

- Cut the overuse of past or present progressive—*was walking, is talking*—and substitute simple past or present—*walked, talks.*

- Spell out almost all numbers in dialogue—exceptions for product names, years, and identification numbers (Route 5, Channel 9).

- Except in unusual circumstances, don't include two digressions set off with dashes in the same sentence.

- Be sure that text set off with dashes, commas, or parentheses has a closing dash, comma, or parenthesis—don't mix dashes, commas, and parentheses.

- Make sure that all sentences have a terminal punctuation mark (period, question mark, or exclamation point) or that they end with an ellipsis or an em dash.

- Never start a sentence with a numeral—spell the number or rewrite the sentence.

- Don't underline; don't use all caps for emphasis (except for children's fiction and then only rarely).

- Don't overuse italics but do use italics to stress a single word, for unfamiliar foreign words (not common foreign words), and for sound words that you want readers to hear (*crack, boom*).

- If you're using AmE rules, use *single* quotation marks only inside a quote that already uses double quotation marks—don't use singles to stress a word.

THE TAKEAWAY

Editing for grammar, punctuation, and spelling will be one of your final steps, though you may check all three at any stage. But typically you'll be editing for these items as you polish. Take the time to get the mechanics right; it isn't likely that you'll be able to proofread for these issues in a single day.

Learn the rules. Know why we have rules—learn what they do for our writing and for our readers. Apply the rules to communicate your story to the reader. And then allow yourself to relax the rules when doing so doesn't harm a story but enhances it.

If grammar and punctuation are hard for you, this might be the time to call in favors or hire a proofreader.

28

COMMON MISTAKES
AND THEIR FIXES‡

THIS LIST OF COMMON writing mistakes—and suggested fixes for them—is useful for those who self-publish as well as those who follow the traditional route to publication with a publisher.

Some of the mistakes listed here are explored in depth in other chapters. You'll find them here, however, because I wanted to give you a go-to list of common problems. These may not be the only weaknesses in your manuscript, but fixing them would take care of a great portion of the common mistakes writers make with novels.

I won't presume to say I know the 10 or 25 most common fiction-writing mistakes of all writers of all time, but this is a list of mistakes that *I* see again and again. I've included a sampling of fixes for these mistakes, though by no means an exhaustive list.

I don't advise that you work on all these mistakes at one time. Some have quick fixes while others deserve thoughtful consideration.

There's no rank or order to the list. And while I'm pointing these items out as mistakes, keep in mind that what may be a weakness for most stories can be finessed into a strength. That is, you may want to play up what is typically regarded as a writing mistake, turn it inside out, and make it work for your story.

Usually, however, you won't want to include these kinds of mistakes in your fiction. They weaken stories and can identify the writer who doesn't correct them as an inexperienced beginner. While you do have to begin somewhere, in the marketplace your stories have to compete with the stories of experienced writers. Give your work all the advantages you can. Your stories can sound fresh and new; they shouldn't sound amateurish.

To compete with experienced authors, create a product worthy of competition. This means cutting out the common mistakes of beginning writers.

Give yourself every marketplace advantage. Eliminating common errors before you submit to agent or publisher or before you publish on your own gives you an advantage, *a great big healthy one*. Use it.

COMMON MISTAKES OF FICTION WRITERS

Writing reports rather than scenes

I see this one frequently. The writer mistakes writing *about* events in report form for writing scenes that engage both characters and readers. If you've been accused of telling rather than showing, if the story is all in your character's thoughts instead of playing out in real time on the page, your fiction may be more report than story.

> **Fixes**: Write scenes. This means characters doing something (including talking) in an established or identifiable place and time (setting). Think interaction—characters using props and responding to other characters. Think motion. Show cause and effect, stimulus and response. Portray a real-time unfolding of events. Cut back on narrative summary and exposition.

Writing boring dialogue

Writers can forget that dialogue should raise the conflict level as well as advance the plot. Dialogue that's bland, too agreeable, or too complete doesn't create conflict. And dialogue with all the *uhs* and *ums* and the tediousness of real conversation doesn't work for fiction. Dialogue shouldn't bore readers, but pull them deeper into story events and into caring about what characters are up to.

> **Fixes**: Write dialogue in incomplete sentences. Have characters deliberately not answer or answer a question that's not asked. Have characters lie. Include subtext. Make characters interrupt one another. Write fictional dialogue that seems real and not real conversations that seem contrived.

Using clichés and common phrases

This error occurs when a writer uses common phrases in place of fresh wording or phrases specific to a particular story and its characters. While I'm suggesting you use words and phrases that are peculiar to your characters, I'm also talking about removing clichés and banal phrases that could be found in any story. Rather than make your story sound familiar or stale, make it sound new.

> **Fixes**: Cut all clichés unless one is exceptionally apt or a character is prone to using them *and* using clichés adds to rather than detracts from the story. Substitute your own words for familiar phrases. Cut common three- and four-word phrases that add nothing to the action, the mood of the scene, or the emotion of the moment and aren't needed for rhythm. One useful practice is to root out unnecessary prepositional phrases—*at this moment, under these circumstances.*

Turning characters into talking heads

This happens when the writer fails to include setting details, character movements, and character interaction with props from the setting. If your characters talk non-stop, without pausing to move *through* or interact *with* the setting, you're essentially featuring bodiless talking heads. While not every section of dialogue must be interrupted by character actions or movement (too much of that creates a new problem), you don't want readers wondering where the characters are or what they're doing. You should make that apparent.

And you definitely don't want to write a full scene with only talking heads. Give readers a sense of time and place, and show characters inhabiting the setting. Think motion and a physical space.

> **Fixes**: Interrupt dialogue with character movement, including quirks and habits that reveal personality and motions that reveal *e*motion. Have characters connect with objects from the setting.

Omitting sensory details

Both characters and readers have senses—put that knowledge to work for your fiction. Omitting sense references can leave stories flat, unable to compete with real-world distractions. Give characters sounds, sights, and scents to respond to. Have the feel of objects and the touch of other characters mean something to them. Characters who react to sensory elements seem real and their reactions help ensnare the reader. Sense-related details make readers feel that they're inside actual places and close to the action.

> **Fixes**: Add something of the senses, beyond what a character sees, to each scene. Consider giving your main character a link to a particular sense, perhaps an overly sensitive sense of smell or hearing. Perhaps physical touch moves her beyond the norm. Use a variety of sense references but make each fit your characters, the genre, and the unfolding plot.

Failing to push or increase conflict

Some writers shy away from conflict, even with imaginary people. But conflict is a primary element of fiction. Your main character should face conflict, react to conflict, and *instigate* conflict. Conflict should be of varying levels and come from multiple sources. And the level of conflict should increase as the story advances.

> **Fixes**: Add conflict to dialogue. Create friction between even the best of friends. Set your characters at odds, whether that means a difference of opinion or a difference in philosophy. Even when there's agreement about a problem, characters could disagree about the action needed to resolve it. Also, give your lead character conflicts within himself, perhaps a struggle between choices. Make sure there's conflict in every scene and that it escalates as the story progresses. Make sure conflict comes to a head in the climax.

Failing to vary the pace

Stories shouldn't maintain the same pace or same intensity throughout. Readers should instead feel a buildup toward a climax. The failure to pick up the pace and/or push the emotional stakes as the story heads toward the climax is a common mistake.

At the two-thirds mark (approximately), if the reader isn't anticipating the ending, isn't feeling that something's about to break open, it's likely that you haven't upped the pace and begun to push the emotions. It's not that you shouldn't also vary pace and introduce emotions earlier as well, but the reader should feel the difference as the story heads toward the showdown. What's at stake for the character, both losses and gains, should be greater. The story should *feel* as if it's moving to an inescapable conclusion. Readers should both think that the lead character can't stop until he solves his problems and feel that they themselves can't put the book down until they discover what ultimately happens.

Use changes in pace throughout a story to change the mood and to influence reader emotions.

Use changes in pace to prime readers for upcoming events.

Use changes in pace when characters would logically slow down or speed up their actions.

> **Fixes**: Starting at about the midpoint of the story, begin to raise the stakes for the characters even more than you have. Introduce more problems and shorten the time available to fix them. Show the emotional toll the adventure is taking on the main character and then add more problems that will challenge his emotions further. As the story's climax approaches, speed the pace by writing shorter sentences. Make paragraphs and chapters shorter. Put more white space on a page. Cut rambling dialogue and make each word count. Reduce description. Or, conversely, include a detailed description of a person or object that the protagonist is focused on to the exclusion of all else.

The ending should be a natural outcome of a story's opening, but you need to give the ending third (or even half) of your story a different feel in terms of consequences. Infuse character actions and words with importance as the story approaches the end.

Misusing flashbacks and back story

No matter how often they're counseled against the practice, many new writers still introduce flashbacks and back story too soon and use them too often.

Readers can't be immersed in the present story if a flashback is included in the first couple of pages or if back story is dumped onto the page and introduced too soon. Flashbacks by definition stop the forward motion of a story. If you need a flashback, add it after the current story is well underway and the main character and his problem are introduced.

Back story can be beneficial for revealing character motivation and necessary history, but it should serve the true story, not be a substitute for story events; it shouldn't take over. This means that back story shouldn't get more page time than current story events. It shouldn't be highlighted at the expense of current events. Except for certain types of stories—for example, a frame story—the majority of the story should take place in the story's present and not the past.

> **Fixes**: Remove flashbacks from the first chapter. Immerse readers in the current story—hook them—before distracting them with side issues. Get them involved with what's happening now before giving them what happened then.
>
> Use flashbacks sparingly. Use other ways to introduce character motivation and history. Present important revelations from the past via a single line or two of back story instead of using full flashbacks. But be miserly with back story as well. Think of it as spice, not a side dish and certainly not the main meal.

Also, when characters go into flashbacks or think about the past, provide a stimulus for their thoughts—don't have them thinking about the past with no prodding. Show the reader what induces the memories. Make flashbacks fit seamlessly into the current story, as if they belong.

Giving readers too much time in a character's head

I definitely see this one a lot, especially in first-person narration, though it's not unknown in third-person POVs. Instead of showing action or putting the emphasis on what's going on around the character, the writer who keeps us in a character's head filters everything through the character. Responses are shown through thoughts alone rather than through a mix of thoughts, dialogue, and physical reactions. Also, the reader is often told what the character hears instead of hearing for himself. Symptoms of this mistake include phrasing such as *I heard a footstep* rather than *a heavy foot found the squeaky third floorboard*.

> **Fixes**: Search for *I*, *he*, or *she thought, felt, heard, saw, noticed*, and so on. Make changes if too much emphasis is placed on the character's ability to notice, see, and hear rather than on the actions or events themselves. If you've given readers more character thought than action, shift the balance toward action and dialogue.

Explaining too much or too often

Unless readers can't possibly catch on without help, writers shouldn't explain dialogue or actions. Evidence of explanations include the phrases *so as to, so that, in order to, as if,* and the words *so, because, like,* and *to*. If you find yourself writing a lot of sentences such as *he peeked through the blinds to see who was inside the room* or *he said it with a little-boy voice so she wouldn't take it too hard*, you'll want to make changes. Readers are smart—let *them* read intent and meaning into actions and dialogue without you bluntly telling them why a character acts or reacts.

If you give readers the dots, even widely spaced ones, they can connect them. You don't need to hold their hands and lead them through your story, pointing out cause and effect along the way.

As if is an especially obvious ploy to explain a character's actions.

> She stood on tiptoe, as if she was too short to get a
> clear view otherwise.

If you tell readers that Sue stood on tiptoe, they'll infer the reason.

Not all explanations use *as if*, though these might be the easiest to find as you edit. And not all uses of *as if* require a change. Yet edit with an eye toward rooting out sentences that slow or stop the action to explain *how* or *why*.

Make motivation clear through word choice and the timing and order of action and reaction instead of blatantly saying he did this because she did that.

> **Fixes**: Don't explain. Make action and dialogue con-
> vey the message. Search for words that explain and
> then rewrite them.

Using wacky grammar

Dangling and misplaced modifiers, absolute phrases that don't make sense, and participial phrases showing simultaneous actions that should be sequential are grammar mistakes I see often. These can be hard to identify in our own writing, but you should catch most on a read-through from hard copy.

> **Dangling modifier**: *Powering down the court, the basket-*
> *ball popped out of his hands.*

> In this example, the subject should be *he* and not *the*
> *basketball—powering down the court, he lost the basketball* or
> *he powered down the court, and the basketball popped out of his*
> *hands.* Or if *the basketball* is the subject, the sentence
> could be rewritten another way—*the basketball popped*
> *out of his hands as he powered down the court.*

Absolute phrase format used incorrectly: *She sang about ballet shoes and tutus, the sun going down.*

The sun going down isn't appropriate for an absolute phrase because it doesn't expand the first part of the sentence or narrow the focus onto one part of it—it doesn't modify the sentence, which is the purpose of an absolute phrase. What *does* work—*she sang about ballet shoes and tutus, her music playing loudly from the speakers* or *the sun having gone down, the night air grew quickly cold.*

Participial phrase used incorrectly: *Racing her horse through the park, she skipped into the restroom to wash her face.*

While she's actively riding the horse, this character can't also skip, on her own two feet, into the restroom. The two actions should be written so they're sequential, or the character needs an action she can perform while she's racing. Both of these work: *After racing her horse through the park, she skipped into the restroom to wash her face; racing her horse through the park, she pondered her stepmother's ultimatum.*

Fixes: Check participles, especially at the beginnings of sentences. They often lead to problem phrases. Not only do you want to correct problems with them, but you also want to make sure they're not used too often to begin sentences. Think variety in sentence construction. Also, since the format and rhythm for absolute phrases stand out, don't overuse absolute phrases.

Repeating words

Sometimes favorite words show up a couple of times on a page. *On every page.* Other times an unusual word, one that calls attention to itself, gets too much play in a story. Even if it's used only three or four times, a word such as *farctate* is going to stand out. The reader will notice—and be at least momentarily distracted. Intended repetition can be powerful; unintended repetition can be annoying.

> **Fixes**: Proofread for repetition. Reduce the number of
> uses of favorite words. Have a critique partner help
> you decide whether intended repetition works.

Writing unlikeable characters

Readers don't have to love every character, not even your main characters. But since they'll be spending a lot of time with your characters, readers should find something in them to admire or latch on to. If readers should be rooting for a character, give them one worth rooting for. Give readers a reason to care whether or not your protagonist succeeds. Even major characters should have weaknesses, but unlikeable characters are not the same as flawed characters.

> **Fixes**: Give characters, especially those who get a lot
> of page time or who should be sympathetic, a couple
> of endearing traits. Or a compelling personality. Ask
> beta readers if they like your leads and want to see
> them succeed or fail. Make changes if readers don't
> want to spend time with your characters.

Switching viewpoint characters within scenes

Viewpoint duties shouldn't bounce from character to character within one scene. Even with the omniscient point of view, which allows us to see into the heads of multiple characters, readers shouldn't have to figure out whose thoughts they're hearing or which character is noticing something taking place in the corner of a crowded room. A single viewpoint per scene helps with emotion and consistency and a stable mood. It also helps the reader get to know a few characters intimately rather than all characters only superficially.

Fixes: Decide who gets to present a scene and maintain that character's viewpoint until the scene changes. Yes, there are exceptions. Yes, the exceptions can work and work well. But the techniques to make this work *require* work. If you need to portray part of a scene through the eyes, reactions, and emotions of one character and another part through the eyes of a second character, explore techniques for how to achieve the best results for doing that seamlessly.

Forgetting character reactions

Characters, especially the major ones, should have reactions to story events, the actions of other characters, and to dialogue. The purpose of including such events, actions, and dialogue is to stir up character response. You should intentionally make things happen so characters respond and then make something else happen in response to their reactions and so forth and so on throughout the book. Remember to have your character respond when his workplace is bombed or his dog dies or he learns his wife left him.

Fixes: Make sure each action, event, or revelation is followed by a response. Vary the level and length of responses. Use thoughts, dialogue, action, and emotion in responses. Ensure that responses fit the character and the action that prompted the response.

Gentrifying the words

This is not a technical writing term, just one I borrowed. Writers often try to pretty-up their phrasing by using fancy-sounding words to make a story feel and sound literary. Unless the entire story has a literary flavor and adheres to other practices that make it fit the literary genre, a few deep or grand phrases here or there won't work. In fact, they'll sound silly and out of place and pretentious. Let your words fit the genre, your characters, and the story as a whole.

Fixes: Change phrases that jump out from the rest of the text, that don't match the story's mood and the characters' personalities. Write poetic and lyrical phrases if doing so fits the story; otherwise, leave them for another book. Cut out purple prose unless a character is making a point or being humorous.

Giving characters words they wouldn't know

Many writers forget that not all characters know what the writer himself might know or would use the same words he'd use. Poor word choices stand out when characters use words they should be unfamiliar with or words that feature in professions or vocations they know nothing about. Also, writers sometimes remember to use the correct words for character dialogue and yet forget when they write character thoughts. Incorrect word use by characters is obvious and may have readers thinking about the mechanics and foundations of the book rather than the story.

Fixes: Edit for word choices. Decide who your characters are and familiarize yourself with the kinds of words they'd use *as well as those they wouldn't use*. Use word choices to reveal characters.

Failing to include chapter-ending hooks

If you don't invite readers to turn the page at the end of a chapter, if you don't give them a reason to turn the page, they might not do it. They might instead put the book down, never to pick it up again. The ends of chapters should satisfy at least some of the story threads that have come before that point *and* entice readers into reading more.

Fixes: Check the last few paragraphs of every chapter. Make sure they give the reader a reason to read on. Think tease and anticipation. Think about planting a question in the reader's mind, a question she must have answered right away.

Ignoring setting and props

Unfortunately, I see this one a lot. Writers give characters a place to act out their story and then walk those characters through the setting without letting them interact with the locations and the props they should find there. Characters don't react *at* the size and beauty of surroundings or *to* the unusual sounds that fill the air. They don't snatch cookies from the tray that's just out of the oven or run their fingers through the cat's fur or use a fingernail to pick at something stuck to the kitchen table.

They don't hear music or react to too much salt on their fries. They don't see colors or note textures or dodge the 20 neighbor children celebrating a daughter's birthday in the living room.

They don't read newspapers or observe holidays or get paper cuts.

But when characters interact naturally with setting, the reader can see and feel it. When characters deal with political news or mention sports events or noteworthy moments in the life of their village, country, or people group, then setting helps frame character. Setting details and character interaction with setting bolster the reader's belief in story events. If the setting is solid and real for characters, then the characters and their events seem solid, real, and *plausible* to the reader.

> **Fixes**: Make sure you've included something of the setting in every scene. This doesn't mean you need to write a paragraph of description for each scene. It does mean that readers should know where a character is and that characters should be more than dolls plopped onto an empty stage. Give your setting more than stage dressing; put in objects that characters can use. Add cultural touches that make each story different. Create a real world and show characters relating to that world. Give readers enough setting so they can picture the feel of a town, understand the belief systems, and see objects, people, and places important to the characters. Fill your stories with the everyday details that give meaning to a human's life.

Overplaying dialect or accents

Using spelling to show dialect and accents has been out of favor for a long time; writers use other ways to convey differences in speech and pronunciation. You don't want readers struggling to understand what a character is saying because you've thrown odd spellings at them. You instead want to convey dialect and accents almost instantly so readers can get on with the story. Dialogue is a report of the words that are spoken, not a visual of *how* they're spoken. Show the *how* through means other than odd or phonetic spellings.

> **Fixes**: Have a character observe, in thought or dialogue, how unusual someone's accent is. A character can guess where another character is from or note how another man drops his *G*s or even appreciate how melodic an accent is. Have a character admit that he has to listen carefully to understand another character's words. Or use an unusual word or two to convey a character's voice or the rhythm of his speech, words that evoke accent or dialect or a character's background, rather than try to portray spoken words as they sound to the viewpoint character.

Making characters oddly self-aware

Real people who think about brushing back their silky raven locks or who note the way their sinewy muscles bulge when they lift weights would be odd. Odd too are characters who think of themselves in ways that real people don't. This problem usually comes down to a viewpoint error.

> If you're giving us thoughts about a character through her viewpoint, make sure to report only what she would really report about herself.

Would you write *Jonathan patted his smoothly shaved cheeks and jaw, noting how the deep cleft in his chin felt especially deep and manly* or something such as *Jonathan picked at his chin, ticked off that he'd missed the same damned spot he missed every time he shaved without a mirror?*

If a character is the viewpoint character, most of the time he'll respond as if he's actually living in his skin and seeing out through his eyes and feeling with his heart. He doesn't see himself from the outside looking in but from the inside looking out. Give him words and descriptions of himself that reflect the direction in which he's looking. Characters can't report what their facial expressions look like (with a few exceptions, of course). But they *can* report how their faces and bodies feel to them, and they can report the emotion behind their expressions. (An omniscient narrator *can* report what a character looks like.)

> **Fix**: This mistake can be tough to find. In every scene, put yourself inside the viewpoint character's head. Understand what the character can see or know, and share only that information. Also, rather than simply report description, put description to work in an active way, in a way that reveals character personality and emotion and not just the character's looks.
>
> In place of *Tia's red hair was wildly curly and reached past her shoulder blades*, try something like *Tia fought her hair for forty-five minutes, until every stubborn curl was glass smooth.*
>
> If you need or want more, expand on your description.
>
> *Then she forced each strand into the extra-strong clip to secure it off her neck. She admired her handiwork from every side. Hmm . . . The color was subdued now too. Maybe she wouldn't have to smile off any more catcalls about being a red-hot mama.*

Hedging

Writers can be guilty of using hedge words—*seemed, sort of, kind of, perhaps, a bit*—in lieu of making assertions. Yet the impact is almost always stronger with a solid declaration in place of the hedge. Writers may not want to antagonize the reader or may not want to be over-bearing, but while we may want to get along with others in our real worlds, we don't want our characters playing nice and being meek.

Don't hedge. Make assertions. Be bold and clear. Make your characters say what they mean. If a character is diffident, that's a different issue, of course. But not all your characters will by shy or unsure or always eager to please. Rather than saying *she noticed that he seemed to be angry*, try *she recoiled at his unusual anger*.

> **Fixes**: Search your manuscripts for hedge words and replace them, when appropriate, with bold statements. (You'll find a list of hedge words in the appendix.) Or simply cut out the hedge words. Give your characters backbones. Make characters stir up trouble by speaking and thinking their minds.

Having characters declare conclusions

When a writer describes a character's expression and then has another character conclude what the expression means—or when a writer skips the description and has a character conclude what another character looks like—the reader is deprived of the satisfaction of drawing that conclusion herself. The reader is also deprived of seeing that first character for herself.

Additionally, when a character states a conclusion that's obvious to the reader, that may annoy the reader. If you imply that readers can't pick up on your clues, they'll notice. Pull readers deep into emotions and story problems by allowing them to draw conclusions.

Rather than saying *Dell's face went from white to red in an instant. He was no doubt mad, and Kelly had no intention of angering him further*, try something such as *Dell's face went from white to red in an instant. Kelly stepped out of the reach of his fists and fought to keep from shaking.* The reader's going to catch on, and you won't have to waste words explaining what Kelly concluded about Dell's expression.

> **Fixes**: Give the reader enough information and let her come to the conclusion you want her to reach. While a very few readers might not catch on, that's better than alienating the majority of readers by spoon-feeding them everything. Remember the advice to show and not tell? Follow that advice for these situations.

Telling in place of showing (and vice versa)

The subject of telling vs. showing gets a lot of attention when writing advice is being tossed around, but telling in place of showing is obviously not the only mistake writers commit. Still, there is a time for showing, a time for telling. And stories can be made immeasurably weaker when important scenes are relayed via summary, the ultimate in telling.

On the other hand, scenes can be needlessly drawn out when an incident that should be summarized is instead made into a scene.

Show key scenes and events for which you want to elicit reader emotions. Show events that turn the story in a new direction. Summarize and tell when there's no reason to include a full scene, when readers don't need to see characters in motion in a particular place.

At a micro-level, describe setting and characters in ways that readers can visualize them—show those places, objects, and people in action or being used. Don't explain why a character reaches to move the hot pan away from a curious toddler—*Abigail pushed the pot to the back burner so Little Frankie wouldn't burn himself.* Show the event in action—*Abigail raced to the stove and knocked the tottering pot back just as Little Frankie reached for the handle.*

> **Fixes**: If there's too much summary without a break, insert a scene. If an important scene is told via summary, rewrite the summary as a scene. If you need to reveal something about a character, show the revelation in action. If a scene seems dull, not important enough to be a scene, or it's too similar to another scene, try substituting summary for the scene.

To relieve telling at the sentence level, replace telling with visuals that the reader can see and leave out the explanations. Fold description and detail into scenes rather than tacking them on as if they were separate from ongoing events. So rather than say *the dog was barking*, try something like *Richard flung his loafer at the baying puppy*. Yes, sometimes you do want the simple sentence, but many other times you don't.

Failing to go all out

When writers commit to the height, depth, and breadth of action and characterization and emotion, they create powerful, even magical, stories. When they fail to go all out, when they hold back out of fear, the story is compromised. Weak. Ineffectual.

For any number of reasons, some writers don't go all out. But those writers do themselves, their stories, and their readers a disservice. Stories with impact are remembered. Characters who stand out are celebrated. Writers who write boldly are read again and again.

Go all out with your fiction. For the reader who's reading you for the first time, you get to make only one first impression, so make it a kicker. Don't hold back; there's no reason to keep anything in reserve. You'll be starting fresh with the next story—give everything you have to the current story. You'll be replenished when it's time to write the next one.

> **Fixes**: Allow yourself to write anything—any word, any situation, any event. Don't censor yourself. Cut out weak phrases in narration and dialogue. Cut out weak events. Cut out weak characters who aren't strong enough to make an impact.

Using too many words

Too many words can make scenes and stories feel bloated, maybe blunted rather than sharp. The effects of a sentence or phrase are almost always stronger with fewer words.

Fix. Reduce the number of words in sentences if you can say the same thing with fewer words. Keep in mind, however, rhythm and intentional repetition that might require more words.

Write with economy and certainty. Rather than say *the creature approached, accompanied by the sound of a hiss*, try *the creature approached, hissing*. Or maybe *the creature hissed as it slithered closer*.

Starting in the wrong place

Starting the story too far back in a character's past is a problem for many writers. There's no reason to explain all the details of the main character's life before you drop the reader into ongoing events.

Fix. Start with the inciting incident or the moments just before the inciting incident begins. You can give the reader details about the protagonist's life later.

Introducing back story or flashbacks before the current story gets started

Readers want to see what's happening at *this* moment in your story world. They want to step into the current story, where something interesting is happening right now. Too much back story that comes before the right-now story grabs the reader can distract. Flashbacks can stop the advance of the current story's events.

Fix. Begin with the current story and save back story and flashbacks for a later chapter.

FINAL WORDS

Keep in mind that there are always exceptions to every rule and every bit of advice, so assume there are exceptions here as well. Sometimes you'll want to commit one of these mistakes and when you do so, when you do it on purpose, it won't be a mistake. However, for the most part, avoid these mistakes in your fiction. And if they slip in, correct them.

Write bold fiction and write to make an impact. If that doesn't happen in your second, third, or fourth draft, use these fixes to make corrections when you edit, especially if you'll be self-publishing and no one else will be pointing out these kinds of errors to you.

Give readers stories they'll remember for all the right reasons. Edit to enhance those reasons.

Part Five

STYLE ISSUES:
LITTLE DETAILS,
BIG EFFECTS

29
EXAMINING WORD CHOICES

WORD CHOICE IS one of my favorite topics as it relates to writing fiction. All other elements being equal, word choice can make or break your story, make it stand out from hundreds of similar stories or blend in with the mountain of nothing-special stories that grows ever higher.

So why include a chapter on word choices in a section on big effects? Because the results of word choices made again and again and again create the big picture of a novel. Word choice is critical when we're considering the impact of a single word as well as when we consider the cumulative effect of words over the course of a story.

From the very first captivating line to the final image or emotion generated by the sentence just before *The End*, word choices touch every page, every element, every pulse and breath of your story. Words frame story; they fill it. They elevate it from letters on a page to romance and action and suspense and adventure.

Word choice influences or reveals tone, mood, pace, dialogue, and subtext; character personality, emotions, and actions; and reader tension and emotions. Word choice is critical to every element.

Words working together can create a harmonious, cohesive perfection of a story. Word choices that fight one another not only don't help a story, they actively damage it.

> Words must fit character—fit character strengths, weaknesses, goals, history, dreams, and motivation. Words must fit how a character moves and thinks and feels. Words not only reveal who a character is but they *make* your character who she is, who she'll be for eternity.

So choose words that fit each character. Choose words that make characters three-dimensional. Memorable. Sympathetic or fascinating or compelling. Choose words to fit a character's education, culture, career, emotions, background, personality, and problems. Choose words to create the character your story needs.

Choose words appropriate for era and genre and setting.

Choose words that keep readers bound to the fiction and to the fictional world. Don't allow readers to be pulled away or distracted. Rather, use word choices to draw them deep and keep them reading.

Common words and phrases make a scene go flat; the right words keep it bubbling.

Words create humor or sorrow. They can make readers cry.

Words carry the power of your story through every page. Words—connected and re-connected and connected again—*are* your story. Take the time to make sure each one—yes, each one—fits. One word out of place can jerk the reader straight out of the fiction and plop her back into her own world. Be relentless—hold readers tight with your word choices.

But don't only be picky about word choices; use words effectively.

Cut out repetition in words, actions, thoughts, characters. Cut out repeated paragraphs or scenes. Be especially mindful of repeated scenes if you've done a lot of editing, copying, and pasting; make sure you keep only the corrected version of the scene or passage.

Vary sentence construction—which may involve changing the forms of words—so that not every sentence displays the same pattern or structure.

> Choosing the right words is one of the easiest ways to make your story unique. Characters who sound like only themselves and not a thousand other characters will help your story stand out. Characters who are more than just bland cardboard cutouts can have your reader paying attention, eager to read more.

Use word choice to convey emotion and tone. Use it to convey everything from the style of a character's movement to the pacing of a chapter or scene to the description of a completely new and never explored fictional world. Use words that your characters would use.

That means you need to be familiar with their backgrounds, education, work histories, and birth places.

Know how your characters think, how they speak, the phrasings and jargon and slang they'd use as well as the phrases they'd never know or use.

Understand how major characters would speak to loved ones, to co-workers, to strangers.

When you edit, give consideration to individual words, to phrases, and to sentences.

Make sure sentences mean what you think they do; make sure words mean what you think they do.

Make sure words create the effect you want or need.

We won't cover every category of words, but let's look at a handful that you're bound to come across as you decide which words fit your scenes.

> Don't worry too much about word choices, especially
> categories of problem words, as you write your first
> draft; just get the story down. A much better time to
> work your magic on word choices is while you're editing.

HEDGE WORDS

Don't allow your characters to hide behind hedge words unless that's part of their personality or because hedging is required for a scene. Let characters speak boldly. The impact is stronger. Memorable. Longer lasting.

Root out hedge words before you publish. These include *sort of, kind of, a bit, maybe, almost, perhaps, seems,* and *somehow.* (See the appendix for a longer list.) Not every use of these words is wrong, but if you find countless examples of these types of words in your stories, you're not creating scenes or story moments as compelling as they could be. Make characters declare with confidence and then deal with the consequences of their brash words.

Clichés

If you find clichés in your manuscripts, cut them out. Unless a character uses clichés and you're emphasizing that use as a character trait—or a character is using a cliché to be humorous—give readers fresh phrases. Give us inventive phrases and new imagery. Give us new similes. Make your stories sound different by using different word combinations. Use phrases that can be found in only one story and spoken by only one character in only very specific circumstances, the circumstances found in your book.

Don't give readers the tired, the common, and the general when instead you can give them vibrant and rare and specific.

You *will* use phrases common to hundreds of stories—sometimes you'll need to write *he raced down the street*. But try to limit such common phrasings. And when the scene calls for freshness, give it to the reader ~~brand-spanking~~ ~~hot-off-the-presses~~ Internet-rumor new. Twitter-rumor new?

Not sure what a cliché is? They are those slick, familiar phrases that come tripping off your fingers without a thought—

> black as pitch
>
> few and far between
>
> went off without a hitch
>
> locked him up and threw away the key
>
> like looking for a needle in a haystack
>
> happy as a clam
>
> it is what it is

Clichés are phrases that at one time were novel. Then they became familiar. Then common. And then they were codified into clichés.

On an edit pass, root out clichés and rewrite.

SIMILE AND METAPHOR

Similes and metaphors help writers create a poetic feel to fiction. They can add beauty and depth. But they can also be too much. They can be used too often or by characters who wouldn't use them.

At the most basic, similes and metaphors are comparisons. They allow writers to create instant images or understanding for the reader. When a character is compared to something else, the reader can easily picture the character or note a specific detail about that character, can understand a character's emotion or motivation. But when similes and metaphors are used by characters who wouldn't use them, they create the wrong feel, a mood that doesn't fit, and may have readers shaking their heads.

But even when comparisons work, when they fit the scene and the character using them, they still may be too much.

Not all characters should speak or think metaphors. Not all should spout clever similes. If every character does, such use reflects the author's hand rather than the characters' personalities.

When you edit, search for similes and metaphors. Similes are easy to find—do a word search for *like* and *as*. For metaphors, make note of them as you create them or look for them during one of your edit passes. Cut out any that don't fit a character or scene. Remove or rewrite any that wouldn't immediately create an image or comparison in the reader's mind. If readers have to work too hard to understand a simile or metaphor, the comparison should go. And reduce the number of them if you find them every couple of pages or several on one page. Let characters speak naturally, without having them show a talent for similes that they might not or should not actually possess.

Use comparisons as spice; don't let them overwhelm.

A Potential Problem with Similes

When you edit, make sure similes actually compare what you intend for them to compare. We'll look at a simile to see how it works.

Frannie dropped Mario like a hot potato.

This simile is also a cliché, but for our purposes, it demonstrates what could be a problem simile.

What's the comparison here? Is this comparing Frannie dropping Mario to the *way* she'd drop a hot potato (*Frannie dropped Mario as she'd drop a hot potato*)? Or is this saying she dropped him as if *he* were a hot potato? Or did she drop Mario in the way a hot potato would drop something?

Some similes can be understood only one way—

> Bobby lifts weights like a circus strongman.

This says Bobby lifts weights the way a circus strongman would; taking this sentence any other way would be difficult, even though it could be worded better. But compared to this, the hot potato simile is confusing. The setup is identical, but the reader has to read it differently to make sense of it. Similes may need to be rewritten so that readers aren't confused.

While you'll usually want to use words your characters would use (such as the common *like* rather than *as*), consider adjustments for similes, at least for some. Use *like* when a noun or pronoun follows and the comparison is noun to noun, and use *as* when a verb follows.

> Zach's tuna surprise tasted like **anchovy bait**.

> She scooped Brody up as if he **were** peach ice cream.

As you edit, make sure similes mean what you want them to mean.

DIALECT

Re-think dialect and accents if you've tried to portray them through spelling. Rendering dialect accurately is difficult, and strong dialect can make the read difficult for readers. Rather than try to convey the peculiarities of a character's speech—and face it, you probably only tried it for one or two characters anyway, not all of them, even though everyone has quirks to their speech—use a choice word or two and word order to convey accent and dialect. Or use another character's reaction to an accent to highlight speech differences. When one character has trouble understanding another or comments on an accent, readers will pick up on what you're saying.

Dialect was once routinely conveyed through odd spellings, but that style of writing isn't in vogue today. And spelling isn't a key to pronunciation anyway. All English speakers would spell the words in the sentence you're reading the same way; they just might pronounce them differently.

Remember that real people will be reading your stories; don't give them long problem passages with odd spellings and weird punctuation. Convey dialect and accent in other ways.

VERBS

Substitute strong verbs for weak ones and change common verbs that you use again and again. *Put, walk, look, touch, had, was, get, sat, stood,* and others of similar style get a workout in most manuscripts. Before you publish, change common verbs to those that fit the particulars of the scene. If the common word suits, that's fine. But use other words, stronger or more accurate words, when they're a better fit.

NOUNS

Strong noun/verb combinations make action and dialogue vivid. Use precise and specific nouns—*German shepherd* rather than *dog, skillet* rather than *pan*—when the viewpoint character would know and use such words. Choose words not only for meaning, since several words could have similar meanings, but for sound, for context, and for how they look on the page and amid other words.

For example, if you've created an unintended rhyme, a change of one of the rhyming words may be called for. The same is true for unintentional or unwanted assonance, consonance, and alliteration. You'll also want to use different words to avoid unwanted repetition.

Choose nouns for their fit to the sentence and mood, to character and emotion, to the effect needed at that moment in the scene. Some nouns should stand out, others should give place to the nouns surrounding them. If you find yourself skipping sections of text as you read because nothing striking stands out, first check to see if the section is truly necessary. If it is but it's not reading as significant, rewrite. Check your nouns and verbs and make sure they say what you intend for them to say and what they need to say.

HETEROGRAPHS

Be aware of heterographs, pairs or groups of words pronounced the same but that have different meanings and different spellings. Most writers are quite aware of the differences between *its* and *it's*, between *there, they're,* and *their.* But typing mistakes do creep in as we write. While editing, check common heterographs and other words that you know you type incorrectly.

UNNECESSARY WORDS

Some words are simply unnecessary. Take out those that take up space without contributing to meaning or rhythm.

Let's consider an example.

She sat down on the chair.

Down when paired with *sit* or *sat*—do you need it? For that matter, do you need *on the chair?* If the chair's important, great. Include it. If not, there's nothing wrong with *she sat.* If you want more detail, try *she sat, eyes closed, and then leaned forward, fingers clasped.*

Do you need to include *up* with *stood?* If the character had been sitting, then saying *she stood, vibrating with rage* works just as well as *she stood up, vibrating with rage.* For the more unusual *she stood down* or *he sat up,* you'll want to include all the words.

What of *she walked across the room to the door?* Might *she walked to the door* or *she crossed to the door* be sufficient?

And how did she move? That might be important to show. Did she stomp or skip or trudge or strut?

We're getting into the nitty-gritty here, but this is important. Extra words can dilute the impact of the action and/or the emotion you so carefully crafted. And common phrasings make one story sound just like any other story.

Yes, you sometimes want and need to include these phrases in all their common glory. But not all the time. Not in every sentence. Not in every paragraph.

Be choosy. Take out the extras that leach the impact from a sentence, that dilute the power of a paragraph or scene.

REDUNDANT WORDS

Redundant words can easily creep into your phrases. Look for them and then remove them. Here are a few to get you started—

> **free** gift
>
> **blend** (or mix, join, or merge) together
>
> circle **around**
>
> **new** recruit
>
> **empty** space

There's no need to say *thought to himself* since people think only to themselves (allowances for paranormals and stories in which characters can mind-talk to others).

These phrases also contain redundancies or unnecessary words:

> he nodded **his head up and down**
>
> she shook her head **side to side**
>
> she shrugged **her shoulders**
>
> he felt his heart pounding **in his chest**

Cut superfluous words when you edit.

PREPOSITIONAL PHRASES

Prepositional phrases often provide necessary detail; other times they get in the way. Check your prepositional phrases. Do you need them? All of them? Even those that come at the ends of sentences to direct the reader's attention away from the main thrust of the sentence?

Prepositional phrases have purposes, but they can also serve to dull a sentence, especially when they're tacked on to a sentence end or strung together half a dozen to a sentence. If you don't need them, cut them.

NOTHING WORDS

A few words are so bland, they nullify a sentence or phrase.

> **Somehow** I had to get home.

> I had to tell her **somehow**.

Somehow tells us nothing—readers already know that something happened *somehow*. The vague word soaks the power from surrounding sentences. Check out your use of the *some* words—*some, something, somewhere, somehow, somebody, someone*. If you can replace them or reword to create a stronger impact, do it.

MELODRAMA

There's no need to go overboard and paint every event, every action, or every spoken word with significance. Melodrama exaggerates to purposely stir the reader's emotions. Yet unless you're writing the *Newest Perils of Pauline*, you're not likely to be writing melodrama. Leave the exaggeration and hyperbole for bedtime stories.

If you find you've given too much attention to common events or character reactions, made them seem important when all you're really reporting is a guy putting on his shoes and socks, cut out the exaggeration and melodrama.

OH AND WELL

Check for the overuse of *oh* and *well,* especially as the first words in a line of dialogue. Most of the time they add nothing to the meaning of the sentence or to the mood or emotion of the scene. Their use may even dilute the impact of the words that come after them.

One character might use either word, but not all characters would. Not every character would begin dialogue with *hey* either. If you're not using *oh, well,* and *hey* to indicate character personality, cut them.

THING

Thing is a placeholder. If you write a sentence using *thing* on a first draft, that's fine. But replace it with a stronger word on a rewrite.

Might a character say *thing* in dialogue? Of course. And every once in a while, *thing* might be a word you deliberately use in your sentences. But do be deliberate. Don't throw *thing* into your stories as if it's a great descriptive word. It's not. It does little for the feel or meaning of most sentences. Readers will pass right over *thing* and the words attached to it. Why use a word or write a sentence that will have no meaning for the reader or the scene or the plot? Dig deep and find a word that works for the story.

IT

We looked at *it* in the grammar chapter. Here I just want to remind you that when *it* is used as a substitute for a stronger word or phrase, one that could nail the emotion of a moment or give readers greater insight into a character, you've created a negative in your scene.

Rather than use the nonspecific *it,* give us particulars. The exact is almost always more powerful than the imprecise.

Using specifics rather than general or imprecise words is a superb way to make a story your own. When you use specifics rather than generalities for your characters, they stand out among generic or fuzzy characters who have no depth or no standout characteristics.

Choosing pinpoint-perfect words is an easy way to create memorable characters, deep emotion, unforgettable or haunting scenes, and involving plots.

When you edit, replace uses of both *it* and *thing* with more precise words when doing so will create a stronger impact.

MODIFIERS

If you're given to overusing modifiers, either adjectives or adverbs, do an editing pass to check them. If there are too many, start cutting.

You know I can't give you a number for how many is too many; every book is different and carries a different style and feel. But you're a reader—how do you feel about modifiers? When adjectives are piled up, do you actually make note of all of them or do they each lose their punch? Is one well-chosen, well-placed modifier stronger than a string of them or a page full of them? Quite often the answer is yes.

At the least, cut back on your favorites, and I'm talking yours here, not the character's. If a character uses adjectives and adverbs, that's different from your use of them. But don't overplay a character's favorite words either. Repetition, no matter the source, is annoying.

Cut back on vague or common modifiers—*very, just, only, some, really, actually.*

If every dialogue tag has an adverb attached, cut some. No, cut most. Unless you're purposely going for an old-fashioned feel, don't constantly pair dialogue tags with adverbs. Doing so will make the story seem outdated and stale, familiar rather than distinct.

Yet no matter what you might have heard, adverbs are not the enemy. You *can* use them. But do be aware of their cumulative effect.

Remember the Tribbles from the *Star Trek* episode "The Trouble with Tribbles"? Tribbles were cute and endearing when there were only a few of them. It was when they multiplied that they proved troublesome. Treat adverbs like Tribbles and keep the number manageable. And don't allow them to congregate in the same paragraph, crowding out other words, leaving no place for anything else.

In addition, make sure the use of adverbs makes sense and adds to the feel of a scene and to reader comprehension. You don't want to use adverbs just because other writers have used them. You don't want to use adverb clichés.

I mentioned romance-ese in the discussion of dialogue, but I also mentioned that romance isn't the only genre to use stock words, often adverbs, borrowed from other books.

As an example, consider the word *reprovingly*. How many of us would ever use the word in a normal conversation? Maybe a handful would use it once or twice in a lifetime. But the word shows up a lot in fiction. And not only shows up, but is used in ways that often don't make sense.

If you use *reprovingly* in a dialogue tag, writing that a character speaks reprovingly, that makes sense. But *frown reprovingly*? Does that work? Maybe. Maybe we can read reproof in a frown. But how about someone shaking their head reprovingly? Can that be done, or is the adverb asked to do more than it's capable of doing? What's the difference between a head shaken reprovingly and one shaken excitedly? Do they look different? I would argue that such a pairing makes no sense, that a writer uses such a phrase because he's read it before. It's an adverb cliché. And it's not only less than exact, it's common, two writing weaknesses you don't want in your fiction.

As for adjectives, they're also useful words, quite necessary for our stories. But not every noun needs two or three adjectives. Sometimes they don't need any. Use adjectives judiciously and in moderation. Rather than listing a string of adjectives to go with a noun, give the reader one strong and memorable adjective. Yes, use multiple adjectives for effect or the sound. But don't imagine that all adjectives must be paired off or travel in packs.

STORY- AND CHARACTER-SPECIFIC WORDS

Use words that fit characters and their circumstances.

Use words and phrases peculiar to your characters, their backgrounds, their situation, their personalities, and their emotions. Rather than write sentence after sentence that could suit any character with any problem in any setting in any book, choose words that can fit only your characters and their situations.

Be selective and specific. You aren't writing anyone's story, you're writing the story of a particular character. Choose words to reflect the character, words that fit no other character in no other story.

Sure, you'll need some common wording. But when it counts, your words shouldn't be common.

Also, your characters don't need to speak perfectly. Let them mess up word choice and grammar. Let them stutter. Let them repeat themselves (within reason). Let them misspeak and misunderstand. Let them coin words and phrases—keeping in mind that the new words of one character shouldn't find themselves in the thoughts and speech of other characters unless those second characters have picked them up on purpose or because of propinquity.

Give characters word groupings that don't match anyone else's.

WRONG WORDS

Words that are the wrong choice—they don't mean what you think they do or they have shadings and you've used them in the wrong context—are nearly impossible for a writer to recognize. Why? Because *you* think a word means something other than what it does mean. That's why you used it in the first place.

If such words are pointed out by beta readers, check them out. Choose more appropriate words if necessary.

As you read your manuscript, note any words you don't typically use. Look them up to be sure they mean what you think they mean.

> This is one duty of an editor that's easily overlooked in the rush to self-publish, but you don't want your books filled with misused or inappropriate words. If you've edited and not had to look up the meaning, the uses, or the nuances of any words, you're not serving the story *as an editor* as well as you should.

This isn't the place for a discussion of prescriptive vs. descriptive grammar other than to say that some readers may find your word use wrong while others will welcome creative uses of words.

STANDOUT WORDS

Be wary of overusing an unusual word; the word will be noticed. If you find an uncommon word that's perfect for one line or scene, resist the urge to use it several more times in the same story. Used once, it'll be refreshing. Used repeatedly, even only two or three times, it will attract negative attention. While a word such as *quondam* might work once—*the quondam chancellor had fled Earth for Nexus Nine twenty years earlier*—use *former* or *onetime* in subsequent mentions of this chancellor. And refrain from using *quondam* to modify other nouns such as *colony*, *partner*, and *lifestyle* in the same story.

TIPS FOR SPECIFIC PROBLEM WORDS

I can't list or give you notes for every problem word since each writer has his or her own problem words, but let's look at a few words you'll want to make note of. I've used a few of these examples to segue into rules, options, and even controversies concerning word use.

Comprise

Many grammar experts tell us to never use the phrase *was comprised of* to mean *made up of*, to not say, as an example, *the corporation was comprised of twenty-three divisions*. They advise instead that we write *the corporation comprised* [contained] *twenty-three divisions* or *the corporation was composed of twenty-three divisions*. They would rightfully remind us that *comprise* means *to contain* or *include*.

Yet a note in *Merriam-Webster Online* says that the use of *comprise* meaning *compose* or *make up* has been around since the late eighteenth century. And that means for over 200 years. So you could argue for such a construction. But you'd have to decide if having such wording pointed out as an error, as it inevitably would be, is worth the fuss. If a character would use the phrase this way, use it. But expect some readers to have a negative reaction. If you or an omniscient character uses *comprise* this way, the reaction may be even stronger.

Impact

The same warning and advice goes for *impact* as a verb meaning *to have an effect on*. Plenty of experts would tell you that this is an incorrect usage, but plenty of people also use it with that definition in mind. What would your character say?

Different

What of the *different from, different than, different to* conundrum? Many vocal prescriptivists (traditionalists?) say we can never use *different to* or *different than*. They usually mean in comparisons, but then someone else hears that rule and says that we can never use such word pairs no matter what. But as fiction writers, we know better. If our characters would use such phrases, then that's what we have them use.

Different from is the traditional wording when we're saying one thing or person differs from another—and when a noun follows *different from*—but *different than* has been used for several hundred years. It's used much more often in AmE than in BrE, but it is used. And often in speech.

> He's different from the man he used to be.

> He's different than the man he used to be.

The second sentence might not bother you much, but it does bother a lot of folks. To some readers, *different than* is akin to nails on a chalkboard. Really sharp nails.

We're not going to discuss reasons for the arguments about *different than*—just know that it is used in spoken AmE and it's accepted more often when it's followed by a clause rather than a noun.

Different to is used primarily in BrE, typically in speech. But its use could also be a problem. Especially for characters who should be using AmE.

"It's different to what I expected," Mary told him.

It's different to the national debt.

But any English speaker would use *different to* in some situations. Thus there shouldn't be a blanket rule against it.

His voice sounds *different to* my ears.

My advice is that you recognize that not all readers will agree with *different than* or *different to*. You'd be safe using *different from* in most comparisons, but as always, consider what a character would say.

Use to/Used to

These same couple of words can be found in several expressions.

I used to read comic books (but now I don't).

I'd gotten used to (accustomed to) the small print.

The cream is used to smooth away wrinkles.

Use *use to*, without the *d*, in a negative expression or in a question in which *did* is included.

Did you use to climb trees?

Didn't you use to climb trees?

But Edgar didn't use to eat snails.

In or Into, On or Onto

There are exceptions, but most of the time you want to use *into* to show movement toward something and *in* to refer to being inside something. (In the same way use *onto* to show movement toward something and *on* for things already on something else.)

Michael dropped his keys **into** his pocket.

Michael dropped his keys somewhere **in** his office.

Michael dropped his keys **in** his pocket. ✗

This last sentence would work if Michael happened to be inside a giant's pocket and he dropped his keys there.

I know, you're wondering if this isn't straining, pushing too hard at a nothing problem when all readers would understand what that third sentence means. Maybe differentiating this way *is* going overboard. But it's also being accurate. And why not be accurate, why not be exact and give a true sense of what we mean, especially since doing so costs only the addition of two little letters? And what if differences in meaning were dramatic?

The boys jumped **into** the car.

The boys jumped **in** the car.

These definitely have different meanings.

The boys jumped into the car, wanting to get their favorite seats.

The boys jumped in the car, ruining the springs in the seats and punching holes into the headliner.

Write accurately to convey the necessary meaning.

When *in* is part of an existing expression and you need to say *in to*, use two words, not *into*. (Same for *on* and *onto*.) Also use two words (or rewrite) when using a single word creates a nonsense phrase.

Charlie's mother finally **gave in to** the urge to pull him out of school.

Lucy **caved in to** Heather's demands.

Ann **held on to** Bo's hand as he went over the ledge.

Alonzo turned into his mother. ✗

Less/Fewer

Use *fewer* for count nouns and *less* for noncount (mass) nouns. Noncount nouns include abstract and collective nouns such as milk, peace, happiness, and clothing.

> Clancy has fewer cavities than Mullins has.

> I had less time to diffuse the bomb than Tia expected.

Literally/Figuratively

Figuratively means symbolically or metaphorically; literally means factually. Yet many people use *literally* to exaggerate something that is quite obviously not literally so.

If a character is using *literal* or *literally* for exaggeration or because he doesn't know better, that can work. But if an omniscient narrator needs to use the correct word, save *literally* for reports of the factual.

Damn/Damned

Using *damn* in place of *damned* is a choice. *Damned* is the typical adjective, but many real-world people use *damn* instead. Which word would your characters use? Characters might use *damn* with some nouns, *damned* with others.

A while/Awhile

Awhile is an adverb meaning *for a time*. *While* is a noun. Use *while* after prepositions and when you need a noun. Use *awhile* to modify a verb. If the phrase already includes the word *for*, do not use *awhile*.

> Stay awhile.

> Stay for a while.

> "Consider my offer awhile."

> Give me a while.

Give me awhile. ✗

She took a while to make up her mind.

She thought a while. ✗

She thought for a while.

Sammy said he'd be back in a while.

She rode her bike for quite a while.

Stay for awhile. ✗

Alright/All right

Spelling should be correct no matter which words you use or how you have your characters pronounce them; pronunciation doesn't guide spelling. *All right* is always two words. Something such as *awriiight*, used in dialogue, is an option, but *alright* is never correct. Spelling the expression as *alright* shows your spelling error, not the character's. Change *alright* to *all right*.

A lot

Alot is incorrect. Make it two words—*a lot*—unless you mean to say *allot* (apportion).

SPELLING WORDS DIFFERENTLY BECAUSE THEY'RE DIFFERENT WORDS

But what of words that are actually different words, not just different spellings? You may have to draw a fine line to determine whether words are different words or simply spelling variations.

If a word is truly a different word—you're not trying to convey dialect or accent, not trying to make a word look and sound different—use the spelling that matches the word. If your characters say *gotta, gonna, wanna, kinda,* and *sorta,* consider spelling them this way.

The difference between these spellings and spelling *all right* as *alright*? When someone says *all right*, they're saying *all right*. Spelling it *alright* doesn't change what they're saying. However, when someone says *gonna*, they aren't saying *going to*. This isn't a function of trying to spell accent or dialect; it's a reflection of the word that's actually used.

That said, make sure you don't go overboard. Use the common faux words such as those I've listed here, but don't smash every word together, even if that sounds like what your character is doing. You're trying to reflect the character's speech (and thoughts) while at the same time making the text clear. If readers have to stop to figure out what you're trying to say, you've done something wrong.

Use a light hand.

Hafta might give your readers pause. As might *ya* in place of *you*. (Is it supposed to be pronounced *yuh* for *you* or *yah* for *yes* or *yay* for *yay*?) Go with the common and recognizable not-quite-real words and pass on those that might confuse the reader. But if you do use such words, use them sparingly and typically only in dialogue or for character thoughts when it's clear that we're in the character's head.

Yet you don't have to spell words this way, even if a character pronounces them as such. Readers will follow the other cues you've given them. Don't try to micromanage their reading experience—let readers picture your characters and imagine their voices as they see fit. Let readers contribute to their own reading pleasure.

Note that *gotta* is a substitute for *got to*—*I've gotta go*—and not *got a*—*he's gotta job now.* ✗

PHRASES OR SENTENCES WITH DUAL OR AMBIGUOUS MEANINGS

As you might not notice incorrect words in your own writing, you might also not recognize when a phrase or sentence can be read two ways. But when there are two ways of reading a phrase, because of wording or punctuation, you can be sure that readers will read a sentence the way you didn't intend it to be read. Garden path sentences (they start out seeming to say one thing but end up saying something else), amphiboly (a sentence that can be taken in more than one way because of sentence structure), and other ambiguities can create sentences with dual meanings. A few examples:

> She bumped into Max wearing her new dress.

Use this only if Max is wearing her dress. Otherwise, try—

> She, wearing her new dress, bumped into Max.

> Wearing her new dress, she bumped into Max.

Or what about this?

> She sang to the kids lying on their cots sweetly.

Putting the adverb where it belongs would give us either of these—

> She sang sweetly to the kids lying on their cots.

> She sang to the kids lying sweetly on their cots.

Another—

> Their dad prompted Giselle to forgive her sister, but
> she ultimately rejected the overture.

Giselle rejected her dad's suggestion or Giselle's sister rejected Giselle's offer of forgiveness?
And another—

> The old support one another.

A reader might assume that this was starting out saying something about an old (adjective) support (noun) rather than the old (noun) supporting (verb) others.
One more—

> Disoriented, Daniel ran into the house. Then he
> whirled around and ran into Bob.

Does this mean Daniel is inside the house or that he collided with it? Did he meet up with Bob or bash into him?

Beta readers can be good for finding these kinds of errors. But if beta readers are not writers themselves, they may never mention some problems they find. And they may not find these types of problems. Beta readers may only point out large-picture issues, not phrase-level problems that they trip over. They may assume that they're just not picking up on some nuance.

Not all professional editors will pick up on such problems either. After all, anyone who reads the sentence as you intended will not see a problem. But someone who's done a lot of reading looking for errors is probably more likely to find this kind of error.

To increase your chances of finding these kinds of phrases or sentences as you edit your own work, be sure you read from hard copy and away from the computer, especially when you're close to publishing or submitting. Read aloud if you've got the time.

ADVERB PLACEMENT

Some adverbs can find a home in many places in a sentence, which is rather cool. Except it's not cool when we tuck an adverb into a spot that makes the sentence nonsensical or changes the meaning.

The easy fix is to keep adverbs next to the words (verbs, adjectives, and other adverbs) they modify, either before or after them, depending on your needs and style. (When modifying adjectives, adverbs go before the adjective.) Don't make readers wait until the end of a sentence for an adverb that should be paired with a word early in the sentence. Yes, such a choice can work to create a particular effect. But generally the modifier should be paired with the word it modifies so readers can process them as a unit. If you wait too long to include the modifier, even if it ultimately makes sense for the reader, he'll have already made note of the words without the adverb and will have to rethink what he read. It's not impossible for readers to catch on, just potentially annoying. And words that are out of place can slow the reader's flow through your scenes.

On the other hand, we usually want to use the word order a character would use in her thoughts and speech.

When the two choices differ, weigh the effects of using each. Should the character stay in character or should clarity for the reader take precedence? Should adherence to a rule come before other options, even if sticking strictly to rules creates a feel too formal for the sentence? You may need to decide adverb placement on a case by case basis.

Sentence adverbs—adverbs that modify the entire sentence and not only a single word—usually go at the beginning of the sentence and are typically followed by a comma. An adverb that's attached to something other than the sentence itself but still finds its place near the top of a sentence could be moved closer to the word it modifies.

Maybe—Haltingly the boy spoke of his love and respect for the girl.

Better—The boy spoke haltingly of his love and respect for the girl, *or* the boy haltingly spoke of his love and respect for the girl.

Worse—The boy spoke of his love and respect for the girl haltingly. (Adverbs can work at the ends of sentences, but this sentence puts too many words between the verb and its adverb. Readers may not remember what *haltingly* is supposed to be paired with.)

To emphasize the adverb—The boy spoke, haltingly, of his love for the girl.

Wrong—Haltingly, the boy spoke of his love for the girl and ran off. ✗ (He didn't speak haltingly *and* run off haltingly, as is implied with the placement of *haltingly* in the position of a sentence adverb.)

Better—The boy spoke haltingly of his love for the girl and ran off.

Sometimes word placement can be fluid, other times it matters greatly where you put your modifiers. Sometimes the placement depends on the modifier itself—adverbs of place, manner, and time often go at the end of a sentence or clause.

Only, just (when it means *only*), *not*, and *also* need to be close to the words they modify. Otherwise the meaning of the sentence is changed, even made nonsensical in some cases. You've probably seen examples of adverb placement that use the word *only* to show the importance of that word placement. I've included my version.

#1 Only the boy's mother ate donuts.

There's one boy (or only one boy has been singled out), his mother ate donuts, and depending on the circumstances already described, either his father didn't eat donuts or the girl's mother (or the girls' mothers) didn't eat them. To make your meaning clear, you could emphasize one of the words or rewrite—

Only the boy's *mother* ate donuts.

Only the boy's mother, not Angie's, ate donuts.

Only the boy's mother, not his father, ate donuts.

As with any text, there are always multiple options

#2 The only boy's mother ate donuts.

There's still only one boy, but the accent is on him being the only boy, and while his mother ate donuts, we don't know if others ate donuts or not. We don't even know if others are present.

#3 The boy's only mother ate donuts.

The stress here is on the fact that the boy has just one mother. This may be in contrast to others, already mentioned, who have multiple mothers. Or it may reflect the boy's wish for an additional mother or a complaint that he had only the one.

#4 The boy's mother only ate donuts.

The focus is on one woman, the boy's mother, and the fact that she ate donuts but did nothing else with them, such as balancing a stack of them on her nose or rolling them across the floor, which might have been the wish of her son.

But there's a second possibility here. This construction could also be telling us that the boy's mother didn't do anything but eat donuts. She didn't go to work, she didn't visit friends, she didn't surf the web. She only ate donuts.

#5 The boy's mother ate only donuts.

#6 The boy's mother ate donuts only.

For both of these sentences, only one mother is of concern, and she ate nothing but donuts. Whether that means on this occasion or for her daily meals must be determined by the surrounding text.

CAREER OR HOBBY WORDS

To create internal ties for your stories, make a list of verbs associated with a character's job or major hobby or interest. Make the list as long and as deep as you can. Stretch as you look for words common to the character's career and then use those verbs when the character thinks and speaks *and* when she's in motion.

You won't use these words only when the character is working at job- or hobby-related tasks, but those are perfect times to use them. When you use these verbs at other times, you'll be subconsciously reminding the reader of what the character does and who she is. You'll be linking story elements, creating and tightening story threads. You'll also be subtly using character-specific words to help readers keep characters straight, more than helpful for large casts or when many characters are of the same sex and similar age.

Do this with several characters, but especially the protagonist, the antagonist, and the protagonist's best friend or sidekick—the characters who get a lot of page time.

During one of your edits, read with the lists in front of you. See where you can play up the ties to a character's background or career or hobby by substituting a related word in place of a general verb.

As an example, for a teacher you could have the following list:

add	explain	read
assess	figure	report
assign	grade	research
brainstorm	graduate	show
coach	instruct	study
compute	learn	subtract
correct	lecture	teach
display	mentor	test
divide	multiply	train
drill	note	tutor
drone on	practice	write
evaluate	quiz	

Let's say this teacher is an amateur detective. After watching her buddy, a police officer, question a witness, she might say, *"Geez, you were* **quizzing** *that guy pretty closely. And then you* **lectured** *him. He's the mailman, not some punk from Crooks-R-Us."* When she's examining info she's uncovered, you might write *Mattie* **added** *up the clues, concluding she had zilch* or *Mattie* **tested** *her conclusions and found them wanting.*

The ways to weave such words into the story are numerous, yet you wouldn't want to overdo this technique of tying words to character. You want the words to create a connection, but you don't want that connection to jump out at the reader so much that he notices or starts to anticipate the use of these career or hobby-related words. Introduce them as an undercurrent, felt but unseen.

You also don't want these words used in places where they don't fit, where it's a stretch that you'd choose the word at all. Choose your words wisely and with an eye toward fit with the character and the story moment—matching the scene, action, or snippet of dialogue.

PROBLEM-WORD LIST

Search for repetition and for common or problem words. Make changes when words are used too often or when they're weak or inconsequential. Get rid of wasteful words and pointless phrases. Substitute words of consequence.

I've included a short list of words you should check, but your own favorite words should make it to this list as well. If you use a word too often, start cutting.

Search for the words and phrases on this list and rewrite if you've used one word too many times or when other wording would be a better fit, would create a stronger impact, or would create a more memorable story moment.

- common adjectives—pretty, nice, beautiful, big, small, old, young

- as (especially when *when* would be a better choice)

- at this (or that) time, at this (or that) moment, at that moment in time, in this situation, for a moment, in a moment

- expletives—there is, there was, there were, there are, it was, it is— these are filler words that contribute little to a sentence's meaning

- for some reason, in some way, somehow, some kind of

- go and *verb* (drop *go* and use a form of the verb instead—*you need to go and check on your mother* becomes *you need to check on your mother*)

- gave (or give) a something (a kiss, a look, a smile) or took (or take) a something (a look, a walk); substitute a verb for the noun—kissed or smiled or walked

- headed toward or headed for

- hedge words—a bit, almost, kind of, maybe, perhaps, seem

- in my life, in this life

- in the direction of (try *toward*)

- it goes without saying

- just, only, that, really, very, suddenly, all of a sudden

- look (any form of the verb)

- pause/ed (be sure a character is truly pausing if you use this verb)

- so as to (try *to*)

- sound preceded by *a something*—a crashing sound, a whispering sound (change to *a crash* and *a whisper* and so on)

- stand, stood, or standing there—you can often drop the *there*

- started to or began to or tried to plus a verb—unless the character has trouble succeeding, don't use *try*, just have him do the action; unless it's important to know he's starting an activity, drop *started to* or *began to* and go straight for the action

- try and *verb* (change *and* to *to*—*try and come to the party* becomes *try to come to the party*)

- suddenly, all of a sudden

- the fact of the matter

- walk (in any tense and paired with *over* or *across*)

YOUR LIST

FINAL WORDS

Be creative, but make sure words fit. And make sure they're accurate.

Make every word count; make each perform double and triple duty. The word that reveals character can also raise the conflict level and influence the reader's emotions.

Choose unique words that fit the story. That means using words that are appropriate for characters, genre, era, setting, mood, impact, and pace. Words should suit all the story elements.

They should be story, scene, and character specific.

Words are powerful. They create worlds and people *out of nothing*. They create friction and conflict from nothing. Choose your story words with care, with consideration for what they can do. Change them to get a sense of what a different word or phrase can do to a scene or event or story. Change words when doing so tips the balance from safe and staid to uncommon and soaring.

Edit boldly with big strokes, changing large sections of text, and edit delicately, one word at a time. Manipulating word choice is the working of craft. *This* is where the magic of story is created, one word at a time, one section or scene at a time, until you've built up and out and beyond your own imagination. Until you've bumped up against the boundaries of possibilities and pushed outward. Until you've fashioned an authentic and living world out of a lifeless void.

30

CUT THE FLAB, PUMP UP THE LEAN

THIS CHAPTER IS your reminder to cut out excess words and words that add nothing to your story.

When it's time to edit, it's also time to snip away.

No matter how pretty or powerful or beloved by you, no matter how brilliantly clever, words that don't contribute in some way, preferably in multiple ways—advancing plot, revealing character, increasing conflict, establishing or changing mood, creating emotions in the reader—need to be changed or cut from a story.

If words, sentences, paragraphs, scenes, or chapters don't work for a story, it's flab the story can't afford to keep. No matter where extra words end up—with characters, events, dialogue or description—they need to be cut if they don't make a positive contribution.

If words are redundant, cut them. If meaning is unclear, clarify. If text is useless, change or delete it.

If words dilute the impact of the action or of surrounding phrases or words, the words that dilute don't belong in your story.

Setting description that drags on and on should be pruned or done away with altogether. A character too similar to another or who has no purpose—who wouldn't be missed if you excised him from the pages—should be cut.

There are no sacrosanct elements that can't be touched as you edit, so start touching.

> Tell your ego to cower in the corner if he can't stand for
> your editing witch to cut his beautifully perfect words.
> And remind him that no words are perfect on their own.
> They need to fit seamlessly into every other story com-
> ponent and if they don't, they need to be adjusted or cut.

Take your liberty and cut away. Removing words will get easier with time and practice and with the revelation of how much stronger a line or paragraph or image becomes once the dross is removed.

> Trust me—your stories will be stronger and more engaging once you allow yourself the liberty to cut words as freely as you added them.

Pump Up What's Left

Of course, cutting is only half the story; you'll also want to enhance the wording left behind.

Substitute powerful and specific verbs for ordinary ones. Use words that only *your* characters would use and only in the circumstances and under the conditions in which they find themselves.

Use descriptive and precise nouns. Be scrupulously particular. Look for words with just the right shading to express motion or emotion, tone or mood.

Finesse a phrase until it does *exactly* what you want it to. Don't settle for almost when you can make it pitch perfect.

And consider not only meaning but sounds and visuals, the way a word sounds when spoken and how it looks on the page.

Some words carry associations based on how they sound, either alone or with other words. If you've got a harsh scene, choose harsh words, maybe guttural-sounding words. Think of words that contain letters with hard consonants. Consider using short and punchy words and short, hard-hitting phrases and incomplete sentences. And yes, this is fiction. You are welcome to—invited to—use sentence fragments and incomplete sentences.

If you need something soft or flowing, choose smoother-sounding words and longer sentences and words with multiple syllables.

Choose your words and sentence style to match the emotion and/or feel of the scene.

Go lyrical or smooth if that's what a scene needs, or go with jarring and rough.

Consider alliteration (repetition of the initial consonant sound in words) or rhyme (words that sound the same, especially at their ending sounds). Consider also assonance (repetition of vowel sounds in neighboring words) and consonance (the repetition of consonant sounds in the middles or ends of words). There's also that childhood favorite—onomatopoeia—words named in imitation of sound.

If doing so fits your genre and the feel or mood you want to create, wax poetic.

Make sure that the words you keep portray character personality, influence emotion, and advance the plot, but also make sure that words are attractive to the ear and the eye so they'll entice the reader and have him turning pages, eager for more.

Cut out what doesn't belong. But pump up the words that remain.

31

MUTE YOUR MESSAGE

WHETHER YOU CALL IT theme or message or character trait, if you've inserted a message into your story, make sure it doesn't overwhelm. Readers are smart—they don't need to be bonked over the head with your pet theory or social philosophy. Include a theme by all means, but shoot for subtle. Make it fit. And make the portrayal of your theme like the lightest of perfumes—just barely noticeable. Don't overwhelm your story with preaching or a message that smothers.

Allow your characters to be themselves. This means they each have opinions. And their opinions may not mesh with yours.

You're not telling your life story in novel form (are you?), so no single character will think as you do. That means political, social, and religious views, if you include them, shouldn't mirror your beliefs. Not for all your characters. Not for many of them. Maybe not for any of them. Let characters go their own ways, even if that means giving them opinions contrary to yours.

You're a creator, not a clone artist. Allow characters their own prejudices, foibles, and quirks. Stretch yourself by writing a thoroughly fabulous character with beliefs contrary to your beliefs.

Yet even when you do this, don't let those beliefs take over. You're writing fiction, so keep it entertaining. You're not trying to convince readers of a position, at least not on the surface, though you might accomplish that very thing. But if readers see your manipulation, your intent to sway them, you've lost them.

Use a light touch. Rather than pound your opinions into your readers, help them open up to new viewpoints through the power of the characters' convictions. Don't tell readers what to think or feel—*give them reasons to think or feel a certain way*. Show them the benefits of a particular belief or the advantage of a specific point of view.

And if you're presenting a theme, even one that's not overtly controversial, don't drown readers in symbolism or too many references to that theme.

Readers are smart; they'll pick up on your theme after one or two references. And if your characters are convincing, readers will see your theme in action.

Fiction is about events and characters. Theme adds depth and can add meaning, but too much emphasis on theme ruins the imaginative feel of fiction. If you've got readers thinking about meaning rather than the story, then they're studying your novel and not enjoying it. There's nothing wrong with a study of literature, of course. But give readers a story to enjoy before you give them a book to analyze.

As you edit, look for your pet opinions and reduce the number of instances of each. Tone them down so they're not prominent in the story. Or cut them out altogether.

SYMBOLISM

Reduce the number of references to symbols. In a full-length novel, you may not need more than three references to a symbol for the reader to recognize its importance.

And make sure that introduced symbols are put to use; don't merely introduce one for the purpose of including one, maybe to give your novel a literary flair. If you point out a red circle that doesn't quite close and that symbol shows up a couple of times in the story, you need to make sure it has meaning or relevance. Also, make sure that such references don't get dropped halfway through the story. If you don't need the symbol after all, cut out all mentions of it. If you do need it, make sure it contributes to your story's theme and resolution and relates in some way to your protagonist.

THE TAKEAWAY

Ensure that your story stands on its own, without your positions in the mouths and actions of all your characters.

And don't fool yourself; you know your pet theories and core be-liefs. Cut them out if they don't belong or they overwhelm. Just as you'd do for your children, allow your characters their own beliefs rather than make them a mouthpiece for yours.

Cut back on sections of character thoughts about a social theory and reduce instances of uninterrupted dialogue that allow a character to espouse a political, religious, or social view without being chal-lenged by an equally persuasive character with an equally valid contrasting viewpoint.

Take yourself out of your novels, at least the part of you that in-sists on preaching or teaching your party line.

Mute your message. Simply tell a story.

WEED OUT
AUTHOR INTRUSION‡

AT THEIR MOST BASIC, author intrusions are story anomalies where the writer has projected herself into the fictional world. These intrusions show up as events, knowledge, or words that don't fit.

Or, to look at intrusions in a slightly different way, consider them places where the writer hasn't sufficiently covered her tracks.

You'll want to cull author intrusion from your novels before you publish or submit them.

In fiction, any time the reader sees a trace of the writer imposed upon the story world or bleeding through the illusion, that writer has intruded—stepped into a place she doesn't belong.

Intrusion is distracting. It's interruptive. It's annoying.

Author intrusion upsets the rhythms of a story. If noticed, it upsets the readers. Author intrusion upsets characters who must adapt to the anomaly.

If one character starts spouting off in favor of the writer's pet crusade, other characters must respond—even if the topic has nothing to do with these characters or their plot. Or if the writer knows characters shouldn't respond because the first character shouldn't be advocating such a viewpoint, she may have other characters ignore what the first character is saying. And this, of course, creates additional problems. Characters *should* respond to what others do and say. When they don't, story ties are loosened. The pattern of action/reaction is broken. The story loses cohesion.

A tip to remember about intruders is that they aren't welcome. Would you rather your readers were moved by your story or ticked off because you plopped yourself into the middle of it?

Readers come to fiction for the characters' stories, for the make-believe that they can imagine is real. They don't come to novels for a writer's opinions.

Of course, not all author intrusion is about a pet cause or the author's stand on an issue.

- When a character suddenly sounds unlike himself for reasons having nothing to do with the plot . . .
- When a character reveals knowledge he couldn't or shouldn't have—not necessarily about story events but general knowledge of the world . . .
- When a setting is burdened with details no one but a specialist (or a writer who overdid the research) would know . . .
- When characters speak as if they all have MFA degrees . . .
- When the plot is about a novice writer trying to pen a best-selling novel . . .

. . . the writer has intruded into the story and left her mark.

IDENTIFY AUTHOR INTRUSION

Author intrusion can be difficult for writers to see because we're used to our own opinions and knowledge; it's part of us and we don't notice anything wrong with it. Seeing our opinions in others, including our characters, wouldn't jar us.

> To clearly see and evaluate a story as something independent of us, we must separate ourselves from our stories. We must step back and study them dispassionately. The ability to do this takes practice and the *willingness* to distance oneself from one's creation, a task especially difficult for beginning writers. Experienced writers should be doing this distancing as a matter of course as they rewrite and edit.

So how can we identify author intrusion? Give yourself the distance I just mentioned by putting the manuscript aside for a time. When you get away from a manuscript—and busy your mind with other tasks and/or work on other stories—you create the distance necessary to come back to a story as a reader would, to see it with fresh eyes. When you've been away long enough—and if you're not writing to deadline, I'm talking weeks and not days here—author intrusion will be obvious when you return to the story.

You can also listen to your beta readers. If they tell you they see your hand or hear your voice in a scene, believe them and cut out the author intrusion.

If a reader tells you that all your characters sound like finance wizards—and you just happen to be a finance wizard yourself—you know that you've intruded into your story.

The same is true if your characters sound like medical professionals, using terms more common to doctors and nurses than to people with no knowledge of anatomy, disease, or medical specialties.

Relying on or overusing words peculiar to an area of expertise or familiarity can be a problem for writers proficient in any profession or discipline—law, music, literature, physics, sports, psychology, and so forth. When you edit, search for words and knowledge common to subjects familiar to you and your profession. And substitute words that fit your characters in place of words that fit you.

Search also for your favorite buzzwords. If they don't fit the character and the story, yank them out. Your books will be stronger for being whole unto themselves, fiction adventures free of your real-world presence.

Don't think that such words can't be used as placeholders or as temporary text in early drafts; use them if you need to as you create. Just remember to substitute character-appropriate words when you rewrite and edit.

WHAT TO LOOK FOR

Author intrusion can enter the fictional world in a variety of ways. Be on the lookout for

- the sensibilities, mindset, or worldview common to your culture and era but which should be foreign or unknown to characters in the story.

- words that you, the writer, would use in places where readers should find words only the character would use.
- knowledge that you rather than the character possess—names of plants or flowers or animals or birds; names of body parts; sports trivia, history, and the workings of mechanical objects or technology; knowledge beyond what a person of the story era would logically have, knowledge beyond a character's education or station or age or experience.
- characters of the opposite sex—relative to the writer—who sound like characters of the writer's same sex.
- phrasing and rhythms that you rather than the character would use.

Items that a character notices should be events, people, objects, and insights that the character—because of his background or history or training—would notice. If he *wouldn't* notice something, no matter how cool that something is, but he does notice and goes on and on about it, that's author intrusion. That's a writer including a fact he discovered, *because he found it fascinating*, even when the inclusion doesn't fit the story.

Author intrusion can be subtle or grossly obvious.

AUTHOR OPINION

If every character has the same political, religious, or social stand and those stands match yours, you have intruded into the story.

> An author who gives all characters the same stance doesn't yet know her characters as individuals, doesn't care to make her characters independent of her, or doesn't understand that story conflict arises from the differences between characters.

When most characters hold the same opinion and a writer makes a dissenting character look especially ignorant or clown-like because of his stance, the writer is revealing her own opinion and most likely using her story to pursue a personal agenda.

While the writer *may* be pitting the independent character against all others to show how strong he is and that he can prevail, the writer who makes a dissenting character look like a fool often wants to put down rather than champion the opinion put forth by that character, especially regarding political, religious, and social issues.

AUTHOR RESEARCH

Author intrusion comes in when a writer has so researched a topic or issue that she can't resist adding her knowledge to a story whether or not the characters would know the same information.

Familiarity and general knowledge are not equal to specialized knowledge. A character can own a car and not know how it runs. And a time traveler going to the past might be able to talk about the wonders of the future but not be able to explain to people in the past how those wonders work or how they were invented.

If your characters know what they typically wouldn't or shouldn't, or they pay attention to issues, knowledge, or events that wouldn't interest them, cut out that author intrusion.

AUTHOR WORD CHOICES

Author intrusion can come into a story with word choices. Some writers like to pretty up their prose, add a dash of the poetic or use fancy words in place of cheap, everyday words. Now, if your character uses the fancy words *all the time*, that's one thing. When he or she waxes poetic only once or twice over the course of a novel—and the waxing's not done for a plot reason (such as making another character laugh)—then the author's hand is obvious.

Writers often add a flourish to a character when they think they've been too earthy or common or just plain normal with their words. But if your characters *are* earthy or common or normal, let their words reflect their personalities. Don't introduce purple prose or fancy words or intricate sentence constructions when the common serves the character, the scene, the story, and the genre.

Cut out word choices that are examples of author intrusion.

Any time a reader can see the writer—word choice, preaching or teaching, a character who doesn't speak or act as he should, setting details that overwhelm (because the writer couldn't hold back after researching for days)—then the author has stuck a toe, a finger, a fist, or even his mind into the fictional world. This intrusion distracts, draws readers away from the story and toward the mechanics and/or the author.

> Author intrusion is *not* an all-knowing narrator sharing his knowledge, knowledge that no one else in the story has. An omniscient narrator *can* know everything. But an omniscient narrator who sounds like the writer trying to teach a history lesson or preach a sermon is a sign of author intrusion.

Author intrusion is also not the skills, the special knowledge, and the personal style that a writer brings to a story to give it richness and distinction. Author intrusion only becomes a problem when those skills, that knowledge, and those styles point outside the story and toward the writer rather than inward toward the characters and their unfolding exploits.

FIXES FOR AUTHOR INTRUSION

- Remove traces of the author by replacing your words with words and phrases common to and appropriate for the characters, and by cutting out references to knowledge a character couldn't possess.

- Give characters their own personalities, personalities strong and independent enough to stand against your will and interests.

- Use setting details to color and enrich a scene, not drown it under facts—no matter how fascinating—that have no bearing on the story.

- Learn the ways you personally intrude and eliminate the intrusions.

Your personality, your skills—your heart and hands and mind—will be all over your writing projects. Just don't let the reader recognize the evidence of your touch inside the story world—no lingering footsteps or fingerprints or stray hairs. Don't let readers catch you running around the corner just ahead of them. Don't let them feel you peering over their shoulders, nudging them into noticing your excellent phrasing or pithy remarks.

Do your work without leaving physical evidence of your passage through the adventure. Let a reader imagine he's the first human outsider to walk through your settings and fiction, the first to love and fear and laugh with your characters.

Write fiction that reveals your characters and their world, not your personality and your world.

Edit yourself out of your stories.

33

BE A MISER
WITH YOUR WORDS

YOU'VE ALREADY READ lots of suggestions for strengthening your stories, tips for framing the fiction elements, for playing some up and others down. Are you ready for one more?

While *you* may be conservative with your words as you create the first draft, many writers are not. And there's no reason to be overly conservative when you know you'll be rewriting, editing, and changing text. But a time to prune words that weigh down or dull the words around them will come. I saved this suggestion for close to the end of the book because it's one you should follow closer to the end of your revising and editing.

CUT WORDS

Using fewer words—to convey meaning, to establish tone or mood, to tell a joke, to reveal character—is almost always better, the effect stronger and more immediate, than using too many words. When you can convey the same meaning and feel with fewer words, do so.

The presence of too many words can delay an effect or create too much distance between cause and effect or between noun and verb. Too many words, even the right ones, can dilute the power of a scene or even a sentence.

Rather than write *she gave him a cunning little smile*, try *she smirked*. Rather than say *he might could use a beer or two*, try *he craved a tall boy*.

Yes, yes, yes, sometimes you want the longer wording for the feel or rhythm and because it reflects the way a character thinks or speaks. If that's your purpose, use the longer phrasing. But you don't always need the extra words. Extra words often add nothing but words. They don't advance plot or reveal a character's personality or add to the mood, and they may dilute tension rather than increase conflict.

Sometimes words do nothing positive and that means, at best, they're neutral and at worst, they harm the scene.

Keep some words to yourself. Hoard them as though they were precious and irreplaceable.

TRICKS FOR CUTTING UNNECESSARY WORDS

Get rid of three-word phrases—often found at the ends of sentences—and cut back on prepositional phrases, especially multiples in a single sentence. Reword when you've got a lot of phrases that exist as a recognizable unit. These phrases are common and do little to distinguish your style. Common phrases, especially if used often, make a story, your story, sound like any other story. You don't want readers thinking *I've read this story before*. You especially don't want them thinking *and it was better the first time*.

Phrases such as *at that time, for the moment, in his life,* and *for that matter* are often tacked to the end of otherwise strong wording, weakening the impact. Root out such phrases in an editing pass. (I read about this trick of cutting three-word phrases a few years ago. I don't know where I read it, but I'm thankful to the word lover who shared it.)

Do the same with prepositional phrases. Look up lists of prepositions and then search your story for them. Rewrite where necessary.

Consider the following illustrations. While you might argue that the first example uses prepositional phrases as a style choice and has a rhythm that works, you probably wouldn't say the same for the second, a true horror.

> He walked down the hall, looked into the first room on the right and then into the one on the left. He checked under the beds, peered over the lintels, and reached into the drawers.

> From across the room and through the window on the wall above the oak chest, he saw birds with fluorescent wings flying in the sky near the maple trees along the fence line beyond the pond and across the meadow. ✗

Another trick is to check the ends of sentences and paragraphs to make sure most sentences finish with memorable words.

Most of the time you'll want to put the strongest images and words last in a sentence, where words automatically receive emphasis. Readers hear and remember words from the ends of sentences; the words resonate.

The second strongest location is the beginning of a sentence. You typically don't want to lose important words and images in the middle of a sentence.

The simplest adjustments, including moving words to a new location in a sentence, can make a considerable difference to the power of a sentence and ultimately to the scene and chapter, creating more punch with little extra effort on your part.

Instead of writing *he pulled her close to himself*, write *he pulled her close*. *For him* (or *her* or *them* or *me*), *to him*, and *to himself* are phrases that often find their way to the ends of sentences, even when they're not needed. Use only as many words as are required to get the point across, and use them in a manner fitting for the scene, the character, and the genre.

As always, there are exceptions. While we want to leave readers with words that resonate—one reason to put memorable words at the ends of sentences and paragraphs—there are times when the meaty words should come first. Consider these sentences—

I was attacked by the snarling madman.

The snarling madman attacked.

If we already know he's a snarling madman, those words don't need to be emphasized. And the passive construction of the first example sets the character and reader apart from the violence of the action, diluting the impact of that action.

The second sentence is engaging and dramatic in a way that's different from the first, and the format would work in many instances. Still, the first sentence can work too. Either setup is a valid option, depending on the needs of the scene.

And while we're talking about passive construction . . .

Don't think that you need to edit all passive sentences out of your fiction, switching passive voice to active. We sometimes need the passive voice.

Sometimes *who* something happens to needs to come first.

> Victor was hit by a car. (passive)

> A car hit Victor. (active)

Sometimes characters don't know who performed an action, or sometimes the identity of the agent is unimportant to the characters.

> "Oh God. Melanie was attacked in the woods behind the college by some lowlife."

Most of your sentences *will* be active voice, but don't ignore helpful uses of passive voice.

Keep Cutting

If you need to, reward yourself for cutting words on rewrites and editing passes. Do whatever's necessary to convince yourself it's okay to cut words. Having a high word count doesn't make a story great. Having the right words for the story, no more and no less, helps make memorable stories.

If wording is in a story to pump you up, to make you feel impressive as a writer, it needs to be cut. Story words serve character, plot, and reader, not the writer's ego. Put your needs aside and take care of the story.

My suggestion for you here is to allow yourself the freedom to cut away. If one chapter ends up being only a page long, that's okay. There's no sacred writing rule carved in stone that says all chapters must be the same length.

Cut dialogue that doesn't contribute enough or that goes on too long without interruption. Cut description that's going to get skipped because *it* goes on too long or because it exists for no purpose other than to merit a tick on your checklist.

Pare action scenes down to the elemental components; toss the fluff. Unless that fluff serves a story purpose.

Cut single words, phrases, paragraphs, sections, scenes, and even chapters. Let cutting be one of your major editing practices.

> You've heard me say (again and again) that any fiction element or any line of text or even any word that doesn't advance plot, reveal character, establish or change mood or tone, increase conflict, or create emotion in the reader should be changed or cut. This is your benchmark for deciding which words stay and which go. You'll also need words for rhythm and clarity, but the major focus is on these five issues.

Most sections of text should accomplish at least two purposes. If they don't, replace them with words that better serve the story. Or simply cut them. When you're editing, you'll often find yourself looking for ways to change words, forgetting that another option is to delete them. Sometimes the best choice is to excise words that don't pull their weight and don't do anything to support or accentuate adjacent words. Let surrounding words breathe—and create striking images to excite the reader—by removing superfluous words. Don't allow unnecessary words to dilute the power and impact of strong words, of the ones that *do* work positively for a scene.

Keep some of your words in reserve; don't use them all in one sentence or one book. Be a miser with your words.

34

THE NAME GAME

BEFORE THE SELF-PUBLISHING ERA, writers might have spent hours, even days, finessing a title for their books, only to discover that publishers also had preferences for titles—with their preferences carrying the greater weight.

While that might seem devastating for an author who knows exactly what the title should be, often the publisher was right. Those who know books and book sales also know what works to draw attention to a book. They don't sit around trying to figure out ways to mess with authors—they want to put out a product that sells. And the right title can sell a book.

If you self-publish, the responsibility for creating the perfect title falls to you. You can solicit advice from friends and fans, but once you name a book, that's its title. So my advice is to pick a good one.

And if you're submitting to an agent or publisher, use your title as a sales tool. Use it to excite interest from people who know nothing about your book except what you've shared in a query letter.

Look for a title that fits. One that fits the story and the feel of the book. If one title gets you through the writing, the rewriting, and the editing, then go with that title as you write and rewrite and edit. But if it doesn't fit the story that you eventually end up with, change it.

> You aren't locked into a title simply because you lived
> with it for the three years it took to write the book.

What do you call the book as you're writing and editing, the full title or a nickname? If your 10-word title has become a 2-word one in your shorthand references, reconsider the title. You've likely narrowed in on the story's heart with your shortcut and *that* should be your starting place for the title.

Run a few titles by your beta readers and your friends and fans. Hold a contest for your fans to choose the title for the next book.

Consider how you want the book to be remembered and choose a title to match.

You can base your title on almost any criteria, but here are a few guidelines and suggestions to get you started.

- Make sure the title fits the book's genre.
- Make sure it fits the target reader's age and sensibilities.
- Base the title on a character's name or occupation.
- Base it on a place name from the book.
- Base it on a place name that a character dreams about.
- Base it on a line from the book.
- Link books in a series by using related titles (include a color, a number, a name, a food dish, a music style, ball team name, or any other category that can be mined for titles).
- Use a detail from the story's setting (mountain or lake name, region, people group, era).
- Consider the tone and/or emotion you want to create and use words that tap into that emotion.
- Make the title easily remembered.
- Make it easily pronounced.
- Make it easily spelled.
- Make sure the title isn't misleading (unless that's intentional).
- Use a play on words.
- Use humor.
- Check your title against slang phrases and words in foreign languages—you don't want to inadvertently name your book something off-color or rude or humorous.
- Imagine what nickname readers (or critics) will give the book based on your title—don't give critics ammunition by neglecting to anticipate a negative nickname.
- While book titles can't be copyrighted, you don't want to name your book after a famous novel. You also won't want to title it the same as five other newly released self-published books. Check out Amazon and Google (or their equivalents) for books with the same title.

Give your book an inventive title, but don't be so clever that a customer looking for it can't remember it. Just like a parent naming a baby, you're giving your book a name that has to last it a lifetime. Consider not only the moment the book comes into the world, but all the other moments ahead for your novel. Give it a title that fits both the novel's present and its future. Think of the long term and name your book accordingly.

CHAPTER TITLES

You may also want to consider chapter titles. Chapters can be numbered, named, or both, and any choice is acceptable. If you title your chapters, think of names that make the read easier for the reader. You don't want readers puzzling over titles, not unless you've actually set them up as part of a puzzle or mystery. Use titles as signposts to help the reader maneuver through your unfamiliar world.

Children's fiction often includes chapter titles, and mysteries do as well. But certainly a lot of adult fiction makes do with chapter numbers only. You don't have to include chapter titles.

Don't be surprised if readers skip chapter titles. Some readers are so caught up in the unfolding adventure that they read only the story, bypassing anything else on the page. Use chapter titles to tickle or to set a mood for the reader, but don't include major story information or clues in chapter titles unless you've let the reader know that's what you've done and you do so consistently.

If you number your chapters, you can include the word *chapter*, but you don't have to. But when you edit, do make sure chapters are numbered sequentially.

THE TAKEAWAY

Titles, for both chapters and novels, are useful to the reader. Use your book's title as a sales tool and as a way for readers to remember the story. Use the title to create anticipation in the reader, to prepare her for your story world and its unique characters.

Titles can be clever or straightforward—find a title that encompasses the adventure, the mystery, the romance, the unique story world, or the events that take place in your novel.

Don't try to encapsulate your whole story in the title; focus on one element or emotion or word.

Use titles to create a mood or a sense of anticipation. Use titles to jumpstart connections to reader emotions.

Prime readers for the events and characters of your story before they even open to the first page.

Don't let titles be merely decorative. Put them to work.

Part Six

FOCUS ON
EDITING

35

SEARCH FOR MISTAKES

THIS CHAPTER'S FOCUS is less on mistakes and wrong choices themselves and more on understanding the need for searching out those mistakes, recognizing that you actually do have to look for them. Use this chapter to help you determine what kinds of errors you're likely to find when you edit.

My advice here is that you should go into an edit looking for mistakes and problem areas *expecting to find them*. While you can passively read your manuscript, hoping that problems will jump out at you—and some will do just that—you also need to purposely hunt for errors, mistakes, and story weaknesses. Read through the various checklists before you make an editing pass in order to keep topics and potential problems in mind. When you take a break and then return to your edit, review the checklists again.

I'm not necessarily talking punctuation or grammar mistakes here, though you can, should, and must look for those. I'm not even talking about choosing the wrong words. I'm talking about story mistakes, big-picture and foundational mistakes that are sometimes so large you can't easily see them. Mistakes that are obvious after someone else points them out. Mistakes that you want to take care of before a reader or a critic wielding a poisoned pen finds them. Mistakes that might require you to try on a new perspective in order to root them out.

If you think an edit is only about looking for punctuation errors and poor word choices, you're missing the major purpose of editing.

EDITING FOCUS

Look at the major areas that need to be edited as two intertwined but separate components: you've got story (fiction) issues and mechanics (writing) issues. And while any mechanics issue or technical problem can affect a story issue, the methods for correcting them are vastly different. Although you need to correct for weaknesses in both components, you won't solve story issues, issues dealing with the fiction elements, by correcting punctuation or grammar or by searching for dropped words. (Though *do* look for missing words as you edit; I find words missing from every manuscript I read. Dropping words is simply a function of our typing proficiencies and the ability to mentally fill in the gap where we expect words to be.)

Plan to edit for both the mechanics—technical issues—and the fiction issues. But give the fiction issues the larger slice of your time.

> Yes, if something has to take second place, let it be
> grammar and punctuation.

You don't know how it pains me to write that last sentence.

Grammar and punctuation are important; the components of both affect what the reader sees and feels. Some readers read punctuation just as easily as they read words and to them, punctuation mistakes are just as annoying as mistakes with words.

Because I'm like you and don't want to make any mistakes in the books I write and edit, I want every punctuation mark to be correct and useful, every sentence to make sense grammatically or to break the rules in a logical way. I choose words and punctuation for myself and my clients with deliberation. I want grammar and punctuation to be perfect, to be so right for a sentence or paragraph that they serve the story while drawing no undue attention to themselves.

My goal is for the mechanics to work in such a way that they're felt, but not overly intrusive. Effective, but inconspicuous. Yet for all my desire for perfection, I'm not perfect and my choices aren't always perfect. Still, I've got to put an edit to rest eventually, and so will you.

Because you have only so many years and months and hours to your life, something might have to give when you edit. And what gives shouldn't be the time spent rooting out plot errors. Therefore you might have to spend less time with the mechanics.

Please don't take this as a license to ignore grammar or punctuation, sentence and paragraph construction, or word choice. And please don't proclaim to your writing group, critique partner, professor, agent, or editor that I suggested ignoring these issues or implied that they're unimportant. They are vital to your story and to your skills as a writer; using them correctly will help you create better stories and make you a better, more exacting technician and artist. But reality says time is not only finite but fleeting and that if you have to take a shortcut as you edit, you need to take it with the mechanics rather than with the fiction elements.

There is, of course, a caveat—you don't have to take shortcuts at all. Recognize that an edit is going to take time and *plan time for editing and proofreading in advance.*

If you do take shortcuts, you *will* end up paying the price. That's a reality as well.

If you can address every issue, technical *and* story related, do so. Make your novel one that readers can follow—because you've given them clear signposts with the mechanics—and enjoy—because you've told a rollicking good story.

And bring a variety of tools to your work. Bring a machete so you can easily cut out large swaths of unnecessary text, including scenes and chapters. And bring the finest scalpel that can be used to excise one word from a section of hundreds.

Don't be timid about cutting anything that needs to be cut. If it doesn't belong in the story that you ended up with, cut it out. Or make changes so that it does fit.

PRACTICAL MEASURES

So then, what practical steps can you take and what should you look for when you edit?

Be open to *any* change. And don't fear trying any approach that looks as if it could make a moment, a scene, a chapter, or a book more powerful, more memorable, more provocative.

There's absolutely nothing wrong with changing a character's occupation, family history, sex, or motivation.

There's nothing wrong with changing setting.

There's nothing wrong with dropping a character or adding one.

> Whatever an edit needs, be willing to take it on. Go for that gusto; you may get only the one chance. Don't let timidity or fear hold you back or down or out. Bold characters, engrossing stories, and unflinching writers are remembered. The timid remain unread.

In a few chapters in this section we'll look at specifics, but first let's consider broad concerns. I'll offer suggestions, but what I really want to do is spur *your* ideas with my questions . . . to help you push past simple answers for solutions and look beyond the questions toward related concerns . . . to use questions to get you to probe deeper.

WHAT TO LOOK FOR AS YOU EDIT

Make time to look at the big picture at least once as you edit, as if you're playing the child's game of *what's wrong with this picture*. Look for elements that don't belong or that need adjusting *and* search for gaps, for missing components. Do this at both the beginning and end of your edits if possible.

Consider searching for what shouldn't be in your story first, before looking for missing elements. It's usually easier to see what's there than what isn't. And you may see gaps when you focus on elements that don't belong. Ultimately, however, do what works for you.

ELEMENTS TO CUT OR CHANGE

▪ Look for story threads, characters, or events that don't belong in the story you ended up with. I won't say the story that you intended to write, because the final product isn't always what we expected it would be. But every story element should fit the final version.

If a story thread you'd intended to use to highlight your main character's motivation didn't pan out, did you remember to remove all references to it?

- Are there scenes where nothing happens or where what happens has absolutely no impact on plot or characters? Cut those scenes.

- Does a character pontificate to his captive audience (and to yours) without interruption? Get him off his soapbox and cut his preaching.

- Do your characters quote songs every couple of pages? Consider cutting a few of the singalongs.

- Is there repetition in scenes or events or dialogue?

- Do characters talk too much? Think too much? Break out into uncharacteristic poetic speech?

- What of continuity errors? Just like films, novels can have problems with continuity. If a character or object appears where he or it shouldn't or in a way that shouldn't happen, that's a problem.

> A character who just shaved off his beard, leaving baby-smooth skin, can't have a scruffy chin in a scene that takes place five minutes later.
>
> * * *
>
> An object that's discovered in a treasure trove can't show up in a scene before the discovery is made. And an object that goes missing can't show up until it's recovered (recognizing exceptions for characters who could be manipulating the object, of course).

- Time needs to make sense in stories. Events, actions, and dialogue all take time, so each must fit into the timeline created by what transpires. A sequence of physical events that can't be forced into the 12-hour time frame you established needs to be corrected. A story that doesn't account for the passage of long stretches of time, not even via narrative summary, needs work.

Check your story events as they relate to the time element—time of year, time of day, month, or season. Ensure that events unfold in the proper order, with events coming before the reactions to events. Deal with the passage of time in a realistic way.

- Are word choices too plain for the genre or setting? Too fancy?

- Did you or your characters get lost in a subplot or digression and not find the way back to the main story?

- Look for problems with logic. Story events have to make sense. If they don't, fix them.

- Look for character motivation. If characters do something odd for them or odd for people in general, they must have a reason and that reason must be relayed to the readers.

   Characters need motivation. If you haven't included it or included the wrong type, readers won't be able to make sense of their actions.

- Eliminate coincidence. While we might buy coincidence in the real world, readers don't buy it in our fictional worlds. Rewrite so coincidence plays no role in your story, especially for critical matters. Especially for the story's resolution.

   A character shouldn't accidentally be in the right place at the right time, and a character with just the right skills or experience or gifts can't be the only one who shows up just as one of his skills or gifts is needed. Set up circumstances in a logical way so events don't come off as coincidences.

   Deliberately search for these kinds of errors and shortcomings and correct them.

MISSING ELEMENTS

Once you've taken care of the elements that are out of place, look at the big picture again and figure out what's missing. This one is a bit trickier. It can be extremely difficult to identify a missing element. We may be able to see gaps, but sometimes it's not a thing that's missing, not an object or person that would fill a gap, it's a layer that's not there. Or maybe just a piece of something that is absent. So you have a great character who works well in most areas of the story, but you get to that one scene . . .

   It's not that the character is the wrong one—you know he isn't because he's so perfect in every other scene. But maybe you neglected to give him an emotion that he now needs to call on. Or maybe what's missing is a logical motivation that would allow him to reach this one decision. Maybe you didn't give him a history that makes sense of his response to other characters, a locale, or an object.

And while readers may never *know* that an element is missing, they will feel it. Feel it so that what should have been a tour-de-force scene for your main character turns into a wet fizzle instead. Feel it so that the emotion created in one scene isn't the one you'd intended nor is it the one needed to spur the character's next action or touch the reader's heart. Readers may feel the lack so keenly that a story that should be outstanding is simply so-so.

> Missing elements are obviously not seen, but their absences are felt. And you, the writer, have got to gain enough distance from your story to feel the absence. That's why you need to look at the big picture and read your manuscript just as any reader would. You can't get perspective if you never put the manuscript down, never get out of it and get it out of you. You've got to get out of the story and examine it from the outside looking in.

My advice here is that you read cold, as if the story is unfamiliar. Get out of your story's feel and emotions and rhythms before you try reading for what's missing. This means stepping away from the story for weeks. Clear your mind of the familiarity of the story and read, from hard copy, as readers would. See what jumps out at you.

And when you read, don't allow yourself to get caught up in the story itself. Not for this step. Analyze rather than appreciate. Evaluate rather than enjoy.

Make sure you've given characters actions and reactions. Make sure that you connected all the dots, that some didn't go missing.

Make sure you have enough characters and enough events to build toward a climax. Make sure you *have* a climax.

Search for dropped story threads, characters left hanging, and unresolved story issues.

MAJOR ELEMENTS TO CHECK

You'll find most of the fiction and writing elements covered in detail elsewhere in this book, but as a reminder of areas to edit, these lists should be useful. In general, consider the following for each element (as applicable):

For the writing elements, make sure

- the element is consistent
- rules are followed (or broken only on purpose)
- variety is stressed
- no element overwhelms the story and characters

For the fiction elements, make sure

- the element is present
- the start or introduction of each element is in the right place and is appropriate
- the element is sufficiently explored throughout the story
- events are logical, characters and dialogue are believable, and setting is consistent
- there's a proper balance of elements for the story in particular and the genre in general—eliminate too much emphasis on one element that comes at the expense of others

Writing Elements

These writing elements focus less on the storytelling and more on the mechanics, although there is some overlap.

- syntax (word order) and diction (word choice)
- grammar and punctuation
- rhythm and the sound of words, phrases, and sentences
- variety in sentence construction
- variety in sentence, paragraph, scene, and chapter length
- unintended repetition
- balance between the elements of action, dialogue, exposition, and description

Fiction Elements

The fiction elements deal with the components of storytelling.

- plot (main and subplots)
- characters (including their motivation and goals)
- setting (including props and references to the senses)
- dialogue (and character thoughts or internal monologue)
- conflict
- theme (make sure it's not overplayed)
- point of view
- style
- tone and mood
- action
- description
- exposition
- pace
- scenes
- symbolism (keep it subtle)
- requirements of the genre (murder for a murder mystery, HEA for a romance, danger for a thriller, etc.)
- rising action (the series of events that add tension and build toward a climax)
- turning points
- setbacks and challenges to major characters
- chapter-ending hooks
- climax
- resolution

YOUR WEAKNESSES

Whether you begin with them or not, you'll want to focus on your acknowledged writing weaknesses when you edit.

If dialogue is tough for you, consider starting your edit by working on dialogue. If remembering to give characters goals is a problem for you, begin your edit with characters and their goals and motivation. If you go too light on the sense elements, check every scene for examples of the senses in play.

Whatever your issues are, tackle them. Don't run from your known weaknesses and problem areas. Don't ignore them, hoping they'll disappear on their own. Instead, strengthen the weak places. Push and prod and pick at your shortcomings until they can't be pushed, prodded, or picked apart anymore.

> If anything seems off, any sentence or plot element or character revelation, delve into the issue to determine what's wrong. It's very easy to push aside the sensation that something is wrong by convincing yourself it's not that bad, but instead of stifling your intuition, go with it. If you feel that something's off, address that feeling, even if you have no idea what's wrong. Deal with any item—word, sentence, paragraph, section, revelation, action, bit of dialogue, character—that grabs your attention in a negative way.

THE TAKEAWAY

When you edit your own work, assume you've forgotten something crucial: major or minor events, necessary character motivations, or even plot connections. Assume that you might need a bolder protagonist or a different subplot. Maybe a different setting or more scenes.

Assume you've included too much of one element and too little of several others.

Your assumptions may be mistaken, which would be fabulous, but taking them with you into an edit will encourage you to look for problems. Assumptions will also help you step back and look dispassionately at your manuscript, a necessity for effective editing.

Search for craft *and* technique problems, weaknesses with presentation as well as with plot and character.

Edit with awareness.

36

WORKING THROUGH THE TEXT

WHEN YOU EDIT, you'll take advantage of both edit approaches that we talked about earlier in this book.

Using the first approach, you'll work on problem issues in the order that works best for you, using an editing checklist to make sure you cover every issue and fiction element. It's likely that you'll also edit areas and items that beta readers or your critique partner noted as needing a second look and areas that *you* suspect have weaknesses. Once you've worked through individual issues and scenes, however, you'll want to use the second editing approach to evaluate the manuscript as a whole. In this chapter we'll look at tips for that second approach, for working through your manuscript from beginning to end. We'll demystify the way an editor makes an editing pass through a manuscript.

During a rewrite and in the first editing approach, you'll likely make changes to a number of scenes *scene by scene* or you'll address fiction elements one at a time. But at some point you need to examine every issue by considering their connections and the flow of the story. You can search for most issues in just a few passes through the text. You won't work out the fixes for the issues all at the same time, but you can hunt for them in the same read-through.

Read Cold

When you take an editing pass through your manuscript (we're talking the second edit approach here), read cold. That means putting the manuscript aside for as long as you can before you edit—a few weeks or a month if possible. You want the feel, the rhythms, and even the exact words of the text to be out of your head when you edit. At this point of the process you want to create a disconnect between you and your story. Whereas a writer immerses him- or herself inside the story world and characters, editors need distance. They need distance for at least one edit pass through the text.

Start writing something else. Read something else. Get back to a hobby. Do whatever works to clear your mind of the story you're getting ready to read.

Creating a separation between writer and story at this stage is tough, but it's a necessity for editing thoroughly and objectively.

Before you begin your editing pass, read through the editing checklists from this book a couple of times to familiarize yourself with the kinds of issues you'll be looking for. If reading the checklists or the chapters on particular fiction elements has you doing more rewriting, that's great; go ahead and rewrite. And then go back to the editing checklists to prepare for your editing pass. Also, prep by making notes regarding problem issues you know the manuscript has. And be prepared to search specifically for problems with technical issues or fiction elements that you know aren't your strengths.

While you can note and change punctuation errors as you make your first edit pass through the text (the first of at least two passes using this edit approach), don't think that you must scour the manuscript for them. Not yet. You should make a separate proofreading pass to check for punctuation errors after you edit.

WORKING THE MANUSCRIPT

Plan to make your first full-manuscript editing pass using a hard copy; mistakes that you overlook on a computer screen can jump out from paper. If you already work with hard copy when you rewrite, try printing on paper of a different color or use a different font. Reading text that looks different from the norm can help you spot errors.

Getting Started

- Print on only one side of the paper—you might need to use the backs for notes. Number the pages. There's nothing more frustrating than mixing up the page order when you're trying to read and edit.

- Double space the text and use margins of at least one inch on every side to allow room for edit notes.

- Start a style sheet. You can do this on the front and back of a single sheet of paper. On the style sheet you'll include spellings of all character names—first, last, and nicknames—spellings of businesses and towns, unusual spelling choices, and unusual punctuation choices. Note whether or not you'll use the serial comma. As you edit, remember to update the style sheet.

- Start a sheet for general notes. You'll be unable to include all your comments and notes on the manuscript itself, so have paper ready for additional notes. (You could use a computer or tablet, but jotting a note on a piece of paper might be easier and keep distractions to a minimum.) In your notes you might remind yourself to check a related thread later in the text, you might make suggestions for a new scene, you might ask questions about a fact or ask yourself if you remembered to cut a reference that you'd meant to remove. Make notes on any issue that comes up.

- Have a handful of pencils, with erasers, ready. Use red, purple, blue or green if you want to; I find regular pencils work just fine.

- Be prepared to spend a couple of days on a long manuscript. It's likely that you'll get fatigued, so there's no reason to be alert for the first quarter of the story only to be fuzzy-headed for the rest. Take breaks every couple of hours. But when you do break and then resume, turn back several pages to get into the flow of the read again.

Some editors read through the text once before making any notations, but since you know the story, consider making notes on the very first pass. This way you'll be more likely to mark everything that catches your eye. If you wait until you read a second time, some items won't pop the way they do on a cold read.

Making note of all possible problems is important because you'll want to recognize items that readers might have trouble with and note those problems in the text *at the place where readers would notice them.* You might find a contradiction, the repetition of a scene snippet that you moved around during a rewrite, or a character in a scene that she couldn't be in. Even if you find an answer to your question or problem later in the text—maybe the answer is addressed in another chapter—you'll know when and where readers might be confused or have questions. You can then rewrite that section to head off reader confusion. Or if the question or problem isn't resolved later, you can address the issue.

Always note or highlight a problem when you first see it; never assume that you'll remember it without a notation. Questionable text and errors become less striking with subsequent reads.

The First Edit Pass

When you make your first edit pass, note anything and everything that strikes you. Unless you plan to make multiple editing passes of the full manuscript for separate issues one or two at a time—which would be overwhelmingly hard and tedious—get in the habit of marking *any* problem. Some issues you'll deal with as you edit— adding a comma or period, transposing words, crossing out text, or changing one instance of a repeated word—but for others you'll only be noting the problem.

Look for and note punctuation or grammar issues, plot or character issues, word choices. Make a notation about boring dialogue or too much description. Any issue, no matter how big or small, should be marked as needing attention. Mark anything even questionable— you can always decide later that there was nothing wrong with a section of questionable text.

While knowledge of a few key proofreaders' marks would be helpful, you could always use your own notations. Still, consider learning standard marks—the paragraph symbol (¶), the curved line for transposed words or letters, the number sign (#) for adding space, the squiggle for deleting a letter or word. Print a page of proofreaders' marks from the Internet if that will help. But don't think you need to learn all the marks. Use what works for you.

You're the one who will need to be able to understand your notes when it's time to make changes to the text. Use symbols and notations that you'll understand.

- Circle (or underline) problem words and note changes above them—*ital* for italics, *def* or *ck* to remind you to check the definition. I reserve underlining for repetition—any underlined words are repeated on the same page or back or forward a page or two. If I'm pointing out the repetition of an unusual word or repetition of a word used too many times in general, I'll circle the word, note *rep* above it, and include a notation on my general notes sheet. That way I remember to check every instance of the repeated word.

- Maybe you want to rethink a word that's not quite right. If there's nothing actually wrong with it but you can't immediately think of a different word, you can circle it and put a question mark above it. Do the same for phrases or sentences you want to reconsider.

- Cross out phrases, sentences, or even paragraphs by drawing a line through them, but make sure you can still read the text.

- Bracket phrases or sentences or even paragraphs that you want to move to another spot on the same page or to the previous or following page. Connect the text to its new location with an arrowed line. For text that needs to go into a different chapter or to a page several pages away, note the page number where it will be moved to. On the new page, mark the exact spot where the text will go. (I use an asterisk to mark where new text will be added.)

- To insert a missing word or letter, write the word or letter above the space where it belongs and point a caret (^) at the spot where the missing word or letter should go.

- If you have an idea for new text to replace something you don't like or that doesn't seem to be working, cross out the old text and insert the corrected text above it. If you don't have room, draw an arrow to the edge of the paper and flip the paper over and write the new text on the back. (Make sure you can read what you've written. Sharp pencils work best.)

- If you know that a scene needs fleshing out or that you need to add a new scene but you aren't ready to rewrite or add, make a notation in the text and include an explanation in your general notes.

Start from the first page and work your way through the story—marking text, making notes, adding to your style sheet. Be consistent with your marks so later you won't have to guess what you meant. Until editing this way feels comfortable, consider exaggerating your notes to eliminate any possibility of confusion.

After the First Pass

Once you finish your first editing pass, again step back from the story (for at least a few days) before heading to your computer to transfer changes to your document. Give the story another chance to grow cool before you start incorporating your changes into the text.

This step of making changes to your story text will take much more time than the first edit pass itself because now you'll be taking the time to revise wording that didn't work. You'll be looking up definitions of words to see if you used the words correctly; you'll also be trying different words to see if a different one might not actually be a better choice in terms of meaning, in terms of sound or rhythm, in terms of flow, and in terms of the look of the word on the page.

This is when you verify grammar rules and do your fact-checking.

You'll also be adding new text to flesh out scenes, adding new scenes, and moving scenes around to create a more dramatic read.

You may spend half an hour rewriting the hook at the end of chapter 1, a couple of hours on a new scene to ramp up the tension right before the climax, and a day or two on the climax itself.

You may have to rework sections of dialogue that are too similar to other sections, change the inciting incident, move a flashback, or introduce a new character. You may have to do all this and more.

Sections of text both where you deleted text and where you added text will need attention; the sections before and after need to be adjusted so that they blend with the changes you've made.

New text will need to be checked to make sure it doesn't contradict details in other scenes or chapters.

You'll also want to be alert for additional problems that you'll notice as you work with the file; not all errors will have made themselves known when you read the hard copy. It's likely that this is a time you'll find words are missing or duplicated. It's also likely that you'll notice extra words, perhaps from when you made a change but neglected to delete all the original words.

Consider this your second editing pass. Don't only make the changes from your hard copy—read each sentence again as you work through the text.

Also, keep in mind that a simple change in chapter 4 might mean you need to make changes in subsequent chapters as well. Or a change to the climax might mean you have to revisit a few earlier scenes, even after you've already been through them.

Don't rush through this step of the editing process. This is where you need to call on your skills and your creativity and make them work together to produce strong scenes and captivating phrases. This is when you'll have to dig deep, when you'll have to try five options for any one issue in order to get at the one that's best for the story.

> It's okay to feel as though you're wrestling with a wild animal at this stage; you'll be working to tame the more extreme elements while at the same time giving the story enough room to show itself as potent and compelling. You'll be learning how changes to one area affect other areas and making use of that knowledge to craft a manuscript into a novel worth getting lost in.

It's at this stage that you'll put everything you know about craft to work. This is the time to apply the suggestions and tips that fill the rest of this book. This is the time to take advantage of your particular strengths to enhance your story.

This is when you strut your stuff and work your magic.

This is where you pair skill with talent, art with craft.

Your goal is to make the unreal real—influencing the course of story events and producing extraordinary fictional phenomena by the hidden control of words, punctuation, and the elements of fiction— without giving away your presence to the reader.

> When you make changes to your file, be sure you change
> everything you noted on the hard copy. At the same
> time, make sure that you don't inadvertently introduce
> new errors. That can and does happen, however. (Which
> is one reason you'll read the full manuscript from hard
> copy at least one more time before you're through.)

Allow yourself a couple of weeks or more for this second editing
pass, especially if you have a complex or fairly long manuscript.
There's no need to rush.

Once you've made major changes, attack word repetition. This is a
great time to replace favorite words in order to reduce repetition and
create variety.

One More Pass

Once you've looked up rules and checked facts, once you've made all
your changes and you've read through scenes where you made major
changes, check the spelling again and then print a fresh copy of the
manuscript. Put it aside for at least several days, a week or more if
that's possible. And then take one more pass through the text.

As before, note any problem areas. If you're pretty sure that the
story events and elements are set the way you want them, you can use
this as your proofreading pass as well. But if you're still making story
changes, don't think that this must be your last pass through the
manuscript; you can always read one more time for proofing. The
caution here is not to rush these final steps.

To remind yourself of what to look for as you proofread, print a
copy of the proofing checklist and keep it next to you for reference.
Include on the proofing checklist problem words or punctuation rules
that give you problems.

After you're finished, make your changes to your file—being especially careful not to introduce errors—and check spelling once again.
If you made more than a few major changes, print at least the chapters where you made those changes and take one more editing pass.
(If you changed a lot of chapters or scenes, print the full manuscript

and read one more time.) Once you're down to only a few changes on an edit pass and you're satisfied with your changes to the text *and* you've proofread for errors, you should now be done. And you can celebrate with abandon.

If no one has read the story before this point, pass the newest version to your beta readers. Yet you probably want at least a few beta readers to have read the manuscript before this stage.

If you typically don't have a lot of typos and punctuation and grammar errors, you might want beta readers to read right after you finish rewriting or after you finish working the first edit approach (before you edit the manuscript from beginning to end). But to give readers a cleaner manuscript and a more enjoyable reading experience, you could ask them to read after you complete your from-beginning-to-end edit. The manuscript won't be fully polished at that stage, but it will be close.

Once all changes are made, including those you'll make while proofreading, consider having one more reader read the manuscript.

If you're planning to self-publish and you'll be formatting for print, you'll get at least one more chance to work through the text as you format. When you format, you may have to change words to eliminate widows and orphans, to make text fall on a page in the most appealing way possible.

Before self-publishing or submitting to an agent or publisher, you may want a proofreader to go through the text.

That's the setup for working through an edit of your manuscript. Let's now consider all the issues, big and small, that you'll want to cover when you edit.

37

THE SUPER-SIMPLE STUFF

EDITING INVOLVES NOT MERELY POLISHING a manuscript, making it pretty, but sometimes gutting it, cutting away the bad parts or even good sections that are technically correct but nonetheless don't work for a particular story, as well as adding necessary components that were missing. The suggestions in this chapter deal mainly with issues that are easy to check and easy to *forget* to check. In this list I've included details that you don't want to forget to check.

Some of these are oddities that don't fit in other editing lists.

The bottom line is that you have to actively search for problems and then fix them. Assume your manuscript is imperfect and then set off on a treasure hunt to discover the imperfections. If you have to, reward yourself for finding and correcting errors before you publish or send a manuscript off.

> The correction of errors in a manuscript is a very good
> thing, so never feel bad that you have to look for errors
> or weaknesses or that you actually find problems.

You want to find errors before readers do. Give yourself time to edit. You can't edit a novel-length manuscript overnight. You can't edit in a single pass. An edit could take weeks or more.

And be prepared to make changes. Recognize that it's okay to change even major story elements.

Let's put these items in list form. That way you can check off each item. But there's no rank or order, except for the final one. Make sure you do that one last.

____ Check for words that don't belong—no *okay* before its time.

____ Use a current dictionary. Look up spelling and definitions for words you're not sure of or that don't look quite right or that might have multiple definitions.

____ Ensure that chapters begin on new pages, that scene breaks are marked, that chapter numbers are consecutive.

____ Check spelling of names (search for common alternative spellings). Your protagonist shouldn't be Allen, Allan, and Alan. Check also for typos in names—Mario, Maria, or Mare for Marie; Brain, Bran, Brine, or Bruin for Brian.

____ Make sure there are no holdovers from when you changed a character's name (or place name). No Sam if you changed his name to John. No Raylene County if you changed the name to Ryburn County. If Ralph is now Irving, make sure there are no stray references to Ralph by name *or* by allusion. *Hey, I bet you were named for that guy from* The Honeymooners *TV show* won't work for an Irving.

____ Make sure you've eliminated placeholders. That is, if you stuck anything—asterisks, number signs, numbers or other symbols, or even words—into the manuscript to mark text you needed to follow up with, make sure you've replaced it with the correct words or removed it. (Tip: Use the same placeholder so you can search for it easily. I use XXX.)

____ Check your facts. This means verifying dates, events, people involved, technology, history, geography, and products. If you're asserting something as fact, you need to make sure you've got the details right. Double check compass directions or the arrangement of buildings and the layout of towns in actual locations.

____ Check spelling of brand names and trademarks. Crock-Pot, Jacuzzi, ChapStick, and Q-tips are all trademarked names.

____ Make sure that all story elements are present—major turning points, the inciting incident, the protagonist's dark moment, the climax, a resolution, challenges for the major characters, and character goals and motivations.

____ Make sure that there's enough white space on pages, that the text isn't too dense for too long.

____ Check character description, especially eye color, hair color, height, race, age, skills, education, and occupation. Have you inadvertently changed one of these details in one part of the manuscript but not in another?

____ While we're talking description . . . be sure you've varied your descriptions. Every time a character shows up, you shouldn't mention his bedroom eyes, his black eyes, his piercing eyes. This holds true for every detail of characters and setting. Use a variety of details; don't repeat too often. That may mean only a handful of mentions of any one particular detail or trait.

____ Make sure characters don't repeat the same habits in the same way, with you using the same words over and over. Establish character quirks, put them to use in selected scenes for specific purposes, and then give characters a variety of actions and responses for different circumstances. Characters can have habits, but those habits shouldn't take over.

____ Do a headcount—a roll call—for each scene. Know who should be there and who *couldn't* be there. Remove characters who don't belong.

____ If you don't have permission to use them *and* they're not in the public domain, cut out quotes from poems and songs. There are limits to using the words of others without permission of the copyright holder, even if you cite references. You *can* refer to poems and songs by title; you don't get to quote from them without the copyright holder's say-so. You have leeway if you use a quote from longer copyrighted works such as novels and movies, but I suggest you check copyright law before you quote someone else's work. One way around the need to obtain permission to quote songs and poems is to make up your own lyrics and poetry. Another workaround is to write in general about a song or poem without quoting the words. If you do obtain permission to quote from copyrighted works, include permissions in your book's back matter.

____ Check your problem words. If you typically misspell or mistype *sight*, *site*, and *cite* or *discreet* and *discrete* or *think* and *thing*, search for every instance of every word and make sure you've chosen the correct one. The search function of your software makes this step easy, so don't overlook or ignore it. A few examples to get you started: *All right* is always two words, never *alright*. *A lot*, not *alot*, when you're talking about many of something. Do you want *disinterested* or *uninterested?* They're not the same. Check for use of *that* and *who*—for people, use *who*. Free *rein*, not *reign*.

____ Run spellchecker.

As I said, this is simple stuff, simple suggestions and practices that can spare you complex headaches. Make the time to proofread and edit. You spent months writing the story—don't cheat yourself out of making it awesome because you don't like cleaning up messes. Your story is worth the time, even if that means you rewrite and proofread and edit multiple times.

38

THE EDITING CHECKLIST‡

THE CHECKLIST IN THIS CHAPTER can be used as a blueprint for approaching an edit or a rewrite. Use it to prepare your manuscript for publication or for submission to an agent or publisher.

Use the questions and your answers to pinpoint poorly developed story elements and areas in the manuscript that need reworking.

One purpose of the checklist is to get you thinking, maybe brainstorming. It should definitely have you assessing your manuscript to see if you dropped the ball with any of the primary fiction elements.

Allow the questions to guide your rewriting. The topics in the checklist are found in nearly every piece of fiction, so it's likely you'll want to at least consider each in relation to your story.

Don't limit yourself to this list as you make changes to your stories, but use it instead as a starting place. At the very least, these are story elements to check and recheck before you publish or submit. If they lead you to other topics, then have a go at those as well.

WHY A CHECKLIST

There are so many components to fiction, how can you be sure you've checked each, weighed the value of each, polished each?

Changes cascade through a story, touching one element and then another, requiring more changes to sections you've already changed and multilevel changes to sections you haven't yet touched. So how do you remind yourself to re-check those story elements that you already looked at?

Where do you even start this checking and polishing?

An editing checklist will give you a framework for working through your story, a way to keep track of the elements you've worked on and those that still need visiting or even revisiting.

A checklist is a reminder of what you're looking for when you edit.

A checklist can narrow your starting place.

Changes in any story element, but especially in large-picture or story-wide issues, will necessitate changes throughout the manuscript. Be ready to evaluate the manuscript again after making large-picture changes. Make sure changes are carried through the story.

THE EDITING PATH

I've already mentioned that I don't believe there's only one path for rewriting and editing; as writers approach their craft in a manner that works for them, so should editors, even when the editor is the writer editing his own projects. Do what works for you and your organizational patterns, yet don't merely wing it, guessing your way through. Learn what to look for and learn how to address problem areas.

Remember the two edit approaches, where you first work through the fiction elements and different sections of text and only afterward work through your manuscript from beginning to end? Both approaches are necessary for finding problems in a fiction manuscript.

Still, you don't have to edit with a specific step 3 following a specific step 2, especially for the first approach. Because of the way your story is structured or the way your mind makes connections, your step 3 may be very different from another writer-editor's step 3—you need to work in a way that makes sense for you. This guide may convince you to edit certain elements in tandem because doing so is more efficient than another order, but don't get caught up worrying about the perfect order of the steps. Just be sure to cover each.

When you begin your edit using the first editing approach, you may want to begin with the major fiction elements or one of the big-picture areas mentioned in this chapter's checklist, but those are just two options. You may instead want to begin with genre concerns.

For science fiction, you may first want to tackle world building—is the story world well established? Are elements of the world clear and consistent? Do setting elements and plot elements mesh?

For a mystery you may first want to make sure that you have enough viable suspects. You may want to make sure clues don't give away too much. You'll definitely want to make sure that readers have enough clues to figure out who the culprit is.

For romance you may want to ensure you've satisfied genre expectations. Did you include a memorable meet between hero and heroine, a memorable first kiss, reasons for the couple to fall in love, and emotional low and high points?

For suspense you'll want to make sure that pacing fits events, that a clock is ominously ticking away, and that danger is ever lurking.

Outside of genre concerns, you may want to focus first on characters (growth and change), on plot (major events and their repercussions), or on setting (milieu, cultural norms, or time and place).

> Where you choose to begin your edit will probably have a lot to do with how you see your story. Consider starting with what you consider the heart of the novel—the romance, the mystery, the patter of witty dialogue, the idiosyncrasies of the fictional world.

Yet once you're done editing that one issue or element (which in reality is never one issue but dozens), don't forget all the other elements of fiction and good writing. You aren't finished editing simply because you've perfected what you consider the most crucial component of your story; there's a whole lot more to your stories than the heart.

- Plot-heavy stories need more than dynamic events. They need characters to flesh them out, characters that fit every other element and characters that readers can care about.
- Character-heavy stories still need plot events that move characters and readers forward in time and place.
- And milieu stories, where setting plays a major role and the main character is often a stranger to the story world, still need characters engaged in meaningful activities.

Start your edit with the heart of your story, but don't ignore or forget the other parts.

As you edit, you'll want to think ahead and anticipate how changes in one element, scene, or plot thread will change elements, scenes, and plot threads later (or earlier) in the story. Scenes, characters, and events are related, so when one changes, you've got to ensure that changes are carried through the whole story.

Also, you'll want to be flexible. Realize that one story may require an approach different from what you've tried before. Don't lock yourself into an inflexible checklist or edit pattern—be aware that each story has its own needs. You may find a unique dilemma that requires an original fix.

No two stories will require the same edit.

Be aware that you may have to work backwards. If an issue needs attention at the end of the story, you'll likely need to change multiple sections earlier in the story to bring about the needed outcome.

Also, allow yourself to think beyond one-step fixes—you may need to layer corrections in order to fix a problem. A weak character may need a new personality quirk, may need to lose part of his history, *and* may need a different character for a sidekick.

Be bold in your prescriptions. On the flip side, don't overlook the simple solution.

Rely on experience, but be open to the unexpected.

Know the rules, yet allow yourself freedom and flexibility.

EDITORS AND WRITERS APPROACH STORY DIFFERENTLY

The distinct areas you'll consider as you edit will be the same areas writers focus on as they create, but the emphasis, since you'll be looking through an editor's eyes, may well be different.

Writers must make sure they include fascinating characters and plots that keep a reader's attention. Editors (and writers who self-edit) will check for fascinating characters and plots as well. They may also consider what additional characters would mean for the story or what a subplot could add.

Writers are often concerned with the story in their heads and with getting that story to the page. Editors are concerned with the elements of the story as written *and* the elements of the story that are not yet on the page—they look to see what's missing. Editors also focus on weeding out distractions from the core story—characters who don't fit, settings that don't work, dialogue that adds nothing, subplots that dilute the main plot, and digressions and other nonproductive elements that neuter the power of the story or actually detract from it.

Editing can be art, but there are standards and practices and even tips and tricks you can bring to your edits to ensure you've been complete in your evaluation and your fixes.

You may have editing specialties, as most people do in the tasks that they perform often. But no editor should overlook important elements simply because she prefers to focus on other elements.

If you tend to focus on the big picture and story-wide issues, take extra time with the details.

And if you're a stickler for details, allow yourself time to thoroughly evaluate the big-picture items.

You'll find suggestions for both the big picture and details in this edit checklist.

What I've done in this chapter is put areas of text and topics that editors look at and *should* look at into lists with a bit of explanation. This way you'll know the areas you'll want to cover in an edit.

You may find that you'll take every topic mentioned here into account *each* time you edit or you may assign certain steps or sections of text to different edit passes (a more likely scenario). You may find some issues that you've never considered as you've worked and reworked your manuscript and find you now need to work those issues into your editing (or even your rewriting).

I'm going to split the elements into big-picture areas and fine-detail areas. I realize there will be overlap, and I'm sure we wouldn't all arrange the areas in the same way. I'm using this method since I think about story in this manner, with story-wide issues that affect the whole manuscript and fine details that can be edited without necessarily making changes to the full story.

Yet as I said, there can be overlap. For example, some fine-detail issues can have great impact on the story as a whole.

WORKING THE CHECKLIST

Rather than passively read this checklist, actively search your manuscript for answers to the questions.

> If a vital element is missing, add it in. If the element doesn't do enough, expand it. If the element is overplayed, tone it down. If an element is in the wrong place, move it. If it doesn't belong, cut it loose.

An example—

Let's imagine that after rewriting a manuscript several times you discover that your inciting incident is no longer strong enough to get your protagonist involved in the story problem. In other words, with the changes you've made to both plot and character, the event that drew the main character into the story, the event that made her *have* to act, either no longer fits the person the main character has become (because of changes to her personality she is no longer motivated to stick her neck out to intervene in the story problem) or is no longer significant enough to get the character involved.

You have the option of changing the character and plot to again match the needs of the inciting incident, or you need to change the inciting incident. Changing the inciting incident may mean writing a completely different event to pull the protagonist into action, or it may mean ramping up the incident you already have, putting a different spin on it, or using it to tap into a trait or motivation of your protagonist other than the one that fit the original inciting incident.

And if you change the inciting incident, you have to change any references to it that no longer fit.

You'll want to answer every checklist question by verifying what's actually in the manuscript. Don't rely on your memory—check what's written on the page. That's what the reader will see, so that's what has to be right, what has to fit every other story element. Working this checklist isn't about mentally affirming your intentions for the story elements. This is about discovering what the story actually says, what's included and what's left out.

After most question sections, I've included a few reminders of what each story element should accomplish through suggestions for steps to strengthen or enhance that element. Yet this chapter is primarily a list for prompting you to look at particular areas, a list to help you keep track of what's been done and what yet needs to be done. More suggestions and explanations for story areas and the fiction elements can be found in other chapters. If a checklist item is unfamiliar, revisit the topic in the chapter devoted to it.

And do keep in mind that while the items on the checklist have been separated from one another as a means of exploring and working with each, in actuality they don't stand alone in a story. Focusing on them as separate issues is necessary at times, but you won't want to forget that making a change in any one issue may require a change in other issues as well.

As you read the questions and consider the action steps, try to look dispassionately at your story, as an outsider would. Examine your characters and story world as if you were an observer and not the creator wholly involved in the characters and events.

Edit with tough love rather than an indulgent attitude. Make changes, even difficult ones, if those changes will make the story more inviting, memorable, or cohesive.

Edit Checklist for _____
(manuscript title)
Version # _____   Date _____

BIG-PICTURE AREAS

Genre

Questions to ask

____ Are genre conventions addressed

____ Is genre evident within a few pages of the story's beginning

____ Does the story try to appeal to too many genres (meaning it doesn't do enough to satisfy only one genre)

____ Are genre conventions pushed so much that the story reads like parody

Steps to take

____ Make sure genre is clear

____ Make sure genre conventions that typically come at certain points (for example, murder at the beginning of a murder mystery) actually occur at the proper time and in the correct (best) order

____ Consider new and creative ways to satisfy genre expectations

____ Ensure that characters and setting fit genre

World Building

Questions to ask

____ If the story world features magic, paranormal, or fantasy elements, is that made clear to the reader early in the story

____ Are the story world's natural laws consistent with each other and throughout the story

____ Are differences between the story world and the real world made clear

____ Is enough made of a supposedly "alien" world to warrant
placing your story there

____ Do the story world's components fit one another and are they
logical for that world

____ Is too much emphasis placed on the story world in some
scenes, not enough in others

____ Is the story world the best one for the characters who walk
through it and the events that take place there

Steps to take

____ Make sure that details and description of the story world are
consistent and logical

____ Keep details and description from overwhelming characters
and events

____ Reveal details about the story world in a variety of ways—
through description; through character interaction with the
world itself; through the dialogue, thoughts, and reactions of
multiple characters

____ Be sure that unusual features or aspects of the story world that
get a lot of attention have something to do with the story
problem or its solution

____ Make sure that characters unfamiliar with the story world
(aliens or time travelers) react to elements of that world that
are unknown to them

Plot

Questions to ask

____ Is plot engrossing; will readers care about story events

____ Is the story headed somewhere in particular

____ Is there enough plot to sustain the story through the final page

____ Are there too many subplots, not enough subplots

____ Are major plot issues resolved

____ Is plot introduced in an engaging way

____ Does the overall story make sense

____ Are there strong hooks (especially at the story's opening and at the ends of chapters); are they logical; are they related to the rest of the plot

____ Are individual plot events engaging, inevitable, believable

____ Is the plot full enough or does it feel thin

____ Are main characters truly challenged by setbacks, or are setbacks flimsy

____ Are challenges strong enough to defeat the main characters

____ Does the premise match the story that's ultimately told

____ Does the ending match the story's beginning

____ Has reader expectation first been whetted and then satisfied by plot events

____ Is there a focus or is the plot scattered

____ Does the story start in the right place

____ Is the inciting incident sufficiently inciting; is it geared specifically to appeal to the main character's goals and motivations; does it fit the genre

____ Has coincidence been removed, or do events rely on flukes

____ Are plot events causally related

____ Is there sufficient *meaningful* action

____ Does plot get lost behind meaningless action

____ Is there rising action that builds to a climax

____ Is there a climax; does it fit what has come before; is the climax momentous enough

____ Are there events that surprise both characters and readers

____ Do events in the middle chapters get lost behind back story and flashbacks

____ Does the risk level for the protagonist progress ever higher; does the protagonist face stiffer challenges and more problems as the story progresses; is the protagonist's task more difficult scene by scene

____ Would a scene or the emotional impact be stronger if different characters instigated a scene's action or if different characters were the recipients of the action

____ Can you pinpoint the story problem, the one the protagonist needs to solve; will readers be able to pinpoint it

____ Does the story problem begin early enough to engage characters and readers; is the story problem big enough that it can't be solved too easily or long before the story's end; *is* it solved by the end; is the story problem solved by the protagonist

____ Do major events take place in scenes, in real time, or are they presented via narrative summary

Steps to take

____ Weed out coincidence

____ Maintain forward movement

____ Include surprises

____ Move characters and events logically from point to point

____ Resolve plot threads

____ Whether you consider the opening event or the event precipitating the protagonist's acceptance of his call to action to be the *inciting incident*, make sure the story has both events

____ Use back story sparingly and blend it so that it doesn't stop story momentum

Make sure

____ the ending is sufficient (in terms of length and depth) when compared to other story sections

____ the ending is inevitable

____ the ending doesn't drag; make it satisfy the reader

____ the black moment and climax are strong enough for the story

____ main characters are involved in the climax and resolution

____ there are enough major plot events

Character

Questions to ask

___ Are lead characters interesting enough

___ Will readers want to spend time with lead characters

___ Will readers care what happens to major characters

___ Do minor characters get too much page time

___ Do lead characters have sufficient motivation to move through the plot, to try to resolve the story problem

___ Does the antagonist complement the protagonist

___ Do major secondary characters have enough to do

___ Are background characters too prominent

___ Do characters have strengths *and* weaknesses

___ Do characters strike sparks off one another

___ Is the viewpoint character in each scene the one with the most at stake

___ Are character goals clear

___ Are characters well-rounded

___ Are all featured characters vital to the plot

___ Are characters sufficiently different from each other

___ Do character words (thoughts and dialogue) and behaviors fit the setting (especially era) and genre

___ Are a character's motivations and personality traits appropriate to produce the reactions they need to generate

___ Do characters react and react to the appropriate degree to events and dialogue

___ Do characters reveal emotions

___ Are characters bold enough for fictional people

Steps to take

___ Make sure there are enough characters to carry the plot

___ Make sure there are no unnecessary characters

___ Give the main character secondary characters to support him

____ Make the antagonist strong enough to take on the protagonist

____ Make the protagonist strong enough to take on the antagonist

____ Fit characters to genre and era

____ Give characters appropriate and sufficient habits, quirks, favorite words, speech patterns, dreams, motivations and goals as well as hot buttons that other characters can push

____ Make characters three-dimensional—include their thoughts, actions, and *re*actions

____ Make the main character unique; make her memorable

____ Give readers reasons to follow major characters through a variety of story events

____ Allow characters to embarrass themselves

____ Allow characters to be wrong

Setting

Questions to ask

____ Is setting conveyed sufficiently

____ Is it appropriate for the story

____ Would a different setting work better

____ Do setting elements fit genre

____ Do setting elements mesh with each other

____ Is setting consistent across the story (except for intentional changes, say, from one location to another)

____ Are appropriate props included in scenes *and* put to use

____ Are multiple senses used to reveal setting details

____ Does the story take advantage of the wide range of setting details (such as laws, religion, politics, weather, holidays, historical events of the story world, and so on)

____ Is setting used to advance plot, to create mood, to increase tension and conflict

____ Are readers given a clear sense of place and time for each scene at the *top* of each scene

Steps to take

____ Make sure setting details are appropriate to story and scene

____ Verify setting details (with other details within the story world and with real-world details, if applicable)

____ Make sure each scene has details that fit the scene

____ Make sure setting doesn't overwhelm action and plot

____ Include props that characters can handle and use

____ Include sense elements (sounds, scents, tastes)

____ Make sure that setting details serve multiple purposes

Dialogue

Questions to ask

____ Does dialogue advance the story

____ Is dialogue appropriate to character

____ Is dialogue appropriate to the scene

____ Does dialogue increase conflict

____ Is there sufficient dialogue; is there too much dialogue

____ Is dialogue too straightforward

____ Does dialogue reveal too much

____ Does dialogue contain too much back story

____ Does dialogue overwhelm other action

____ Do characters sit or stand around talking in too many scenes or in back-to-back scenes

____ Does the same character always initiate dialogue

____ Does the same character always get the best dialogue

____ Does dialogue include effective subtext

____ Do characters preach or teach from a figurative soapbox

____ Does dialogue reveal character emotions

____ Does dialogue raise reader tension in scenes where it should

____ Are characters allowed emotional rants at dramatic moments

____ Do characters talk too long without interruption

____ Do all scenes of dialogue have the same rhythm and pattern

Steps to take

____ Use genre-appropriate dialogue tags

____ Reduce overuse of names in dialogue

____ Keep adverbs in dialogue tags to a minimum unless genre allows for them

Make sure

____ characters sound sufficiently different

____ it *is* dialogue and not conversation

____ no character speaks on and on without interruption

____ scenes don't have only talking heads, all talk and no movement or no sense of where the characters are

____ dialogue doesn't serve as an info dump

____ characters don't overuse their favorite words and phrases; make sure characters do use supposed favorite phrases more than once

____ that all characters don't use the same common words or phrases—for example, *oh, well,* or *hey*

____ that character emotions affect dialogue

____ dialogue advances plot

Description and Detail

Questions to ask

____ Does description in a scene overwhelm action and dialogue

____ Does setting description match genre and scene locations

____ Do details fit smoothly into the narrative or do they seem tacked on

____ Do details of character description tell too much

____ Do characters note and/or remark on details (of setting or characters) when they should be too busy to notice

____ Do characters describe their own looks or expressions when they can't see themselves

____ Do all places (rooms, buildings, outdoor areas) get the same attention to detail; should all locations be described in full

____ Do descriptions include a variety of elements—color, size, sound, smell

____ Is too much description given to common objects

____ Are important objects or symbols overemphasized

____ Is setting description sufficient; could readers use a more detailed sense of setting

____ Are setting details conveyed early in the story and early in scenes with new locations

____ Do details match what the viewpoint character would notice

____ Do characters have knowledge of details they shouldn't have (for example, knowledge of a dress's designer, the name of a type of shrubbery, the year a car was first produced, or how radio waves work)

____ Are descriptions clichéd; are details too vague or common

Steps to take

____ Cut details unimportant to the plot; show only the features of an object or a character that another character would notice

____ Cut details that sound like a play-by-play of common actions or activities (such as driving a car or entering a home); use summary rather than a full report of a character's every step

____ Put description of both characters and setting in words the viewpoint character or the speaker would use

____ Allow readers to imagine characters for themselves by including only necessary description

____ Weave details and description into action and dialogue so that description doesn't sit baldly on the page

Make sure

____ setting description doesn't go on for too long

____ some details of a new setting are included with scene changes

____ characters don't describe what they can't know

____ description of both setting and character includes unique details relevant to the story

____ setting details enhance mood

Scenes

Questions to ask

____ Do scenes feature a variety of character groupings

____ Do scenes make up the majority of the story when compared to summary

____ Do scenes end with hooks

____ Do scenes advance and redirect plot

____ Are characters or situations different at the end of every scene

____ Do scenes feature different settings (when a story allows for it)

____ Is every scene necessary

____ Does the mood in a scene match the events of that scene

____ Would a scene be more effective if it were shorter (or longer)

____ Does pace vary in adjacent scenes

Steps to take

____ Give scenes variety in length, format, depth, and pattern

____ Give scenes discernible starting and ending moments

____ Use a variety of settings for scenes (or play against variety and stick to only a few settings)

____ Give scenes a purpose

____ Eliminate unproductive scenes

____ If a scene marks a change in setting or viewpoint character, be sure to highlight the changes early in the scene

Make sure

____ the number of scenes is sufficient for the length of the story

____ the balance of scene to exposition favors scenes

____ individual scenes satisfy and that they are different in terms of action events, character combinations, dialogue patterns, and type of conflict

____ scenes are in the best order to cause problems for the character and induce tension in the reader

____ scenes (and chapters) end with hooks

____ the length of scene events matches references to passing time

____ scenes contain characters doing something somewhere and at a particular time for a specific length of time

Point of View/Viewpoint Character

Questions to ask

____ Is the right POV used for the story, for each scene, and for the genre; would a different POV be more appropriate or more effective

____ Is POV clear

____ Is POV maintained within scenes

____ If POV changes at the top of scenes, is there a logical pattern to the change throughout the story

____ Who should be the viewpoint character in each scene; why

____ Should there be multiple viewpoint characters

____ Are there too many viewpoint characters

____ Does the viewpoint character change willy-nilly midscene

____ Do word choices reflect the viewpoint character

____ Does a viewpoint character know more than she could know

____ Is the narrative distance too distant for the genre or story style

Steps to take

____ Make sure that the viewpoint character doesn't change within scenes (no head-hopping)

____ Change the story's POV if doing so would create a stronger impact or would enhance genre elements or mood

____ Change narrative distance, as necessary, through word choices

____ Make sure viewpoint characters know only what they could really know (characters don't know what they look like without seeing their reflections)

____ Use a change in POV or viewpoint character to bring story and character closer to the reader or to hold the reader at a distance when necessary

____ Use an omniscient POV to present a wide or distant or all-encompassing view of a scene/setting at the beginning of a chapter even for other POVs (except for first-person POV)

Pace

Questions to ask

____ Does pace vary from scene to scene

____ Is the pace of each scene appropriate for genre, events, and location in the plot

____ Does pace influence tone and mood

____ Does pace increase/decrease tension

____ Does pace pick up as the story pushes toward the climax

Steps to take

____ Verify that pace increases with rising tension (if appropriate) and as the climax approaches

____ Make sure that pace changes

____ Shorten scenes and chapters to speed pace

____ Lengthen scenes and chapters to slow pace

Conflict

Questions to ask

____ Is there sufficient conflict in each scene and between characters; does conflict exist between the right characters for the scene's needs

____ Does conflict escalate

____ Are there different levels and types of conflict, different sources of conflict

____ Does conflict always start the same way—with the same character, over the same issue, concerning the same subject

____ Is some conflict resolved sooner than other conflict

____ Does conflict show up in dialogue, in actions, and in thoughts

____ Does conflict push characters into making irrational or unintended responses

Steps to take

____ Use conflict to create tension

____ Make characters and readers uncomfortable

____ Increase the intensity of conflict as the story progresses

____ Make sure every scene has at least one type of conflict

____ Ensure that there's conflict between characters and between the protagonist and his own desires

____ Make sure characters respond to conflict and problems

____ Make sure that not all issues are resolved too quickly or too easily or with similar solutions

Exposition/Narrative Summary

Questions to ask

____ Does summary take the place of scenes when it shouldn't

____ Are critical events conveyed via summary rather than scene

Steps to take

____ Limit exposition and summary so the story doesn't read like a school or business report

____ Include either when you need to move the story along, when a scene isn't necessary; use summary for transitions

____ Make sure key events aren't relayed via summary (use scenes)

Timeline

Questions to ask

____ Is the timing of events accurately conveyed

____ Does the timeline make sense; can events take place as written

____ Does the order of scenes match the timeline

____ Have you included time markers, especially at the beginnings of scenes

____ Have you allowed enough time for action and events and for the passage of time between events

____ Do events play out on the right days, in the right (and most effective) order

____ If you include days of the week with dates, do they match those on the real-world calendar

Steps to take

____ Make sure readers can understand the timeline without any chance of confusion

____ Make sure that events can play out in the timeframe you've indicated that they do

____ Create a story calendar for reference—include events (times, dates, characters present), the time necessary to complete those events, and the time between events

____ For series books, keep a record of events that overlap

Tone/Mood/Feel

Questions to ask

____ Is the story's mood consistent and does it change only when you intend it to (for example, with the revelation of events or at the entrance of a new character to a scene)

____ Is a scene's mood clear and unambiguous

____ Does mood fit genre and story events

____ Is setting used to address and manipulate mood

____ Do the viewpoint character's tone and a scene's mood work together or do they struggle against each other

____ Do word choices match tone and mood

____ Does the story have a particular feel; does the feel match story events and character actions

____ Does the story feel like one story, or do elements compete in a way that makes the story seem disjointed

____ Does the viewpoint character's tone match his personality and the events of the story as a whole and the events of the scene in particular

____ Does pace match a scene's mood

Steps to take

____ Make sure that tone (of the narrator/viewpoint character) and mood (of the scene) are what you intended and are appropriate for story events, genre, scene, and character

____ Make sure that tone and mood are consistent unless something acts to change them

____ Make sure there are no mixed messages because words don't match the intended tone or mood

____ Ensure that tone and mood and the feel of your story are established right away through word choice, setting details, and/or character actions

____ Decide on mood and tone as early as possible so they can direct the story in the direction you want it to go

____ Don't shy away from changing tone or mood if they don't fit the story that ultimately evolves

Balance

Questions to ask

____ Is one element too noticeable

____ Are some elements ignored

Steps to take

____ Ensure balance between elements; make sure no single element overwhelms

____ Balance sections, scenes, chapters, and acts

____ Balance character thoughts, dialogue, and actions with exposition, description, and summary

____ Make sure the number of scenes given to each viewpoint character meets the needs of the plot and that the balance creates the feel and effect the story needs

____ Balance words in sentences, sentences in paragraphs, paragraphs in scenes (they don't need to be the same length, just of a pleasing and effective balance)

____ Make sure that relatively unimportant props, characters, and events aren't given too much attention

____ Make sure the "message" or theme doesn't overwhelm plot

Beginning

Questions to ask

____ Does the story opening hook the reader

____ Is genre obvious within the first page or two if not in the first few paragraphs

____ Does the story start too big, with no place to go

____ Does the story begin too blandly

____ Is there too much setup before anything actually happens

____ Have you told readers (or yourself) that the plot really kicks in at about page 50 (if yes, the story starts at the wrong place)

____ Does the story start too far back in the main character's past

____ Does the story open with current story or with back story

____ Can readers identify the story problem; does it raise in readers a question that needs to be answered by story's end, something such as *how is Sam going to fix this* or *how will Betsy get out of this mess*

____ Have you introduced too many characters in the first few pages; do readers need a cheat sheet to keep up with characters and relationships

____ Does the story go too long before the first major event, first bit of dialogue, or introduction of the protagonist

____ Does the beginning feature something after the initial hook that keeps readers interested

____ Does the inciting incident happen close to the top of the story

____ Are introductions of protagonist and antagonist memorable; are they suitable for genre and for the balance of the story

____ Could the story start at a different place or with a different element and should it

____ Is the story world easy to visualize

____ Are important setting details (especially time and place) made clear fairly early

Steps to take

____ Make the beginning engaging, intriguing, alluring, welcoming

____ Satisfy genre requirements

____ Give readers a character to latch on to

____ Make the reader have to turn those first pages

Ending

Questions to ask

____ Is the climax dramatic enough; is it big enough for all that came before

____ Is the climax long enough to balance other story elements without dragging on for too long

____ Does the end answer the major story problem; does the ending arise out of the story problem

____ Will the end satisfy the reader

____ Does the end set up the next book in a series

___ Does the ending (last scene, action, word, or section of dialogue) resonate

___ Would a different ending be more dramatic or emotional, more satisfying

___ Does the ending satisfy genre expectations

___ Does the ending take place onstage as a scene

___ Are all plot problems resolved by the story's end

___ Does the epilogue fit the climax and the rest of the story

___ Do the main characters drive events of the ending

___ Are the main characters on stage for the climax

___ If there's an epilogue, does it drag

___ Does the ending fit your protagonist, his traits and gifts, his skills and goals

___ Does the ending show what the protagonist learned or how she changed

___ Is the final image a clear one

Steps to take

___ Make the ending memorable

___ Make the ending fit all that has come before

___ Make the ending satisfy the story problem as well as the reader

___ Cut fluff that distracts from essential components of the end

___ Make the climax sufficiently dramatic

___ Give readers a resolution to bring them down from the high of the climax

Theme and Symbolism

Questions to ask

___ Are theme or symbolism overemphasized (pointed out in too many scenes or by too many characters)

___ Are symbols introduced and then forgotten

___ Are there too many symbols or symbols that compete

____ Is overt symbolism necessary or would the story be more effective without it

____ Do the protagonist's actions and beliefs present a clear picture of a unified theme

____ Do the changes in the protagonist by the story's end (changes that highlight theme) reflect the theme that was overtly stated

____ Do word choices fit and accentuate the theme

Steps to take

____ Take the spotlight off themes and symbols; underplay them

____ Let theme evolve naturally without manipulation by you

FINE-DETAIL AREAS

Spelling, Grammar, Punctuation

Steps to take

____ Each must be checked; never assume they're correct

____ Maintain consistency in all three

____ Use a style sheet to keep track of unusual choices

____ Learn the rules; apply the rules; break the rules when doing so creates conflict or drama or engaging literary moments

____ Limit extraneous punctuation, especially commas

____ Reduce use of ellipses, dashes, semicolons, colons, and exclamation points if you tend to favor them

____ Edit out word repetition

Emotion

Steps to take

____ Give characters a variety of responses in terms of action, thought, expression, dialogue, and physical movement

____ Give each character different go-to emotional responses

____ Surprise characters occasionally with the depth of their own emotional responses; surprise characters with the emotional responses of other characters

____ Include more than one major emotional event per story

____ Purposely tap into reader emotion; make sure multiple scenes push the reader's emotional buttons

____ Push the emotional elements; don't hold back, especially if emotional elements bother you personally

____ Extend emotional scenes occasionally; be sure not to stop the emotional punch too soon

Make sure

____ you've shown character emotions

____ characters display more than one emotion

____ emotional responses (the response itself and the level of the response) vary according to events and to the character

____ you drive major characters to an emotional blowout, showdown, or meltdown

____ the emotional response of one character, especially an unexpected response, produces reactions in other characters

____ key scenes are designed to rouse reader emotions

____ to use words that intentionally produce emotional responses in the reader as well as in characters

Style

Steps to take

____ Enhance your personal writing style (diction, syntax, and subject matter) as long as it serves the story, but reword when style upstages story events or characters

____ Cut uses of literary or poetic devices that draw too much attention to the mechanics of the story at the expense of plot and characters

___ Make sure the style is cohesive

___ Reduce the use of literary devices that overwhelm (such as too many similes in general or too many or metaphors in the dialogue or thoughts of multiple characters)

___ Reduce overuse of your favorite sentence constructions, phrases, or sentence patterns; look for multiple prepositional phrases in the same sentence, the use of absolute phrases in sentence after sentence, multiple sentences starting with participial phrases, and a great number of chapters, scenes, or paragraphs starting with expletives (*there were, it was*)

___ Check favorite passages and determine whether they serve the story or merely reflect your strengths; rewrite phrases and sections that don't match the character, the genre, the scene's mood, the intended emotion of the scene, or the action

___ If any one line stands out as being grandly poetic or artistic or simply too different from surrounding text, rewrite

Fact-checking

Steps to take

___ Check dates of actual events and the availability of products and technology by date and location

___ Verify details of inventions and technology, historical events, sports statistics, spelling of product and place names; give special attention to story details concerning era and culture—anything that *can* be verified *needs* to be verified.

Word Choices

Steps to take

___ Delete unintended repetition and unintended rhyme

___ Make sure words are appropriate for character, era, scene, genre, and the emotional impact of a scene

___ Cut out unnecessary words (especially redundant ones)

____ Check to see how humor affects character, scene, mood, and plot, and cut humor if it's inappropriate

____ Make sure verbs say exactly what they need to say

____ Remove or rewrite weak phrasing

____ Take out clichés and replace with fresh phrases that fit the character and the current moment in the character's life

____ Make every sentence and each word count

____ Change words that impede the flow of phrases and sentences

____ Consider substituting common words for fancier-sounding words that readers might not know, especially when a character is supposedly too emotional or too busy to come up with the fancier words (tip: check out the differences between Anglo-Saxon and Latinate words and their effect on mood, meaning, and rhythm—chew vs. masticate, lie vs. prevaricate, think vs. cogitate)

____ Reduce the number of mentions of character names in general and in dialogue in particular

____ Replace the imprecise *it* and *thing* with more precise words

____ Replace odd spellings of dialect and accent with the correct spelling and use word choice or word order to hint at accents

____ Reduce overuse of your favorite words

____ Check for multiple uses of highly unusual words; even two uses of a standout word may be too much

____ Check for overuse of *just, some, very, walk, look, put,* and *that*

____ In first-person narration, check the use of *I, me, mine,* and *my,* and rewrite when any of the words is used too many times in total or too many times in proximity to itself

____ In first-person narration, check the use of *I* at the beginnings of paragraphs; rewrite sentences for variety when necessary

____ Check paragraphs to make sure there's variety in the first word

____ If you use adverbs freely, make sure they don't overwhelm; change verbs and cut out adverbs when possible to create the same or stronger effect using only a verb

____ If you use a lot of adjectives, make sure that some nouns and pronouns go without adjectives

____ Ensure variety in adjective use; make sure not all nouns get only one adjective or that not all nouns have three

____ If a character supposedly speaks tersely, cut both adverbs and adjectives from his speech and thoughts

____ Cut or replace hedge words that are used too often or that create weak rather than bold statements (see the appendix for a list of hedge words)

____ Cut or replace filter words used too often or used in ways that force too much distance between the event and the reader (see the appendix for a list of filter words)

Sentence Construction

Steps to take

____ Verify variety in sentence construction and sentence length

____ Be aware of possible problems (dangling modifiers and concurrent vs. consecutive actions) when starting sentences with present participles

____ For effect or variety, join short sentences or shorten long ones

____ If a word or phrase gets too much attention because it's at the beginning or end of a sentence and you want to hide or de-emphasize it, move it to the center position of the sentence

____ Remove three-word phrases (especially prepositional phrases) from the ends of sentences if they add nothing to meaning, aren't necessary for rhythm, or dull the impact of the sentence

____ Consider rewording when back-to-back sentences end with the same word(s) in order to avoid a dulling effect

Make sure

____ unusual phrasings (such as absolute phrases) are used sparingly

____ to reduce the overuse of sentence fragments

___ you've included some sentence fragments, especially for
character dialogue and thoughts

___ some dialogue trails off or is cut off, but reduce excessive use
of interrupted dialogue

___ strong words, strong images, and words you want to empha-
size are at the ends of sentences

Rhythm

Steps to take

___ Ensure variety in rhythm without producing annoying patterns
or rhymes; rewrite to cut out unintended rhythms or rhymes

___ Consider giving a few characters unique sentence construc-
tions, phrases, or slang to influence the rhythm of their
speech, but don't overdo

___ Vary the way rhythms are interrupted—let patterns gradually
change or sharply interrupt rhythms with a phrase or sentence
that sounds completely different

Clarity

Steps to take

___ Make sure that each section, bit of dialogue, scene, and
chapter is clear

___ If *you* trip over a phrase, a sentence, or even a word, rewrite it

___ Make sure that words and phrases aren't ambiguous unless
you're using ambiguity for effect or a specific purpose

Explanation/Preaching/Teaching

Steps to take

___ Cut out long, boring, or story-halting explanations for why
characters do what they do

___ Make necessary explanations compelling and brief

____ Remove text of a character preaching one of your pet causes

____ Cut out explanations for how unfamiliar or imaginary technology works; instead, show the technology in action

____ Rewrite dialogue that allows a character to present his philosophy without challenge or interruption from other characters

____ Cut out or rewrite encyclopedic descriptions or dictionary definitions that bring the story to a standstill

____ Cut out sections where you, the author, are teaching readers something that's cool or fascinating to you

Back Story and Research

Steps to take

____ Cut out back story that proves unnecessary to the plot

____ Cut out back story that's repetitive

____ Cut out back story that delays the story's true opening

____ Make sure you've used multiple methods for conveying back story, especially if you've included a lot of it; use exposition, dialogue, thoughts, and flashbacks

____ Cut or change any sections that read like the results of writer research and don't fit the story's style, genre, or flow

____ Cut out info dumps in thought, exposition, and dialogue

____ Show a character's back story in action

____ Resist the urge to tell everything *you* know about your characters and the story world; you'll know much more than you'll ever use in a story

Flashbacks, Prologue, and Epilogue

Steps to take

____ Limit the number of flashbacks; keep readers in the present story as much as possible (allowances for stories that switch between the past and the present)

____ Use the epilogue to hint at other stories in a series

Make sure

____ the first flashback comes after an event in the story's present; this may mean no flashback in the first several chapters (I recommend that flashbacks not be included in the first chapter)

____ the prologue is necessary; if you can include details from the prologue in the story itself, rewrite and cut out the prologue

____ the epilogue is necessary; make sure it doesn't leach the impact from the final chapter; make sure it doesn't go on too long

GENERAL QUESTIONS AND REMINDERS

- Is the story written so that the reader will care about the main character and his dilemma?

- Is the story entertaining?

- Is there enough *story* to the story? Does enough happen?

- Is the story different enough to catch a reader's attention?

- Does the story move fast enough?

- Does the story capture the reader's mind or heart, perhaps both?

- Does the story adhere to genre expectations?

- Put story elements (scene, event, section of dialogue, or bit of description) to work—make each do double or triple duty when possible. For example, make dialogue advance plot *and* raise the conflict level *and* reveal character.

- Remember the reader—don't edit in a vacuum. Make sure that readers will be able to understand events, event order, character motivation, and dialogue.

- Cut out anything—word, sentence, paragraph, scene, chapter, character, event, setting detail, symbol, or plot thread—that doesn't advance the main plot, reveal character, establish/change tone or mood, increase conflict, *or* influence reader emotions.

FINAL WORDS

This checklist could go on for much longer and in more detail, but I hope it gives you a helpful go-to list of the areas to look at when you edit *and* gives you ideas for other areas to edit.

May I suggest that you look closest at those areas that don't appeal to you or that give you the biggest headaches? Take time to review the elements of fiction that you're weakest in. Why not strengthen them, help yourself to be an even stronger editor and ultimately a stronger writer?

Take all the time needed to work your way through your edits. Editing, good editing, doesn't happen in an instant. Don't be surprised if you spend as many days—maybe more—on an edit as you do working on a first draft. A good edit deserves the time.

And a good book deserves an outstanding edit.

39

EDITING CHECKLIST: THE SHORT VERSION

WHILE THIS IS a shorter checklist than the previous one, the questions and your answers are still indispensable to your edit process. Use this checklist to home in on specifics of the story as a whole.

Don't hem and haw, dithering with your answers to these questions. If you're not sure, can't decide whether your story accomplishes what these questions aim to get at, then head back in and make changes. You didn't work as diligently and for as long as you did only to take a shortcut now that you've reached the end. If these questions and your answers expose an issue that needs either exploring or correcting, get to it.

And allow these questions to bring other questions to mind; that is, don't limit yourself to only these issues.

CHECKLIST QUESTIONS

____ Does the story entertain? What makes it entertaining—humor, emotion, tricky mystery, quirky characters? Can the entertaining elements be played up and enhanced?

____ Are events logical?

____ Do characters react? React to events, to dialogue, to the expressions and body posture of other characters? If not, give them reactions.

____ Does the story go somewhere either literally or figuratively?

____ Do word choices fit characters and genre or do they sound like you? Do word choices sound like a grad student with a master's in literature rather than what they should sound like, the expressions of your characters?

____ Does the main character change? Grow? Mature? Regress?

____ Do plot events take place in the correct/best order?

____ Does the end complete the beginning and flow from the middle chapters? That is, does the story ending match the problem that was posed in the beginning and the complications that were raised in the middle?

____ Are all major story threads, including subplots, resolved? Did you consider resolving the major secondary plot before the ending? Did you consider resolving both the main plot and the major secondary plot with the same climax? It's not too late to see what a change might mean in terms of impact.

____ Did you plant clues (and not only for mysteries) for your ending throughout the story?

____ Does the protagonist—not someone else—solve your main story issue? If not, rewrite. Also, make sure the story problem/issue is not resolved by means of a fluke, happenstance, or coincidence.

____ Does the end satisfy? Does the final action, last bit of dialogue, final image or final line resonate? If not, set it ringing.

____ Can readers follow easily?

____ How's the balance? Do we spend too much time in a character's head, with little page and story time for dialogue and events? Or is too much explained via dialogue? Do characters ever shut up? Does description overwhelm action?

____ Are there contradictions—in events, in revelations, in character thought, in motivations? If so, resolve them.

____ Have you written story clichés instead of introducing fresh plots and situations? Change anything that sounds like another book, especially outstanding plot elements of other books. If a character is waking from a dream to open your story, change the opening. That's been done and done and done—give your readers something new. And unless you can introduce a twist that's spectacularly original and arresting, don't end a scene with a character falling asleep.

____ Have you written a stereotypical character, one without nuance and shadings? If a stereotype rather than a character is walking through your story, make changes. This is especially important for major characters.

____ Have you prepared the reader for the next book in a series, introducing the right characters, conditions, and recurring or connecting themes and talismans?

RECOMMENDATIONS

Check bothersome elements

Check those half dozen items you kept meaning to check as you wrote and rewrote and polished. You know what I'm referring to: the character who overheard a critical message but who had no reason for being in that scene to overhear, much less a reason for hiding behind a door; the name of the antagonist's second banana that never sat right with you; the protagonist's dreadfully weak motivation for getting involved in a battle he had no interest in.

Whatever they are, those changes you intended to make but never made—those little niggling problems that prodded you a little but not enough to follow through on as you were writing and rewriting—go back and change them now. If you felt more than once that there was a problem, you need to address that problem. Yes, even now, this close to publication or submission.

Include variety

Look for variety at scene (and chapter) beginnings and ends. If you start or end every scene at the same location or with the same kind of thought or action or with a character looking off into the distance, planning retribution, change a few. This is an easy one to check, so do it. Readers will tire of the same character opening every chapter, racing to whatever it is she's racing toward. And they'll tire of endings that feel or sound the same, that seem to leave the main character in the same dilemma, maybe only burdened with an additional weight.

Eyeball the text

Do a visual check. Paragraph after paragraph shouldn't start with *I* or a character's name or the words *it was* or *there was* (or any permutations thereof). The story shouldn't run for pages and pages without dialogue. The story shouldn't run for pages and pages with *only* dialogue, especially that of just one character.

Check for homophones (words that sound alike but have different meanings and are often spelled differently), unintended word repetition, missing words, and missing punctuation (especially closing quotation marks and periods).

When you write and edit, it's easy to inadvertently put two punctuation marks together. Search for two periods together, two commas together, a comma followed by a period, and a period followed by a comma. Couldn't decide between a question mark and an exclamation point? Search for the combination and pick one.

Look for two spaces between sentences and change them to a single space.

Check words at the ends of sentences. Ending back-to-back sentences with the same words can deflate sentences, making them flat.

Names

Review character and place names. Make sure names are sufficiently different in terms of spelling, number of letters and syllables, sound, and their look on the page. If you're trying to confuse the reader, that's one thing. If you're not, make sure you don't do so accidentally.

Add full names and nicknames of all named characters to your style sheet. Duplicate or similar names tend to stand out when they're grouped together.

Hooks

Make sure there are chapter-ending hooks. The ends of chapters should bring some event or story thread to a conclusion, but at the same time, chapter endings must pull readers forward. Make sure each chapter has a hook sufficient to compel readers to turn the page.

No, you don't need to treat each chapter ending like an old-time serial and tie a character to the railroad tracks just as a train is approaching in order to get readers to turn the page. But you do need to provide a reason for readers to keep reading. Set up expectation and infuse readers with anticipation.

Help

Enlist help. You know at least some of your strengths and weaknesses—get help for your weak areas. Ask a friend or fellow writer to proofread for grammar and punctuation if you're not clear on all the rules. (At the same time, start getting clear. Read a grammar book or two or three. Read one every year. Learn how to use your tools in new ways.)

Word count

Check the word count. Does it fit the genre? Self-publishing allows you to write as many words as you want to, yet that doesn't mean you should go wild. And e-publishing may bring changes to traditional word counts, but there's no reason not to be familiar with the typical word counts for your genre, at least as a benchmark. If you're following the traditional publishing route, stick to the guidelines.

Here are general guidelines on word counts, though these numbers aren't set in stone. Children's fiction obviously uses fewer words, but so does YA (young adult), even though many adults read it. The newer category of new-adult fiction has a wide range, with stories able to accommodate an audience of different ages and tastes.

Word counts for adult fiction:

- short story: up to 7,500
- novelette: 7,500 to 20,000
- novella: 20,000 to 50,000 (some recommendations note a maximum of 40,000)
- novel: over 50,000 (some say a minimum of 40,000); typical 80,000-100,000
- new adult novel: 60,000-85,000 (maybe up to 90,000)

Word counts for children's fiction:

- picture books: up to 500 (absolute maximum of 1,000)
- early readers: anything from 200 to 2,500
- chapter books: 6,000 to 10,000 (even up to 25,000)
- middle grade: 30,000 to 45,000
- young adult: 45,000 to 70,000 (maybe 75,000)

Keep in mind that there are exceptions and allowances at both ends of these ranges. There are also sub-categories that could further refine these counts.

> The *maximum* standard word count for an adult novel is about 110,000 words (some recommendations say 130,000 words). Anything from 80,000 to 110,000 is common, with many novels falling in the 90,000 to 100,000 range.

While these are general word counts, science fiction, fantasy, epics, and historicals allow for higher word counts in both adult and children's fiction.

The romance genre has word count standards of its own.

- category romance 55,000 words
- single title 90,000 to 110,000 words (75,000 minimum)

There's also variety in the mystery/thriller genres. Cozy mysteries are typically shorter, with maybe as few as 65,000 words, though even that word count could be higher.

Another consideration regarding word count has to do with audience expectation. Readers accustomed to novels of 95,000 words may not be happy with a 60,000-word novel. And those who like short stories and novellas might become antsy (or bored) with an 85,000-word offering.

If you're self-publishing, don't assume that word count doesn't matter. If you're writing a longer-than-normal genre novel, consider that you might need more characters, more events, and more scenes.

Reduce word count

If your novel (especially a first novel) is 145,000, 190,000, or 250,000 words, start cutting. First novels with high word counts are often a sign of the writer's love for his own words and his unwillingness to cut even the most blatant examples of weak writing. Reduce your word count; don't let your editor, who is you at this moment, indulge the writer.

Also, consider making your 280,000-word epic three books rather than one. You could make a lot more money for the same number of words, and your readers may truly enjoy not having to push through a 1,000-page behemoth.

FINAL WORDS

Be ruthless in your editing. As you allowed yourself freedom when you wrote, give yourself freedom to edit, using all the tools of writing and revision to make your story internally consistent and strong as well as appealing to readers. Don't stifle, spank, or constrain your inner editor while he's working.

Think like an editor, not a writer, when you edit.

40
EDITING CHECKLIST:
THE ULTRASHORT VERSION

SOMETIMES YOU JUST WANT to know if a story meets basic require-ments. The questions in this chapter go to the heart of story essen-tials. You'll want to be able to answer with an unequivocal *yes* to each; *maybe* or *sort of* will not do. If you can't convincingly answer yes to these, you've got work to do.

To get a feel for what work a story still needs, you may want to use this checklist before you tackle your major editing tasks. On the other hand, you may want to visit this checklist once you're finished the bulk of your editing to see if you've covered the big issues.

____ Does the story entertain? Are events actually interesting?

____ Does the story satisfy?

____ Does every scene serve a purpose?

____ Is there a character the reader can root for?

____ Have you included elements to engage the reader's emotions?

____ Do plot events make sense? Is the story comprehensible?

____ Do character motivations make sense?

____ Do story events *and* characters hold the reader's attention?

____ Do major events take place in scenes, unfolding in real time in front of the reader, rather than being conveyed via summary?

____ Does the story conform to genre?

____ Did you maintain narrative tense?

____ Is setting made clear?

____ Is point of view consistent, at least within scenes?

____ Have you proofed for spelling?

41

TIPS FOR PROOFING‡

BY THE TIME your story is nearly ready to be published, you've read it dozens of times while searching for ways to strengthen every element. But there comes the time when you need to finish the rewriting and editing in order to take on proofreading duties instead.

For many writers, proofreading is no fun. You may dread it, or you may laugh and wonder if you need your eyes checked after you find obvious errors on the tenth read of a section of text when you never noticed the error on the first nine passes. Yet no matter which proofing or editing pass you're working on, try the tips in this chapter to create a clean manuscript.

Proofing doesn't need to be drudgery—make a game out of it if that helps. Pay yourself (in dimes or M&M'S or minutes of pleasure reading) for every error you find.

Allow me to encourage you to face proofreading with a positive attitude. Whether you intend to self-publish or pursue traditional publishing, you must proofread your stories or hire someone to do it for you. Or you could twist the arm of a friend, maybe nudge a buddy with the memory of a recent favor you did for her.

There'd be nothing wrong with proofreading your own writing and having someone else do it too. It's likely that you'll find words you want to change once you start to look at the fine details of your stories, changes a proofreader couldn't anticipate. But a proofreader who isn't you is likely to find errors that you, with your familiarity with the text, overlook again and again.

PROOFING TIPS

- Read from hard copy.

- Take out your favorite fine-toothed comb and go through your manuscript line by line, word by word.

- Read with a ruler or use a piece of paper to cover the text so you can concentrate on a single line at a time.

- If you always read from hard copy anyway, change the font when you proofread—if the text looks different, errors often jump out. Print on paper of a different color. Or print two pages on the same piece of paper to simulate the look of a printed book.

- Read away from your computer and in a room other than the one where you write. Try proofreading at a library or in the conference room at your office. Use the kitchen, the back deck, a coffee house.

- Note anything unusual, jarring, confusing, or simply wrong.

- Proof cool, not when the story's fresh in your head. This may mean you can't publish when you thought you could. *Wait.* The story will be better for it.

- If anything bothers you—even the slightest, teeniest bit—fix it. If you're bothered, you can be guaranteed that readers will be as well. Don't pooh-pooh little problems, thinking that no one will notice them. Readers will notice. And once they notice a few little problems, you'll have a big problem.

- Change or mark anything that strikes you—don't assume you'll remember, because you won't. Get the problem down somewhere. Directly on the text is good.

- Read out loud. Yes, this feels silly, but you'll find duplicate words, places where words are missing, spelling errors, and passages where readers could trip over words. At the least, read dialogue aloud.

- You could proof for punctuation and repeated or missing words by reading, sentence by sentence, backwards. Yet while you will find errors, this doesn't seem a prudent use of time. You might want to try it for select paragraphs, scenes, or chapters. If you don't work backwards, proof from the last chapter to the first rather than from first to last. Shake up your brain by examining the story in a new way.

- Do a visual check of chapter titles and scene breaks—are they all formatted the same? Are titles numbered correctly?

- Try text-to-speech software that speaks your text to you.

- Read by scenes or by chapters.

- Turn off the TV and music. Give your full attention to the task.

- Make multiple proofing passes, each for several issues.

- Always check sentences and paragraphs after you make changes.

- Make your final proofing pass thorough. You'll be rushing to publish, but don't rush those final steps. Don't hurry through 350 pages in an afternoon. A good proofreading requires time.

Find those niggling little errors that are hiding in your stories and ruthlessly do away with them. And remember that proofreading should come only after rewriting and editing, after major changes and minor adjustments. It's easy to introduce new mistakes into the text even when you're making minor changes, so save proofreading for the final stage. You won't want to have to proofread again and again.

What to Look For

When you proofread, you'll spend a lot of time checking the mechanics and less time with the fiction elements, though you should be alert to problems with both.

Scenes. In addition to checking grammar, punctuation, and spelling, you'll want to be alert to inconsistencies between scenes. For example, you may find one character doing something in one scene but find a reference to a different character performing that action in another scene. You may find a character in a scene when she couldn't possibly have been there because she was off doing something else while the scene played out.

Spelling. When you proofread, you'll want to do one more check of the spelling of character names, place names, and business names. This is even more critical if you changed names while you were writing the story.

Checking facts. I assume that by this point in your process of story creation that you've verified facts, but if not, now is the time to verify. Check the dates of events and verify the parties and outcomes involved. Check the spelling of the names of real groups, companies, and product brands.

Format. When you submit to agents and editors, you want formatting to be consistent as a signal of professionalism. When you're self-publishing, a consistent format helps you (or the service you hire) maintain consistency with the published book. Items you'll want to check include paragraph indents, line spacing, font type and size, and margins. Using styles for your fonts and page setup makes formatting infinitely easier. If you've never used styles for your manuscripts, learn how to set them up.

A Proofreading Checklist

You'll want to be alert for a wide variety of errors when you proofread. Check for the following:

____ missing words and repeated words

____ misspelled or misused words

____ missing or incorrect punctuation

____ double punctuation marks at the ends of sentences

____ missing closing quotation marks

____ missing periods before closing quotation marks

____ missing punctuation in dialogue

____ overuse of dashes, ellipses, or semicolons

____ missing second dash or comma of a pair (check asides, digressions, and nonessential clauses)

____ inconsistencies in capitalization or hyphenation (your style sheet will come in handy to proof these issues)

____ missing capital letter for the first word of a sentence

____ numerals used in place of words

____ symbols used in place of words

___ sentences inadvertently cut off

___ extra character spaces between words (this can be easily fixed using search and replace)

___ word repetition in neighboring paragraphs

___ overuse of *I* or *there was/were/is*

___ the same words to begin consecutive sentences or paragraphs

___ the same words at the ends of successive sentences

___ overuse of words you didn't realize you used again and again

___ overuse of words you know you use again and again

___ missing or wrong chapter numbers

___ missing scene break markers

___ page after page of long, dense paragraphs

___ page after page of dialogue without dialogue tags or without a pause for physical action

___ timeline errors

___ inconsistent formatting

___ placeholders that were never changed or removed

___ notes to yourself within the text

___ bookmarks that can be removed

___ text highlighting that no longer serves a purpose

___ duplicate scenes or paragraphs

___ typos and errors you consistently make

THE TAKEAWAY

Proofreading requires an eye for detail, but it doesn't have to be an intolerable task. And it's especially important that it's done well if you intend to self-publish.

Proofreading before you submit to agents and publishing houses and before you self-publish will help you put the cleanest product possible before your readers. Don't skimp on this vital step of manuscript preparation.

42

THE DON'TS

MUCH OF THE ADVICE in this book focuses on what you can and should do as you write, rewrite, and edit on your journey to either self-publish or submit your manuscript. This chapter focuses on what you shouldn't do. Consider this your *don't list*.

- Don't publish your first draft—it's not good enough to be called a novel.
- Don't plagiarize.
- Don't feature a would-be novelist as your protagonist. That's been done so many times, it should be a genre all its own. Find a different career for your protagonist. When experts advise *write what you know*, this is not what they have in mind.
- Don't clone the newest best-seller; write your own plot. The story will end up so much more involving if the plot has meaning for you.
- Don't open with a flashback. Actually, don't include a flashback in chapter 1.
- Don't end a scene or chapter with a character yawning and going to bed *unless* you want to put readers to sleep as well.
- Don't dump background information into the story in clumps—think of lightly spicing scenes rather than drowning them under back story.
- Don't try to appeal to three or four genres in the same book.
- Don't hold back. Let characters do and say what they must to make the story an entertaining one. A memorable one. A unique one.
- Don't use coincidence or the handy deus ex machina to resolve the story problem. Make the characters and their skills—plus the circumstances that you created—resolve their predicament.
- Don't preach, teach, or overwhelm the reader with research.

- Don't be deliberately deaf when friends, family, and beta readers you trust tell you that your manuscript isn't ready or your skills aren't up to the task yet. Writers have to be bold and persistent, stubborn even. I understand that. But we don't have to be pig-headed. Don't be like the truly clueless contestant in a talent show who's the last to know he has no talent. Believe in yourself, yes, yes, yes. But do so for a legitimate reason, because you've told a good story well. Because you've learned the rules of good fiction and put them to work in your stories. Do be bold. Don't be a laughingstock.

DON'T RUSH YOUR EDITS

A good edit of a good book takes a good long time. My novel edits average between 60 and 80 hours. That means some take less time, but others take more. And this is only *my* time with a manuscript. This doesn't include the time the writer will then need for reworking scenes or finding the best phrasings where I've suggested a change. (This is typically only the time required for the second editing approach of the two we looked at; *you'll* be working through both approaches for each of your manuscripts. That's a lot of time you'll need for editing.)

I'll give you a real-life example of the time editing can take. As I was finishing the edits for this book, I spent over 20 hours one week editing and reworking a single chapter. *One chapter.* Admittedly, I doubled the word count and had quite a few facts to verify. And the chapter really needed my attention—it wasn't complete by any measure, even though I'd thought it was after I made an editing pass of the whole book.

You may run into the same kind of issue or problem chapter when you edit. My advice for when you do? Take your time. And plan edit time into your schedule. Then double that estimate.

Let's say you spend 80 hours going through your manuscript, first marking changes on hard copy, pointing out weak scenes or too much dialogue or description—whatever the issues are—and then making changes in your file. That's two full work weeks. And it's more than two weeks if you don't have the time to devote 40 hours in each of those weeks to editing on top of your other responsibilities.

In addition, an estimate of 80 hours may be too low. You may need much more time for editing.

You already know that editing isn't only making changes to punctuation, grammar, and word choice. Sometimes you have to rewrite entire scenes. Sometimes you have to create threads from one event forward and backward to link to other events and to characters. That may mean a lot of time spent just figuring out what those links will be before you can begin writing the changes.

So your editing time may have just jumped to well over 100 hours. That's a lot of hours after the hundreds of hours you've already invested writing. But spending hours editing a novel manuscript is necessary for creating well-written and entertaining fiction.

It does end, I promise, this task of editing. But you can't edit a novel in a few days. The activities I've talked about in this book, all these steps, changes, and possibilities, are going to take weeks, maybe months, to complete. Invest that time. Don't rush your edits.

The good news is that in general, editing and rewriting should demand less time with successive novels because you'll incorporate knowledge gained from past projects into the early drafts of new ones; you won't continue to make the same errors, especially foundational or big-picture errors. Complex stories or those in a genre new to you may require more rewrites and more editing time, but on the whole, the time required for rewrites and edits should decrease with successive novels.

The simple truth? Experience will make you a stronger writer.

EXCEPTIONS

Are there exceptions to the rules, even these *don'ts*? Yes, always. And I typically recommend breaking the rules if doing so serves the story. (This book even includes a chapter on exceptions.) But I'm going to take a different tack here.

Sometimes the rules serve you best. Try abiding by them before breaking them. See if you can make a scene or a bit of dialogue work by keeping to the rules, by doing what others have proved will work.

If you have to work relentlessly, trying one option and then others and then even more to fit a rule, you just might create some awesome writing. Some solid, strong, cohesive, and beautiful writing.

Don't always look for a way out. Not the easy way. Work the issue through and show us what you're made of, what you've got in you. What you can do with a couple of words on a page.

Any writer can force a fix, leaving a mess in his or her wake. But if you work the problem—finesse it a little or maybe a lot—you may come up with a sublime fix that fits seamlessly with the surrounding text. And isn't that what you want, a story that runs smoothly, with no bumps to be tripped over and no seams showing?

> Writing is not about shortcuts, although there are valid and useful shortcuts. Writing is about putting words and story together and making the whole package work well using what you have. It's you and your skills pitted against compromise and settling for less than the best. Don't give in. Don't give up. Don't take the easy—the common—way out.

Part Seven

PUTTING IT ALL TOGETHER

43
KEEP THE READER IN MIND

UP TO THIS POINT we've focused primarily on the major fiction elements and on key sections of stories; in particular, exploring ways to refine those elements. But there are many other components to consider when we rewrite and edit long fiction. And there are multiple directions from which to approach an edit.

We have to examine the components, but we also need to evaluate novels as a united whole. Some changes to story will affect more than one component, and some fixes can only come from knowledge of the way story elements join and combine to form that unified whole.

Readers, while they may note favorite sections of a story or favorite characters, typically see stories as a unit, a book, not as thousands of pieces. Let's next consider those readers to make sure we've made their experience a positive one.

I've already mentioned that readers need to be satisfied by a story's ending, but let's examine a few other issues concerning readers.

Readers will be coming to your novels to read stories, not to weigh the components individually. And you need to be able to see your stories in their fullness, as a reader does.

You need to be able to see—and manipulate—what the reader sees. Because no matter how great you think your book is in terms of craft or technique, if the reader isn't satisfied, the book has failed.

You'll never satisfy everyone, but you're not writing for everyone. You're writing for the reader who's come to your story expecting something in particular—a book in a certain genre or featuring a particular character. An adventure. An escape.

Maybe your readers come to solve the puzzle or mystery you set before them. Maybe they want a psychological thriller or want to delve into the psyche of a tortured character.

Whatever they come for, you want to leave them satisfied. Maybe in a way different from the way they anticipated they'd be satisfied, but satisfied nonetheless.

What did you promise in your promotional materials? In the blurb? On the first page? Does the novel deliver on those promises? If not, you need to change either the story or the promises. Story and promises need to match on an elemental level.

A writer and reader share implicit promises, a contract. The reader expects an entertaining read, maybe some surprises, maybe a few facts. Maybe she expects her mind to be stimulated, her senses aroused, her emotions given a workout.

She definitely expects to accept the events unfolding on the page. She expects that you're a writer skilled enough to make her believe what's happening to your characters. *She suspends her disbelief.* She has to. Because she *knows* what's happening on the page isn't really happening. Yet she allows her heart and mind to pretend otherwise.

> That's a powerful force, that suspension of disbelief. A reader who opens a novel ignores everything she knows about reality in order to pretend to believe that what happens to your characters has truly happened and thus changed their lives, those lives that don't really exist in those bodies that don't really breathe and that are powered by hearts that don't actually pump blood.

Many readers can not only believe in a series of imaginary events and unreal characters, they can project themselves into the fiction. When readers imagine themselves as the protagonists of your stories, they're inside the story world. The events happen to *them.* The emotions are real. *They* are fighting to save the world, solve the murder or find love.

They laugh and they cry. They're angered or stirred to passion. They have very real physical, emotional, and mental responses to the words on a page.

The people, places, and events of fiction become part of the readers' thoughts and memories. Had you considered that? Your story world and your characters become a part of their very real three-dimensional lives. Not only can readers step into the story world, but the elements of that world can cross into the reader's world.

> Good fiction stays with a reader for more than a moment. For more than the couple of hours it takes to read the book. For more than a day or two.
>
> For some readers, the effect of a story lasts a lifetime.

Readers can learn your story world so well that they know its streets and sounds, its scents and rhythms, better than most of the physical locales in our world.

What a thought! Your readers can know your fictional world—where to find a killer latte, where to hide from a mob boss, where a noteworthy death took place—in more detail than they know a neighboring real-world town.

Have you given them a compelling world to remember? Locales and events and characters that resonate, that echo, inside them? That pulse with vitality and significance? Have you given them worlds and events they can and *want to* lose themselves inside?

Although readers are primed for immersion into story worlds, eager to get lost in a world different from their own—one with its own laws, consequences, and possibilities—that immersion doesn't happen with every book. But it can happen with yours.

Your stories can have the reader rooting for the protagonist and against the antagonist. Your skills can have the reader feeling genuine emotions when a child is struck by a car or buddies share a joke or one character convinces another character to adopt a stand antithetical to the reader's own moral code. You can convince readers that the town or country or planet of your story world really exists, with streets that are walked and houses that are lived in.

Readers open books ready to believe—you simply have to issue an impossible-to-refuse invitation in the first pages and then keep readers lost in the fiction with every word, event, section of dialogue, and scene you write.

Easy? Not all of it. Maybe not most of it. Not for every writer. We need to work at creating that imaginary world and the characters who will ensnare readers so much that they can't put the book down until they've finished reading it. And each writer needs to work harder at some writing skills and fiction elements than at others.

But the good news is that you get more than one attempt; the first draft isn't the end. Your first version of chapter 1 isn't the one you have to go with. You get to change and cut and add and tweak until your story is a masterpiece.

Just keep in mind that such a project can take months, even years. But writing a book isn't a race, not in terms of who finishes first. Writing a novel is about quality, not speed, so take your time and fashion your story idea, that tiny kernel of an idea, into a book that readers, multiple readers, will be unable to turn away from.

And remember to include those components that will keep the reader lost in your story world: characters that capture the reader's attention, if not his admiration; a plot that intrigues, that isn't so basic that the reader can guess every event before it happens; dialogue that sizzles, that sets the reader on edge; a setting that's so perfect for the story that your reader can see it, can see your characters moving through the space you created for them to play in. A place that readers can taste and touch and smell.

Treat your story world and all its components as real. Make readers feel that you're describing actual places, people, and events.

MAKING THE IMAGINARY REAL

Imagine the holodeck from *Star Trek*.

You know what I'm talking about, right? On Jean-Luc Picard's *Enterprise*, the holodeck could be programmed to host any scenario. Once the details were programmed, the holodeck, a small room in reality, became a full world.

The people weren't boxed in, constrained by walls, but able to move around freely, the setting changing and expanding with them.

You want the same for your story people and their world. You want that world to expand as wide and as high as it needs to for your characters to play out their adventure. You don't want readers able to feel the front and back covers of your books, as if you're constraining the characters with boundaries from the real world. You want to make your story world as expansive as it needs to be to support the characters, the locales, and the drama of the story.

At the same time, you don't want the seams to show. Every so often on *Star Trek*'s holodeck, the walls would be visible, the boundaries of the programmed world evident. And when people saw the walls, the imaginary world was compromised.

When the suspension of disbelief is gone, readers will no longer believe in your story. They won't believe your characters. They won't believe that the events they see have veracity.

Keep readers inside your fiction by keeping the seams hidden. Help readers lose themselves in your fictional world, if only for a couple of hours, long enough to see what happens to these characters they've discovered, characters at critical stages of their lives.

The purpose of the zillions of suggestions in this book is to help you achieve this goal.

But we won't forget about you, the writer. You also come to the reader/writer contract with expectations.

- You expect readers to give you a fair shake, an opportunity to wow them.
- You expect readers to finish the book you've slaved over.
- You expect respect as a writer.

But the onus comes back to you for all of this, for your side of the bargain as well as the reader's. If you don't write convincing fiction and a book worth reading, you're the one who's broken the contract.

Readers don't help you create, so you can't take it out on them if your book fails in major or even minor ways. They can't be expected to love a book that goes nowhere or that sounds like the last five best-sellers or that gets lost in its own plot threads. Readers, however, *can* love good fiction, stories that entertain with characters they want to follow around—or pretend to be—for a few hours.

Do whatever you can to get and keep readers reading. If that means entice, overwhelm, push, prod, or pull, if it means captivate or titillate, if it means confound and amaze and shock and satisfy, if it means mystify or stump, puzzle or bewitch, then that's what you need to do. Try anything. Try everything. Get readers lost in your fiction and keep them lost. Don't do anything to expose the edges of your story world, the boundary that separates story from life. Keep readers looking inward to the characters and unfolding events. Hide the underpinnings, the mechanics, and the support structure. Make the fiction compelling and authentic, strong and convincing, persuasive enough to hold the reader's attention against real-world intrusions of the most potent sort.

Give readers what they want, what they expect to find in a novel, and they'll give you what you want. It's a worthwhile trade.

WAYS TO SATISFY READERS

Readers can find satisfaction with your stories in multiple ways. Which also means they can find dissatisfaction in multiple ways. Your job is to increase satisfaction for them, increase the opportunities *for* that satisfaction, and decrease opportunities for dissatisfaction.

Satisfy readers with the quality of your writing

Readers should find engaging prose and understandable scenes. While characters can be confused and readers could be kept in the dark on purpose, readers shouldn't be confused about what you've written. While meaning and purpose may be shrouded, readers shouldn't have to guess that a car has crashed, a couple has broken up, or a murder has been committed. They shouldn't have to read and reread to make sense of a passage or a scene.

Check your words. Are they fresh, or are your sentences loaded with clichés? Readers expect a new story to contain new wording. Simply put, don't copy the phrases of others.

Yes, you may have a basic plot that's been used thousands of times before. But you don't have to use the same words. And why should you? Your characters are different. Their predicaments are different. The setting is new. *The needs of this story are different from those of any story that has come before.*

So use fresh phrases, and not the common. Not the clichéd. Not the ho-hum.

Satisfy by the way you handle common fiction elements

Readers have read many, many books before coming to yours. They'll expect that you can handle the most basic of writing tasks with skill. After all, every other writer does, so why wouldn't you?

Readers can forgive errors, so I'm not saying they look for perfection. But they've read stories that start with the perfect opening. They've fallen in love with characters. They've been shocked by a character's meltdown or a story's emotional climax. They've grown to expect certain quirks of a genre. And all the good elements they've become accustomed to in other books they subconsciously expect to find in yours.

Give them that good stuff. Don't shortchange them.

Satisfy by crafting a well-written story.

Satisfy by completing what you start

Finish the story that you start. If you open with a mystery, solve the mystery and don't change midstory to a horror story.

Wrap up subplots; readers will notice if you don't. If you made subplots or secondary characters fascinating and worth reading about, readers will want to know what happens with them.

Complete the protagonist's character arc. If he's supposed to grow, make sure he does. If he's supposed to learn a valuable lesson, be sure he learns it. And make sure the learning costs him. No-cost lessons produce little emotion in the reader. And the reader will assume the lesson won't produce long-lasting change in the character.

Refuse to skip steps. Don't rush through the events that reveal your character, that push his personality traits, negative and positive, to the fore.

Satisfy through fascination

Grab the reader's attention and keep it.

Satisfy by entertaining

Write a book the reader can't put down. Write a book the reader will want to savor. Or write a book that the reader can't help but race through.

Make sure the reader doesn't regret spending time within your fictional world.

Satisfy through resonance and meaning and involvement

Give readers someone to root for. Something to fight against or fear. Something to ponder. A dream to imagine.

Make readers feel.

Allow them to get involved by making them think.

Inspire them to contemplate story moments in a search for meaning. Don't always tell or explain. Instead, sometimes make the reader work to understand what's going on. Rather than allow your characters to blurt out every minor conclusion about another character's motivation or about the significance of story events, allow the reader to draw her own conclusions. Let her draw conclusions about characters. About the meaning of clues. About the significance of a wink, the curl of a lip, a shoe turned on its side and forgotten in the middle of the floor.

Engage the reader at every level to make the read satisfying.

QUESTIONS TO ASK

Consider these questions to determine whether your story will appeal to readers. If your answer isn't indicative of reader satisfaction, rewrite until it is.

- Does the opening make promises, both explicit and implied? Did you satisfy those expectations?
- Does the ending answer the major story question? The promises? Does the ending resonate or is it easily forgotten?
- Does the story meet all the conditions of the genre?
- Is the story long enough? Is it too long?

- Are story events credible?
- Are there opening and ending hooks in each chapter?
- Is there too much bloat—too much exposition, back story, flashback, explanation—in the middle chapters? Are there too many uninspiring story threads? Does the number of characters overwhelm?
- Is there enough story? Are there enough threads and sub-plots? Does the story go anywhere, somewhere unexpected and original or at least fascinating? Are there enough scenes, scenes that look, sound, and feel different from one another?
- Do you pair different combinations of characters to create different kinds of scenes, different styles of tension?
- Is there enough variety in setting from scene to scene?
- Is there enough conflict? Enough variety in the type and levels of conflict?
- Did you make character strengths and weaknesses work both for and against major characters? Did you remember to *give* characters both strengths and weaknesses?
- Are secondary characters interesting? Worth spending time with? Are the main characters of a sort that readers will want to spend hours with?
- Have you been too heavy-handed with theme or symbolism? Too free with favorite social, religious, or political theories? Too preachy?
- Have you straitjacketed your characters, maybe making them politically correct rather than individually quirky?
- Did you resolve all plot twists, even if resolution doesn't mean a happily-ever-after?
- Have you copied other books or writers and not in a good way? Did you clone a best-seller, ultimately not writing your own story or in your own style?
- Have you remembered you have readers, or do you treat them cavalierly, assuming that you don't have to consider their needs? Have you included tidbits, temptations, and draws throughout the story to keep them turning pages?

- Did you provide stimulation for the readers' senses, their minds, and their emotions?
- Did you delight, surprise, or shock readers? Did you achieve this more than once?
- Did you offer possibilities?
- Did you give your best?
- Was the story resolution, the answer to your story problem, inherent in the problem itself?
- Did your protagonist solve her own issues or did you rely on coincidence or divine intervention or happenstance?
- Did you finish the story that you started? If you changed course midstory, you need to change either the opening or the ending. What you set up is what you have to conclude, and what you conclude has to arise from the setup. It's not too late to make changes. Do it. Trust yourself. If you see a story problem, so will your readers.

FINAL THOUGHTS

Readers should be satisfied by your story, though not necessarily pleased with all your choices. They should find inevitability in the way story events play out. They shouldn't be able to guess every thought, word, or action before they read it, but once they do read it, they should feel that yes, that's exactly what should have happened.

Your stories should satisfy because you're providing a product and you want your customers happy. You want them coming back for another serving.

Satisfy readers by giving them what they expect; surprise readers by giving them the unexpected.

Give them something they didn't know they were missing and in a way that they recognize the valuable gift you've shared with them.

Reward readers for choosing your book.

44

Write for the Characters, Edit for the Readers

CREATE A STORY that holds together for the characters and their situation, but don't forget the man or woman, boy or girl who will be reading the story. You must get your story down and make sure its logic *is* logical, at least internally. But once you've got the story put together, you must also make sure readers will enjoy it. This will take rewriting and a few editing passes. It might involve compromise.

Early drafts are all about the story—plot and character, events and dialogue, setting, rising conflict, and climax; when you write and rewrite, you settle details in your mind and get them on the page. What you do in editing is make those events clear for the reader.

No, that isn't right. You don't make events clear, you make them *story*. Readers don't read events and dialogue, they read stories.

When you create fiction, you erase the line between real and make-believe. You give fiction life. And you engage the reader.

This means you choose the words that make the best impression. The *right* impression. Words need to do exactly what you need them to do—create a mood or tone, direct or misdirect reader attention, stir up reader emotions. You have to choose the right words and use them in the most effective combinations to achieve your objectives. Some words work, others won't fit.

> A story isn't done when the events are laid out in some logical order. It's complete when the story elements are capable of capturing and holding the interest of your readers. A story doesn't exist alone on a page, perfect in a pristine, untouched state. A story lives when readers find life in it. When humans are moved by it. When it plays out in an imagination other than the writer's.

And thus you're tasked with your second duty as a writer—crafting not only a solid work of fiction, but one that readers will enjoy, manipulating words and scenes so readers can get lost in the world, characters, and events you create.

The cause of the reader's enjoyment doesn't matter, so you might write a love story or a mystery or a literary masterpiece. But if you don't consider the reader, don't choose words, events, scene order, pacing, tone, emotions, and all the elements that will attract *and* hold an audience, pulling readers deep and making them care, your story has failed. No matter how great the premise of your book, if you can't execute the production of it in a way that captures the reader, the story doesn't work. Good ideas are not the same as great stories.

When you *create* your story, when you dig out the plot and clothe your characters with flesh and guts and depth, don't give the reader a first, a second, or a third thought; no writer should create with the audience (or an editor) looming over his shoulder, ready with praise or censure. Writers instead need to be free to create without fear.

Now, you might consider the reader *before you begin*, wondering what he might enjoy in a story, but beyond that, readers shouldn't partake in the creation of a novel, not in the early-draft stage.

While the writer creates, his mind should be filled with plot and setting, dialogue and event, character action and reaction, and not the possible responses of readers. The act of writing, of creating, is for the story itself. Only when you're ready for edits and final revisions should you imagine a reader holding your book in her hands. And *then* you work your craft to find ways to keep the reader turning pages.

Write early drafts for the character and the story world, but edit with the reader in mind.

ATTRACT THE READER

There are dozens, probably hundreds, of ways to attract readers, maintain that hold on their attention, and then satisfy them. Let's look at a few to make sure you've included them in your book before you release it.

Hook your reader from the first page, word, and image

Readers could be doing anything other than reading your book. Snare them right away with something they'll want to pursue. Whether this is dazzling wording, a murder, an intriguing tone, a mystery, or something equally compelling, you've got to attract the reader from page 1. If readers know you and know you'll deliver, you might get a few more pages to tempt them. If you're unknown, you don't get a lot of time to hook readers. Offer something yummy, whatever *yummy* means for the genre.

Make sure the plot doesn't sag, drag, or stop before the end

Make sure readers don't skip sections because nothing's happening. If nothing's happening, make something happen.

Dialogue is something happening. A character reaching an insight is something happening. You don't have to explode buildings or crash planes to keep the reader's attention. While those might be valid events for one story, they may not be for yours. Use what works for your story, but definitely use something. Even character-driven stories must have events.

Check each scene, especially those in middle chapters. Make sure something notable unfolds in each. Make sure each carries conflict.

Create an impact readers can feel. Recognize that a character's low point is a high point for the reader. Make that low point count.

Make sure characters face turning points, dramatic junctures that change their lives and create memorable moments for the reader.

Make sure you've given readers a character to root for

If you don't create a likeable main character, at least give readers one they're willing to follow through the length of a novel.

Read your story as a reader would

Read from hard copy. Try to read as if you've never seen the story before. If you trip up—over characters, events, word choices, punctuation, too much dialogue, or repetition—make corrections.

Hone passages until they create an emotional impact

The story may work, but it also must appeal. If your story is flat, inflate it. If it's dead, give it life. (Or put it out of its misery.) Substitute engaging words for dull ones. Use words that move people, that tap into emotions. Yes, purposely manipulate your readers' emotions.

Don't like the word *manipulate*? If I said *touch the readers' emotions*, would that sit better with you?

You do want readers to feel, so direct their emotions. Rage, fear, lust, relief, joy, or sorrow—rouse an emotional response in the reader.

They want you to do it.

Now, they don't want to *feel* manipulated. They don't want to feel the strings, as if you were a puppeteer. But they want your character's plight or adventure to mean something. They want to experience wonder or fright with your characters. They want to laugh or cry or smile. They may want to hide under the bedcovers.

Give them an emotional component with your fiction. Appeal to their brains, yes, but to their feelings as well.

Check each scene. Determine which emotion the scene is supposed to elicit; make sure there *is* an emotional element to the scene. If there isn't one, rewrite. If it's wrong or the emphasis is off, rewrite.

Use word choice and character reaction to direct reader emotions. If the character is convincingly afraid, if she reacts with fear, the reader will feel the anxiety. If the character trembles with rage, you've probably got the reader's emotions involved as well.

Build up the emotional response by piling on problems

If you don't have enough story problems, add more. If the tension isn't high enough, raise the stakes. If the mood isn't intense enough, set a clock ticking. If characters and readers need a shock, shock them by killing off a character or pushing one past his limits.

Use foreshadowing to vary the reader's emotional response

Use anticipation. Sometimes you want a surprise, with no heads-up about upcoming story events. But if you can get readers anticipating events with dread—and with ever-increasing dread as the events approach—you've got those readers experiencing emotion.

Include resolutions

Be sure you included resolutions at the end of the story—and earlier for secondary plots that finish before the end. If you enticed or teased the reader to pull him deep, be sure you made good on your tease. Conclude side stories and bring teases to satisfactory ends.

You can bet readers will be looking for the resolution of every plot thread, so follow through and satisfy their curiosity. If you leave plot issues or character relationships incomplete, the reader will feel the letdown. And no matter how strong the resolution of the main plot, the reader won't be sated. Not fully. Finish what you start.

Edit boldly

Edit with an eye toward boldness, both your characters' and your own. Don't allow characters to hold back when they should challenge another character—instead, give them scenes where they cut loose and embarrass themselves and others. A character who has reason to be embarrassed is an active character, one who's revealing his agitation. Give him something to lose. Help him reveal his volatility as well as his vulnerability.

> Don't allow yourself to hold back—say it, write it, include it. Whatever you thought of when you began to write a scene and then backed away from, write that into the story. The effect will be stronger. The impact will be stronger. And the reader response will be greater.

This isn't a time to write safely. You've got a story to tell, so tell the whole hairy wonderful thing.

Take advantage of depths and heights, and obliterate boundaries. Don't hesitate to take the safety off. Refuse to be a fainthearted writer with a hesitating pen.

Write a story bold enough to engage your readers.

45

THAT ONE OTHER THING

EVERY WRITER HAS ONE, that one issue, problem, or story weakness that finds its way into every manuscript.

Whatever weakness is common to your stories—and you know what it is, don't you, the one problem your critique partner nails every single time, the one weak element your beta readers all mention—make sure you address that issue, correct the problems it creates, and eliminate story weaknesses.

If you don't push the emotional component in your climax and resolution, check each manuscript and start pushing.

If you forget to include a sufficient number of viable suspects in your mysteries, start reworking characters until they can't help but look guilty.

If you omit reasons for a couple to fall in love with one another in your romances, start brainstorming reasons they couldn't help but fall in love with each other.

I've included this chapter near the end of the book, but you should be working on this issue—whatever it is for you—as early in the editing and rewriting process as you can. If this *thing* is a weakness in every manuscript, attend to the issue before it becomes a flaw in your next story.

If you typically forget subtext, deliberately take time to add it in from beginning to end. If you skip sense elements in your settings, visit every scene and add something that can be appreciated by a character's senses. But use variety and make sure your additions fit in every way.

Add color and sound if characters wander through a colorless or silent world.

Add humor if it's appropriate.

Add description or props if characters live on a bare stage.

Add characters if your main character lives in a world empty of living beings.

Add conflict if all your characters get along all the time.

Cut out repetition or explanations that drag down pace.

Raise the stakes more than once.

Cut out tedious back story that's essential knowledge only for you.

Use a light touch with literary and poetic elements. And definitely cut purple prose unless you're using it humorously.

If you're prone to using clichés, cut, cut, cut. Rewrite with phrases that reflect your style and the story's peculiarities.

Add whatever it is that your stories always lack. Or remove what you typically include but never need.

Whatever that other thing is for you and your stories, work and rework it in an editing pass of its own. Conquer that weakness and turn what used to be an inadequate element into an outstanding hallmark of your fiction.

46

PLAY UP YOUR STRENGTHS

WE'VE COVERED A WHOLE LOT of editing issues to this point. But let's turn our focus from the elements of fiction and particular story issues to you, the writer. Your sensibilities, your outlook and skills play a major role in any work you create. There's no reason to ignore your contributions to your stories.

In the next few chapters, we'll concentrate on you.

A good edit will not only focus on problem areas, it will also address a story's (and the writer's) strengths. And when you're the editor, you need to make sure you highlight your strengths, play them up as necessary without allowing them to overwhelm other areas of the story or the other novel components.

Do you know them, your strengths?

You might be able to guess at your story's strong points—maybe beta readers have all mentioned the same high points. But have they also let you know what you do well as a writer? You'll want to focus on story strengths as well as your own skills when you edit.

> Don't simply get rid of weak writing—play up the good stuff and give it a prominent place to shine.

If humor is a benefit for the story, make sure you use it. Whether it's sprinkled in or blended more liberally, make humor productive. Don't let it be a once-only moment.

If your dialogue is sharp or witty or especially cutting, if you use it to raise the emotional level for both character and reader *and* it works for the story, make sure you've not allowed too many pages to go by without such dialogue. If sharp action is your trademark, make sure to include it in ways that make the action stand out, yet without overwhelming dialogue or description. If you know how to convey character motivation with a single image or how to layer emotion until readers are howling with laughter or tears, or if you know how to craft chapter-ending hooks that keep readers turning pages deep into the night, make use of those skills.

Always include elements that enrich the story, and don't hide your gifts. Make them work for characters, plot, genre, setting, dialogue, and the impact you want to provoke in the reader.

Check your manuscript for its strengths and yours, and add more to highlight those strengths if it's appropriate to do so.

A WARNING

You won't want to confuse writing strengths with the presence of standout or attention-grabbing phrases and sentences. I'm not advising you to add eloquent sentences that will stop readers in their tracks so that they can marvel over your skills. You actually *don't* want to do that. You don't want occasional phrasing so noteworthy that readers are enraptured and they stop reading to admire it. Instead, you want readers so enraptured by the unfolding story and the characters' problems that they can't stop reading.

If readers are focused on the mechanics of a story, you've lost them; they're no longer caught up in the fictional world.

Remember the scene in *The Wizard of Oz* when the hand of the real power behind the wizard is seen?

"Pay no attention to that man behind the curtain," the great and powerful Oz says. But it's too late; Dorothy and company have already seen the setup. All the power and mystery is shown to be fake once the mechanics are revealed.

In your stories you don't want the mystery uncovered, the foundations exposed. At least not while readers are enjoying the adventure. Save revelations for tidbits on your website. Maintain the fiction while the story unfolds.

Now, if you're writing metafiction, that's truly a different story. For metafiction, the underpinnings can be gleefully revealed.

You do want to write great sentences, but they should serve the fiction, not your ego. You want readers, reviewers, and critics admiring how well you put together a story, not just a single sentence here or there. You want readers admiring how the story elements fit smoothly, not how one stands out.

And yes, literary novels are known for beautiful phrasing. Some genre novels are as well. And some authors are known for how they string words together. But those words serve the story. They often *make* the story. They fit. You want to work your strengths so that they're balanced throughout the book, not included just here or there. Keep the focus on the fiction and not on the man or woman behind the keyboard. You're creating a story world and an adventure for a set of characters. They, not story mechanics, are the focus. Help readers get lost in your fiction, lost to your reality; don't remind them they're reading fiction. Don't encourage them to escape the fantasy for their own reality.

You also won't want to overplay your strengths. Too much wise-cracking is annoying. Too much of *any* element can annoy. No matter how beautifully rendered, description and dialogue shouldn't take over or come at the expense of action, especially as a story climbs toward the climax.

Action shouldn't crowd out dialogue. Dialogue shouldn't replace action. Thought shouldn't overshadow action and events.

The elements you handle well should enhance your fiction, not overwhelm the elements that give you trouble.

Still, do look for opportunities to play up the good stuff. *Your* good stuff.

47

Flouting the Rules, Flaunting Your Style

WE HAVE TO AT LEAST touch on the subject of writing rules.

You're writing fiction, so you have leeway with rules that doctoral candidates writing dissertations don't get. And you're a professional writer—or hope to be one—which allows you much more flexibility and latitude than a student with a strict teacher. Yet . . .

I know, there's always a *yet* or a *but*. But the truth is that rules exist for reasons, one of which is to make meaning clear for readers. And if you flout a rule at the wrong time or in the wrong way, you risk confusing readers so much that they have trouble following your plot. If your choices confound readers, you're likely to lose those readers.

You can argue successfully to break the rules; you can argue for style allowances; you can try for something fresh, an innovative style different from the stylings of other writers in your genre. But your words have to make sense, and readers need to be able to understand what's happening in your stories.

Just recently I was reading a grammar book (I have to look up those odd rules too), and I was struck by the rigid advice of the grammarian. I understand that she wrote her advice for all writers and she was simply advocating best practices, yet her recommendations seemed to allow no latitude, no freedoms. When you read such advice—any writing advice, for that matter, including mine—don't feel constrained by the recommendations or think that all rules apply in all situations all the time. Rules do work, of course. But breaking those rules can also work.

I'm not advocating that you toss writing rules out the window or stomp all over them; I'm suggesting that you learn the rules, both of writing in general and fiction in particular, and that you understand the reasons for those rules so that you can in turn choose not to abide by them when you want to create a certain effect or result.

I could easily go back and forth between listing reasons to stick to rules and reasons to break them, but your circumstances and needs will be different from the needs of other writers and so you'll need to decide when following the rules enhances your writing and when straying from those rules is the more effective option.

Adherence to the rules may work in almost every situation—so you follow the rules. You make the read logical and clear for the reader. You make it entertaining.

But if by breaking a few rules or breaking a single rule a time or two you can make a story an outstanding piece of literature, you should be trying that. You'd better be trying that. I sincerely hope you're trying that.

Be bold. Try something fresh. You'll never know what you can create unless you push beyond the orthodox. Be willing to succeed wildly by being willing to fail spectacularly. Risk-takers achieve more than others because they try what others fear to try; they give themselves more options. Sure they fail; pioneers and explorers do fail. But they also succeed in breathtaking ways. We're only talking about breaking writing rules, but you too can succeed in breathtaking ways. Don't let fear stop you.

At the same time, learn the rules that will help you achieve success.

> Many rules that some writers fuss about are the very ones that can turn their bland stories into captivating adventures, their flat characters into memorable originals. Most of the time, most rules are going to be exactly what you need. Not always. Not every time. But often enough that you should know the rules intimately, know them so well that you can manipulate them to exceptional effect.

If up to this time you've only been messing around with writing, hadn't really expected to finish a novel, hadn't expected to need to know all the intricacies of writing and fiction but now find yourself in need of knowledge and a grounding in the rules of writing, grammar, and punctuation, that's okay. At least you know that you need to learn some rules. My advice to you is *start learning*. Take on any of the topics you found in this book and learn what you don't know; fill in the gaps. I guarantee that once you know some of the rules regarding both writing and fiction, your second project will prove to be better written than the first, your next better than the previous.

As for those who all along had every intention of writing and publishing a novel, I hope you'll allow me to be blunt. If you want to be taken seriously as a writer, if you want to write a critically acclaimed novel, if you want to be published and read by the masses *and yet haven't picked up a grammar guide or a book on the craft of writing in decades*, you show little evidence of intending to create reader-worthy fiction.

Reference books not only contain rules and suggestions, they offer *proven* rules and suggestions. Grab some of that knowledge and experience for yourself and put it to work in your stories.

Don't imagine that you need to do it all on your own, that you can't use tools that others created. Use the tools made especially for fiction writers and get on with the task of writing. Learn what the tools can do and use them to create masterpieces.

Search for writing resources online—the information is there for the taking. Take a class or two on either writing or fiction, maybe both. Join a writers group. Gather information that you don't have.

Learn and use the rules because they can help you write clearly, help you say exactly what you want and need to say. And remind yourself not to get so knotted up about rules that you can't write. Don't hide from or fear rules—master them.

And break the rules for reasons of style when doing so doesn't harm the story or the reader's understanding and enjoyment of it.

THE TAKEAWAY

Rules are helpful. They're not always the answer for every writing situation, but knowledge of the rules may be exactly what you need to solve your story problems and to craft enthralling fiction.

48

EXCEPTIONS

I'VE SUGGESTED QUITE A FEW rules for you to consider and included exceptions for them as well.

This is where some of the true crafting of editing and writing comes into play, in knowing when and how you can challenge rules and make exceptions.

I wish I could tell you that all rules are valid one hundred percent of the time, but I can't because they're not. And that's good. Our stories and styles would be much less like us and more homogenized if the rules didn't allow for exceptions, if we really had no options.

> Sometimes you need a dialogue tag other than *said*, sometimes a hedge word is the only choice, and sometimes you want the unwieldy mess of a string of adjectives that stretches on for days.

Writers have options, and I advise you to revel in the opportunities that options provide.

Try an unusual sentence construction. Try an unusual mix of POVs. Try using more dialogue than usual, more exposition than is recommended, more viewpoint characters than you'd normally find in a book of the genre you write.

If your experimentation doesn't work, then rewrite. But at least be willing to try something different.

Maybe you don't want to experiment until you can wield the rules without constantly having to refer to reference books, but recognize that writing and editing require both the skills of the craftsman and the inventiveness of the artist. You do get to be creative with your writing and with your editing. You still want to be consistent, but you aren't a robot and you don't create mechanically. Yes, you use writing rules and standards so that your story ends up a cohesive whole rather than several million unrelated bits, *and* you use the mechanics of writing to guide the reader. But even the mechanics can be creative in the hands of one who knows how to manipulate them.

Acknowledge that there are always exceptions and allowances—for genre, for style, for clarity, for character peculiarities, for sound and rhythm, for dealing with competing rules—but follow the rules most of the time; don't imagine that your case is always different. Yet follow your instincts too. You can always change anything that doesn't work.

Don't always assume an exception is the best choice, but don't be afraid of exploring exceptions.

49

Talk to Yourself:
Ask Some Questions

We've looked at both general writing issues and fiction issues, at both technical and story concerns, and now it's time to make sure you've covered everything.

I'm going to lay out this chapter in the form of questions. Look at both the questions and your answers and consider the unasked variations of each question too. Make necessary changes to your manuscript based on your answers.

You can answer questions in one of two ways—open book or closed book. And you might want to try both, closed book first.

Try answering the questions without looking at your story text; address the questions based on your perceptions of the story rather than on the words on the page. And move beyond the questions you see here. Let these questions lead you to others and let both questions and answers lead you to the final tweaks in your story.

Once you've answered the questions without looking at the manuscript, see if your answers are actually true. That is, next check the manuscript to see if your answers match what's actually on the page.

As an example, one question asks if the mood you achieved in the opening was the one you wanted to set. While you know what you intended, what mood did your words actually produce? Did you use the right word choices to create what you wanted to create? Might the opening need to be changed to match the feel of the rest of the story?

Or if the opening achieves what you wanted it to but the balance of the story is off, will you rewrite much of the story or can you be satisfied with the story you did create?

These questions get at assumptions—do the story elements on the page achieve what you assume they do and what you set out to do? And are you willing to accept what you created, even if what you ended up with wasn't what you planned for back at the beginning?

Does the story on the page match the one in your head? Have you included everything necessary to make the two match? Did you truly write the story you think you did? And if you didn't, if your head story and the page story aren't the same, are you willing to make changes to lessen the disparities? Do you even need to, or is the story on the page a better, more cohesive, more entertaining one than the story in your head?

FUNDAMENTAL QUESTIONS

- What's the story about in one sentence? Is the story meaning clear in every scene?

- Does the book try to be too many stories in one—mystery, romance, coming-of-age YA, suspense, dystopian science fiction, fantasy—rather than just one complete story true to its foundations? Are there too many unrelated or competing elements that keep the story fragmented?

- What do you want the story's first page to do for the reader? What mood or emotion do you want to set? Have you succeeded? How? Is the initial mood carried through the story and into other chapters and scenes? Can you pinpoint exactly where and how that happens? Did you abandon the opening promises or fulfill them?

- Could you make any element clearer? Play up any fiction element? Reduce the use of any element?

- Could you induce more emotion in the reader? What about less?

- At story's end, what emotion do you leave the reader with? What image? Have you given the reader a takeaway, something to remember the story by? Have you set something resonating in the reader?

- What image/tone/emotion do you *want* to end with? Have you included it?

- What's your opening hook? Does it come early enough?

- Is the genre clear from the early pages?

- Are there too many references to theme or symbols?

- What's the point of the story? When does that point become clear?

- What's the theme? Is it really what you think it is, or is the theme you intended not the one that's laced into the narrative?

- What's the lead character's low moment? Will the reader recognize it as such?

- What's the high point of the story for the reader? Why is it the high point? Can you play it up even more?

- Did you include foreshadowing? Should you?

- Will readers want to spend time with your characters? How have you made characters endearing? Fascinating? Memorable? Have you crafted character and plot in such a way that readers will look forward to seeing a character in subsequent scenes?

- Have you done the best job you can at this stage in your career?

RECHECKING THE BASICS

We've focused on these issues before, but take one more opportunity to make sure major story elements do all they can to produce a strong and entertaining book.

- Does the story open in the right place? If there's a flashback or too much back story on the early pages, fix the opening.

- Do chapters end and begin with hooks that make readers turn the page? One of your goals is to keep the reader from putting the book down, especially at scene or chapter breaks. Will your hooks achieve that goal?

- For every scene, ask *what happened in this scene.* Was the plot advanced? Was conflict increased? Is tension higher? What's new and different for the characters and the readers from scene to scene?

- Have you fulfilled the promise of the opening page(s)? Solved the mystery? Saved the world?

- Did you tell a good story exceptionally well?

- Does the story have highs and lows? Does it build to a climax? Does it *have* a climax? Does it have a resolution? Does it lose momentum in the middle?

- Did you make the reader care?

- Did you tell the story with the fewest words that would accomplish your plot goals and fit your style?

- Did your protagonist solve his problem or did you introduce a deus ex machina ending? If the major problem was solved by someone other than your story lead, you've got a bigger problem than he had. If your story problem is solved through coincidence, you've got a problem. If the answer to the problem falls out of the sky or appears from out of the blue, if it costs your main character nothing to obtain it, you've definitely got a problem.

- What (image, scene, theme, character, event, symbol, or object) did you forget to include? Can you add it at this stage? Would it improve the story? Is the story better without it?

- Which scene would you cut—because the story doesn't need it anymore—if the writing in it wasn't so fantastic? (Cut the scene, no matter how great the writing, if it no longer fits the story.)

- If you're writing the first book in a series, have you set up the next book through the first one? Introduced a character necessary for other books? Left a plot thread open-ended without messing up the integrity of the current story? Offered a tantalizing hint about the next story at the end of current one?

YOU ASK THE QUESTIONS

No doubt you can come up with more questions. And you should.

Take time away from the keyboard to devise your own questions. If you're still caught up in the mood and plot of your story, pick up another novel, thumb through it, and ask questions about it.

Why did the writer open chapter 1 where he did? What about chapters 2, 3, and 4? Why did he introduce the antagonist in such a low-key way? How did the author convey character motivation? Was it sufficient or could you not get involved because you didn't buy it as a true motivating force for what followed?

What strikes you as a component that works especially well for the novel? One that doesn't? What are the highlights and the strong elements? What are the weaknesses?

I'm not asking you to analyze a novel. I am suggesting that you get out of *your* story world and look at story in general. Figure out what attracts you. See what pulls you deep. See, also, what prevents you from engaging with a piece of fiction. Then go back to your manuscript and pinpoint where you included the elements that draw you to story. Did you cover each sufficiently? Were you overbearing with one or more elements?

Too little character motivation and too much explanation often haunt the works of new novelists and early drafts. But any writer can emphasize the wrong elements or ignore others. Take the time to step outside your story to devise a list of questions to ask of stories in general, not thinking of your plot or characters or setting in particular, and then go back to your story and look at those areas.

> Make changes if your main character's motivation is only in your head and not on the page. Make changes if you explain too much, depriving readers of the opportunity to engage in a deep way. If the story is all surface, with story events and character thoughts easily observed, with every detail spelled out, readers have no reason to delve deep or pay close attention.

Think of ways to draw readers beyond surface revelations.

If you give readers everything easily, with no effort required, there's no reason for them to push for more. No reason they'd expect more. No reason to remember your story as one that challenged their minds or their emotions.

TAKE YOUR TIME

At this stage in your writing, you're likely ready to kick your current book out into the world. You've written and rewritten and edited and polished. The manuscript has been through your critique partner and critique group, your beta readers, and your spouse. You're tired of it. You're deep into the next writing project and you want this one off your plate already. But don't rush. Please don't rush.

Who knows your characters and their travails better than you do? No one. If you asked others to edit, critique, or format your manuscript, walk yourself through your story one more time after those others are finished with it. Let the last fingers to touch your story be yours. Let the final changes and polish be what *you* bring to the story. Take the time to make sure you got everything right. (Exceptions when your novel is in a publisher's hands.)

Don't shortcut through these final stages. And don't assume that edits and rewrites will always take months and years.

As you produce manuscript after manuscript, you'll automatically begin to include elements that you didn't know to include in early drafts of your first stories. And once that happens, these final steps will go faster. You'll know where you included symbolism and foreshadowing, know exactly the sections of text you used to reveal the main character's motivation and goals. With experience, you may not need as much time for any one aspect of writing or editing. But until you reach that level, take time with the final steps.

Ask and answer questions. And yes, rewrite one more time if the story requires it. Don't give up so close to the finish line. Give your all at every stage, not only the early ones. Push here at the end too.

Allow every step of the process to accomplish what it should—the crafting of a plausible, entertaining, and comprehensible story.

50

Smoothing Out
the Big Picture

ONCE YOU'VE PRODDED, pulled, and plucked at your story, cutting out words and adding others, make sure you haven't left it a mess of jagged, ragged pieces, an improperly stitched garment with its frayed seams showing. After slashing and repositioning words, you need to smooth out the traces of your changes. And you need to do this at two levels.

You need to smooth out rough edges at the word level, making new words fit the existing words in your sentences, and you need to make sure that the action, dialogue, or description portrayed by the new words fits the other actions, dialogue, and description of the same section of text and of the story as a whole.

You may do this as a matter of course when you edit, but you'll still want to examine the big picture when you're done. See if passages have a pleasing rhythm and flow. Make sure the story doesn't judder or jerk to a stop at paragraphs where you reworked a line of text. But if it does, rewrite again.

Keep smoothing and polishing until no seams show, until no stray words or punctuation pokes out, ruining the otherwise smooth read. No one said you get only one chance to make changes, so rework each section until you're satisfied.

As you edit, after you make changes, go back several paragraphs—or even to the beginning of the scene or to the end of the previous scene—and read for flow and clarity. Read to ensure that you haven't added unintended repetition or errors with your changes. Read through the changes and into the paragraphs that follow.

Make sure you haven't made flow or rhythm or even meaning worse by your changes.

Heart and Soul

And make sure you haven't cut the heart from your story. Snipping away can expose the true story to light and fresh air, but cutting too much may not only make your story bleed, it may succeed in killing the story, draining the very elements that give it life.

Whatever the heart of your story, whatever pushes fervor or emotion through the other story components, make sure you don't cut that element off or allow it to shrivel up. Get rid of what holds your story back, but fuel the soul, the personality and passion that make your story unique.

Damming the Flow

Once you've finished the majority of your changes, read with flow in mind. See if you can read with ease.

Although you want to create a certain feel or rhythm in your scenes and stories, you won't want to direct readers so thoroughly that you've got them stopping and starting every few lines for pauses. Don't be so exact with the tiny details, with dashes, ellipses, and tons of commas, that you cut off the story's flow and forward motion. (This is especially helpful advice for the final third of your story.)

Make choices—italics or no italics, commas or dashes—that take into consideration not only the needs of a sentence or paragraph but of the scene, chapter, and story as well.

Be precise, but don't let the million and one choices you make for specific sentences and words add up to a sterile or rigid story.

Mess with details, yes, yes, yes. But mess with the big picture as well. Make sure detail and big picture work together to produce the story you want to present, a cohesive whole that engages and entertains the reader.

If after you've made all your detail-level changes you look at the big picture only to find what looks like a pixelated image—or maybe sharp edges of story components standing out rather than blending smoothly—you're still not quite done. You want a story whose parts fit seamlessly without drawing attention to their edges and connection points, the places where one part ends and another begins.

Picture the image made from a 1000-piece puzzle. When your story is truly finished, you want it to look like the image on the puzzle box, smooth and whole. You don't want it to look like the puzzle itself, with the lines between the pieces showing clearly, as if the pieces fit but don't quite meld into a seamless picture.

The puzzle does show the image clearly, but it also shows the individual pieces, the foundations of the image.

In a novel you don't want to show the individual building blocks. You want a seamless final image.

51

KNOWING WHEN
THE STORY IS FINISHED

WHEN YOU'RE THE EDITOR and publisher of your books, you get to decide when they're ready to face the world. Even if you're submitting in the traditional manner, you have to decide when the story is truly done. But how do you decide that?

To start with, if you've written only a first draft, the story isn't ready for publication.

That's dogmatic of me to say, I know. And yet it's true.

As an editor, I don't often speak in absolutes, saying you can't do this or you can't try that. There are almost always multiple options, and I like to tell writers about their choices. Yet on this issue, I'll be intractable: do not publish or submit a novel's first draft.

The first draft is incomplete. It's boring. It's missing story threads and links. It has too many characters. It's repetitive. It's confusing. It doesn't start in the right place. There aren't enough emotional tugs. Sentence rhythms are repetitive, verbs are uninspired. There's too much telling. Too much back story. Too much explanation.

You've included too much detail in some scenes, not enough in others. The characters sound alike and nothing happens. Or too much happens because you've inadvertently written a melodrama.

One character is allowed to preach several times about a societal ill, while another acts in ways contrary to his stated motivations.

All the characters notice a room's furnishings or *no* character has a reaction to sounds or scents. Characters, even the youngest children, sound like MFA grads. They're beyond clever with quips, puns, and striking metaphors.

Characters are all good or all bad, or you've given your good guys supposed flaws, but only by telling us about them. We never see those flaws in action, never see how they create problems for the characters. Never see how those flaws drive character choices.

You ended the story, but you didn't finish it. Readers won't know why events happened as they did or what the fallout would mean for the main characters.

Your love story is less about love than it is about deceit, your mystery less of a whodunit than a who-cares, your science fiction so filled with implausibilities that no reader, much less one who cares about the possibilities and the future of science, would recommend it.

I know, I know—*your* first draft isn't like that.

Are you sure?

Maybe you're smiling as your remember your first manuscript and how you thought that writing *the end* meant that you really were finished. Maybe you're thinking, *Get on with it already, I know this stuff.*

Unfortunately, not every writer knows or believes that a first draft is woefully incomplete. Most new writers don't value the power of editing and rewriting until they compare a first draft with the fifth or sixth, until they see exactly what a quality edit and focused rewriting can accomplish.

I want you to believe, however. Believe that your story isn't done, not even close, when you finish the first draft. If you hold the first view, thinking a story is done once it's on the page, no changes necessary for format or mechanics or plot, let me recommend that you check out resources on the craft of fiction writing and learn more about what to do after completing that first draft. Give yourself an education on what it takes to write and complete a novel manuscript. Run through exercises to see what rewriting can accomplish.

But beyond this point about a first draft not being ready, how else can you know if your story is finished and ready to be published? If you're self-publishing, you've cut out the middlemen who make this decision for traditionally published novels, so what do you need to know to make this decision yourself?

- If you've been through a handful of drafts, addressed story issues and the mechanics, you're probably getting close.
- If beta readers can't find anything negative and have no questions and say they whipped through the story, unable to put it down, you're probably close.

- If you're deep into another project and nothing from this one is tugging at you, demanding a hundredth look, you're probably extremely close.
- If you've been through multiple drafts *and* beta readers can't find problems with the story *and* you're deep into another manuscript *and* you can step away for a couple of weeks and then come back to the story without finding issues that need to be addressed, you're probably ready to publish. I can't say you won't want to make minor changes, but if you're not completely ready, you're likely close enough to publishing that you can smell the scent of the newly printed book.

If you're the publisher, you have to pick the time to publish. There are issues to consider other than the story itself, of course, such as other releases and the responsibilities the rest of your life puts on you. But when the story's ready, truly ready, then do it. Publish your novel knowing that you've done your part to make it the best you can.

You may well cringe 10 years from now, seeing what you allowed yourself to publish, but you can't wait forever. If you've done the prep and the writing and the rewriting and the editing, if you've used beta readers who know what they're doing and you listened to them, editing not only story issues but editing with the reader in mind, you can't do much more. Not if you're self-publishing and self-editing.

As a reminder, you're not trying to publish your first manuscript, right? While you should definitely rewrite and edit that one for the practice, it's likely that no one should self-publish a first effort.

I'm suggesting that project number three or four or five should become your first published book. As a first *draft* isn't ready to be published, a first *novel* isn't ready to be published. Unfortunately for the first novel, it's likely never going to be ready, not unless you scrap most of what you've done and rewrite with only the basics in common with the first version. A first novel, as I said in the introduction, should be celebrated but not published.

You can rant at me for telling you this, but I'd rather you rant now and at me than bemoan later when you learn all that you didn't know when you were writing your first novel.

A first of anything will not be a masterpiece. It can't be. But your second and third and fourth stories will be immeasurably stronger. In fact, a first effort will suffer so much in comparison to subsequent stories that they'll seem to have been written by different writers.

In effect, they *will* have been written by different writers.

> Start your career out on a high level. Use the first couple of manuscripts as training and don't rush your first novel to print. You know what first efforts are like in other fields—don't be blinded to the fact that they're no different in the writing field. First novels are still first efforts, no matter how much mystique we attach to them.

Advice that will serve you and your reputation well? Offer no story before its time. Don't publish the first or second manuscript, and don't publish any manuscript before it's truly ready.

Write. Rewrite. Edit. Rewrite some more. Check with beta readers. And give the public the best you have within you. Give them a story worth paying for and characters, plot, and a writing style that they'll enjoy spending a few hours with.

Make buying and reading your novel worth their while.

If you're submitting to agents or publishers rather than self-publishing, you still want to present the best product you can. But don't revise forever. Start submitting once you've rewritten and edited, once you've taken your story as far as you can on your own.

DOUBT AND FEAR

As you study your manuscript, trying to decide whether or not it's ready for the public, it's quite likely that doubt, in many guises, will gnaw at you.

Doubt may be strong and latch onto frustration when you're faced with that one final issue that seems impossible to solve. Doubt may pound at you in the early morning hours when you can't sleep because you're wondering if you're ever going to be successful, wondering if the five years you'd given yourself to publish before giving up have been a waste of time.

Doubt can be helpful as a necessary check to rushing rashly into something you're not ready for, yet doubt can also be disabling, a true impediment that blocks your way.

Expect doubts at every stage and deal with them. Prove to the doubts why they're wrong. Show them how you've dealt with their worries by correcting the problems they pointed out or fussed over.

And then, as you draw close to publishing, remind both doubt and yourself that you took care of those earlier issues already. (If you didn't, however, you still need to deal with problems. Ignoring story or mechanics issues doesn't solve them.)

But what happens if you're close to publishing and you discover a major blunder in your storytelling and realize you need to yank out the story's guts and rewrite? Can you, could you, *should* you start over if you find a better way to frame the plot, if you discover a stronger motivation for your protagonist, one that would change many of the story's underpinnings, if you recognize that a different tone or mood would suit better?

Could you start over? My first recommendation is that you need to be very sure that a change at this stage would truly make a difference to the degree that you think it would. My second word of counsel is to suggest you search your motivation. If you're not just putting off publication because you're afraid of exposing your words to the public, then making a major change at this stage *might* be worth tackling. But don't hide your fear behind a trumped-up excuse. Have your moment of doubt, and then explore the reasons behind it. If you're only delaying your novel's release because of doubts, don't blame the story. Don't search for phantom problems in the manuscript to justify your fears.

If you're sure that a major change in the story *would* solve a significant issue that had been niggling at you or that you hadn't seen earlier, then do consider a delay in publication and rewrite.

Of course you can stop to rewrite, even close to publication. If the story will be exponentially better for it, you should rewrite. Make your changes, even if that means you'll release the book later than planned. You're in charge when you self-publish, so you make the decisions.

This also means that you get to deal with the consequences.

For example, if readers are clamoring for the next novel in a series, you may tick them off with a delay. You have to weigh the costs of your choices. Is a delay okay if it means releasing a truly phenomenal book, or is it better to get something out there if you made a promise to do so?

Too many elements will go into any such decision, so I can't make it for you. But I can tell you that making major changes at the last minute is not unheard of and may be just what your story needs.

However, don't let fear and doubt derail your publication schedule. Change the story if you have legitimate reasons for doing so, but if you've made it this far, don't let fear of your story's reception be an impediment to publication.

> If the story's not ready, that's a valid reason to delay. But *you* not being ready is a whole other issue. Don't let your fears get in the way of your novels. Deal with fear and story issues separately. Make the story as good as it can be—not perfect, because it won't be, but entertaining and logical. Vet it through respected readers and not only those who love you. Get a professional opinion or two if that's possible and feasible.

And when you've done it all, if the verdict is a thumbs-up, release your characters into the world. *Then* deal with your insecurities.

If the verdict says the story isn't ready, then do some more work. Or if necessary, start or resume work on a new project. If a story doesn't have what it takes, there's absolutely nothing wrong with scrapping it and starting fresh. Of course, optimally you'd like to discover a dud of a story much earlier in the process, but it's never too late to have your eyes opened. If you've written crap and you recognize that it's crap, don't publish it. Give us your best instead.

We'll wait.

52

FINAL THOUGHTS

PUBLISH OR SUBMIT the best story you can produce. If your current story isn't ready, if your skills aren't yet up to writing, revising, and editing a novel, then wait. Don't wait forever, of course. But do wait. Wait until you've got the skills worthy of telling your story and a story worthy of readers.

But engage in active waiting. And that means keep writing.

And while you're waiting and writing, learn. Learn to write and rewrite and edit. Learn what you should be doing. Learn what works, what doesn't, and why.

Discover what you don't know. And then turn what you don't know into stuff you do know.

> Lots of people can write. Many can write well. Some of those who write well can write novels. Every novel is an achievement; not every novel is worth an audience.

There's no effortless magic to writing and editing, no hocus-pocus or abracadabra. Both writing and editing require hard, intensive work, and the magic is anything but effortless. But creating a first draft gives you material to work with, something to work your craft on, and editing wields the power to transform lifeless stories into life-rich adventures. Good editing draws fictional worlds out of dark voids and into bright reality.

Good editing doesn't breathe life into a story—good editing allows a story to breathe on its own.

Respect your readers by giving them a story worth their time and money. Readers can't regain time spent reading your book—have you made the read worthwhile? Are you providing value?

Don't be afraid to make changes before you self-publish or before you submit to agents and publishers. Don't assume that other writers don't make major changes to stories. And don't ever assume that your text is set in stone. If a character doesn't work, even if he's your protagonist or antagonist, change him. If that means a major rewrite that takes three months, then why not rewrite? A rush to publication may damage your sales and your reputation.

And remember that there are always multiple options for changes. Even for the simple change of a single word you've got more than one option. The choice you ultimately settle on after careful thought could well steer your story into just the place you'd imagined it going.

Don't settle for so-so wording. Fine-tune, tweak, cut, or substitute more powerful words. Or maybe add subtler words.

Give a passage a new focus, a different shading, a different tone. Maybe a different rhythm. Add subtext. Add meaning.

Don't shy away from changes but sever attachments to the first words put down on the page and use an editor's eyes to strengthen the story, no matter how many words end up being changed or cut.

If the story needs fixing, fix it. Don't worry that someone else beats you to publication. Do it right when you understand what right means for your story. Don't willingly put out a book that you know could have been a hundred times better with only a small (in terms of the large picture) time investment.

> When you rewrite and edit, recognize that you'll need to add *and* you'll need to delete. You may need to trim, you may need to gut. You may need to build up, you may need to tear down. Think not only in terms of the presence or absence of an element but in terms of degree and length, depth or distance or time. You may have to adjust text using a combination of strategies.

Remind yourself that there's power in fiction. Remind yourself also that much of that power comes from details, from the buildup of chains of action and reaction, stimulus and response.

Every detail, the smallest elements you include, contributes to the final product. Pay attention to those details. Make sure that they fit one another and the cumulative picture you're trying to create. Put in what will make strong story and powerful fiction. Cut out what dilutes the impact of other elements.

Add in the good stuff. Cut out what's weak or unnecessary, anything that doesn't belong.

And remember that you might not know whether a detail belongs until you've been through several drafts. What appeared in the first draft might not fit the story that emerged after draft 5.

The wise writer, editor, or writer-editor will cut out what no longer belongs, no matter how well written. No matter how attached he or she is to words that haven't earned their place.

RULES AND INSTINCTS

There are always exceptions to any rule. Put the suggestions I've outlined here into practice, knowing that they'll work for most situations, but don't think that you can't try something different. Go with your instincts when you think a different approach might be better. Yet be aware of the possibility of fixing one story weakness only to create two or three more.

There are reasons why some choices are better than others—the effect is stronger or one choice makes events clearer for readers—so understand that what you want to do may not be the best choice. We follow writing rules because writers discovered they worked.

Your situation, however, might be different, and you might need another option. But don't be stubborn, wanting to do only what you want, if the result is a poorer story or a confusing read. Learn why rules have been established and learn why keeping them is sometimes the best choice by far. If breaking a rule doesn't cause unintended negative consequences, try it. But do expect that the breaking of a rule could lead to results you hadn't anticipated.

MY HOPES FOR YOU

Let me take a moment to suggest that you get a professional to edit your manuscripts if you intend to self-publish; an edit is worth the money. While I gave you a lot to think about and try, I can't roll all an editor's knowledge into one book. Walking through a writing project with an editor is a marvelous learning experience, one I can, will, and do recommend.

If you don't hire an editor, at least have that outside eye—friend or colleague—help you out. And prep the story the best you can on your own. Just because you skip the middlemen—publishers, agents, and editors—don't also skip their duties; those fall to you when you self-publish. Take them seriously and give editing as much consideration as you gave the writing of your novel.

I can't guarantee that you'll have sales through the roof or secure an agent or publishing contract if you follow the suggestions in this book. I can guarantee that your stories will be stronger.

A book such as this one can give you general advice, advice and suggestions for strengthening *a* novel. An editor with manuscript in hand can give you specifics for strengthening *that* novel.

My hopes for you:

- I hope what you read here was encouraging and helpful. Maybe challenging. If anything made you stop your rush toward publication to go back to correct an issue or problem area, that's great. There's no point in publishing a book with errors that can be corrected.
- I hope you learned something new or were reminded of a truth you'd forgotten so that you're now looking at writing, rewriting, and editing in ways that will help you turn out even higher-quality books.
- I hope reading this guide was worth your time, that you found not only what you were looking for but also what you needed. I hope you found the unexpected.
- I hope this guide will be useful for all your writing projects for many years to come.

As you no doubt discovered when you wrote your first novel, you can't learn all the ins and outs of putting a novel together unless and until you go through the process step by step; you can't know what's involved until you put your hand to the work. In the same way, you can't know the complexities and benefits of an edit until you and your editor explore that adventure together.

Self-edit all your manuscripts, but hire an editor when you can. You'll be pleased and so will your readers.

The tips and suggestions in *The Magic of Fiction* are only a substitute for an editor who digs into the meat of your novels and puts her hands on your characters and their adventures, but they should fill the gap between having no editor and hiring an editor for your self-published novels. They'll definitely help you prepare manuscripts for submission to editors and publishers.

Whether you're self-publishing or submitting to publishers in the traditional manner, rewrite and edit your projects creatively and competently as a way to make your stories stand out.

And one more wish for you—I hope that these suggestions not only help you improve your stories but help you grow as a writer. I hope they make the writing process more enjoyable, more efficient, a true delight filled with satisfaction.

I wish you great success with your first novel and your tenth and the one that proves to be your last after a long and fruitful career. Here's hoping I see your books on the best-seller lists.

In the meantime, write well and edit wisely. Work that powerful fiction magic. Craft words into story and your stories into art.

MY STYLE SHEET

I thought you might wonder about a few of my style choices and options for *The Magic of Fiction*.

A/B

- and yes—no comma between the words (this is solely a style choice—we typically include a comma between these two words)
- anymore and any more—I've used both. I used *anymore* as one word meaning *any longer,* in the AmE usage of a negative
- back story—two words
- best-selling, best-seller—hyphenated

C/D

- chapter 1—no cap, numeral
- co-worker—hyphenated
- deus ex machina—no caps and no italics (except as needed for emphasis)
- dialogue rather than dialog
- do's and don'ts*****—an apostrophe with *do's* but *must-dos* and *how-tos*

E/F

- fact-checking—hyphenated

G/H

- Head-hopping—hyphenated

I/J

- The Internet (capped), otherwise internet

K/L

M/N

- mid—no hyphen after *mid* for most compound words
- make sure/make sure that—the elliptical construction (without the *that*) is used in many instances
- mind-talk—hyphenated
- nonfiction—no hyphen
- non-stop—hyphenated

O/P

- placeholder—one word
- pig-headed—hyphenated
- page 1, page 10—no caps, numerals

Q/R

- reader—*the reader*, usually singular, thus *the reader's* for the possessive; yet sometimes *readers* (plural) and thus *the readers'* (plural possessive)

S/T

- sync rather than synch

U/V/W

- which—okay to use it for *that* in some restrictive clauses
- writers group—treat this as attributive and not possessive

X/Y/Z

*I remember MS-DOS and still tend to read *dos* as *DOS* or as the Spanish *dos* (two). Very rarely do I read *dos* as if it were pronounced like *dues*. Reading it correctly can be especially confusing when *Dos and Don'ts* (*DOS and DON'TS*) are capitalized, as in a title. My spelling of *do's* with an apostrophe in *do's and don'ts* is a deliberate choice. In your own stories you'll probably only need *dos and don'ts*, but if you wrote *do's and don'ts* for clarity, (most) readers wouldn't chase after you with pitchforks. Some style guides do allow for the apostrophe.

Punctuation

- Serial comma? Yes

- No comma before *too* or *either* at the ends of sentences or before and after *too* midsentence (exceptions before names in dialogue)

- I purposely didn't use question marks in long lists of questions. To match this format, I also didn't use periods in similar lists that didn't contain questions.

Miscellaneous

- While I varied the use of *he* and *she* on purpose for examples, the balance is tilted toward *he*. There is no slight intended to females.

- My go-to words (words and phrases I use noticeably often):

  at least
  just
  make sure (this manuscript only)
  only (not only)
  probably
  rather than
  simply
  some
  something
  sometimes

HEDGE WORDS
AND FILTER WORDS

Hedge Words

a bit	hardly	perhaps
a little	kind of	possibly
a tad	maybe	probably
a touch	might	seem
almost	mostly	some
any	nearly	sometimes
apparently	occasionally	somewhat
appear to	partially	sort of
guess	partly	suppose

Filter Words

asked	noted	saw
decided	noticed	smelled
felt	observed	tasted
heard	realized	watched
knew	recognized	

Short Fiction

While the advice and suggestions in this book have dealt with all types of fiction, the decided focus has been on long fiction, typically novels and novellas. And while short stories and novelettes contain many of the same elements as long fiction, there are differences. I want to address some of those differences now.

The shortest short story will feature character, plot, and setting—all necessary elements of long fiction—as well as theme and conflict. Yet even with the presence of the same major elements, the feel of a short story differs from the feel of a novel.

Rhythms and pacing are different. Some elements—such as dialogue—may be missing altogether. And even similar elements may be treated differently in short fiction—for example, theme may well be more critical to most short stories than to many novels.

The short story has little time to build—events must unfold right away. And since there are fewer events in short fiction, obviously there are many fewer scenes. And yet events and scenes are still important. The events in short fiction will stand out, will take all the focus, so they must accomplish their goals without fumbling.

You'll find far fewer characters in short fiction—maybe only one—so you'll need to choose characters that fit your story by every measure. And since you'll likely have only one viewpoint character, you've got to choose the character most affected by story events. If not that, the one who can best convey the thrust of the story. Or one with a distinct voice.

Words have to be just right. Since there are so few, each will be influential and noted by the reader.

While theme and character insights may play a larger role in short fiction than in long fiction, dialogue may play a much smaller one. And that means you must use other means to convey information to both characters and readers.

There isn't room for much back story in short fiction, especially in the shortest of short stories. Back story and scene setting may be reduced to a sentence or two before the inciting incident begins. There's no place for flashbacks and long explanations of what's gone on before this one moment in the main character's life. (Exceptions for short stories that are themselves flashbacks.) Think of short fiction as compressed when compared to long.

There's no fluff, no room for indulging the writer. Every word must pull its weight, and those that don't must be excised.

There are fewer layers in short fiction and typically only the major plot—no subplots.

Subtext is important in short fiction; it allows the writer to convey more than one message with the same words—the obvious surface meaning and the hidden message of the subtext. Practicing subtext in short stories is a great tool for perfecting it.

Setting is likely to be less important in short stories. Yet on the other hand, it may be the major focus of any one story.

Tone and mood have their places in short fiction, but they'll be unlikely to change over the length of the story.

A short story may consist of only one scene, a true departure from long fiction. But that scene still needs to have a purpose and it needs to lead characters and readers somewhere.

Unlike in most long fiction, the protagonist in short stories may remain unchanged by story events.

Most (though not all) short stories take place in a narrow time frame—a few hours, a day, or a week.

The short story must still have a beginning, a middle, and an end. There must be an inciting incident, a plot complication, a climax and/or a turning point, and a resolution, even if it's only a line or two. And conflict still needs to show up.

The ending might feature a twist or a surprise, a disclosure shocking enough that it wouldn't work in a novel where readers expect to be able to guess what will happen. Readers, however, are prepared to expect the unexpected in short fiction.

Although the coverage of the fiction elements won't be as deep in short stories as it is in long fiction, most elements will be present, and those that are need to be clear, consistent, and potent.

Sources

"Comprise." Def. 3. *Merriam-Webster Online.* Merriam-Webster. n.d. Web. 3 May 2015.

Einsohn, Amy. *The Copyeditor's Handbook: A Guide for Book Publishing and Corporate Communications, with Exercises and Answer Keys.* 2nd ed. Berkeley: University of California Press, 2006. Print.

Garner, Bryan A. *Garner's Modern American Usage.* Oxford: Oxford University Press, 2003. Print.

"Magic." Entries 1 & 2. *Shorter Oxford English Dictionary.* 6th ed. 2007. Print.

New Hart's Rules. Oxford: Oxford University Press, 2005. Print.

Sabin, William A. *The Gregg Reference Manual: A Manual of Style, Grammar, Usage, and Formatting.* 10th ed. New York: McGraw-Hill/Irwin. 2005. Print.

Stilman, Anne. *Grammatically Correct: The Writer's Essential Guide to Punctuation, Spelling, Style, Usage and Grammar.* Cincinnati: Writer's Digest Books, 1997. Print.

Strunk, William Jr., and E. B. White. *The Elements of Style.* 4th ed. New York: Longman Publishers, 2000. Print.

The Chicago Manual of Style. 16th ed. Chicago: The University of Chicago Press, 2010. Print.

Walsh, Bill. *Lapsing into a Comma: A Curmudgeon's Guide to the Many Things That Can Go Wrong in Print—and How to Avoid Them.* New York: McGraw-Hill, 2000. Print.

Whitman, Neal. (2011, January 13). How to Write Dialogue. [Web log post]. Retrieved February 15, 2016, from http://www.quickanddirtytips.com

Index

Acknowledgments

The Magic of Fiction was a three-and-a-half-year effort of fun powered by the art of patience. My thanks to all who helped bring this book to fruition. All errors in the text are mine, the kudos are yours. Thank you for your support, encouragement, and wisdom.

The Gang, fellow writers on the path as we put our dreams into words: Lisa Brackmann, Dale Cozort, Olivia Cunning, Judi Fennell, Kat Sheridan. You guys are a bigger help and support than I can say, and more inspiring than you will ever know. Kat, I'm so sorry I asked you to read this when it was still a jumble of messy words. But thanks for sharing your insights and your skills in turning a phrase.

The Writin' Wombats, a group of writers growing into their craft who let me tag along with them. You are the best.

The Hill contingent—Tracey, Rick, Mark, and Paula. Thanks beyond thanks to you all. You realigned my thinking and my approach, both very productive changes.

Sherrill Ward. Thanks for lending me your eyes, your pickiness (just what the book needed), and for going the extra mile.

Mom, you're the most encouraging and unflagging supporter any writer, daughter, or woman could ever have. I felt—and needed—your support all the way through.

Dad, you're not here to see this one, but I know you imagined it. Thanks for passing on your love of the written word. There could have been no better gift.

My clients and the readers at *The Editor's Blog*, your encouragement was both goad and balm. Thank you.

Writers from the past, I couldn't have had better role models and inspiration. Thank you not only for the entertainment but for arousing the need to understand how you did it so exceptionally well time after time after time.

Present-day writers, I hope we continue to encourage each other for many years to come.

Future writers, I can't wait to see the worlds, characters, and adventures you bring to the page.

About the Author

Beth Hill is a freelance fiction editor who loves to see the power of words released through stories. Some of her favorite childhood memories feature fights with her father over who would get to read the newly arrived *Reader's Digest Condensed Books* first. She writes articles on all aspects of the craft of writing at The Editors Blog (TheEditorsBlog.net), where writers, editors, educators, students, and anyone who wants to get the words right can find tips on technique and answers to questions about writing in general and fiction in particular. She lives in the Southeastern U.S., travels much less than she'd like to, and dreams of visiting every place recommended in the local newspaper's travel section but only *most* of the settings featured in the stories she loves. (www.anoveledit.com)